Fundamental Aspects of Turbulent Flows in Climate Dynamics

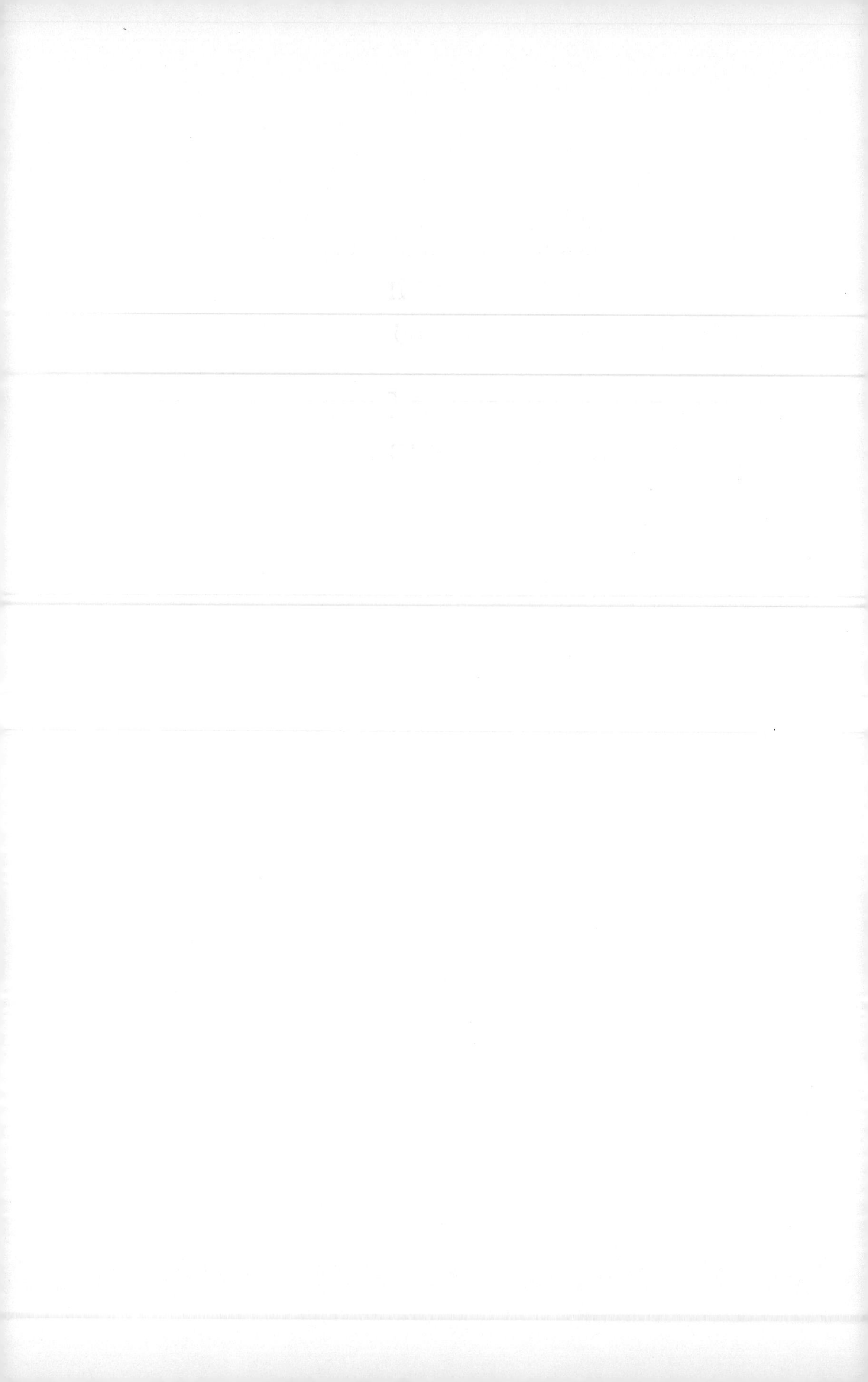

Lecture Notes of the Les Houches Summer School:

Volume 109

Fundamental Aspects of Turbulent Flows in Climate Dynamics

Edited by

Antoine Venaille, Freddy Bouchet, Tapio Schneider, Christophe Salomon

OXFORD
UNIVERSITY PRESS

OXFORD
UNIVERSITY PRESS

Great Clarendon Street, Oxford, OX2 6DP,
United Kingdom

Oxford University Press is a department of the University of Oxford.
It furthers the University's objective of excellence in research, scholarship,
and education by publishing worldwide. Oxford is a registered trade mark of
Oxford University Press in the UK and in certain other countries

First Edition published in 2020
Impression: 1

Published in the United States of America by Oxford University Press
198 Madison Avenue, New York, NY 10016, United States of America

British Library Cataloguing in Publication Data
Data available

Library of Congress Control Number: 2019952628

ISBN 978–0–19–885521–7

DOI: 10.1093/oso/9780198855217.003.0001

Printed and bound by
CPI Group (UK) Ltd, Croydon, CR0 4YY

École de Physique des Houches

Service inter-universitaire commun
à l'Université Joseph Fourier de Grenoble
et à l'Institut National Polytechnique de Grenoble

Subventionné par l'Université Joseph Fourier de Grenoble,
le Centre National de la Recherche Scientifique,
le Commissariat à l'Énergie Atomique

Directeur:
Christophe Salomon, laboratoire Kastler Brossel, Ecole Normale supérieure,
PSL research University, Sorbonne Université, Paris, France

Directeurs scientifiques de la session:
Freddy Bouchet, Directeur de recherche au CNRS
Tapio Schneider, Theodore Y. Wu Professor of Environmental Science and
Engineering, Caltech, Pasadena, USA
Antoine Venaille, Chargé de Recherche CNRS, ENS de Lyon, laboratoire de physique
Christophe Salomon, Directeur de Recherche CNRS

Previous sessions

I	1951	Quantum mechanics. Quantum field theory
II	1952	Quantum mechanics. Statistical mechanics. Nuclear physics
III	1953	Quantum mechanics. Solid state physics. Statistical mechanics. Elementary particle physics
IV	1954	Quantum mechanics. Collision theory. Nucleon-nucleon interaction. Quantum electrodynamics
V	1955	Quantum mechanics. Non equilibrium phenomena. Nuclear reactions. Interaction of a nucleus with atomic and molecular fields
VI	1956	Quantum perturbation theory. Low temperature physics. Quantum theory of solids. Ferromagnetism
VII	1957	Scattering theory. Recent developments in field theory. Nuclear and strong interactions. Experiments in high energy physics
VIII	1958	The many body problem
IX	1959	The theory of neutral and ionized gases
X	1960	Elementary particles and dispersion relations
XI	1961	Low temperature physics
XII	1962	Geophysics: the earth's environment
XIII	1963	Relativity groups and topology
XIV	1964	Quantum optics and electronics
XV	1965	High energy physics
XVI	1966	High energy astrophysics
XVII	1967	Many body physics
XVIII	1968	Nuclear physics
XIX	1969	Physical problems in biological systems
XX	1970	Statistical mechanics and quantum field theory
XXI	1971	Particle physics
XXII	1972	Plasma physics
XXIII	1972	Black holes
XXIV	1973	Fluids dynamics
XXV	1973	Molecular fluids
XXVI	1974	Atomic and molecular physics and the interstellar matter
XXVII	1975	Frontiers in laser spectroscopy
XXVIII	1975	Methods in field theory
XXIX	1976	Weak and electromagnetic interactions at high energy
XXX	1977	Nuclear physics with heavy ions and mesons
XXXI	1978	Ill condensed matter
XXXII	1979	Membranes and intercellular communication

XXXIII	1979	Physical cosmology
XXXIV	1980	Laser plasma interaction
XXXV	1980	Physics of defects
XXXVI	1981	Chaotic behavior of deterministic systems
XXXVII	1981	Gauge theories in high energy physics
XXXVIII	1982	New trends in atomic physics
XXXIX	1982	Recent advances in field theory and statistical mechanics
XL	1983	Relativity, groups and topology
XLI	1983	Birth and infancy of stars
XLII	1984	Cellular and molecular aspects of developmental biology
XLIII	1984	Critical phenomena, random systems, gauge theories
XLIV	1985	Architecture of fundamental interactions at short distances
XLV	1985	Signal processing
XLVI	1986	Chance and matter
XLVII	1986	Astrophysical fluid dynamics
XLVIII	1988	Liquids at interfaces
XLIX	1988	Fields, strings and critical phenomena
L	1988	Oceanographic and geophysical tomography
LI	1989	Liquids, freezing and glass transition
LII	1989	Chaos and quantum physics
LIII	1990	Fundamental systems in quantum optics
LIV	1990	Supernovae
LV	1991	Particles in the nineties
LVI	1991	Strongly interacting fermions and high Tc superconductivity
LVII	1992	Gravitation and quantizations
LVIII	1992	Progress in picture processing
LIX	1993	Computational fluid dynamics
LX	1993	Cosmology and large scale structure
LXI	1994	Mesoscopic quantum physics
LXII	1994	Fluctuating geometries in statistical mechanics and quantum field theory
LXIII	1995	Quantum fluctuations
LXIV	1995	Quantum symmetries
LXV	1996	From cell to brain
LXVI	1996	Trends in nuclear physics, 100 years later
LXVII	1997	Modeling the earth's climate and its variability
LXVIII	1997	Probing the Standard Model of particle interactions
LXIX	1998	Topological aspects of low dimensional systems
LXX	1998	Infrared space astronomy, today and tomorrow
LXXI	1999	The primordial universe
LXXII	1999	Coherent atomic matter waves
LXXIII	2000	Atomic clusters and nanoparticles
LXXIV	2000	New trends in turbulence
LXXV	2001	Physics of bio-molecules and cells

LXXVI	2001	Unity from duality: Gravity, gauge theory, and strings
LXXVII	2002	Slow relaxations and nonequilibrium dynamics in condensed matter
LXXVIII	2002	Accretion discs, jets, and high energy phenomena in astrophysics
LXXIX	2003	Quantum entanglement and information processing
LXXX	2003	Methods and models in neurophysics
LXXXI	2004	Nanophysics: Coherence and transport
LXXXII	2004	Multiple aspects of DNA and RNA
LXXXIII	2005	Mathematical statistical physics
LXXXIV	2005	Particle physics beyond the Standard Model
LXXXV	2006	Complex systems
LXXXVI	2006	Particle physics and cosmology: the fabric of spacetime
LXXXVII	2007	String theory and the real world: from particle physics to astrophysics
LXXXVIII	2007	Dynamos
LXXXIX	2008	Exact methods in low-dimensional statistical physics and quantum computing
XC	2008	Long-range interacting systems
XCI	2009	Ultracold gases and quantum information
XCII	2009	New trends in the physics and mechanics of biological systems
XCIII	2009	Modern perspectives in lattice QCD: quantum field theory and high-performance computing
XCIV	2010	Many-body physics with ultra-cold gases
XCV	2010	Quantum theory from small to large scales
XCVI	2011	Quantum machines: measurement control of engineered quantum systems
XCVII	2011	Theoretical physics to face the challenge of LHC Special Issue 2012 Advanced data assimilation for geosciences
XCVIII	2012	Soft interfaces
XCIX	2012	Strongly interacting quantum systems out of equilibrium
C	2013	Post-Planck cosmology
CI	2013	Quantum optics and nanophotonics
Special Issue	2013	Statistical physics, optimization, inference, and message-passing algorithms
CII	2014	From molecules to living organisms: An interplay between biology and physics
CIII	2014	Topological aspects of condensed matter physics
CIV	2015	Stochastic processes and random matrices
CV	2015	Quantum optomechanics and nanomechanics
CVI	2016	Integrability: From Statistical Systems to Gauge Theory
CVII	2016	Current trends in atomic physics
CVIII	2017	Effective field theory in particle physics and cosmology
CIX	2017	Fundamental aspects of turbulent flows in climate dynamics

Publishers

- Session VIII: Dunod, Wiley, Methuen
- Sessions IX and X: Herman, Wiley
- Session XI: Gordon and Breach, Presses Universitaires
- Sessions XII–XXV: Gordon and Breach
- Sessions XXVI–LXVIII: North Holland
- Session LXIX–LXXVIII: EDP Sciences, Springer
- Session LXXIX–LXXXVIII: Elsevier
- Session LXXXIX: Oxford University Press

Preface

The climate sciences have made impressive progress over the past decades, thanks to theoretical advances, vastly more and improved observations, and increases in computer performance that now allow extensive simulations with general circulation models (GCM). This has led to the unambiguous realization that the climate is and will be warming as a result of anthropic emissions of greenhouse gases. Yet it is also clear that our abilities are limited to predict the energy, momentum, water, and carbon cycles that shape our climate. Our abilities to predict these cycles are limited because they all crucially depend on turbulent flows. Turbulence is at the core of what shapes climate. Turbulent fluxes of energy, in concert with radiative energy fluxes, control the Earth's temperature distribution. Turbulent fluxes of momentum control the distribution of winds, which drive ocean circulations. And turbulent fluxes of water vapor control clouds and their effect on Earth's radiative energy balance, as well as the pattern of precipitation and evaporation that determines which areas of Earth are arid or humid.

Future breakthroughs in our understanding of these turbulent flows and in our ability to model them will most likely come from a combination of advancing our fundamental understanding of turbulent flows, our numerical simulation capabilities, and our observing systems. Physicists, mathematicians, and climate scientists all have important roles to play, bringing together expertise in statistical mechanics, fluid dynamics, nonlinear dynamics, and the climate sciences.

The aim of the summer school "Fundamental aspects of turbulent flows in climate dynamics," held in Les Houches in August 2017, was to survey what is known about how turbulence shapes climate, what role it plays in climate change, and to outline where progress in this important area is within reach, given today's computational and observational capabilities. The summer school gathered participants from different fields, spanning the climate sciences, fluid dynamics, astrophysics, statistical physics, mechanical engineering, and applied mathematics. Experts surveyed tools and concepts from statistical physics and turbulence theory, ocean dynamics, large-scale atmosphere dynamics, clouds, and turbulent moist convection. The program consisted of nine core lectures:

1. Turbulence theory, statistical mechanics, and dynamical systems approaches:
   - **Henk Dijkstra:**
     Dynamical systems analysis of climate variability.
2. Ocean turbulence:
   - **Paola Cessi:**
     i) From transformed Eulerian mean to thickness-weighted average.
     ii) Parameterisation of eddy fluxes.

- **Raffaele Ferrari:**
  i) Abyssal ocean circulation.
  ii) Deep-ocean mixing and abyssal circulation revisited.
- **Bill Young:**
  i) Tides and a little about the energetics of ocean turbulence.
  ii) The zeroth law of turbulence and its discontents.
  iii) Waves and turbulence on a beta-plane.

3. Large-scale atmosphere turbulence:
   - **Isaac Held:**
     i) Quasigeostrophic dynamics and turbulence.
     ii) Idealised models of the climate of tropical cyclogenesis.
   - **Ted Shepherd:**
     Barotropic aspects of large-scale atmosphere turbulence.
4. Clouds and moist convection:
   - **Caroline Muller:**
     Clouds and turbulent moist convection.
   - **David Romps:**
     Theory of tropical moist convection.

The core lectures were complemented by shorter presentations by visiting lecturers. These additional lectures covered a wide range of more specialised topics, from more applied aspects of the climate sciences to new theoretical approaches in geophysical fluid dynamics:

- **Freddy Bouchet:**
  Statistical mechanics and rare event algorithms in climate.
- **Oliver Bühler:**
  The Gage-Nastrom spectrum and wave-mean flow interactions.
- **Thierry Dauxois:**
  Abyssal mixing in the laboratory?
- **Luc Deike:**
  Wave breaking in ocean-atmosphere interactions.
- **Ken Golden:**
  Modeling fluid processes in the sea ice system.
- **Peter Haynes:**
  A fuctuation-dissipation theorem in climate?
- **Valerio Lucarini:**
  Melancholia states in the climate system.
- **Brad Marston:**
  Direct statistical simulation of geophysical flows.
- **Alan Newell:**
  Wave turbulence.
- **Richard Peltier:**
  Ocean turbulence and global climate variability.
- **Thierry Penduff:**
  Characterizing the chaotic variability of the global eddying ocean.

- **Tapio Schneider:**
  The future of clouds.
  Turbulent flows in climate dynamics.
- **Geoffrey Vallis:**
  Climate change: uncertainties, time scales, thermodynamics and dynamics.
  The structure of the atmosphere and its response to global warming.
  Simple models and parameterization for moist convection.
- **Jacques Vanneste:**
  Geometric generalized Lagrangian mean theories.
- **Antoine Venaille:**
  Waves, symmetries, and invariants in geophysical fluids.
- **Achim Wirth:**
  A fluctuation-dissipation relation for the ocean-atmosphere system.

All lectures except one have been recorded. They can be viewed at the Les Houches youtube channel. Links to the videos, the presentation slides, and to additional materials for the lectures are also available at the school website.

Fifty-four early-career participants attended the school (graduate students, post-doctoral fellows, and early-career researchers). Their active participation contributed to the success of the school, be it through presentations on their research, tutorials and journal clubs they led, and research projects on which they collaborated with the lecturers. One of the most rewarding experiences of this school was the lively and friendly atmosphere the participants created through informal scientific discussions during the days and into the nights: after lectures and during lunches, hikes, and evening drinks, which smoothly interpolated from science to jam sessions on a diverse array of musical instruments.

In this book, the first two chapters are lectures on clouds and moist convection by Caroline Muller and David Romps. The third chapter contains lectures by Henk Dijkstra on dynamical system approaches to climate dynamics, including tutorials dealing with a hierarchy of geophysical flow models. The fourth chapter provides lectures by Ted Shepherd on large-scale atmospheric circulations. We hope that this set of lectures, together with the videos and slides that are available, will provide a helpful introduction to climate dynamics and turbulence and will serve as a reference for this active and important field. The summer school introduced a new generation of early-career scientists to these problems, and our hope is that this book and the accompanying materials will broaden the reach of the school.

Acknowledgment

The organisers wish to express their gratitude towards the administrative staff of the Les Houches School of Physics, especially Murielle Gardette, Anny Glomot, and Isabel Leliévre. They provided efficient and competent support before, during, and after the session, which we much appreciate. A number of participants have been very active in taking and editing notes during lectures, which were invaluable in preparing this book. We also warmly thank Thibault Jougla and other participants who took pictures and gathered them during the school, including those used in this book.

Funding

Les Houches Physics school is affiliated with University Grenoble Alpes, UGA, Institut National Polytechnique de Grenoble, INP, Centre National de la Recherche Scientifique, CNRS, Commissariat à l'énergie atomique, CEA, and Ecole Normale supérieure de Lyon, ENS-Lyon. This session was also partially funded by:

- Formation permanente du CNRS.
- Ecole Normale Supérieure de Lyon.
- Région Rhône-Auvergne, and Université de Lyon 1 UCBL.
- The ERC TRANSITION grant (F. Bouchet, through the European Research Council under the European Union's seventh Framework Programme FP7/2007–2013 Grant Agreement No. 616811).
- Travel grants to some participants by the Climate and Large-scale Dynamics Program of the U.S. National Science Foundation.

Participants of the summer school during the “cloud hike”.

Contents

List of participants

Organizers

BOUCHET, FREDDY
CNRS, Ecole Normale Supérieure de Lyon, France

SCHNEIDER, TAPIO
Caltech, Pasenada, USA

VENAILLE, ANTOINE
CNRS, Ecole Normale Supérieure de Lyon, France

Lecturers

CESSI, PAOLA
Scripps, University of California San Diego, USA

HENK A. DIJKSTRA
Utrecht University, The Netherland

FERRARI, RAFFAELE
MIT, Cambridge, USA

HELD, ISAAC
GFDL/NOAA, Princeton University, USA

MULLER, CAROLINE
LMD ENS Paris, France

DAVID M. ROMPS
University of California, Berkeley, USA

THEODORE G. SHEPHERD
University of Reading, UK

VALLIS, GEOFFREY
University of Exeter, UK

YOUNG, WILLIAM
Scripps, University of California San Diego, USA

Invited Seminars

BÜHLER, OLIVER
Courant Institute, New York University, USA

DAUXOIS, THIERRY
CNRS, Ecole Normale Supérieure de Lyon, France

DEIKE, LUC
Princeton University, USA

GOLDEN, KEN
University of Utah, USA

HAYNES, PETER
Cambridge University, UK

LUCARINI, VALERIO
University of Reading, UK

MARSTON, J. BRADLEY
Brown University, USA

NEWELL, ALAN
University of Arizona, US

PELTIER, RICHARD
University of Toronto, Canada

PENDUFF, THIERRY
CNRS, Université Grenoble Alpes, France

VANNESTE, JACQUES
University of Edinburgh, UK

WIRTH, ACHIM
CNRS, Université Grenoble Alpes, France

Students and Other Participants

ALEXANDER, ROMEO
Courant Institute, New York University, USA

AYET, ALEX
École Normale Supérieure, Paris, France

BALWADA, DHRUV
Courant Institute, New York University, USA

BARPANDA, PRAGALLVA
The University of Chicago, US

BECKEBANZE, FELIX
Universiteit Utrecht, The Netherlands

BEMBENEK, ARKADIUSZ
McGill University, Canada

BEUCLER, TOM
MIT, Cambridge, USA

BODNER, ABIGAIL
Brown University, USA

CHANG, CHIUNG-YIN
Princeton University, GFDL, USA

CHEN, TING-CHEN
McGill University, Montreal, Canada

CONSTANTINOU, NAVID
Scripps, University of California San Diego, USA

COPE, LAURA
DAMTP, University of Cambridge, UK

DAVIS, GÉRALDINE
Ecole Normale Supérieure de Lyon, France

DEMAEYER, JONATHAN
Institut Royal Météorologique, Bruxelles, Belgique

DEREMBLE, BRUNO
LMD, Ecole normale supérieure, Paris, France

FROMANG, SEBASTIEN
CEA/Saclay, Service d'Astrophysique, France

GALLET, BASILE
CEA/Saclay, Service de Physique de l'Etat Condensé, France

GUO, JIAHUA
Harvard University, Cambridge, USA

HASSANZADEH, PEDRAM
Rice University, Houston, USA

HELFER, KEVIN
Delft University of Technology, The Netherlands

HELL, MOMME
Scripps, University of California San Diego, USA

HORNE IRIBARNE, ERNESTO
LMFA, École centrale de Lyon, France

HOSSEIN, AMINI KAFIABAD
McGill University, Montreal, Canada

HOWLAND, CHRISTOPHER
DAMTP Cambridge University, UK

JOUGLATHIBAULT
LEGI, Grenoble-Alpes Université, France

KANG, WANYING
Harvard University, Cambridge, USA

KHATRI, HEMANT
Imperial College London, UK

KUTSENKO, ANTON
Jacobs University, Bremen, Germany

LE REUN, THOMAS
IRPHE, Marseille, France

LEPOT, SIMON
CEA/Saclay, Service de Physique de l'Etat Condensé, France

MONTEIRO, JOY
Stockholm University, Sweden

PARÉS PULIDO, CARLOS
ETH Zurich, Swizerland

PENN, JAMES
University of Exeter, UK

PLUMLEY, MEREDITH
University of Colorado, Boulder, USA

RAGONE, FRANCESCO
University of Milano-Bicocca, Italy

RENAUD, ANTOINE
Laboratoire de Physique ENS de Lyon, France

SEELEY, JACOB
University of California, Berkeley, USA

SERAZIN, GUILLAUME
LEGOS/IRD, Toulouse, France

SHIBLEY, NICOLE
Yale University, USA

SHUKLA, VISHWANATH
Ecole normale supérieure de Lyon, France

SIMONNET, ERIC
INLN, CNRS, Valbonne, France

TARSHISH, NATHANIEL
Princeton University, USA

THALABARD, SIMON
Observatoire de la Côte d'Azur, Nice, France

UCHIDA, TAKAYA
Columbia University, New York, USA

VAN KAN, ADRIAN
Universität Heidelberg, Germany

WAGNER, GREGORY
MIT, Cambridge, USA

WANG, HAN
Courant Institute, New York University, USA

WANG, LEI
The University of Chicago, USA

XIE, JIN-HAN
University of California, Berkeley, USA

YANG, DA
University of California, Berkeley, USA

YANKOVSKY, ELIZABETH
Princeton University, GFDL, USA

YU, SUNGDUK
University of California, Irvine, CA, USA

ZEMSKOVA, BARBARA
University of North Carolina at Chapel Hill, USA

ZHANG, XIYUE
California Institute of Technology, Pasadena, USA

ZHANG, GAN
University of Illinois at Urbana-Champaign, USA

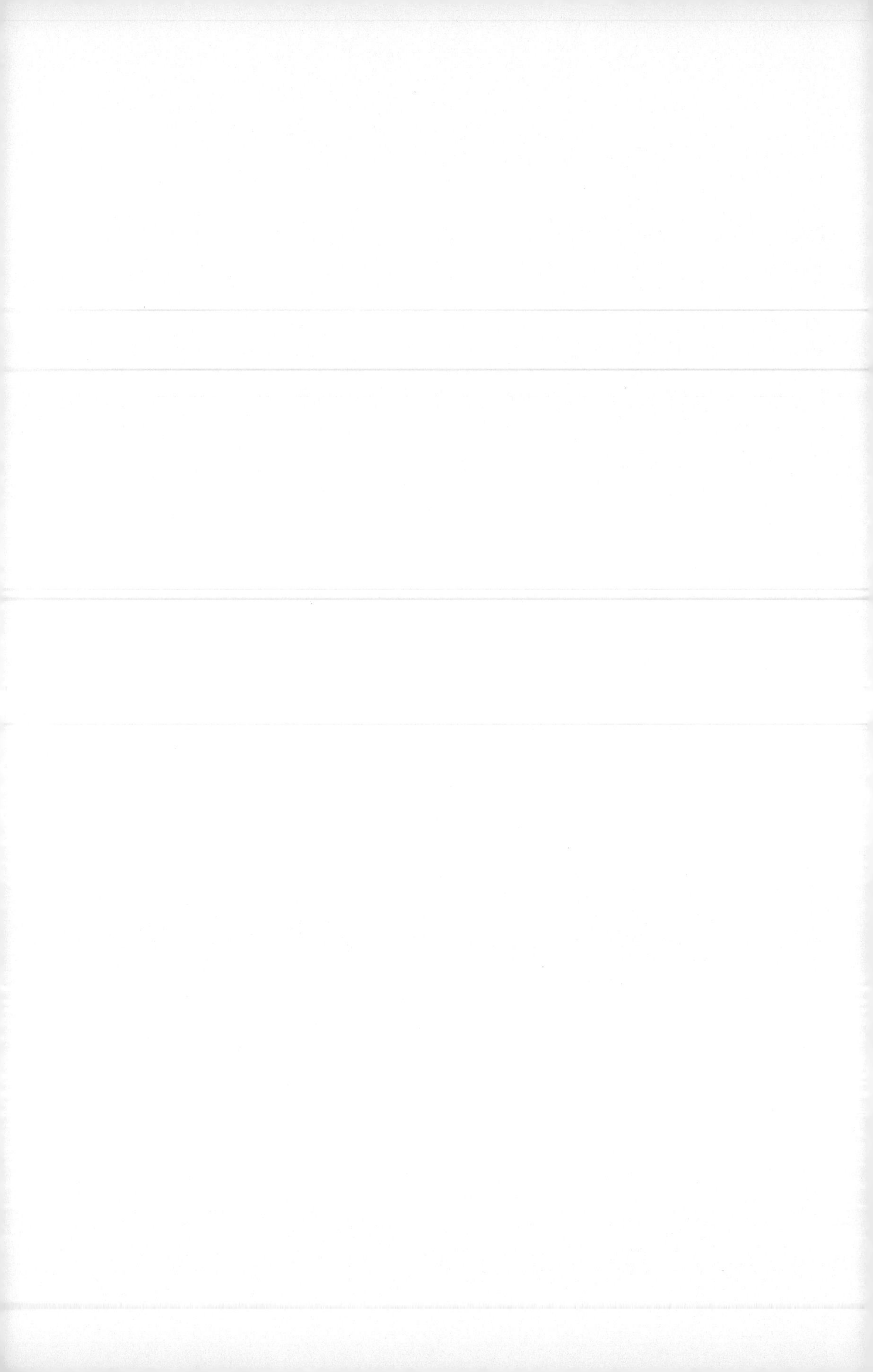

1
Theory of tropical moist convection

David M. Romps

Department of Earth and Planetary Science, University of California, Berkeley, CA
Climate and Ecosystem Sciences Division, Lawrence Berkeley National Laboratory, Berkeley, CA

Romps, D. M., *Theory of tropical moist convection* In: *Fundamental Aspects of Turbulent Flows in Climate Dynamics*. Edited by: Freddy Bouchet, Tapio Schneider, Antoine Venaille, Christophe Salomon, Oxford University Press (2020). © Oxford University Press.
DOI: 10.1093/oso/9780198855217.003.0001

Chapter Contents

1.1 Introduction

These lecture notes cover the theory of tropical moist convection. Many simplifications are made along the way, like neglecting rotation and treating the atmosphere as a two-dimensional fluid or even reducing the atmosphere to two columns. We can gain an immense amount of insight into the real atmosphere by studying these toy models, including answers to the following questions: what is the dominant energy balance in the tropical free troposphere; what sets the temperature structure of the tropical free troposphere; what happens to the pulse of heating deposited into the atmosphere by a rain cloud; why does the tropical atmosphere have the relative-humidity profile that it does; and what sets the amount of energy available to storms? These notes attempt to give the first-order answers to these questions in a format that is accessible to beginning graduate students. We begin with a discussion of atmospheric energy.

1.2 Dry thermodynamic equations

Fluids are governed by conservation laws: conservation of mass, conservation of energy, and conservation of momentum. Each of these conservation laws, when written down as an equation, prognoses (i.e., predicts or governs) the evolution of the fluid's mass, energy, and momentum, respectively. Sometimes, we write down those governing equations in terms of closely related variables. For example, we might rewrite the equation for energy in terms of an equation for temperature T. Or, we might rewrite an equation for momentum as an equation for velocity $\vec{u}$. But, no matter how the equations may be written in the end, they are all derivable from equations that plainly state the conservation of mass, energy, and momentum.

The best way to derive these conservation equations is to start in Eulerian form. An equation in Eulerian form has a term that is an Eulerian time derivative of some quantity. An Eulerian time derivative is just a partial derivative with respect to time, $\partial/\partial t$. (It may seem silly to give $\partial/\partial t$ a special name like "Eulerian time derivative," but this is necessary to distinguish it from the "Lagrangian time derivative" d/dt, which is also commonly used in the study of fluids.)

In Eulerian form, we can write any conservation law as

$$\text{Storage rate of } X \text{ in the box} + \text{Export rate of } X \text{ out of the box} \\ = \text{Sources of } X \text{ in the box}, \quad (1.1)$$

where X is either mass, momentum in one of the three independent directions, or energy. Here, the "box" is some box-shaped region—perhaps a cube—that has a fixed size, shape, orientation, and position with respect to the chosen coordinate system (typically, x, y, and z). It is most important that this box be stationary: the fluid can and will pass through the box, but the box that we consider must not move. For simplicity, we will imagine a box whose edges are parallel to the x, y, and z axes and that have lengths L_x, L_y, and L_z, respectively; see Figure 1.1.

In equation (1.1), the "storage rate" or "tendency" is the rate at which the amount of X in the box is increasing. The "export rate" or "divergence" is the rate at which

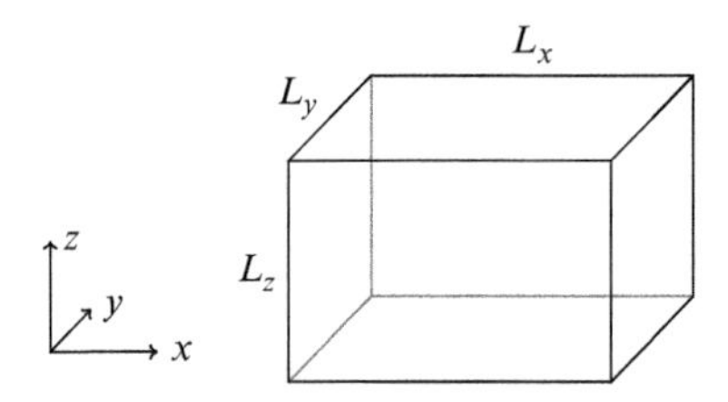

Fig. 1.1 Imaginary box, fixed in space. You may think of this box being infinitesimally small. We derive equations describing the mean quantities of the fluid in this box, as the fluid passes through this box. Eventually, we take the limits of L_x, L_y, and L_z to zero, such that the box reduces to a single fixed point in space.

X is being carried by the fluid out of the box by passing through the walls of the box. The "sources" are any addition of X to the box (or, if negative, subtraction of X from the box) through means other than being carried into or out of the box by the fluid flow.

To write out Equation (1.1) in more detail, note that the amount of X in the box is equal to the volume of the box V times the density of X. So, the storage rate is[1] ∂_t of the volume of the box V times the density of X. But, since V is constant in time,

$$\text{Storage rate of } X \text{ in the box} = V\partial_t(\text{density of } X).$$

The export rate of X is equal to the net rate at which X is carried outwards across the faces of the box. Let us consider the two faces whose normals are aligned with the x axis. The rate at which X passes through one of those faces is equal to the area of the face $L_y L_z$ times[2] u times the density of X. The net export across the two faces with $\hat{x}$ normals is then

$$(L_y L_z)\left[(u \times \text{density of } X)|_{+L_x/2} - (u \times \text{density of } X)|_{-L_x/2}\right],$$

where the subscripts $-L_x/2$ and $+L_x/2$ indicate that the expressions should be evaluated at the location of these faces, which are at positions $-L_x/2$ and $+L_x/2$ relative to the box's center. Now, if we imagine that our box is small compared to the spatial variations in u or the density of X, then we can write this as

$$\begin{aligned}
&(L_y L_z)\left[L_x \frac{(u \times \text{density of } X)|_{+L_x/2} - (u \times \text{density of } X)|_{-L_x/2}}{L_x}\right] \\
&= (L_y L_z)\left[L_x \partial_x (u \times \text{density of } X)\right] \\
&= V\partial_x(u \times \text{density of } X).
\end{aligned}$$

[1] Here and throughout, the partial derivatives $\partial/\partial t$, $\partial/\partial x$, $\partial/\partial y$, and $\partial/\partial z$ will be abbreviated as ∂_t, ∂_x, ∂_y, and ∂_z. This is simply a matter of convenience: it reduces clutter and saves ink.

[2] Here, we adopt the standard meteorological convention of referring to the three components of the fluid velocity by u, v, and w, corresponding to x, y, and z axes, respectively.

Similarly, the net exports through the two $\hat{y}$-normal and two $\hat{z}$-normal faces are

$$V\partial_y(v \times \text{density of } X)$$

and

$$V\partial_z(w \times \text{density of } X),$$

respectively. Altogether, the net amount of X being exported through the faces of the box is:

$$\text{Export rate of } X \text{ out of box} = V\vec{\nabla}\cdot(\vec{u} \times \text{density of } X).$$

The only thing left to figure out, then, is the set of sources for X. For mass, there is none:

$$\text{Sources of mass to the box} = 0.$$

Although the diffusive fluxes of mass, momentum, and energy can be important, especially near the surface, we will ignore diffusion for simplicity. For momentum, there are gravity and pressure forces:

$$\text{Sources of momentum to the box} = V\vec{g} - V\vec{\nabla}p.$$

Here, $\vec{g} = (0, 0, -9.81 \text{ m s}^{-2})$ is the gravitational acceleration vector and p is the fluid pressure. Noting that the pressure of a fluid is isotropic (the same in all directions) and recalling that pressure is simply force per area, the pressure-gradient term $-V\vec{\nabla}p$ in the previous equation can be derived by considering the forces on the faces of the box. For energy (by which I mean the sum of internal energy, kinetic energy, and gravitational potential energy), the sources that we need to worry about are radiation and pressure work:

$$\text{Sources of energy to the box} = VQ - V\vec{\nabla}\cdot(p\vec{u}).$$

Here, Q is the net radiative heating per volume with units of W m^{-3} and the last term represents the energy added to the box by being pushed by adjacent fluid at the faces of the box. Like the pressure-gradient term in the momentum equation, the $-V\vec{\nabla}\cdot(p\vec{u})$ term can be derived by considering the force-times-distance work performed on the parcel of air at the faces of the box.

Putting it all together, denoting the density of mass, momentum, and energy by ρ, $\rho\vec{u}$, and ρE, and dividing by the constant V, we get

$$\partial_t\rho + \vec{\nabla}\cdot(\rho\vec{u}) = 0 \tag{1.2}$$

$$\partial_t(\rho\vec{u}) + \vec{\nabla}\cdot(\rho\vec{u}\vec{u}) = \rho\vec{g} - \vec{\nabla}p \tag{1.3}$$

$$\partial_t(\rho E) + \vec{\nabla}\cdot(\rho E\vec{u}) = Q - \vec{\nabla}\cdot(p\vec{u}), \tag{1.4}$$

where E is the specific[3] energy of the fluid and the pressure is specified by the ideal gas law to be $p = R\rho T$, where R is the specific gas constant of air.

[3]The term "specific" means "per mass." Therefore, E has units of J kg^{-1}.

The energy equation (a.k.a., the thermodynamic equation) plays a prominent role in these lectures because energy is tightly connected to the topics of buoyancy and atmospheric convection. Although there are many different "energy" or "thermodynamic" variables for dry air, they are all functions of[4] temperature T and also, possibly, pressure p or height z. Therefore, we can write a general thermodynamic variable for dry air as $f(T,p,z)$. At a given height, the buoyancy b of a dry parcel in a dry atmosphere is defined in terms of the temperature of the parcel T_p and the temperature of the environment at the same height T_e as

$$b = g\frac{T_p - T_e}{T_e}, \tag{1.5}$$

where $g \approx 10$ m s^{-2} is the magnitude of the gravitational acceleration. By this equation, a dry parcel is neutrally buoyant—i.e., will remain at that height in a stratified atmosphere if initially motionless—if and only if its temperature equals the temperature of the environment at the same height. Since the heights of the parcel and environment are the same, and since the parcel can be assumed to be the same pressure as its immediate environment so long as it is moving slowly compared to the speed of sound, a dry parcel is neutrally buoyant if and only if it has the same T, p, and z as its environment. In other words, a dry parcel in a dry environment is neutrally buoyant if and only if the parcel and its environment have the same energy (measured in terms of whatever thermodynamic variable we want). It is this tight connection between buoyancy and energy that puts energy front and center when we study convection.

1.2.1 Energy $E = c_v T + u^2/2 + gz$

What is the E in Equation (1.4)? For a dry atmosphere, the energy in the box is a sum of three types: internal energy, kinetic energy, and gravitational potential energy. Therefore, E can be written as

$$E = \underbrace{c_v T}_{\text{internal}} + \underbrace{u^2/2}_{\text{kinetic}} + \underbrace{gz}_{\text{gravitational}}, \tag{1.6}$$

where $c_v \approx 700$ J kg^{-1} K^{-1} is the specific heat capacity of air at constant volume, u is a shorthand[5] for $|\vec{u}| = \sqrt{u^2+v^2+w^2}$. Note that we made choices about what constitutes "zero energy." For the internal energy, we have chosen "zero internal energy" to be at absolute zero. For the kinetic energy, we have chosen "zero kinetic energy" to be when $\vec{u} = 0$ in our chosen reference frame. For the gravitational potential energy, we have chosen "zero gravitational potential energy" to be at $z = 0$ in our chosen reference frame. We are always free to make these choices, or for that matter, any other set

[4]For one of the thermodynamic variables, there is an explicit dependence on the wind speed, but as we will see, this dependence is negligible and can be ignored for most purposes.

[5]Note that u is used for both the x component of the wind and for the magnitude of the velocity. This overloading of the variable u is typical. Context should make it clear which meaning is being used.

of choices. To see why, note that we can multiply Equation (1.2) by any constant we want and add it to Equation (1.4); that effectively adds that constant to E, which can be interpreted as adding that constant to any one of the internal, kinetic, and gravitational energies, thereby changing where their zero-point values occur.

To understand the Earth's tropical atmosphere, we must understand its energetics. In particular, we need to understand how air parcels are able to move up and down in a stratified atmosphere. Moving laterally in the tropics is pretty simple, but moving up and down requires an addition or removal of energy, either through phase changes of water or through radiative heating. Since that up-and-down movement is utterly critical to how the atmosphere works, we need to understand its energetics.

Regarding the energetics, the simplest thing we can try to understand is the difference in energy between air at the bottom of the troposphere and air at the top of the troposphere. Let us consider a static atmosphere; this lets us ignore the kinetic piece, whose contribution is small even in the real atmosphere.[6] For our comparison, we will use nice, round numbers. For the surface air, we will use $T = 300$ K and $z = 0$. For air at the tropopause, we will use $T = 200$ K and $z = 15$ km. See Figure 1.2. At these two heights, we have:

$$
\begin{aligned}
E \text{ @ surface} &= 700 \times 300 + 10 \times 0 \\
&= 210{,}000 \text{ J kg}^{-1} \\
E \text{ @ tropopause} &= 700 \times 200 + 10 \times 15000 \\
&= 290{,}000 \text{ J kg}^{-1} \\
\Delta E &= 290{,}000 - 210{,}000 = 80{,}000 \text{ J kg}^{-1}.
\end{aligned}
$$

Therefore, the tropopause air is higher in energy by 80,000 J/kg.

Is this the right way to calculate the energy difference? The answer to that depends on what you are hoping to learn. If we are interested in the movement of air up and down in the atmosphere, the answer is no: this difference in E is *not* the energy that we must extract (by, say, radiative cooling) from a parcel at the tropopause to make it descend in a neutrally buoyant way down to the surface. Why? There is the pressure term on the right-hand side of the governing equation for energy, $-\vec{\nabla} \cdot (p\vec{u})$, that prevents us from interpreting ΔE in this way.

1.2.2 Internal energy $c_v T$

What about internal energy? Is it the "right" way to think about the energy difference between the lower and upper troposphere? To find out, we need to derive the governing equation for internal energy. This will not be a new equation; it can be derived from the equations we already have.

[6] The highest winds in the atmosphere are found in the upper-tropospheric jets, which can hit speeds of 100 m/s (~200 mph). That corresponds to a specific kinetic energy of $100^2/2 = 5000$ J/kg, which is equal in energy to a temperature increment of about 7 K since $c_v = 700$ J kg^{-1}. Most windspeeds, however, are much smaller than this. Even a 50 m/s wind (~100 mph) corresponds to an equivalent temperature increment $[(50 \text{ m/s})^2/2/c_v]$ that is less than 2 K. Therefore, we can safely ignore the kinetic piece in our order-of-magnitude energy calculations.

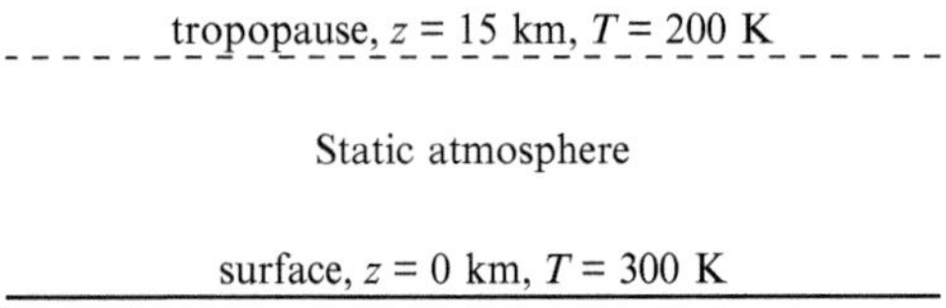

tropopause, $z = 15$ km, $T = 200$ K

Static atmosphere

surface, $z = 0$ km, $T = 300$ K

Fig. 1.2 For the comparison of the energies of air at the surface and tropopause, we will assume that the tropopause is at 15 km and that the temperatures of the surface air and tropopause air are 300 and 200 K, respectively.

To get there, it will make things easier to first define the "Lagrangian derivative" d/dt, which is related to the Eulerian derivative $\partial/\partial t$ by

$$\frac{d}{dt} = \partial_t + \vec{u} \cdot \vec{\nabla} . \tag{1.7}$$

The interpretation of the Lagrangian derivative is that it gives the rate of change following a parcel of fluid. Contrast this with the Eulerian derivative, which gives the rate of change at a fixed point in space.

The mass equation (a.k.a., the continuity equation) in (1.2) can be rewritten in a slightly different form that we will find useful. Also, by using the continuity equation on the momentum and energy equations, they, too, can be put into a similar form. The result of these efforts is

$$\begin{aligned} \partial_t \rho + \vec{u} \cdot \vec{\nabla} \rho &= -\rho \vec{\nabla} \cdot \vec{u} \\ \partial_t \vec{u} + (\vec{u} \cdot \vec{\nabla}) \vec{u} &= \vec{g} - \frac{1}{\rho} \vec{\nabla} p \\ \rho \partial_t E + \rho \vec{u} \cdot \vec{\nabla} E &= Q - \vec{\nabla} \cdot (p \vec{u}) . \end{aligned}$$

These equations are similar in the sense that their left-hand sides all have an Eulerian derivative of something plus $\vec{u} \cdot \vec{\nabla}$ operating on that same thing. By the definition of the Lagrangian derivative in Equation (1.7), this can be written as

$$\frac{d}{dt} \rho = -\rho \vec{\nabla} \cdot \vec{u} \tag{1.8}$$

$$\frac{d}{dt} \vec{u} = \vec{g} - \frac{1}{\rho} \vec{\nabla} p \tag{1.9}$$

$$\rho \frac{d}{dt} E = Q - \vec{\nabla} \cdot (p \vec{u}) . \tag{1.10}$$

Equation (1.9) can be turned into an equation for kinetic and gravitational potential energy by dotting with $\vec{u}$,

$$\frac{d}{dt} \left(\frac{1}{2} u^2 + gz \right) = -\frac{1}{\rho} \, \vec{u} \cdot \vec{\nabla} p .$$

Multiplying by ρ and subtracting from Equation (1.10) gives

$$\rho\frac{d}{dt}(c_vT)=Q-p\vec{\nabla}\cdot\vec{u}. \tag{1.11}$$

Let us compare the surface and tropopause. At the surface, $T=300$ K. At the tropopause, $T=200$ K. Therefore,

$$\begin{aligned}c_vT \text{ @ surface} &= 700\times 300\\ &= 210{,}000\ \text{J kg}^{-1}\\ c_vT \text{ @ tropopause} &= 700\times 200\\ &= 140{,}000\ \text{J kg}^{-1}\\ c_v\Delta T &= 140{,}000-210{,}000=-70{,}000\ \text{J kg}^{-1}.\end{aligned}$$

The tropopause air is *lower* in internal energy by 70,000 J/kg.

Does this difference in internal energy tell us about the energy that must be added or removed to bring a tropopause parcel down to the surface? Certainly not! If we believed that, then we would think that we have to heat a tropopause parcel to get it down to the surface. This is not right. The problem is in the remaining pressure term: $-p\vec{\nabla}\cdot\vec{u}$ (pdV work).

1.2.3 Enthalpy $h=c_pT$

Let us add $\rho d(RT)/dt$ to both sides of Equation (1.11). On the left-hand side, this gives $\rho d(c_pT)/dt$, where $c_p=c_v+R\approx 1000$ J kg^{-1} is the specific heat capacity at constant pressure. The right-hand side becomes

$$\begin{aligned}&Q-p\vec{\nabla}\cdot\vec{u}+\rho\frac{d}{dt}(RT)\\ &=Q-p\vec{\nabla}\cdot\vec{u}+\frac{d}{dt}(\rho RT)-RT\frac{d}{dt}\rho\\ &=Q-p\vec{\nabla}\cdot\vec{u}+\frac{d}{dt}p+RT\rho\vec{\nabla}\cdot\vec{u}\\ &=Q-p\vec{\nabla}\cdot\vec{u}+\frac{d}{dt}p+p\vec{\nabla}\cdot\vec{u}\\ &=Q+\frac{d}{dt}p.\end{aligned}$$

In the third line, we have used Equation (1.8) on the last term. In the fourth line, we have used the ideal gas law. The result is the enthalpy equation,

$$\rho\frac{d}{dt}h=Q+\frac{d}{dt}p, \tag{1.12}$$

where $h=c_pT$ is the specific enthalpy for dry air. Recall that "specific" means per mass. What is enthalpy? Enthalpy is the sum of internal energy plus pV. For a box of volume V and mass M, its specific pV is pV/M. This equals p/ρ since $M/V=\rho$, and $p/\rho=RT$ by the ideal gas law. Therefore, by adding $d(RT)/dt$ to both sides of the internal-energy equation, we changed our "X" from internal energy (which, per mass, is c_vT) to enthalpy (which, per mass, is c_pT).

Let us compare the surface and tropopause. Again, the surface and tropopause temperatures are 300 and 200 K, respectively. Therefore,

$$c_pT \text{ @ surface} = 1000 \times 300 \tag{1.13}$$
$$= 300{,}000 \text{ J kg}^{-1} \tag{1.14}$$
$$c_pT \text{ @ tropopause} = 1000 \times 200 \tag{1.15}$$
$$= 200{,}000 \text{ J kg}^{-1} \tag{1.16}$$
$$c_p\Delta T = 200{,}000 - 300{,}000 = -100{,}000 \text{ J kg}^{-1}. \tag{1.17}$$

The tropopause air is *lower* in internal energy by 100,000 J/kg.

This is still not the relevant thermodynamic variable for calculating the cooling needed to bring a parcel to the surface. We still have a pesky pressure term on the right-hand side of Equation (1.12): dp/dt, which corresponds to the pressurization of the parcel.

1.2.4 Potential temperature θ

To get rid of that pesky pressure term, let us divide both sides of Equation (1.12) by ρT. That produces

$$c_p\frac{d}{dt}\log(T) = Q/(\rho T) + R\frac{d}{dt}\log(p).$$

This can be written as

$$c_p\frac{d}{dt}\left[\log(T) - \frac{R}{c_p}\log(p/p_0)\right] = \frac{Q}{\rho T},$$

and then as

$$\frac{d}{dt}\log(\theta) = \frac{Q}{c_p\rho T},$$

or as

$$\frac{d}{dt}\theta = \frac{\theta}{c_p\rho T}Q. \tag{1.18}$$

Here, θ is called the potential temperature, which is defined by

$$\theta = T\left(\frac{p_0}{p}\right)^{R/c_p}. \tag{1.19}$$

The variable θ is the temperature that a parcel of air (with an initial pressure p and temperature T) would have if adiabatically compressed or expanded to pressure p_0. It is conventional to set $p_0 = 1$ bar $= 10^5$ Pa, which approximates the surface pressure. Note that we finally have an equation with no pressure terms on the right-hand side. As we cool a parcel to bring it from the tropopause to the surface over time Δt, Equation (1.18) tells us that the change in its potential temperature is

$$\Delta\theta = \frac{1}{c_p}\int_0^{\Delta t} dt\,\frac{\theta}{T}\frac{Q}{\rho}. \tag{1.20}$$

Our ultimate goal is to find the specific cooling (J kg^{-1}) that is required to bring a tropopause parcel down to the surface. By the definition of Q, which is net heating per volume per time, the net specific heating of the parcel during time Δt is

$$\int_0^{\Delta t} dt\,\frac{Q}{\rho}.$$

For the sake of intuition, it is sometimes convenient to talk about a heating or cooling in terms of Kelvins. When we refer to "x K of heating," we usually mean "the Joules per kilogram of heating that would raise the temperature of an air parcel by x K at constant pressure." These are simply related by a factor of c_p. Specifically; we have the following correspondence:

$$\int_0^{\Delta t} dt\,\frac{Q}{\rho}\quad [\text{J/kg}] \qquad \Longleftrightarrow \qquad \frac{1}{c_p}\int_0^{\Delta t} dt\,\frac{Q}{\rho}\quad [\text{K}].$$

Note that the right-hand side of (1.20) is not quite equal to this: Equation (1.20) has a factor of θ/T inside the integral. Nevertheless, we can approximate that factor.

Let us compare the surface and tropopause. At the surface, $T = 300$ K and $p = 10^5$ Pa, so $\theta = 300(1)^{R/c_p} = 300$ K. At the tropopause, $T = 200$ K and $p = 0.13 \times 10^5$ Pa, so $\theta = 200(1/0.13)^{R/c_p} = 360$ K. We do not know the time-averaged θ/T, but we can approximate θ and T in that ratio as averages of their tropopause and surface values, which are $(360 + 300)/2 = 330$ K and $(200 + 300)/2 = 250$ K, respectively. Then,

$$\begin{aligned}
\Delta\theta &= \frac{1}{c_p}\int_0^{\Delta t} dl\,\frac{\theta}{T}\frac{Q}{\rho} \\
&\approx \frac{1}{c_p}\frac{330}{250}\int_0^{\Delta t} dt\,\frac{Q}{\rho} \\
\Rightarrow \quad \frac{1}{c_p}\int_0^{\Delta t} dt\,\frac{Q}{\rho} &\approx \frac{250}{330}(360 - 300) \\
&\approx 45 \text{ K}.
\end{aligned}$$

This is roughly the amount of cooling needed to bring a tropopause parcel down to the surface. We were forced to make an approximation, however, so we cannot trust this to be quantitatively exact.

1.2.5 Entropy $c_p \log\theta$

It is worth noting at this stage that $c_p \log\theta$ is the entropy of dry air. We can derive its governing equation from (1.18), which gives

$$\frac{d}{dt}(c_p \log\theta) = \frac{Q}{\rho T}.$$

Note the familiar "heating divided by temperature" term on the right-hand side. And, note this equation does not contribute any new information not already present in our governing equations for mass, momentum, and energy; in fact, we have derived this entropy equation purely from the conservation of mass, momentum, and energy.

1.2.6 Dry static energy $\text{DSE} = c_pT + gz$

Potential temperature is nice because it is conserved for adiabatic ($Q = 0$) processes, but with its weird exponent and a source that is not exactly equal to specific heating, it is inconvenient. For example, in the calculation of the cooling needed to bring a parcel of air from the tropopause to the surface, we could only get an approximate answer when evaluating Equation (1.18) with pencil and paper. A more convenient equation can be obtained from the enthalpy equation so long as we do not mind invoking hydrostatic balance. Assuming that the atmosphere is hydrostatic and that we cool or heat parcels slowly enough that they are always at their equilibrium height (i.e., their density equal to the environment's density), then

$$\begin{aligned}\frac{d}{dt}p &= \partial_t p + \vec{u}\cdot\vec{\nabla}p \\ &= w\partial_z p \\ &= -w\rho g \\ &= -\rho\frac{d}{dt}(gz).\end{aligned}$$

Here, we are simplifying matters by assuming that the atmosphere has no horizontal or temporal variations in pressure (a good approximation for the tropics), and we have used hydrostatic balance in the third line to equate $\partial_z p$ and $-\rho g$. Using this result to rewrite the dp/dt term in Equation (1.12), the enthalpy equation becomes

$$\rho\frac{d}{dt}(c_pT) = Q - \rho\frac{d}{dt}(gz),$$

or

$$\frac{d}{dt}\text{DSE} = Q/\rho, \tag{1.21}$$

where $\text{DSE} = c_pT + gz$ is the dry static energy. Now, we have a very clean relationship between a function of the parcel's state (DSE) and the specific heating (Q/ρ).

Let us compare the surface and tropopause. At the surface, $T = 300$ K and $z = 0$. At the tropopause, $T = 200$ K and $z = 15$ km. Therefore,

$$\begin{aligned}
\text{DSE @ surface} &= 1000 \times 300 + 10 \times 0 \\
&= 300{,}000 \text{ J kg}^{-1} \\
\text{DSE @ tropopause} &= 1000 \times 200 + 10 \times 15000 \\
&= 350{,}000 \text{ J kg}^{-1} \\
\Delta\text{DSE} &= 350{,}000 - 300{,}000 = 50{,}000 \text{ J kg}^{-1}.
\end{aligned}$$

The tropopause air is *higher* in dry static energy by 50,000 J/kg. Dividing by $c_p = 1000$ J kg^{-1} K^{-1}, this corresponds to 50 K. So, we see that our approximate calculation of 45 K from the θ equation was pretty close to the actual answer.

Needless to say, DSE is super useful. It has gotten us the amount of cooling needed to bring a parcel from the tropopause to the surface, or, vice versa, the amount of heating to bring a parcel from the surface to the tropopause. In the absence of heating, DSE should be approximately conserved. For example, if we lift a parcel from the surface to the tropopause without any heating, then its original DSE of 30×10^4 J/kg is conserved, so the temperature becomes $(30 \times 10^4 - 10 \times 15000)/1000 = 150$ K. Not surprisingly, that is 50 K less than the temperature of the tropopause air; this is the 50 K that must be added as we lift the parcel if we want it to be neutrally buoyant at the tropopause.

Note that we can restate all of this very simply. Conservation of DSE implies that $dT/dz = -g/c_p = -10$ K/km. This is just the dry adiabatic lapse rate, which is well-known by all atmospheric scientists.

But, we cannot use conservation of DSE blindly. If we lift the surface parcel to 40 km in the stratosphere, what will the temperature of the parcel be? As we saw previously, a parcel with a temperature of 300 K at the surface has a DSE of 300 kJ kg^{-1}. At 40 km, the parcel's DSE would be

$$\text{DSE} = 1000T + 10 \times 40000,$$

where T is the unknown temperature of the parcel there. To solve for T, we use conservation of DSE, which tell us that this expression is equal to 300 kJ kg^{-1}. Therefore,

$$1000T + 400000 = 300000 \tag{1.22}$$

$$\Rightarrow \quad 1000T = -100000 \tag{1.23}$$

$$\Rightarrow \quad T = -100 \text{ K}. \tag{1.24}$$

Negative temperature! What went wrong? Can we not lift a parcel to 40 km? Of course we can. That is a totally physical thing to do. And, since negative temperatures are meaningless, it is conservation of DSE that must have failed. We will find out why in Section 1.7.

1.3 Tropospheric energy balance

Clear air cools radiatively through infrared emission by about 1 K per day (10^{-5} K/s). Since there are 10 tons (10^4 kg) of air overlying each square meter of surface, that corresponds to about

$$Mc_p\left(\frac{1}{c_p}\frac{Q}{\rho}\right) = 10^4 \times 1000 \times 10^{-5} = 100 \text{ W m}^{-2}.$$

That is a lot of cooling. How is this balanced? By the definition of the Lagrangian derivative in Equation (1.7), we know that

$$\frac{d}{dt}\text{DSE} = \partial_t\text{DSE} + u\partial_x\text{DSE} + v\partial_y\text{DSE} + w\partial_z\text{DSE}.$$

In the tropical free troposphere, $\partial_t T$ is nearly zero, as are $\partial_x T$ and $\partial_y T$, which are often approximated as zero in the weak temperature gradient (WTG) approximation (Sobel *et al.*, 2001). Therefore, Equation (1.21) can be approximated as

$$w\partial_z\text{DSE} \approx Q/\rho.$$

In other words, radiative cooling of clear air is balanced by descent of the clear air (vertical advection of higher DSE from aloft). This is illustrated in Figure 1.3. We can draw the same diagram in terms of T. This is shown in Figure 1.4.

Note that the clear air is everywhere sinking. What makes that possible? Where does that air come from? Why is there a seemingly endless source of air at high altitudes? The answer is that the high-altitude air is supplied by clouds! Clouds are the only things that can power their way up through the atmosphere to dump air at high altitudes. Clouds, therefore, are fundamental to the mass balance and energy balance of the troposphere. In these lectures, the word "cloud" will refer exclusively to

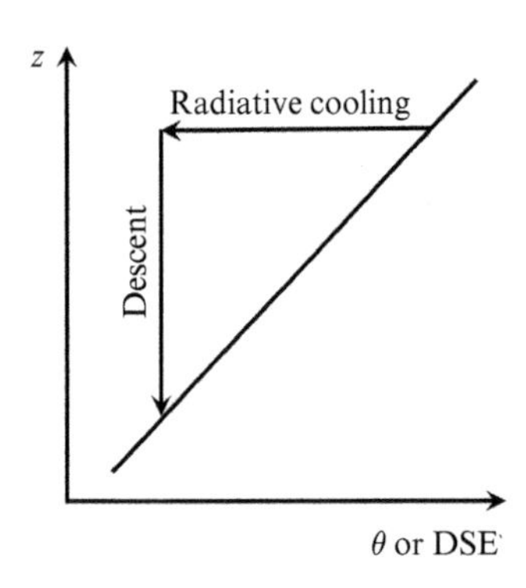

Fig. 1.3 A schematic of the clear-sky thermodynamic balance from the perspective of θ or DSE. Clear-sky radiative cooling moves the parcel to the left in this diagram. Since θ and DSE are conserved for adiabatic processes, descent of the parcel moves the parcel downward in this diagram. In a steady state, Lagrangian parcels move, but they move along the existing thermodynamic profile, which keeps the profile constant in time.

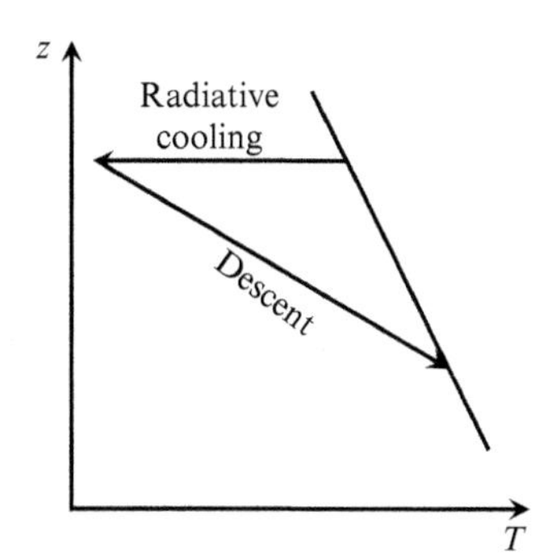

Fig. 1.4 A schematic of the clear-sky thermodynamic balance from the perspective of T. Clear-sky radiative cooling moves the parcel to the left in this diagram. Since an adiabatically descending parcel has a dry-adiabatic lapse rate $g/c_p = 10$ K/km that is larger than $-\partial_z T$, descent of the parel moves the parcel down and to the right in this diagram. In a steady state, Lagrangian parcels move, but they move along the existing temperature profile, which keeps the profile constant in time.

precipitating cloud updrafts. In the taxonomy of clouds, these are the cumulonimbus and the precipitating cumulus. While non-convecting clouds like stratus and cirrus help set the overall temperature of the planet through their interaction with radiation, they do not play the same fundamental role in the energy budget of the tropical troposphere that precipitating cloud updrafts do.

Convecting clouds typically rise so quickly that radiation does not have time to act on them in any significant way. Instead, the energy balance in a column of rising cloud is between vertical advection and latent heating. Denoting convecting cloud by a subscript c, we can think of this as

$$w_c \partial_z \text{DSE} = Q_{c,\text{condensation}}/\rho > 0\,.$$

Now, some of the condensates that form within the cloud end up evaporating in the environment, either because cloudy air detrains into the environment and evaporates or because rain falls through the environment and evaporates. This produces an additional cooling of the environment, so we should write the DSE balance in the environment, denoted by a subscript e, as

$$w_e \partial_z \text{DSE} = \left[Q_{e,\text{radiation}} + Q_{e,\text{evaporation}}\right]/\rho < 0\,.$$

The atmosphere's energy cycle works like this: The Sun heats the ocean, the ocean cools itself by evaporating water, the resulting water vapor is used by clouds to power their way to the upper troposphere, that causes subsidence everywhere else by continuity, and that adiabatic heating by subsidence is matched by radiative and evaporative cooling. Sounds simple enough, but there are a lot of questions:

- What sets the value of ∂_zDSE or, equivalently, $T(z)$?
- What sets $Q_{e,\text{radiation}}$ or, equivalently, what sets the distribution of humidity?

- What sets $Q_{e,\mathrm{evaporation}}$ or, equivalently, what is the fate of condensed water?
- How is $Q_{c,\mathrm{condensation}}$ affected by the turbulent entrainment of dry air?

These are some of the biggest unresolved questions in atmospheric science.

1.4 How do global climate models work?

In Earth's atmosphere, cloudy updrafts have a typical width of around 1 km. Global climate models (GCMs), on the other hand, have a typical grid spacing that ranges from 25–200 km. Therefore, the GCM grid spacing is much too large to resolve cloudy updrafts, at least not motions that faithfully represent true moist convection.

To understand how GCMs deal with this problem, it is sufficient to consider a single column of a GCM. In fact, a single column of a GCM is often isolated and used for research purposes all on its own. Isolated in this way, we call such a thing a single-column model (SCM). But how can an SCM possibly capture the dominant energy balance in the clear air? As we have learned, the radiative cooling of clear air is balanced by having the clear air sink. In an SCM, however, there is nowhither for the air to go, and nowhence to come.

Since the cloudy updrafts cannot be resolved explicitly, their effects must be parameterized. Fortunately, in addition to being small, cloudy updrafts also occupy a small fraction of area: a typical fraction of area that is occupied by precipitating cloudy updrafts is on the order of 10^{-3}–10^{-2}. This small area fraction is a consequence of the disparate rates of heating and cooling in precipitating updrafts and the environment. The radiative cooling of the environment is about 1 K/day, whereas a deep-convective cloud traverses the depth of the troposphere by adding 50 K to its DSE from latent heating in about one hour; these two rates of heating (1 K/day and 50 K/hour = 1200 K/day) differ by three orders of magnitude. Therefore, to have an energy balance, the area fraction of deep convective updrafts must be, on average, about 10^{-3}. Of course, there are large-scale regions of the tropics where the area fraction of precipitating updrafts exceeds 10^{-3}, made possible by the export of energy to neighboring regions of the tropics, so an area fraction of 10^{-2} is possible. Either way, the area fraction of precipitating cloud updrafts is small. As a consequence, there are two conceptual frameworks that we could use for parameterizing cloudy updrafts in an SCM. Both take advantage of the fact that cloudy updrafts occupy a very small area.

In the first framework, we let the GCM grid column represent just the clear air, and let convection be an appropriate source or sink of air at each height. This is depicted in Figure 1.5a, in which a blue tube represents cloudy air being removed from the lower part of the clear-air-only grid column and deposited into the upper part of the column. Let us define the mass flux of cloudy air M as the kilograms of air per second that go up the tube divided by the horizontal area of the grid column. By mass continuity, the vertical velocity w of the air in the grid column in between the tube's inlet and outlet must be given by

$$w = -M/\rho. \tag{1.25}$$

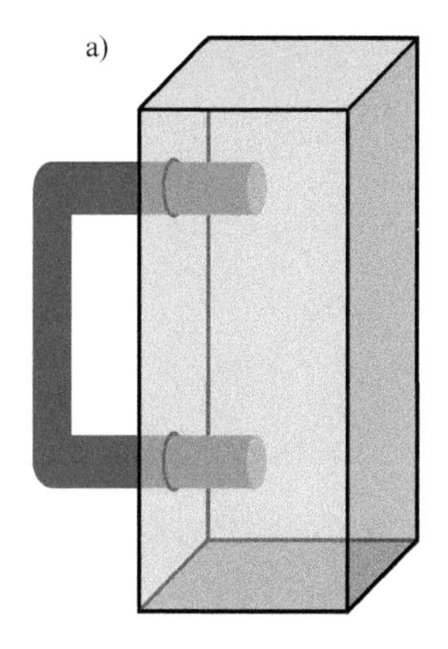

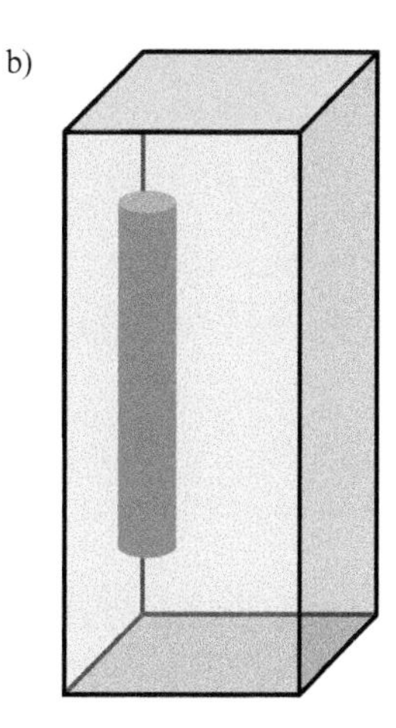

Fig. 1.5 Two possible frameworks for incorporating moist convection into a GCM grid column. (a) In the first framework, we think of all of the air in the grid column as being clear environmental air, and we imagine that the convection is a sink and source of mass throughout the column, which we can visualize as cloudy air moving upward through tubes outside the grid column. (b) In the second framework, we think of the air in the grid column as including both the clear environmental air and moist convection, so the tube carrying cloud updrafts lies within the grid column. This second framework is the one used in most, if not all, GCMs.

In a steady state, this subsidence must be balanced energetically by radiative and evaporative cooling. Therefore, the vertical velocity of the column is related to those processes by

$$w\partial_z \text{DSE} = (Q_{\text{radiation}} + Q_{\text{evaporation}})/\rho. \tag{1.26}$$

In this first framework for parameterizing convection in a GCM, the convection must be parameterized in two places: the M in the mass equation and the $Q_{\text{evaporation}}$ in the energy equation. (In practice, convection must also be parameterized in the momentum and humidity equations, but we are ignoring those for simplicity.) Do not be confused by the fact that there are two equations here for w. The way to think about this is that, in a steady state, the convection is governed by $Q_{\text{radiation}}$: to achieve that steady state, the convection is providing the right M and $Q_{\text{evaporation}}$ to satisfy both equations.

In the second framework, we let the GCM grid column represent an average over all the air: cloudy updrafts and clear air. This is depicted in Figure 1.5b, in which a blue tube representing the cloudy updrafts is within the grid column. In this second framework, the vertical velocity w, which now represents an average of cloudy and clear, must be zero in a steady state: there can be no net vertical movement of mass in a steady-state closed box. Therefore,

$$w = 0. \tag{1.27}$$

If $w = 0$, how is energy conservation satisfied? Even though there is no net vertical movement of mass, 99–99.9% of the air in the grid column is descending at levels between the tube's inlet and outlet. This is because the tube itself (the cloudy updrafts) occupy only 0.1–1% of the horizontal area. So, the mass flux in the tube is still causing the vast majority of the column to sink even though it does not register in the column's w. The energy balance is now

$$0 = Q_{\text{radiation}} + Q_{\text{evaporation}} + Q_{\text{subsidence}}\,, \tag{1.28}$$

where

$$Q_{\text{subsidence}} = M\partial_z \text{DSE}\,.$$

Since the vertical velocity of the clear environment is $w_e = -M/\rho$ by mass conservation, this is basically the same as Equation (1.26), but written with the subsidence term on the right-hand side. In this second framework, the convection must be parameterized in only one place: the sum of $Q_{\text{evaporation}} + Q_{\text{subsidence}}$, which is the convective tendency for dry static energy.

To the best of the author's knowledge, all GCMs are written with the second framework in mind, depicted in Figure 1.5b. This has the advantage of treating the cloudy updrafts as contained within the grid column (as they are in reality), but it has the disadvantage of hiding a lot of advection. In an SCM, stuff in the column (water vapor, trace gases, momentum) must be advected downward by the convective parameterization. And advection is one of the hardest things to do well in any numerical simulation of fluids. So, it is important to be aware that the dynamical core (dycore, for short) is not the only piece of a GCM responsible for the challenging numerical task of advecting fluid.

With either approach, the balance that is achieved in this single column is referred to as radiative-convective equilibrium (RCE). As its name implies, this is a steady state in which radiative cooling is balanced with convective heating. Typically, this refers to solutions in which there is no net ascent in the column (i.e., for approach 2, $w = 0$). RCE is an excellent starting point for understanding the structure of the tropical atmosphere, and we will study RCE further in sections 1.10 through 1.13.

1.5 Rigid-lid gravity waves

As opposed to an SCM, a column in a GCM has neighbors so it is no longer "single." And, since a grid column can import and export mass through its lateral boundaries, its w is no longer required to be zero even in a steady state. If there is a lot of cloudy mass flux in the column, then w will be positive, indicating that the column is ascending on average. If there is very little cloudy mass flux, then w will be negative (due to the fact that the environmental air is subsiding to balance the radiative cooling). To a first approximation, we can think of the clear air as descending at the same speed everywhere in the free troposphere, so it is the variation in cloud ascent that causes a column's w to have one sign or the other.

For example, consider the Hadley cell. The deep tropics has, on average, more cloudy ascent than clear-air descent, so the average w is positive there. Nevertheless, the vast majority of the air in the deep tropics is descending because the area fraction

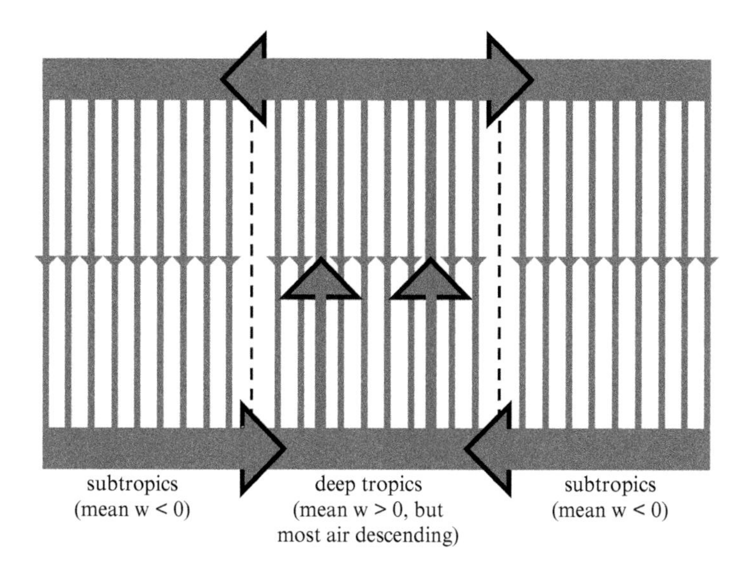

Fig. 1.6 Schematic of the Hadley cell. In the deep tropics, cloudy updrafts move air rapidly from the lower troposphere to the upper troposphere. That air then descends throughout the deep tropics and subtropics. Even though the area-averaged vertical velocity w is positive in the deep tropics, the vast majority of the air in the deep tropics is descending.

of convection is small. In the subtropics, the average w is negative because there is relatively little cloudy mass flux. On average, therefore, the deep tropics imports air at low altitudes and export air at high altitudes, and vice versa for the subtropics. See Figure 1.6 for a schematic of the Hadley cell. Note that the Hadley cell is not simply a pair of conveyor belts; instead, air is pumped into the upper troposphere of the deep tropics by moist convection, and that air then descends throughout the deep tropics and subtropics.

This description is appropriate for a steady state, but what happens if a column of the atmosphere has a sudden surplus or deficit of convection? How does it communicate that to all the other columns of air in the tropics to establish a new circulation? Consider a two-dimensional atmosphere (x and z) that is split up into adjacent columns. Imagine that, initially, w is zero in each column; in other words, the upward cloudy mass flux in each column is exactly balanced by the downward flux of environmental air. Then, imagine that one of the columns briefly has more moist convection than normal. What happens? By mass conservation, the environmental air in that column must briefly descend more than normal. That puts the subsidence out of balance with the radiative cooling, causing the column to heat up. Using Equation (1.21) for DSE, this is expressed mathematically as

$$\rho\partial_t \mathrm{DSE} = Q_{\mathrm{radiation}} + Q_{\mathrm{evaporation}} + M\partial_z \mathrm{DSE} > 0\,,$$

which is caused by M briefly exceeding its steady-state value of

$$-(Q_{\mathrm{radiation}} + Q_{\mathrm{evaporation}})/\partial_z \mathrm{DSE}\,.$$

Now, the column is warmer than its surroundings. Recall that the environmental air occupies 99–99.9% of the column, so the temperature of the column is basically the same thing as the temperature of the environment: if the column has a warm anomaly, that means the environment has a warm anomaly. Since warm air rises, a circulation develops between the column and its nearest neighbors, allowing the column to have $w > 0$ through a brief ascent (or a brief decrease in the descent rate) of the environmental air. That brief ascent causes the column to cool because ascent advects the column's air up the DSE gradient, i.e., for adiabatic ascent ($w > 0$), the equation $\partial_t \mathrm{DSE} = -w\partial_z \mathrm{DSE}$ tells us that $\partial_t \mathrm{DSE} < 0$. Of course, by mass conservation, this means that the column has exported some air laterally in the upper troposphere (i.e., near the tropopause) and imported some air laterally in the lower troposphere (i.e., near the surface). This is only possible if its neighboring columns descend, i.e., have $w < 0$. So, their environmental air warms up a bit. Being warmer, they now want to ascend, and they do, but that causes *their* neighbors to descend, and so on. This is a gravity wave.

Describing gravity waves in a compressible atmosphere with a realistic stratification is a pain in the neck. Fortunately, we can work with a simplified system to get some physical intuition for these waves. The simplest system with gravity waves is the 2D shallow-water system. But, such a system does not allow us to think about vertical structure and vertical propagation of waves. For that, we need to work with a Boussinesq fluid.

The Boussinesq equations describing hydrostatic linear perturbations to a two-dimensional, nonrotating, stratified fluid at rest are

$$\partial_t u = -\frac{\partial_x p}{\rho_0} \tag{1.29a}$$

$$0 = -\frac{\partial_z p}{\rho_0} + b \tag{1.29b}$$

$$\partial_t b = -N^2 w + Q \tag{1.29c}$$

$$0 = \partial_x u + \partial_z w\,, \tag{1.29d}$$

where u is the horizontal speed, w is the vertical speed, ρ_0 is a constant density, p is the pressure perturbation, b is the buoyancy, N is the Brunt–Väisälä frequency, and Q is the buoyancy source or, in other words, the heating. Let there be a rigid lid at H, where H is the tropopause.

With this system of equations, we will want to understand what happens when we have an isolated pulse of heating. This isolated pulse of heating can be thought of as either the subsidence warming generated in the vicinity of a single cumulonimbus, or as the heating of a column of atmosphere due to a positive anomaly in the convective mass flux in that column. Either way, if we imagine that the vicinity of the cumulonimbus is small (or that the column that got anomalously heated is small), then we can approximate that heating as being localized as a Dirac delta function in x. Likewise, if the heating is deposited quickly, then we can think of the heating as being localized in time. On the other hand, the vertical structure of the heating could be anything. To simplify matters, we will use sine functions to describe the possible vertical structures. (These sine functions can be used to construct any vertical structure of heating that is zero at the surface and tropopause.) Let m be the vertical wavenumber of the chosen sine function: $m = n\pi/H$, where n is an integer. Then, a heating that is localized in x, localized in t, and has vertical wavenumber m is described mathematically by

$$Q(x,z,t) = B_0 \sin(mz)\delta(x)\delta(t)\,. \tag{1.30}$$

Here, B_0 is the horizontally integrated amplitude of the resulting buoyancy anomaly at $t = 0^+$. In fact, Equation (1.29c) tells us that the buoyancy at time $t = 0^+$ is simply

$$b_m(x,z,0^+) = B_0 \sin(mz)\delta(x)\,, \tag{1.31}$$

where we will keep a subscript m on this buoyancy to remind us that this is the solution with that vertical wavenumber. The question, then, is how this buoyancy evolves in time. In other words, what is $b(x,z,t)$ for $t > 0$?

To begin, we must first obtain from Equations (1.29) a single equation for b. The reader can verify that these equations can be combined to yield

$$\partial_t^2 \partial_z^2 b + N^2 \partial_x^2 b = \partial_t \partial_z^2 Q\,. \tag{1.32}$$

Since we already know the buoyancy at $t = 0^+$, and since $Q = 0$ for all $t > 0$, we are interested in the homogeneous part of this equation, i.e.,

$$\partial_t^2 \partial_z^2 b + N^2 \partial_x^2 b = 0\,. \tag{1.33}$$

This looks a lot like a wave equation.

To make any further progress, though, we need to make an assumption about the boundary condition at the tropopause. It is typical to treat the tropopause as a rigid lid. This is tantamount to assuming that the static stability of the stratosphere is infinite; i.e., $N = N_1 > 0$ in the troposphere, where N_1 is finite, and $N = N_2 = \infty$ in the stratosphere. That infinite stratification implies that $w = 0$ at $z = H$. Since w also equals zero at the surface, i.e., at $z = 0$, we have a finite domain in the vertical, and this implies that the normal modes of the system are discretized. In fact, from looking at Equation (1.33), we can guess them pretty easily:

$$\sin(mz)f(x + Nt/m)$$

and

$$\sin(mz)f(x - Nt/m)\,,$$

with m an integer multiple of π/H and f an arbitrary function.

These solutions are waves of buoyancy that retain their vertical structure and propagate either to the left or the right with speed N/m. Therefore, for the initial buoyancy given in Equation (1.31), the solution must be a delta function moving either to the left and/or the right. In fact, by the symmetry of the problem, there must be equal delta functions moving to the left and the right. Therefore, the solution is

$$b_m(x,z,t) = \frac{B_0}{2}\left[\delta(N_1 t/m + x) + \delta(N_1 t/m - x)\right]\sin(mz)\mathcal{H}(H-z)\mathcal{H}(t)\,. \qquad (1.34)$$

In the absence of dissipation, these pulses will propagate forever. As more and more moist convection happens, the domain fills up with more and more of these pulses, adding more and more kinetic energy. When does the growth in kinetic energy ever stop? In this system, never.

1.6 Leaky-lid gravity waves

In the real troposphere, of course, gravity-wave kinetic energy does not grow *ad infinitum.* Why? Because the tropopause is not a rigid lid. In other words, the stratification of the stratosphere is not infinite. Instead, N_2 is positive and finite. This allows waves to propagate into the stratosphere where they grow in amplitude due to the decreasing density, causing the waves to break and convert their energy to heat. For these tropospheric-centric lecture notes, we are interested not in the details of that wave breaking, but in what the escape of wave energy from the troposphere does to the pulses of heating in the troposphere.

Consider a semi-infinite atmosphere in the vertical, where N is piecewise constant in height,

$$N = \begin{cases} N_1 & 0 \le z \le H \\ N_2 & H < z \end{cases}\,. \qquad (1.35)$$

For $N_2 > N_1$, this is a simple analogue for Earth's atmosphere in which the troposphere is capped by the more stratified stratosphere. In this system, we have to be a bit more careful when we describe the heating. In principle, we could add heating to the stratosphere. In practice, however, moist convection does not appreciably penetrate into the stratosphere,[7] so we are still only interested in heatings that are confined between $z = 0$ and $z = H$. Therefore, we just need to be clear that our wavenumber-m heating pulse and the resulting initial buoyancy are restricted to $z < H$, which we can do with the Heaviside unit step function $\mathcal{H}$,

$$b_m(x,z,0^+) = B_0 \sin(mz)\delta(x)\mathcal{H}(H-z)\,. \qquad (1.36)$$

How does this evolve in time? Is (1.34) the solution? No, it is not. Since there is no longer a rigid lid, w is no longer constrained to be zero there, and the normal modes are now quite different. However, $b_m(x,z,t)$ can be derived analytically; for details, see Edman and Romps (2017).

[7]Deep convective clouds can sometimes overshoot into the stratosphere, but that effect is much too small and irrelevant to be bothered with for our purposes here.

Although the expression for $b_m(x,z,t)$ is a bit complicated, its behavior is simple. There are still two pulses of buoyancy: one that travels left and one that travels right. And, as in the rigid-lid case, the pulses are initially delta functions and they travel away from the origin at a speed of N/m. But, there are two big differences from the rigid-lid case: the stratosphere jiggles with waves, and the pulses of buoyancy in the troposphere "melt." By "melting," I mean that each pulse spreads out, growing in width. As it turns out, that width grows linearly with time. As a function of time, the full-width half-maximum of each pulse is

$$\text{FWHM} \approx \frac{N_1}{N_2}\frac{\pi N_1 t}{Hm^2}\,. \tag{1.37}$$

Since the integrated buoyancy within each pulse is finite, this also means that the buoyancy in each pulse is finite valued for all $t > 0$.

Let us put some numbers to these things. Let us take $N_1 = 0.01$ s^{-1}, $N_2 = 0.025$ s^{-1}, and $H = 15$ km as characteristic values for Earth's tropics. Deep heating throughout the troposphere will project strongly onto a vertical wavenumber of $m = \pi/H$, which is referred to as the first-baroclinic mode.[8] For this wave,

$$\begin{aligned} d\text{FWHM}/dt &\approx \frac{N_1}{N_2}\frac{HN_1}{\pi} \\ &\approx \frac{.01}{.025}\frac{15\times 10^3 \times .01}{3} \\ &= 20 \text{ m/s}. \end{aligned}$$

Meanwhile, for a first-baroclinic wave, the horizontal group velocity is

$$\begin{aligned} |c_{gx}| &= N_1/m \\ &= \frac{HN_1}{\pi} \\ &\approx \frac{15\times 10^3 \times 0.01}{3} \\ &= 50 \text{ m/s}. \end{aligned}$$

So, we see that the speed at which each pulse widens is comparable in magnitude to its speed of propagation.

How can we understand this behavior? Putting a plane wave $b_m \propto \exp(-i\omega t + ikx + imz)$ into

$$\partial_t^2 \partial_z^2 b_m + N_1 \partial_x^2 b_m = 0\,,$$

we find

$$(-i\omega)^2 (im)^2 + N_1 (ik)^2 = 0\,,$$

[8] In general, we refer to waves with $m = n\pi/H$ as the nth-baroclinic mode.

which can be written as

$$\omega = \pm N_1 k/m\,.$$

This is the dispersion relation for hydrostatic gravity waves in the troposphere. Note that $\partial\omega/\partial k$ gives the N_1/m expression used for the horizontal group velocity previously given. The vertical group velocity is given by

$$c_{gz} = \frac{\partial \omega}{\partial m} = \mp N_1 k/m^2\,.$$

Taking the plus sign to consider wave packets traveling upwards, we get $N_1 k/m^2$. To get an estimate of the residence time of the wave energy in the troposphere, we divide H by this speed, which gives

$$\tau_{\text{no lid}} \approx \frac{m^2 H}{N_1 k}\,.$$

This is the timescale with no lid, i.e., with $N_2 = N_1$. When $N_2 > N_1$, there is some wave reflection at the tropopause, trapping wave energy for longer. The result of that reflection is that the residence timescale is increased by a factor of N_2/N_1; see Edman and Romps (2017) for details. Therefore, the residence timescale for a wave with wavenumbers k and m is

$$\tau_{\text{leaky lid}} \approx \frac{N_2}{N_1}\frac{m^2 H}{N_1 k}\,.$$

In the tropics, $N_2/N_1 \approx 2.5$ and $H \approx 15$ km. The key thing for us to note is that this timescale is proportional to $1/k$, so higher horizontal wavenumbers decay faster. A wave with a first-baroclinic ($m = \pi/H$) vertical structure and a 100-km horizontal wavelength will decay on a timescale of

$$\begin{aligned}
\tau_{\text{leaky lid}} &\approx \frac{N_2}{N_1}\frac{\pi^2}{HN_1 k} \\
&= 2.5\frac{\pi^2}{15 \times 10^3 \times 0.01 \times (2\pi/10^5)} \\
&= 2.5\frac{\pi}{3 \times 10^{-3}} \\
&\approx 2500 \text{ s} \\
&< 1 \text{ hour}\,.
\end{aligned}$$

After an hour, what is left in the troposphere? In this case, not much: the sine wave has mostly disappeared after an hour. What if the pattern were not sinusoidal, but had a pattern that repeated horizontally every 100 km? In that case, there would be higher-k components at the beginning, but those would decay away in even less time than 1 hour because the residence timescale goes like $1/k$. On the other hand, if there were components with wavelengths much greater than 100 km, then those components would still remain after 1 hour.

The longest-lived first-baroclinic wave would be the wave with the longest possible horizontal wavelength. On Earth, the maximum lengthscale is set by the planet's circumference of 40,000 km. For a wave with that horizontal wavelength, the timescale would be 400 times as long as for the 100-km wavelength, and that is equal to about 10 days.

It is important to recognize that the vertically propagating waves do *not* remove the horizontally averaged buoyancy from the troposphere. The horizontally averaged buoyancy belongs to the $k=0$ component, which has an infinite residence timescale. The propagation of waves out of the troposphere simply smooths the buoyancy horizontally until, finally, it is horizontally uniform.

1.7 When and why does DSE conservation fail?

In Section 1.2.6, we saw that using conservation of DSE could generate negative temperatures, which is clearly unphysical. The problem is with the DSE equation that we derived,

$$\frac{d}{dt}\mathrm{DSE} = Q/\rho .$$

Although this is how the DSE equation is almost always written, this is missing a term that can be quite important in certain cases. To find out what went wrong in the derivation, and to correct it, we must go back to the enthalpy equation,

$$\rho\frac{d}{dt}h = Q + \frac{d}{dt}p .$$

To treat the dp/dt term properly, we need to distinguish between the pressure and density of the Lagrangian parcel (p and ρ) and the pressure and density of the environment at the same height but far from the Lagrangian parcel (p_e and ρ_e). Then, to invoke hydrostatic balance, we need to make two reasonable assumptions: 1. that the environment is hydrostatic far from the parcel (i.e., with $\partial_z p_e = -\rho_e g$ there) and, 2. that $p(z) = p_e(z)$ (which does *not* require hydrostatic flows around the parcel). With those two assumptions,

$$\begin{aligned}\frac{dp}{dt} &= \frac{dp_e}{dt} \\ &= w\frac{dp_e}{dz} \\ &= w\partial_z p_e \\ &= -w\rho_e g \\ &= -\rho_e\frac{d}{dt}(gz) .\end{aligned}$$

Substituting into the enthalpy equation, we get

$$\rho\frac{d}{dt}h = Q - \rho_e\frac{d}{dt}(gz) .$$

Next, we add $\rho d(gz)/dt$ to both sides to make $\rho d\text{DSE}/dt$ on the left. Because $\rho_e \neq \rho$ in general, we get

$$\rho \frac{d}{dt}\text{DSE} = Q + (\rho - \rho_e)\frac{d}{dt}(gz).$$

Dividing by ρ, this can be written as

$$\frac{d}{dt}\text{DSE} = Q/\rho - bw\,, \tag{1.38}$$

where

$$b = g(\rho_e/\rho - 1) \tag{1.39}$$

is the parcel's buoyancy. Using the ideal gas law and the fact that $p = p_e$, the reader can confirm that Equation (1.39) is identical to Equation (1.5).

For adiabatic processes, Equation (1.38) tells us that

$$\frac{d}{dz}\text{DSE} = -b\,.$$

In other words, if the Lagrangian parcel is positively buoyant, then its DSE decreases as it moves upwards. If it is negatively buoyant, its DSE increases as it moves upwards. We can write this as a conservation law by noting that convective available potential energy (CAPE) is the vertical integral of a parcel's buoyancy from its current height to some reference height above (e.g., its level of neutral buoyancy),

$$\text{CAPE} = \int_z^{\text{LNB}} dz'\, b(z')\,.$$

Note that,

$$\frac{d}{dz}\text{CAPE} = -b\,.$$

Therefore, we can write the general conservation law for a dry adiabatically lifted parcel as

$$\frac{d}{dz}(\text{DSE} - \text{CAPE}) = 0\,.$$

In other words, $\text{DSE} - \text{CAPE}$ is conserved for an adiabatically lifted parcel. When water is involved, the correct statement is that *moist* static energy (MSE) minus CAPE is conserved; see Romps (2015) for details.

Let us return to that example of lifting a surface parcel to 40 km. Using an original temperature of 300 K and conserving DSE, we got the nonsensical temperature of -100 K. Now, let us use conservation of $\text{DSE} - \text{CAPE}$. That can be written as

$$
\begin{aligned}
\frac{d}{dz}(c_pT+gz) &= -b \\
&= -g\frac{\rho_e-\rho}{\rho} \\
&= -g\rho_e/\rho+g \\
\Rightarrow \quad c_p\frac{dT}{dz} &= -g\rho_e/\rho \\
&= -gT/T_e \\
\Rightarrow \quad \frac{dT}{dz} &= -\frac{g}{c_pT_e}T \\
\Rightarrow \quad \frac{d}{dz}\log(T) &= -\frac{g}{c_pT_e} \\
\Rightarrow \quad T(z) &= T(0)\exp\left[-\int_0^z dz'\frac{g}{c_pT_e(z')}\right].
\end{aligned}
$$

From this equation, we see that T is always non-negative. For an isothermal atmosphere, this is simply

$$T(z)=T(0)e^{-gz/c_pT_e}.$$

In other words, the temperature of the parcel undergoes an e-folding reduction for every distance c_pT_e/g that it ascends. For $T_e = 300$ K, this is $1000\times300/10=30$ km. So, by 40 km, the parcel has experienced only a little more than one e-folding of its temperature: $300\times\exp(-40/30)=79$ K.

To make contact with the standard dry-adiabatic lapse rate, let us take the expression for the $T(z)$ of a dry parcel in an isothermal atmosphere and Taylor expand in terms of z. This gives

$$T(z)=T(0)-\frac{T(0)}{T_e}\frac{g}{c_p}z+\frac{T(0)}{2}\left(\frac{g}{c_pT_e}\right)^2 z^2+\ldots.$$

Written this way, we see that the parcel's initial lapse rate is not g/c_p, but $T(0)/T_e$ times g/c_p. Consider the case where $T_e=300$ K. If $T(0)=303$ K, then the parcel's initial lapse rate will be 1% larger than g/c_p. If the parcel is heated by a flame to 1000 K, then the parcel's initial dry-adiabatic lapse rate will be a whopping 33 K/km. If, on the other hand, the parcel begins with $T(0)=T_e$, then its initial lapse rate will be exactly g/c_p and the third term on the right-hand side becomes the leading correction. That third term on the right-hand side remains negligible compared to the second term on the right-hand side so long as z is much less than c_pT_e/g, which is exactly the e-folding distance for $T(z)$.

1.8 Moist thermodynamic equations

What happens if there is water vapor? Since water vapor can condense, we have to account for the internal energy of the water vapor to properly track the energy. The energy of an air parcel is then approximately given by

$$E = c_v T + q_v E_{0v} - q_s E_{0s} + u^2/2 + gz\,, \tag{1.40}$$

where q_v is the vapor mass fraction (i.e., the fraction of the parcel's mass that is water vapor), q_s is the solid mass fraction (i.e., the fraction of the parcel's mass that is ice), E_{0v} is the difference in specific internal energy between vapor and liquid at the same temperature, and E_{0s} is the difference in specific internal energy between liquid and solid at the same temperature. This expression is approximate because it does not account for the differences between the heat capacities of dry air, water vapor, liquid water, and ice. Those differences must be taken into account in any quantitatively accurate treatment of atmospheric thermodynamics (see Romps 2008), but are not at all necessary for understanding the basics. Therefore, in this expression, we pretend as though dry air, water vapor, liquid water, and ice all have the same heat capacity c_v. This is an acceptable approximation because the total mass fraction of water does not exceed a few percent in Earth's tropics.

Note that the liquid-water mass fraction q_l does not appear in this definition of specific energy. That is because we have chosen to define the specific internal energy of liquid water as equal to the specific internal energy of dry air at the same temperature. By this choice, a kilogram of liquid water has the same energy as a kilogram of dry air with the same T, u^2, and z. Because liquid water can evaporate or freeze, we are *not* free to make the same choice for water vapor and ice; instead, the values of E_{0v} and E_{0s} must be given their empirical values. If water were able to convert to dry air, then that would have eliminated the freedom we have to define the internal energy of liquid water equal to dry air.

Proceeding as before, the specific internal energy e is simply the specific energy E minus the specific kinetic and gravitational pieces,

$$e = c_v T + q_v E_{0v} - q_s E_{0s}\,. \tag{1.41}$$

To get specific enthalpy, we must add to this the specific "pV," which is p/ρ. We will assume that liquid and ice have no volume[9] so that they contribute nothing to "pV." Therefore, $p = (q_a R + q_v R_v)\rho T$, where $q_a = 1 - q_v - q_l - q_s$ is the dry-air mass fraction, R is the specific gas constant of dry air, and R_v is the specific gas constant of water vapor. Adding p/ρ to the specific internal energy, we get specific enthalpy $h = e + (q_a R + q_v R_v)T$, or

$$h = c_p T - q_t RT + q_v L_c - q_s L_f\,,$$

[9]The density of air at 1 bar is about 1 kg m^{-3}, whereas the density of water is about 1 ton m^{-3}, so the specific volume of liquid is about 1000 times smaller than that for dry air.

where $c_p = c_v + R$, $q_t = q_v + q_l + q_s$ is the total water mass fraction, $L_c = E_{0v} + R_v T$ is the specific latent heat of condensation, and $L_f = E_{0s}$ is the specific latent heat of freezing. The $q_t RT$ term is small compared to the errors introduced by neglecting the differences in heat capacity between dry air and the three phases of water, so we can safely ignore this term for the level of accuracy we hope to achieve here. Therefore, we can write our expression for the enthalpy as

$$h = c_p T + q_v L_c - q_s L_f \,. \tag{1.42}$$

We can then define something perfectly analogous to the dry static energy by adding gz to the specific enthalpy. Rather than calling it the dry static energy (DSE), however, we refer to it as the moist static energy (MSE) to emphasize that water is involved. Adding the specific gravitational potential energy to the enthalpy, we get $\text{MSE} = h + gz$, or

$$\text{MSE} = c_p T + q_v L_c - q_s L_f + gz \,. \tag{1.43}$$

The E, e, h, and MSE equations are then

$$\rho \frac{d}{dt} E = Q - \vec{\nabla} \cdot (p\vec{u}) \tag{1.44}$$

$$\rho \frac{d}{dt} e = Q - p\vec{\nabla} \cdot \vec{u} \tag{1.45}$$

$$\rho \frac{d}{dt} h = Q + \frac{dp}{dt} \tag{1.46}$$

$$\rho \frac{d}{dt} \text{MSE} = Q - \rho b w \,. \tag{1.47}$$

With E, e, h, and MSE defined in this way, we must interpret Q strictly as a radiative heating; we can no longer think of Q as encompassing latent heating, too. Instead, with these definitions, latent heating does not alter E, e, h, or MSE; e.g., for MSE, it simply moves energy between $c_p T$, gz, $q_v L_c$, and, if freezing, melting, deposition, or sublimation are involved, $-q_s L_f$.

1.9 Moist-adiabatic lapse rate

A common convention, and the one that we adopt here, is to denote saturation quantities by an asterisk. So, for example, if we define p_v to be the vapor pressure of water vapor, then $p_v^*(T)$ is the saturation vapor pressure at temperature T. Note that p_v^* is a function of temperature only. Similarly, q_v^* is the saturation water-vapor mass fraction; it is a function of temperature and pressure. For a warm cloud, i.e., one that has no ice, we can approximate q_v as q_v^* because the cloud always stays within 1% of a relative humidity of one. Therefore, given the cloud's MSE, pressure, and height, we can calculate its temperature. For a cloud with a mixture of ice and liquid, its q_v is more uncertain because it lies somewhere in between the saturation value with respect to liquid and the saturation value with respect to ice; the precise value is determined by time-dependent kinetic effects. To avoid those complications, we will simply ignore ice and assume that we are dealing with warm clouds. With the assumption that $q_s = 0$, we can write a cloud's MSE, which is equal to its MSE*, as

$$\text{MSE} = \text{MSE}^* = c_p T + q_v^*(p,T)L + gz \quad \text{(warm cloud)},$$

where we henceforth drop the subscript "c" on L_c since there will be no ambiguity going forward that L is the latent heat of condensation. If the cloud's buoyancy is negligible, and if the cloud's lifetime is brief compared to the time it would take radiative heating to have any significant effect, then, by Equation (1.47), we can approximate its MSE as conserved.[10] Then, assuming we know the MSE of the cloud, and given z and p, we can solve the previous equation for T numerically (i.e., using a root solver). In that way, we can construct the entire temperature profile of the cloud as it rises through the troposphere.

What implication does this have for the temperature profile of the atmosphere? Well, one common and convenient approximation is to say that convection adjusts the temperature of the atmosphere to a moist adiabat.[11] To be precise, an atmosphere with a moist-adiabatic temperature profile is an atmosphere whose temperature profile is the same as that of a saturated air parcel that is adiabatically lifted through it. Let us derive the expression for a moist adiabat in such an atmosphere.

First, we have to figure out how q_v^* varies in the vertical. Since q_v^* is approximately given by[12]

$$q_v^* = \frac{Rp_v^*}{R_v p},$$

we can take ∂_z of this and divide by q_v^* to find

$$\partial_z \log(q_v^*) = \partial_z \log(p_v^*) - \partial_z \log(p). \tag{1.48}$$

So, to figure out how q_v^* varies in the vertical, we need to find $\partial_z \log(p_v^*)$ and $\partial_z \log(p)$.

From the Clausius–Clapeyron relation, we know that p_v^* varies with temperature according to

$$\frac{d}{dT}\log(p_v^*) = \frac{L}{R_v T^2}.$$

Defining $\Gamma = -\partial T/\partial z$ as the lapse rate, we can multiply this by Γ to get

$$\partial_z \log(p_v^*) = -\frac{L\Gamma}{R_v T^2}. \tag{1.49}$$

This gives us one of the terms needed on the right-hand side of Equation (1.48).

[10]This ignores convective entrainment, which we will later see is important. The effect of entrainment would show up in Equations (1.44–1.47) through diffusive terms, which we have neglected. The turbulent eddies would shear out our cloudy parcel until spatial gradients in its vicinity become so large that the diffusive terms start to matter, and the properties of the environment would begin to diffuse into the parcel.

[11]Again, this statement neglects the effects of entrainment. The lapse rate with entrainment will be treated in Section 1.12.

[12]The approximation here is to keep using R, the dry-air gas constant, for the moist air. For small q_v, this is a good approximation.

For the other term, we can use hydrostatic balance,

$$\partial_z p = -\rho g \, .$$

Using the ideal gas law to write ρ as p/RT, we get

$$\partial_z \log(p) = -\frac{g}{RT} \, . \tag{1.50}$$

This is the second term needed on the right-hand side of (1.48).

Combining (1.48–1.50), we get

$$\partial_z \log(q_v^*) = -\gamma \, , \tag{1.51}$$

where

$$\gamma = \frac{L\Gamma}{R_v T^2} - \frac{g}{RT} \, . \tag{1.52}$$

This is the fractional change in q_v^* with height.

We are now ready to derive the moist-adiabatic lapse rate. By definition of a moist-adiabatic atmosphere, the temperature of adiabatically rising clouds matches the temperature of the environment, so the cloud buoyancy is zero and, therefore, the cloud MSE is conserved (i.e., constant in height). Since clouds are saturated, this means that MSE* is conserved as well, which means that $\partial_z \mathrm{MSE}^* = 0$. This fact can be written as

$$\begin{aligned}
0 &= \partial_z \mathrm{MSE}^* \\
&= c_p \partial_z T + L \partial_z q_v^* + g \partial_z z \\
&= -c_p \Gamma - L q_v^* \gamma + g \\
&= -c_p \Gamma - L q_v^* \left(\frac{L\Gamma}{R_v T^2} - \frac{g}{RT} \right) + g \\
&= -\Gamma \left(c_p + \frac{q_v^* L^2}{R_v T^2} \right) + g + \frac{q_v^* L g}{RT} \, .
\end{aligned}$$

Solving for Γ, we get

$$\Gamma = \frac{g + \dfrac{q_v^* L g}{RT}}{c_p + \dfrac{q_v^* L^2}{R_v T^2}} \, . \tag{1.53}$$

This is the moist-adiabatic lapse rate.

In very cold temperatures, terms multiplied by q_v^* are small, so $\Gamma = g/c_p = 10$ K km^{-1}. This makes sense: in cold climates, water vapor is so scarce that its presence should have a negligible impact on the lapse rate. This is true in the tropical upper troposphere. On the other hand, at the bottom of the tropical free troposphere, q_v^* is roughly 0.02 and cannot be neglected. Using $R \approx 300$ J kg^{-1} K^{-1}, $R_v \approx 500$ J kg^{-1}

K^{-1}, and $L \approx 2.5 \times 10^6$ J kg^{-1}, we can find Γ at the bottom of the tropical free troposphere to be

$$\Gamma = \frac{10 + \frac{0.02 \times 2.5 \times 10^6 \times 10}{300 \times 300}}{1000 + \frac{0.02 \times (2.5 \times 10^6)^2}{500 \times 300^2}} \tag{1.54}$$

$$= 4 \text{ K km}^{-1}. \tag{1.55}$$

If we average 10 and 4 we get 7 K km^{-1}, which is very close to the value of 6.5 K km^{-1} that is often taken as a representative lapse rate for the troposphere.

1.10 Bulk-plume model

So far, we have neglected convective entrainment, which is the turbulent mixing—and subsequent diffusion—of environmental properties into clouds as they rise through the atmosphere. The simplest representation of a convective atmosphere that includes entrainment is called the bulk-plume model. To be more accurate, we could call this a two-bulk-plume model: one of the plumes is for the ascending air and the other plume is for the descending air. By "bulk" we mean that the properties of each plume are horizontally homogeneous.

Let us denote one of the plumes by a subscript c for convecting clouds, and let us denote the other plume by a subscript e for environment. For conservation of mass, we can approximate the density of the cloud and environment as equal, so we will not bother with a subscript on ρ. Let us denote the area fraction of the cloud and the environment by σ_c and σ_e, respectively. These are related by $\sigma_e = 1 - \sigma_c$. Let us denote the vertical velocity of the cloud by w_c and the vertical velocity of the environment by w_e.

Finally, we will assume that the atmosphere is in radiative-convective equilibrium (RCE). This means that there is no large-scale ascent or descent, just like in a single column of a GCM that is physically isolated from its neighbors. In RCE, conservation of mass requires that $\sigma_c w_c + \sigma_e w_e = 0$. We call $\sigma_c \rho w_c$ the convective mass flux or, since there is usually no ambiguity as to which mass flux we are referring, we simply call it the mass flux. We denote this by M. Note that the convective and environmental mass fluxes are equal and opposite; when we need to be careful with signs, we might write these as M_c and M_e, respectively. Note that $M = \sigma_c \rho w_c$ has units of kg m^{-2} s^{-1}. In particular, $M(z)$ is the kilograms of convective air passing upward per second through an average square meter of horizontal area at height z. Note that this is the mass flux for an average area of the total domain, not for an average area of the convective plume, which would simply be ρw_c.

We are almost ready to write down the continuity equations for the two plumes. But, we first need to recognize that mass can move from one plume to the other. If this were not possible, then air could not move in the plumes at all: the troposphere has a lower and upper boundary, so for mass to ascend in one plume, it must eventually move into the other plume so that it can descend. Let us denote by $e(z)$ the kilograms of air per second that are entrained into the convective plume from the environmental plume in an average cubic meter of total atmosphere at height z. Similarly, we can define $d(z)$ to be the mass that is detrained from the convective plume into the environmental plume.

Now, we can write the two mass-conservation equations as

$$\partial_t(\sigma_c\rho)+\partial_z(\sigma_c\rho w_c)=e-d \tag{1.56}$$

$$\partial_t(\sigma_e\rho)+\partial_z(\sigma_e\rho w_e)=d-e. \tag{1.57}$$

Since $\sigma_e=1-\sigma_c$ and $\sigma_e\rho w_e=-\sigma_c\rho w_c$, these are redundant equations, so we need only keep one of them. We will retain the first one.

By scale analysis, we can reduce the complexity even further. For a column of atmosphere that is hundreds of kilometers wide with a large ensemble of cloudy updrafts, σ_c will vary on timescales of about a day or longer. Convective properties will vary in the vertical on a lengthscale comparable to the depth of the troposphere. And, empirically, the characteristic updraft speed and convective area fraction are about 10 m s^{-1} and 10^{-3}. Altogether, the characteristic scales of t, z, w_c, ρ, and σ_c are, respectively,

$$T=10^5 \text{ s} \tag{1.58}$$

$$H=10^4 \text{ m} \tag{1.59}$$

$$W_c=10 \text{ m s}^{-1} \tag{1.60}$$

$$P=1 \text{ kg m}^{-3} \tag{1.61}$$

$$\Sigma_c=10^{-3}. \tag{1.62}$$

Therefore, the magnitudes of the terms on the left-hand side of (1.56) are $\Sigma_c P/T=10^{-8}$ kg m^{-3} s^{-1} and $\Sigma_c PW_c/H=10^{-6}$ kg m^{-3} s^{-1}. Therefore, the first term (the storage) is 100 times smaller than the second term (the divergence), so it does not enter into the dominant balance and can be neglected. In fact, to reach this conclusion, we do not have to assume anything about the magnitudes of ρ and σ since they appear in both terms on the left-hand side. For example, the tendency would still be 100 times smaller than the divergence if we took the magnitude of ρ to be $P=0.1$ kg m^{-3} (appropriate for the upper troposphere) and/or $\Sigma_c=10^{-2}$ (appropriate for a more intensely convecting atmosphere). The large difference in magnitude between the two terms on the left-hand side of (1.56) is caused by the fact that mass transits the depth of the convecting layer in a time that is much shorter (about 10^3 seconds) than the timescale over which M varies (about a day, or 10^5 seconds).

Neglecting the tendency term, the continuity equation for a bulk-plume atmosphere (with no large-scale ascent or descent) becomes

$$\partial_z M=e-d. \tag{1.63}$$

Introducing the fractional entrainment rate ε (units of m^{-1}) and fractional detrainment rate δ (units of m^{-1}), which are related to e and d by $e=\varepsilon M$ and $d=\delta M$, we can write (1.63) as

$$\partial_z M = M(\varepsilon - \delta)$$

or

$$\partial_z \log(M) = \varepsilon - \delta\,.$$

Next, let us consider how a passive tracer gets transported by the bulk plumes. Let us denote the mixing ratio of the tracer in the two plumes as $\phi_c(z)$ and $\phi_e(z)$. If the tracer has no sources and sinks, i.e., it is just advected by the plumes, then the tracer obeys

$$\partial_t(\sigma_c\rho\phi_c) + \partial_z(\sigma_c\rho w_c\phi_c) = e\phi_e - d\phi_c \tag{1.64}$$

$$\partial_t(\sigma_e\rho\phi_e) + \partial_z(\sigma_e\rho w_e\phi_e) = d\phi_c - e\phi_e\,. \tag{1.65}$$

By the same argument, the tendency in the first equation does not enter into the dominant balance and can be neglected. But, that argument cannot be made for the environment's tendency: the timescale for variations in ϕ_e is comparable to or smaller than the timescale for environmental mass to transit the depth of the troposphere. In fact, the timescale T for variations in ϕ_e can be thought of as advection dominated (i.e., dominated by subsidence). Letting L denote the length scale of vertical variations, which can be less than H if ϕ_e has many oscillations in the vertical, then the scales for Equation (1.65) are

$$T = L/W_e \tag{1.66}$$

$$L \leq H \tag{1.67}$$

$$W_e = \Sigma_c W_c = 10^{-2} \text{ m s}^{-1}\,, \tag{1.68}$$

where the last line is obtained from conservation of mass ($\sigma_e\rho w_e = -\sigma_c\rho w_c$). With these scales, the terms on the left-hand side of (1.65) are of the same order of magnitude, so both terms must be retained.

Since $\sigma_e \approx 1$, we can approximate the tendency in Equation (1.65) as $\rho\partial_t\phi_e$. Therefore, we can approximate these equations as

$$\partial_z(M\phi_c) = e\phi_e - d\phi_c \tag{1.69}$$

$$\rho\partial_t\phi_e - \partial_z(M\phi_e) = d\phi_c - e\phi_e\,. \tag{1.70}$$

Using Equation (1.63), we can write (1.69) as

$$\partial_z\phi_c = \varepsilon(\phi_e - \phi_c)\,. \tag{1.71}$$

This tells us that entrainment is trying to relax ϕ_c to ϕ_e on a length scale of $1/\varepsilon$ as the cloud rises. If we add (1.69) and (1.70), we get

$$\rho\partial_t\phi_e = \partial_z\left[M(\phi_e - \phi_c)\right]. \tag{1.72}$$

This tells us that the tracer is conserved: the storage of tracer in a layer of the atmosphere is equal to the convergence of tracer into that layer by the convective

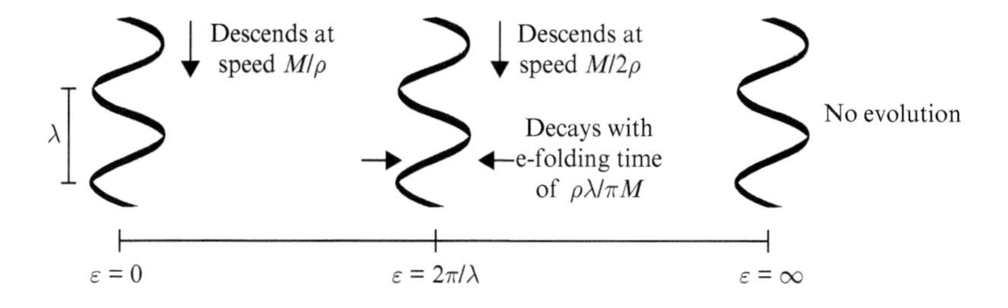

Fig. 1.7 The response of a sinusoidal tracer profile to moist convection with $\delta = \varepsilon$ and three values of ε: zero, the vertical wavenumber of the sinusoid, and infinity.

plume, $-\partial_z(M\phi_c)$, plus the convergence of tracer into that layer by the environmental plume, $-\partial_z(M_e\phi_e) = \partial_z(M\phi_e)$.

To get a feel for how the tracer evolves, let us consider the simplifying case of $\partial_z M = 0$. We can then take a look at three scenarios:

- If $\varepsilon = 0$, Equation (1.71) tells us that $\partial_z\phi_c = 0$, so ϕ_c is constant in height. Therefore, by (1.72), $\rho\partial_t\phi_e = M\partial_z\phi_e$. In other words, the ϕ_e profile simply advects downwards at a speed M/ρ.
- In the limit of $\varepsilon \to \infty$, Equation (1.71) tells us that $\phi_c = \phi_e$; i.e., the exchange of mass into and out of the convective plume is so fast that the properties of the convective plume are identical to that of the environment. By Equation (1.72), this tells us that $\partial_t\phi_e = 0$. In other words, the ϕ_e profile does not evolve: the initial $\phi_e(z)$ is simply frozen in time.
- For intermediate ε, the effect is to cause the profile to descend and decay. (I say "decay" rather than diffuse because the effective diffusivity is a function of vertical wavenumber, so it is not strictly a diffusive process.) The fastest decay occurs when $\varepsilon = m$, where m is the vertical wavenumber. In that case, the e-folding timescale is $2\rho/Mm$ and the subsidence speed is $M/2\rho$ (see Romps 2014*b* for details). Therefore, the distance that the sinusoid descends in one e-folding timescale is $1/m$, i.e., a wavelength divided by 2π, i.e., about one-sixth of a wavelength. In other words, the tracer pattern decays away rapidly.

These three scenarios are depicted in Figure 1.7. As ϵ is increased from 0 to ∞, the descent rate decreases from M/ρ to 0. On the other hand, the decay rate of the sinusoid is non-monotonic as ε is increased from 0 to ∞: it starts at 0, reaches a peak value when $\varepsilon = m$, and then goes back to zero.

1.11 Free-tropospheric relative humidity

The previous section has given us a feel for the transient evolution of tracers in the moist-convecting atmosphere. More relevant to climate, however, is the application of the bulk-plume equations to the steady-state profile of relative humidity. Water vapor is the dominant greenhouse gas and shortwave absorber, so it is critically important to understand the processes that set its distribution.

In the derivation that follows, we will let $q_v(z)$ represent the water-vapor mass fraction in the environment. Since the environment occupies 99–99.9% of the horizontal area at each height, $q_v(z)$ is also an excellent approximation for the specific humidity averaged over the entire area (both convection and environment) at height z. Therefore, we will interchangeably refer to q_v as the specific humidity of the environment and of the entire atmosphere.

For the convective plume, we will make two simplifying approximations. First, we will assume that the convective plume carries no condensates. This may sound a bit silly (after all, clouds are only visible because of their condensates), but the ratio of the condensate mass fraction to the water-vapor mass fraction is quite small within moist convection in the lower troposphere. And, although we do not allow the convective plume to lift condensates, we still allow the convecting plume to condense water vapor; we just imagine that the resulting condensates are removed from the convective plume quickly, with some fraction rapidly falling to the surface and the remainder rapidly evaporating into the environment.

Second, we assume that the temperatures of the two plumes are equal at each height. This "zero-buoyancy plume approximation" was introduced by Singh and O'Gorman (2013). This may also sound a bit silly (after all, clouds only rise because they have some positive buoyancy), but that buoyancy is of only secondary importance to the atmosphere's water budget. Furthermore, the typical buoyancy of tropical moist convection (expressed as an effective temperature difference) is only about 0.3 K (Romps and Öktem, 2015), which is quite small, indeed. With these two approximations, the convective plume's mass fraction of total water is simply equal to the environment's saturation humidity, $q_v^*(z)$.

To begin, we will construct the bulk-plume equations for water vapor in RCE, i.e., in an atmosphere with no net ascent or descent. Let M denote the convective mass flux (units of kg m^{-2} s^{-1}), e and d denote the entrainment and detrainment rates (units of kg m^{-3} s^{-1}), c denote the condensation rate (units of kg m^{-3} s^{-1}), and α the fraction of condensates formed at height z that evaporate into the environment. For analytic solubility, we will assume that this fraction of condensates formed at z also evaporates into the environment at height z. Note that the precipitation efficiency PE is equal to $1-\alpha$. We can then write down the following equations for the steady-state convective mass flux M, the humidity within clouds q_v^*, and the humidity within the environment q_v:

$$\partial_z M = e - d \tag{1.73}$$

$$\partial_z (M q_v^*) = e q_v - d q_v^* - c \tag{1.74}$$

$$\partial_z (-M q_v) = d q_v^* - e q_v + \alpha c. \tag{1.75}$$

Since M is the total mass flux and q_v is a mass fraction (as opposed to a mixing ratio), there should technically be a $-c$ on the right-hand side of Equation (1.73) to account for the loss of mass due to condensation. For small q_v^*, as in Earth's atmosphere, this term has a negligible impact and its inclusion greatly complicates the equations, so it has been omitted.[13] Defining the fractional entrainment and detrainment rates as $\varepsilon = e/M$ and $\delta = d/M$, the mass flux M can be eliminated from these equations to yield

$$\partial_z q_v^* = \varepsilon(q_v - q_v^*) - c/M \tag{1.76}$$
$$-\partial_z q_v = \delta(q_v^* - q_v) + \alpha c/M\,. \tag{1.77}$$

Writing q_v as $\mathrm{RH}q_v^*$, we can write the left-hand side of (1.77) as

$$[1 - (1/\gamma)\partial_z \log(\mathrm{RH})]\,\mathrm{RH}\gamma q_v^*$$

where $\gamma = -\partial_z \log(q_v^*)$ as before. Since $1/\gamma \approx 2$ km in the tropics, the second term in these square brackets is negligible so long as the fractional variations in relative humidity (RH) are small over that distance. Averaged over large horizontal areas, this is certainly true, so we can neglect that term and approximate these equations as

$$-\gamma q_v^* = \varepsilon(\mathrm{RH} - 1)q_v^* - c/M \tag{1.78}$$
$$\mathrm{RH}\gamma q_v^* = \delta(1 - \mathrm{RH})q_v^* + \alpha c/M. \tag{1.79}$$

These two equations can be solved for RH and c/M, giving

$$\mathrm{RH} = \frac{\delta + \alpha\gamma - \alpha\varepsilon}{\delta + \gamma - \alpha\varepsilon} \tag{1.80}$$
$$\frac{c}{M} = \frac{\delta + \gamma - \varepsilon}{\delta + \gamma - \alpha\varepsilon}\gamma q_v^*\,. \tag{1.81}$$

This derivation of Equation (1.80) is replicated from Romps (2014*a*).

This expression for RH is particularly easy to understand if $\alpha = 0$. In that case, Equation (1.80) simplifies to

$$\mathrm{RH} = \frac{\delta}{\delta + \gamma}\,. \tag{1.82}$$

Note that $1/\delta$ is the lengthscale over which convection moistens the environment towards saturation (by detraining saturated air into the clear air as it subsides), and $1/\gamma$ is the lengthscale over which subsidence drives RH towards zero (by adiabatic compression of the subsiding air, which drives up q_v^*). The relative humidity is set by the balance between these two processes. If δ is large, then the moistening effect of

[13] This choice is analogous to the treatment of mass in the Boussinesq equations, in which density is held constant for the purposes of the conservation-of-mass equation even though it is effectively removed and added by the "heating" Q in the equation for buoyancy.

convection wins out over subsidence-driven drying, and RH is close to unity. If δ is small, then the subsidence-driven "drying" dominates,[14] and RH is close to zero.

In the free troposphere, the relative humidity profile tends to have maximum values in the lower and upper troposphere, and a minimum in the middle troposphere. We are now in a position to understand this characteristic "C" shape of the RH profile. In the lower troposphere, γ is small because Γ is small and T is large. In the upper troposphere, δ is large because the mass flux is decreasing with height towards zero. In both places, these facts push RH closer to one than zero. In the middle troposphere, both δ and γ are moderate and, in fact, tend to be of comparable magnitude, i.e., around 1/(2 km). That drives RH to values around a half.

Equation (1.80) also allows us to see how biases in a convective parameterization will affect free-tropospheric RH in a GCM. A convective parameterization that has too little entrainment will also have too little detrainment (since the mass flux M and, therefore, $\partial_z M$ are largely constrained by clear-sky radiative cooling, and $\partial_z M = e - d$), and this will tend to produce a free troposphere that is too dry. And, not surprisingly, a convective parameterization that has too high a precipitation efficiency (i.e., too low an α) will also produce a free troposphere that is too dry.

The precipitation efficiency is notoriously difficult to quantify in observations. For an atmosphere with no net ascent, however, we can place a bound on the precipitation efficiency simply by measuring RH. Solving (1.80) for α, we get

$$\alpha = \mathrm{RH}\frac{A}{B}, \tag{1.83}$$

where

$$A = \gamma - (1 - \mathrm{RH})\frac{\delta}{\mathrm{RH}} \tag{1.84}$$

$$B = \gamma - (1 - \mathrm{RH})\ \varepsilon\,. \tag{1.85}$$

Since α and RH are positive by definition, either A and B are both positive or both negative. To determine their sign, consider B. By Equation (1.78), B is equal to the gross condensation rate c divided by the mass flux M and q_v^*, all of which are positive. Therefore, A and B are both positive. Since δ is generally bigger than ε, δ/RH is almost certainly bigger than ε, so $0 < A < B$. Therefore, $A/B < 1$ and so $\alpha < \mathrm{RH}$. Since $\mathrm{PE} = 1 - \alpha$, this implies that $\mathrm{PE} > 1 - \mathrm{RH}$. In other words, an observation of RH automatically provides a lower bound on PE. Figure 1.8 plots PE and $1 - \mathrm{RH}$ for a cloud-resolving simulation of RCE, where PE(z) is the net condensation above height z divided by the gross condensation above height z. As expected, PE is bounded from below by $1 - \mathrm{RH}$.

[14] The word "drying" is in quotation marks here because the adiabatic subsidence of a parcel does not change its q_v; it only increases is q_v^*, thereby leading to a decrease in RH. Therefore, it is only a drying from the perspective of *relative* humidity.

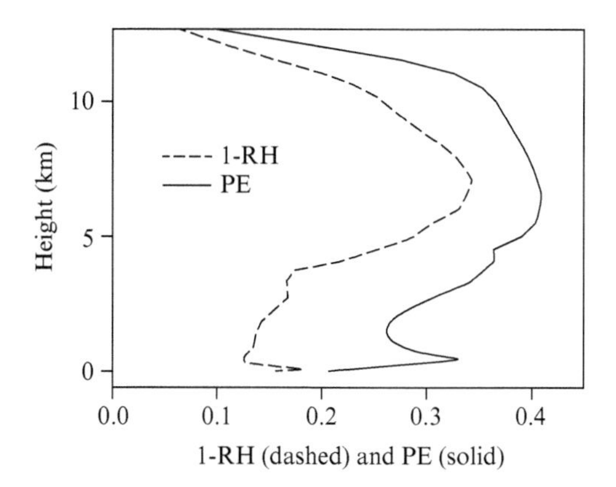

Fig. 1.8 (left) Profiles of (dashed) $1-\text{RH}$ and (solid) precipitation efficiency for a cloud-resolving simulation of RCE. Adapted from Romps (2014*a*).

1.12 Moist-entraining lapse rate

In Section 1.9, we derived an expression for the moist-adiabatic lapse rate. In reality, the lapse rate of the tropical free troposphere is larger than that for a moist adiabat; the real atmosphere is much closer to the temperature of entraining moist convection. Following Romps (2016), we can derive an expression for the moist-entraining lapse rate by assuming that M, RH, and PE (i.e., $1-\alpha$) are all constant with height. The constancy of M with height then implies that $\varepsilon=\delta$, and the constancy of RH and α then implies that ε and δ are both constant.

To set up the problem, we must write down two expressions for the vertical derivative of MSE* that can be combined to give an expression for Γ. Using the zero-buoyancy plume approximation, MSE* of the environment is equal to MSE* of the convection because their temperatures are equal. Recalling the definitions $\text{MSE}^*=c_pT+Lq_v^*+gz$ and $\gamma\equiv-\partial_z\log(q_v^*)$, we can write

$$\partial_z\text{MSE}^* \;=\; -c_p\Gamma+g-L\gamma q_v^*\,.$$

Using Equation (1.52) for γ, we can write this as

$$\partial_z\text{MSE}^* \;=\; g\left(1+\frac{q_v^*L}{RT}\right)-\Gamma\left(c_p+\frac{q_v^*L^2}{R_vT^2}\right). \tag{1.86}$$

The second equation for MSE* is obtained by writing down the bulk-plume equation for the updraft MSE,

$$\begin{aligned}\partial_z\text{MSE}^* &= \varepsilon(\text{MSE}-\text{MSE}^*)\\ &= \varepsilon L(q_v-q_v^*)\\ &= \varepsilon(\text{RH}-1)Lq_v^*\,.\end{aligned} \tag{1.87}$$

The assumption of constant M, RH, and α implies that ε is proportional to γ. Let us define the constant a as $a = (1-\alpha)\varepsilon/\gamma$. The entrainment rate, detrainment rate, the relative humidity from Equation (1.80), and the condensation rate from (1.81) can then be written as

$$\varepsilon = \delta = \frac{a\gamma}{1-\alpha} \tag{1.88}$$

$$\mathrm{RH} = \frac{\alpha + a}{1+a} \tag{1.89}$$

$$\frac{c}{M} = \frac{\gamma q_v^*}{1+a}. \tag{1.90}$$

Substituting (1.88) and (1.89) into (1.87), we get

$$\partial_z \mathrm{MSE}^* = -\frac{a}{a+1}\gamma L q_v^*. \tag{1.91}$$

Note that $\gamma L q_v^* = -L\partial_z q_v^*$, so this can be written as $\partial_z \mathrm{EMSE}^* = 0$, where

$$\mathrm{EMSE}^* = c_p T + gz + \frac{Lq_v^*}{1+a} \tag{1.92}$$

is a conserved variable for entraining parcels in the zero-buoyancy plume approximation much like MSE* is conserved for adiabatic parcels; we call this the entraining moist static energy (EMSE).

Finally, equating the right-hand sides of (1.86) and (1.91) and using (1.52) to express γ in terms of Γ, we can solve for Γ to find

$$\Gamma = \frac{(1+a)g + \dfrac{q_v^* L g}{RT}}{(1+a)c_p + \dfrac{q_v^* L^2}{R_v T^2}}. \tag{1.93}$$

If the entrainment rate is zero (i.e., $a = 0$), then the moist-entraining lapse rate reduces to the moist-adiabatic lapse rate given in Equation (1.53).

More interesting is the limit of infinite entrainment (i.e., $a \to \infty$), in which case the moist-entraining lapse rate reduces to the dry-adiabatic lapse rate g/c_p. This is consistent with Equation (1.90), which tells us that the condensation rate goes to zero. At the same time, however, Equation (1.89) tells us that the atmosphere approaches saturation. We can understand all of this as follows. An increase in the entrainment of subsaturated environmental air reduces the condensation rate and, therefore, steepens the lapse rate, pushing it towards the dry adiabat. Meanwhile, an increase in entrainment implies an increase in detrainment, which moistens the environment, pushing it towards saturation. For a very large entrainment rate, the environment is nearly saturated, but the entrainment rate is large enough that the entrainment of the slightly subsaturated environmental air places the condensation rate at a value near zero.

1.13 Analytical theory for CAPE

In the previous section, we learned that EMSE*, defined in Equation (1.92), is constant in RCE when M, RH, and PE are constant. We can use this fact to derive an analytical expression for CAPE following Romps (2016). From the fact that saturated EMSE* is constant with height in the environment, we know that

$$c_pT + gz_e(T) + \frac{Lq_v^*[p_e(T),T]}{1+a} = c_pT_{\text{cb}} + \frac{Lq_{v,\text{cb}}^*}{1+a}, \tag{1.94}$$

where T_{cb} is the cloud-base air temperature, $q_{v,\text{cb}}^*$ is the cloud-base saturation water-vapor mass fraction, $z_e(T)$ is the height profile as a function of environmental temperature, and p_e is the pressure profile as a function of environmental temperature.

CAPE is the vertical integral of the buoyancy of a parcel as it is lifted *adiabatically* through the atmosphere. The temperature of this adiabatically lifted parcel is governed by the MSE equation, given in Equation (1.47). There, we see that the MSE of the parcel decreases with height in proportion to its buoyancy. To good approximation, we can neglect that change in MSE so long as the characteristic height over which its buoyancy is most significant (typically about 10 km in the upper troposphere) is small compared to the scale height c_pT/g (which is about 20–30 km).[15] Therefore, we will use strict conservation of MSE to approximate the properties of the adiabatic parcel. (Equations 1.95–1.97 are provided in note 15.)

[15]To see why, imagine that we calculate the buoyancy of an adiabatically lifted parcel using conservation of MSE (i.e., neglecting the adiabatic decrease in MSE) and obtain from this a characteristic temperature anomaly (difference in temperature between a parcel and its surroundings) of ΔT. If we had properly accounted for the decrease in MSE, then the correction to the parcel's MSE would be

$$\delta\text{MSE} \sim -\text{CAPE}.$$

Here, we are denoting corrections by a δ, not to be confused with the fractional detrainment rate. In the upper troposphere, where q_v^* is small, this must be expressed as a change in temperature or, equivalently, a correction to ΔT on the order of

$$\delta\Delta T \approx -\text{CAPE}/c_p\,.$$

Defining H as the characteristic height over which ΔT is most significant, then the correction to the CAPE will be on the order of

$$\delta\text{CAPE} \sim H\delta b \tag{1.95}$$

$$= Hg\frac{\delta\Delta T}{T} \tag{1.96}$$

$$\approx -\frac{Hg}{c_pT}\text{CAPE}, \tag{1.97}$$

and this is small if $H \ll c_pT/g$, i.e., if the height over which the buoyancy is expressed is small compared to the scale height $c_pT/g \approx 20-30$ km. In the current tropics, CAPE tends to be dominated by high buoyancy over about 10 km in the upper troposphere, the depth of which is small compared to 20–30 km. Therefore, for a first-order approximation of CAPE, it is appropriate to calculate adiabatic-parcel ascent using strict conservation of MSE.

For the adiabatic or "undiluted" parcel, we then know that

$$c_pT + gz_u(T) + Lq_v^*[p_u(T),T] = c_pT_{\mathrm{cb}} + Lq_{v,\mathrm{cb}}^*\,, \tag{1.98}$$

where $z_u(T)$ and $p_u(T)$ are the profiles of height and pressure, respectively, as functions of undiluted-parcel temperature. If we subtract (1.94) from (1.98), we get

$$g\,[z_u(T) - z_e(T)] + Lq_v^*[p_u(T),T] - \frac{Lq_v^*[p_e(T),T]}{1+a} = \frac{a}{1+a}Lq_{v,\mathrm{cb}}^*\,.$$

Thanks to the fact that $Lq_v^*/RT \ll 1$ through most of the troposphere,[16] $q_v^*[p_u(T),T]$ can be approximated as $q_v^*[p_e(T),T]$. Therefore, this simplifies to

$$\Delta z(T) \approx \frac{a}{1+a}\frac{L}{g}\left(q_{v,\mathrm{cb}}^* - q_v^*\right)\,, \tag{1.99}$$

where $\Delta z(T) \equiv z_u(T) - z_e(T)$. Figure 1.9 shows plots of z_e and z_u for three different cloud-base temperatures and $a = 0.2$.

To get CAPE, we need the area between the two temperature curves plotted on z and T axes. This is usually expressed as

$$\mathrm{CAPE} \approx \frac{g}{T_0}\int_{\text{cloud base}}^{\text{tropopause}} dz\,\Delta T(z)\,, \tag{1.100}$$

where T_0 is a characteristic tropospheric temperature (e.g., the average of the surface and tropopause temperatures), the tropopause is the assumed level of neutral buoyancy for the undiluted plume, and $\Delta T(z)$ is the temperature difference between

[16]The values of $q_v^*[p_u(T),T]$ and $q_v^*[p_e(T),T]$ are related to each other by

$$\begin{aligned}
q_v^*[p_u(T),T] &= \frac{Rp_v^*(T)}{R_v p_u(T)} \\
&\approx \frac{Rp_v^*(T)}{R_v\,\{p_e(T) - [z_u(T) - z_e(T)]\rho_e g\}} \\
&\approx \frac{Rp_v^*(T)}{R_v p_e(T)\,\{1 - [z_u(T) - z_e(T)]g/RT\}} \\
&\approx \frac{Rp_v^*(T)}{R_v p_e(T)}\,\{1 + [z_u(T) - z_e(T)]g/RT\} \\
&\approx q_v^*[p_e(T),T]\,\{1 + [z_u(T) - z_e(T)]g/RT\}\,.
\end{aligned}$$

Using this more accurate expression for $q_v^*[p_u(T),T]$, we get

$$\Delta z = \frac{a}{1+a}\frac{L}{g\left(1 + \frac{Lq_v^*}{RT}\right)}\left(q_{v,\mathrm{cb}}^* - q_v^*\right)\,.$$

By comparison to (1.99), we see that accounting for the difference between $q_v^*[p_u(T),T]$ and $q_v^*[p_e(T),T]$ modifies Δz by a factor of $1 + Lq_v^*/RT$. At 300 K, Lq_v^*/RT is about 1/2, and it decays exponentially as temperature decreases. Therefore, over the vast majority of the troposphere for cloud-base temperatures below about 310 K, we can ignore this factor.

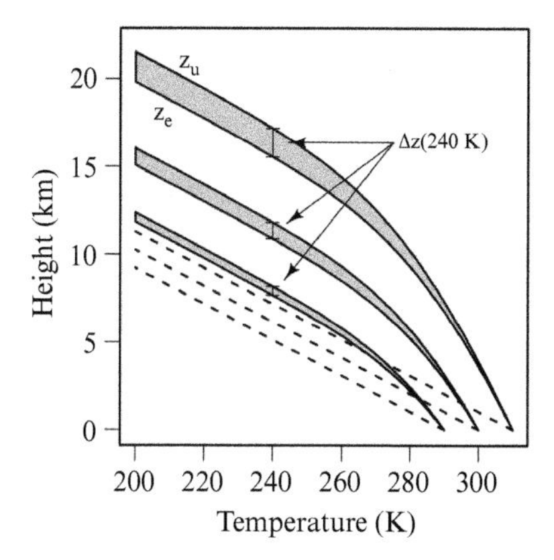

Fig. 1.9 For $a = 0.2$ and surface temperatures (really, cloud-base temperatures) of $T_s = 290$, 300, and 310 K, profiles of (solid) environmental and non-entraining-parcel temperature profiles can be calculated using the analytical expression in Equation (11) of Romps (2016) and (dashed) dry adiabats. Note that CAPE is proportional to the shaded area between the two temperature profiles.

the undiluted plume and the environment at height z. But, another way to write this is

$$\text{CAPE} \approx \frac{g}{T_0} \int_{T_{\text{tropopause}}}^{T_{\text{cloud base}}} dT\, \Delta z(T) \,. \tag{1.101}$$

The integrals in (1.100) and (1.101) are identical. For our purposes, though, it is much more convenient to evaluate the integral in Equation (1.101). Plugging in our expression for Δz, this becomes

$$\text{CAPE} \approx \frac{g}{T_0} \int_{T_{\text{tropopause}}}^{T_{\text{cloud base}}} dT\, \frac{a}{1+a} \frac{L}{g} \left(q^*_{v,\text{cb}} - q^*_v \right) .$$

Over most of the temperature range of the troposphere, $q^*_v \ll q^*_{v,\text{cb}}$, so we can further approximate this as

$$\text{CAPE} \approx \frac{g}{T_0} \int_{T_{\text{tropopause}}}^{T_{\text{cloud base}}} dT\, \frac{a}{1+a} \frac{L}{g} q^*_{v,\text{cb}} \,.$$

At this point, nothing inside the integral depends on T, so this integrates trivially to give

$$\text{CAPE} \approx \frac{a}{1+a} L q^*_{v,\text{cloud base}} \frac{T_{\text{cloud base}} - T_{\text{tropopause}}}{T_0} \,. \tag{1.102}$$

As expected, CAPE increases with the entrainment rate, i.e., with a. Most importantly, we see that CAPE increases in proportion to q^*_v at the cloud base; this means that CAPE experiences Clausius–Clapeyron scaling, increasing exponentially with surface temperature, which is closely tied to the cloud-base temperature. This dependence of

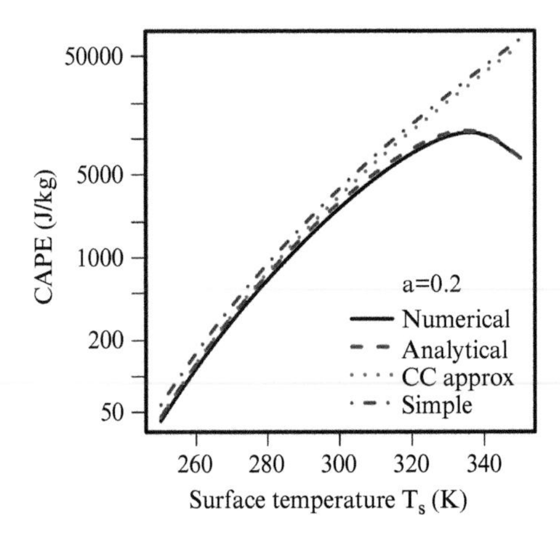

Fig. 1.10 CAPE as a function of surface temperature T_s (really, cloud-base temperature) for $a = 0.2$ as calculated using (black solid) numerical integration, (blue dashed) the analytical expression for CAPE given by Equation (12) of Romps (2016), and (red dotted) the approximate analytical expression for CAPE in Equation (17) of Romps (2016), which exhibits CC scaling. Also plotted is (purple dashed-dotted) the simple approximation for CAPE given here in Equation (1.102). Adapted from Figure 5 of Romps (2016).

CAPE on surface temperature is illustrated in Figure 1.10; note the log axis. This exponential dependence on surface temperature has implications for the intensity of storms since CAPE is the reservoir of energy that storms can tap to generate damaging winds, hail, and lightning.

1.14 Future directions

Toy models of the atmosphere, e.g., parcel models, Boussinesq equations, and bulk-plume equations, are powerful tools for guiding our understanding of the atmosphere. As we have seen here, these models have provided explanations for the energy balance of the tropical troposphere, the "melting" of tropospheric gravity waves, the temperature structure of the convecting tropical atmosphere, the relative humidity profile in the tropics, and the processes that set CAPE. Despite this progress, however, there are many questions left to answer. An exhaustive list is impossible, but we can list a few here that relate to the topics covered in these lectures. With regards to the leaky lid, how does energy apportion between tropospheric and stratospheric heating, the latter caused by the breaking of vertically propagating wave energy? What sets the profile of cloudiness from detrained convection, and how does it relate to the profile of relative humidity? What determines the spectrum of cloud updraft sizes? If CAPE sets the upper limits on updraft buoyancy and speed, what determines the spectrum of actual cloud buoyancies and speeds? What determines the convective entrainment rate? And, which results can be extended to the midlatitudes, where planetary rotation is important? There is much to do, and simple, analytic models will continue to play an essential role in future progress.

Acknowledgments

I am particularly grateful to Freddy Bouchet, Antoine Venaille, and Tapio Schneider for the invitation to participate in the Les Houches Summer School on Fundamental Aspects of Turbulent Flows in Climate Dynamics, where these lectures were given. Thanks are also due to Tom Beucler, Rodrigo Caballero, Dale Durran, Nadir Jeevanjee, Yi-Chuan Lu, Zhihong Tan, and Tiffany Shaw, all of whom offered suggestions and corrections that greatly improved these notes. This material is based upon work supported by the National Science Foundation under Grant 1535746.

References

Edman, Jacob P. and Romps, David M. (2017). Beyond the rigid lid: Baroclinic modes in a structured atmosphere. *Journal of the Atmospheric Sciences*, **74**(11), 3551–66.

Romps, David M. (2008). The dry-entropy budget of a moist atmosphere. *Journal of the Atmospheric Sciences*, **65**(12), 3779–99.

Romps, David M. (2014*a*). An analytical model for tropical relative humidity. *Journal of Climate*, **27**(19), 7432–49.

Romps, David M. (2014*b*). Rayleigh damping in the free troposphere. *Journal of the Atmospheric Sciences*, **71**(2), 553–65.

Romps, David M. (2015). MSE minus CAPE is the true conserved variable for an adiabatically lifted parcel. *Journal of the Atmospheric Sciences*, **72**(9), 3639–46.

Romps, David M. (2016). Clausius–Clapeyron scaling of CAPE from analytical solutions to RCE. *Journal of the Atmospheric Sciences*, **73**(9), 3719–37.

Romps, David M. and Öktem, Rusen (2015). Stereo photogrammetry reveals substantial drag on cloud thermals. *Geophysical Research Letters*, **42**(12), 5051–7.

Singh, Martin S. and O'Gorman, Paul A. (2013). Influence of entrainment on the thermal stratification in simulations of radiative-convective equilibrium. *Geophysical Research Letters*, **40**(16), 4398–403.

Sobel, A. H., Nilsson, J., and Polvani, L. M. (2001). The weak temperature gradient approximation and balanced tropical moisture waves. *Journal of the Atmospheric Sciences*, **58**(23), 3650–65.

2
Clouds in current and in a warming climate

Caroline Muller

CNRS, Laboratoire de Météorologie Dynamique, École Normale Supérieure Paris

Lecturer picture from the summer school to be added by us:)

Muller, C., *Clouds in current and in a warming climate* In: *Fundamental Aspects of Turbulent Flows in Climate Dynamics.* Edited by: Freddy Bouchet, Tapio Schneider, Antoine Venaille, Christophe Salomon, Oxford University Press (2020). © Oxford University Press.
DOI: 10.1093/oso/9780198855217.003.0002

Chapter Contents

2.1 Introduction

We see them in our everyday lives. They make skies and sunsets even more beautiful, inspiring painters all over the world. But what are clouds? What are the physical processes occurring within a cloud? Do they all look alike, or are there different types of clouds? Why? Beyond our small human scale, how are clouds distributed at large, planetary scales? How do they couple and interact with the large-scale circulation of the atmosphere? What do the physics of cloud formation tell us about the hydrological cycle, including mean and extreme precipitation, in our current climate and in a warming world? What role do they play in the global energetics of the planet, for instance, by reflecting the incoming shortwave radiation from the Sun and by reducing the outgoing longwave radiation to space, because of their high altitudes and thus, cold temperatures? These are the questions that will be addressed in these five lectures.

The two first lectures will review well-understood aspects of cloud distribution and physics, which can also be found in various classical textbooks (which will be referred to at the relevant places). More specifically, the first lecture, *Cloud fundamentals*, will describe the fundamental properties of clouds: global distribution, cloud types, cloud visualization from satellites in space, and link with the large-scale circulation. The second lecture, *Cloud formation and physics*, will focus on the physics of clouds. We will briefly review the important results from atmospheric thermodynamics, and their implications for convective instability and cloud formation.

Then the last three lectures will address three key open questions about clouds in our current and in a warming climate. The third lecture, *Organization of deep convection at mesoscales*, addresses the issue of spatial organization of convection (here and in the following, convection refers to overturning of air within which clouds are embedded). The most spectacular example of organized convection is arguably the tropical cyclone, with its eye devoid of deep clouds, surrounded by the eyewall where winds among the strongest on the planet are found. Despite the extreme weather and thus, the strong societal impact of organized convection, the physical processes at stake are not fully understood. Recent advances on this topic will be presented. Clouds are also tightly linked with precipitation and the fourth lecture, *Response of the hydrological cycle to climate change*, will review recent results on the response of the hydrological cycle to climate change, including both mean and extreme precipitation. The fifth and last lecture, *Clouds in a changing climate*, will review the effect of clouds on climate sensitivity (climate sensitivity refers to the temperature increase at equilibrium in response to a doubling of carbon dioxide concentrations), how this effect is quantified, as well as recent theoretical advances on the response of clouds to climate change including the so-called "fixed anvil temperature" or (FAT) hypothesis.

These last three topics are still very active areas of research, and for each we will review the state-of-the-art and present some recent advances made possible in recent years by the increased computational power as well as increased fundamental understanding of moist convection.

2.2 Cloud fundamentals

2.2.1 Spatial distribution of clouds: Overview

What are clouds? The definition from the World Meteorological Organization of a cloud is a "hydrometeor consisting of minute particles of liquid water or ice, or of both, suspended in the atmosphere and usually not touching the ground. It may also include larger particles of liquid water or ice, as well as non-aqueous liquid or solid particles such as those present in fumes, smoke or dust." In other words, clouds are suspensions of liquid and ice water in the atmosphere. Note that, although there is water vapor in clouds—in fact there is water vapor everywhere in the troposphere, this is not what we see. Indeed, our eyes are not sensitive to water vapor, instead what makes a cloud visible are the liquid and/or ice particles that it contains.

Looking at a daily weather map of deep clouds, see e.g., the website (EUMETSAT, 2017), confirms the diversity of cloud dynamics (see Figure 2.1 for a snapshot). This map shows a one-year long evolution of weather and clouds derived from infrared satellite measurements, which are sensitive to cloud top temperatures, thus to high and deep clouds reaching cold high altitudes. The distribution of clouds is not uniform and varies greatly with latitude.

The rich dynamics of deep clouds include small-scale, "pop-corn"-like, deep convection in the tropics, notably convection associated with the diurnal cycle above tropical continents (e.g., central Africa close to the equator). In the tropics, corresponding to the rising branch of the Hadley circulation known as the inter-tropical convergence zone (ITCZ), deep clouds yield cold cloud-top temperatures. Deep clouds

Fig. 2.1 Snapshot from the 2017 "Year of Weather" online one-year long animation of high clouds from satellites. ©EUMETSAT 2017.

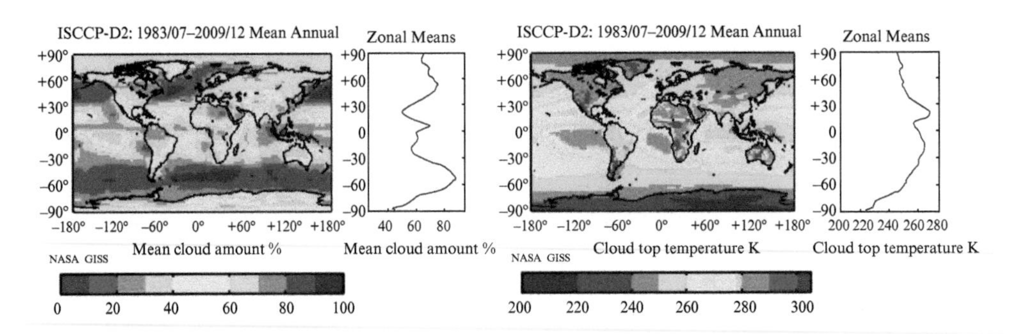

Fig. 2.2 Time-averaged (1983 to 2009 estimated from ISCCP) distribution of cloud amount (fractional area covered by clouds, left) and cloud top temperatures (right) as a function of latitude and longitude. Also shown are zonal means as a function of latitude (blue curves). From ISCCP data (Rossow and Schiffer, 1999).

can span the whole depth of the troposphere, from the top of the planetary boundary layer, to the tropopause, around 15 km at tropical latitudes.

Also notable at mid latitudes (around $\pm 45°$ latitude) are large-scale cloud systems associated with extra-tropical cyclones and their associated frontal systems. Deep clouds are embedded in frontal low- and high-pressure systems typical of those latitudes. More precisely clouds and high water vapor concentrations can be found on the eastward side of cold fronts.

Smaller cloud areal coverage is found in the subtropics (centered around $\pm 30°$ latitude), i.e., in the subsiding branch of the Hadley circulation, as can also be seen in the time-mean spatial distribution of cloud amounts and cloud top temperatures Figure 2.2. The data is from the ISCCP project, whose website provides useful information and data on clouds (ISCCP, 2009; Rossow and Schiffer, 1999). In the subtropics, warmer cloud-top temperatures are consistent with the occurrence of shallow clouds (typically one to two kilometers in height).

Globally, clouds cover a large fraction of our planet, about two thirds (Figure 2.2). The zonal mean makes clear that high cloud coverage is found in the tropics (close to the equator, within 10° latitude or so) and at mid latitudes (centered around $\pm 45°$ latitude). The largest cloud cover is over the Southern Ocean, and more generally larger cloudiness is found over oceans than over land.

Clouds are thus key actors of the climate system, as they cover a significant fraction of the planet. Indeed, depending on their thickness and their height, clouds can interact with the Earth radiation budget in different ways. Clouds cool the planet by reflecting some of the incoming shortwave radiation from the Sun. Clouds also warm the planet by trapping some of the longwave radiation emitted at the Earth surface, thus reducing the radiative cooling to space. Those radiative effects of clouds make them crucial ingredients of the global energetics. We will come back to this in the last lecture Section 2.6.

Consistently, understanding clouds, their coupling with a large-scale circulation, and how it impacts climate sensitivity, has been identified as one of the World Climate Research Programme (WCRP) grand challenge (Bony Stevens, Frierson, Jakob,

Kageyama, Pincus, Shepherd, Sherwood, Siebesma, Sobel, *et al.*, 2015). WCRP grand challenges represent areas of emphasis in scientific research in the coming decade, identifying specific barriers preventing progress in a critical area of climate science.

2.2.2 Cloud classification

Clouds are classified based on their appearance and altitude (Houze Jr, 2014). The classification is based on five Latin roots:

- *Cumulus*: heap, pile;
- *Stratus*: flatten out, cover with a layer;
- *Cirrus*: lock of hair, tuft of horsehair;
- *Nimbus*: precipitating cloud;
- *Altum*: height.

Cumulus refers to clouds with some vertical extent, typically resembling "cotton balls." Stratus refers to clouds with some horizontal extent, typically with a flat large horizontal cover. Cirrus characterizes the thin, filamentary aspect of the highest clouds almost entirely composed of ice crystals. Nimbus simply indicates precipitation reaching the ground, and altum is used to characterize mid-level clouds.

The roots are combined to define ten cloud types, shown on Figure 2.3 and listed next from low to high (according to the height of cloud base):

- low clouds (cloud base below 2 km): cumulus, cumulonimbus, stratus, stratocumulus, nimbostratus;
- middle clouds (cloud base between 2 and 6 km): altocumulus, altostratus;
- high clouds (cloud base between 5 and 12 km): cirrus, cirrocumulus, and cirrostratus.

Note that the cumulonimbus is classified as a low cloud because of its low cloud base. It may sound couter-intuitive to call it a low cloud given its significant vertical extent. Historically, clouds were classified according to cloud base because cloud observers were on the ground, making it difficult to estimate the cloud height. But now that modern observations are from satellites in space, it becomes more common to classify clouds based on their cloud top height. The cumulonimbus would thus be called a high cloud, or even better a deep cloud.

2.2.3 Visualization from space (IR, VIS, WV)

A powerful tool to investigate cloud properties and distribution is visualization from satellites in space. Clouds can be visualized in several channels, including the infrared channel, giving the emission temperature which helps detect high cold clouds; the visible channel, giving access to the albedo which helps detect low and high clouds thick enough to reflect sunlight; and the water vapor channel, which gives information on the flow and the water vapor advection (Figure 2.4). Note that the VIS (visible) map has partial coverage, as information is not available at night. The interactive website of the University of Wisconsin-Madison (SSEC, 2018) allows the browsing of views from various geostationary satellites and is a useful resource to become familiarized with these products.

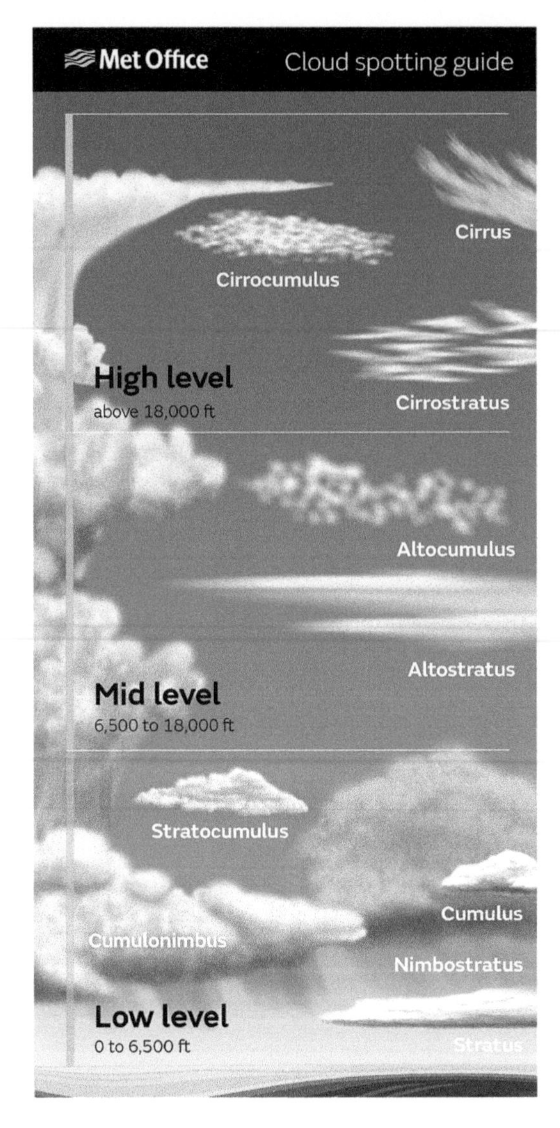

Fig. 2.3 Cloud classification. Figure from the Met Office online cloud spotting guide http://metoffice.gov.uk. © British Crown copyright, Met Office.

2.2.4 Link with the large-scale circulation

Clouds are tightly coupled to the large-scale circulation. Indeed, clouds form where there is upward motion, for reasons that will be discussed in Section 2.3 (briefly, colder temperatures at higher altitudes favor the condensation of water vapor into cloud liquid or cloud ice). In this section, we describe the distribution of clouds at planetary scales (thousands of kilometers), and its relationship with the Hadley and Walker global cells, as well as Monsoon systems. Then we review the distribution of

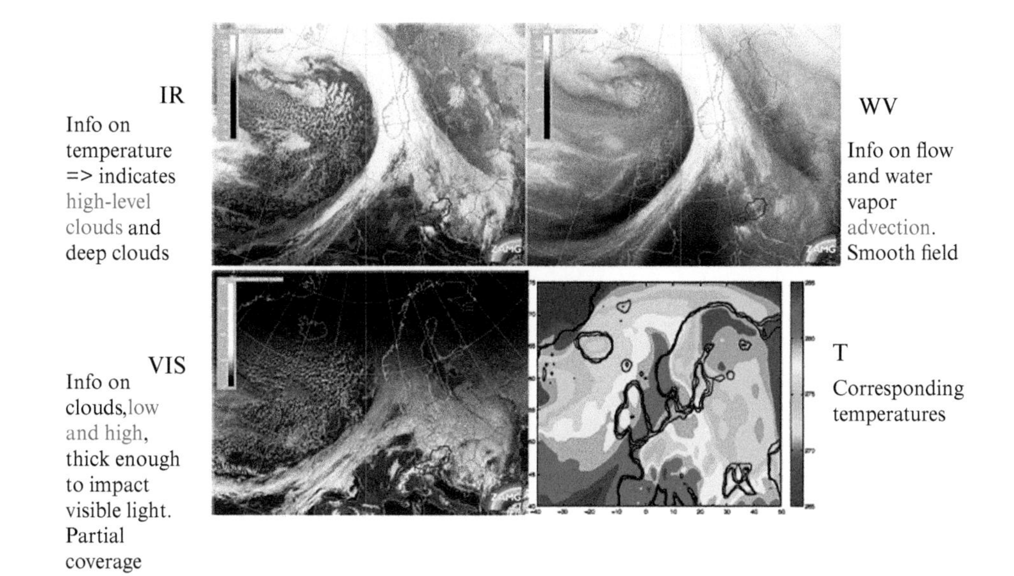

Fig. 2.4 Cloud visualization from space in the infrared, water vapor and visible channels, from the Zentralanstalt für Meteorologie und Geodynamik (ZAMG) website (courtesy: Guillaume Lapeyre; data from ERA40 (Uppala *et al.*, 2005 Quart. J. Roy. Meteor. Soc.)).

clouds at synoptic scales (hundreds to thousands of kilometers), and its interaction with equatorial waves and mid-latitude frontal systems.

We focus on tropical, subtropical, and mid-latitude clouds which have specific sets of dynamics. In other words, we will not discuss polar clouds. We note in passing that there is also organization of convection at mesoscales (a few hundred kilometers), taking the form of mesoscale convective systems (these include squall lines, mesoscale convective complexes, and tropical cyclones), whose link with the large-scale circulation is still not fully understood, and is the subject of active research. We will come back to this in Section 2.4.

Planetary scales

Looking at sections of cloud fraction and circulation around the intertropical convergence zone (ITCZ) shows a clear correlation between cloud fraction and large-scale upward motion, with deep convection in the tropics, and shallow convection in the subtropics where there is large-scale descent (Figure 2.5). Deep clouds (i.e., clouds spanning the whole depth of the troposphere, from the surface to the tropopause) are found in the ITCZ, which corresponds to the rising branch of the Hadley cell in the tropics. Conversely, in regions of large-scale descent such as the descending branch of the Hadley cell in the subtropics, deep convection is suppressed by the stability and dryness of the middle troposphere. Clouds are thus confined to the planetary boundary layer (from the surface to 2 km or so). Consistently, precipitation tends to be larger in the tropics and smaller in the subtropics. The cloud fraction and precipitation

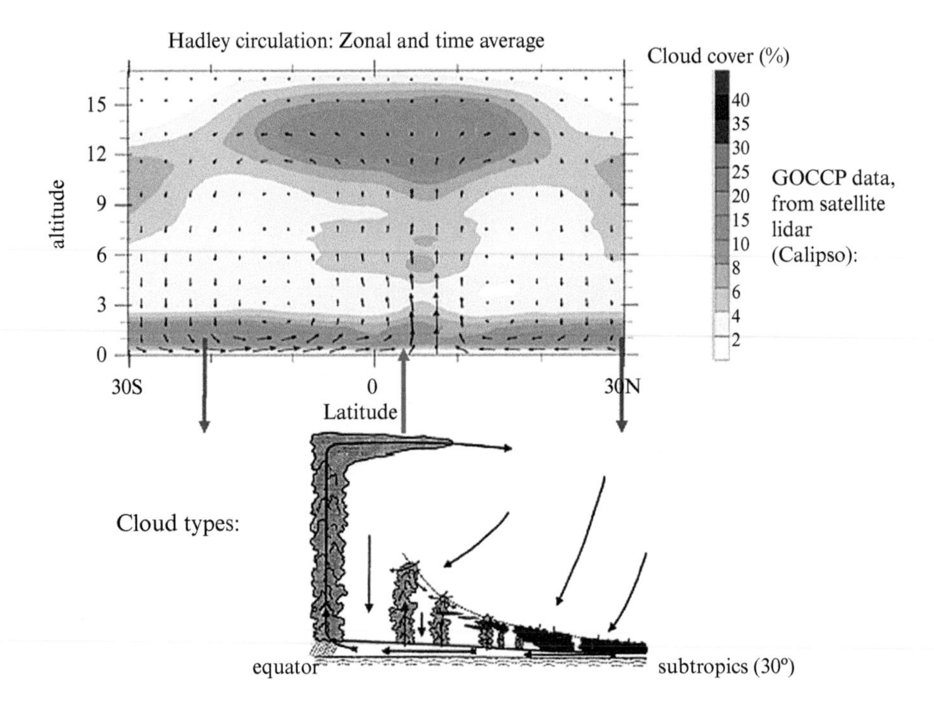

Fig. 2.5 Top: Cloud fraction as a function of height and latitude, zonally and temporally averaged (green), along with the mean circulation (arrows) from the CALIPSO-GOCCP product (courtesy: Gilles Bellon). Bottom: Schematic of the latitudinal distribution of clouds, with deep clouds in the tropics and shallow clouds in the subtropics (adapted from Emanuel, 1994, Chapter 14); © 1994, Oxford University Press, Inc.

map varies seasonally, accompanying the meridional motion of the ITCZ around the equator (the location of the ITCZ is linked to the global energy balance including insolation differences and ocean heat transport).

Clouds are also embedded within the Walker cell, with deep convection occuring above the warm waters of the warm pool, corresponding to the rising branch of the Walker cell. Looking at the El-Niño Southern Oscillation (ENSO), which is the main mode of inter-annual variability of the Walker cell, we can see that the deep clouds move zonally, following the zonal shift of the upward motion. Both Asian and West African monsoons have signatures in cloud fraction and cloud content as well, similarly consistent with the location of upward motion.

Synoptic scales

The synoptic scale has more subtle dynamics. In the tropics, the Coriolis parameter is small, and an important source of synoptic variability comes from equatorial waves. In the extratropics, the Coriolis force is dynamically important, and the leading order dynamics is quasi-geostrophic. This leads to the formation of synoptic frontal systems (fronts refer to regions with strong horizontal temperature gradients; see e.g., the strong temperature gradients found over Europe in Figure 2.4), within which clouds are embedded, as described in more details soon.

- Equatorial waves
  Let's start with the tropical atmosphere and see how equatorial waves lead to convective organization. Adopting the shallow-water formalism of Matsuno for the tropical atmosphere (Matsuno, 1966), we can write the inviscid shallow-water equations linearized around a state of rest. Assuming the Coriolis parameter, f, linearly proportional to distance from the equator (i.e., $f = \beta y$ a suitably valid approximation for motions in the tropics), the equations in usual notations are:

$$\frac{\partial u}{\partial t} - \beta y v = -g\frac{\partial \phi}{\partial x}, \tag{2.1}$$

$$\frac{\partial v}{\partial t} + \beta y u = -g\frac{\partial \phi}{\partial y}, \tag{2.2}$$

$$\frac{\partial \phi}{\partial t} + H\left(\frac{\partial u}{\partial x} + \frac{\partial v}{\partial y}\right) = 0, \tag{2.3}$$

  where ϕ denotes geopotential height, and H the depth of the undisturbed layer. Note that this system does not necessarily support plane wave solutions in (x, y, t) since one of the coefficients, βy, depends on the coordinate y. However, this system yields wave solutions in (x, t) whose amplitude varies with y, i.e., solutions of the form $\propto \hat{A}(y)e^{i(kx+\omega t)}$. Specifically, one finds various types of trapped waves whose amplitudes decay in the y-direction.

  The applicability of shallow water theory to equatorial convectively coupled waves is by no means obvious. However, the impressive match obtained by Wheeler and Kiladis (Wheeler and Kiladis, 1999) between observed equatorial variability (based on observed outgoing longwave radiation anomalies, see also (Kiladis, Wheeler, Haertel, Straub, and Roundy, 2009) for a review) suggests that a portion of deep convection in the tropics is consistent with this theory. Agreement is also seen on Hovmoller diagrams of outgoing longwave radiation Figure 2.6.
- Frontal systems and clouds
  In the extratropics, cold and warm fronts are ubiquitous. Cold fronts refer to cold air masses advancing into warmer air. They tend to have sharp edges with high slope (Figure 2.7) and deep convection. Warm fronts refer to warm air moving towards colder temperatures and tend to have a shallower slope (Figure 2.7). These fronts are for instance visible on Figure 2.4, where sharp temperature gradients are clearly seen to be strongly correlated with cloud cover. Indeed, as cold air meets warm air, the warm air rises, thus giving rise to ascent and to cloud formation.

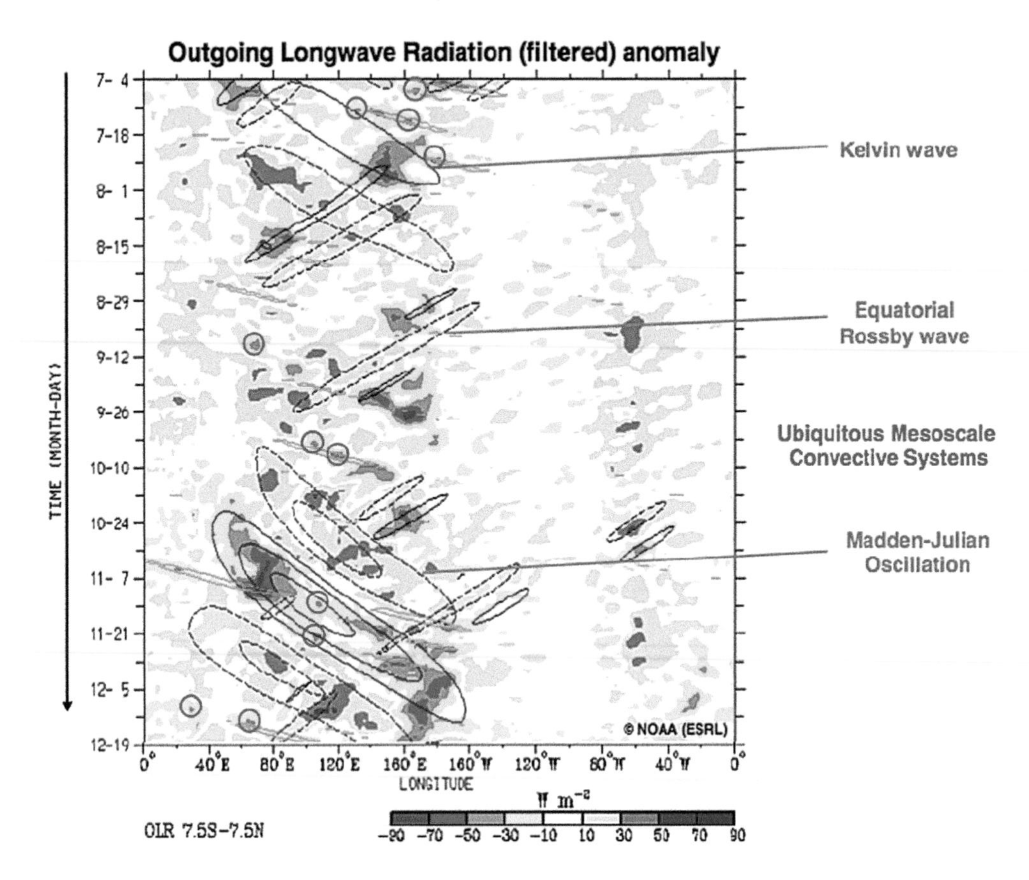

Fig. 2.6 Time-longitude (Hovmoller) section of OLR anomaly averaged from 7.5S to 7.5N (time-mean and seasons removed, from ESRL-NOAA, courtesy: Gilles Bellon). Contours are anomalies filtered for the total OLR for specific regions of the wavenumber-frequency domain corresponding to the MJO (blue contours), Kelvin waves (green contours), and equatorial Rossby waves (black contours). Beyond the synoptic equatorial waves, we can also note the numerous smaller-scales (hundreds of kilometers) cloud clusters (red contours); these are mesoscale convective systems and will be discussed in Section 2.4.

2.3 Cloud formation and physics

In the previous section, we saw that deep clouds are typically found in locations with large-scale upward motion and are suppressed in regions of large-scale subsidence. In this section, we discuss the physics of cloud formation, which will clarify this observation. The main references for this part are the two textbooks (Emanuel, 1994) and (Bohren and Albrecht, 2000).

2.3.1 Atmospheric thermodynamics: dry convective instability

The parcel method

Cloud formation is closely related to the convective movement of air. Thus, a key question is: What makes the air move? Note that, although temperature decreases with height, the cold air aloft is not heavier and thus does not "fall" to the ground,

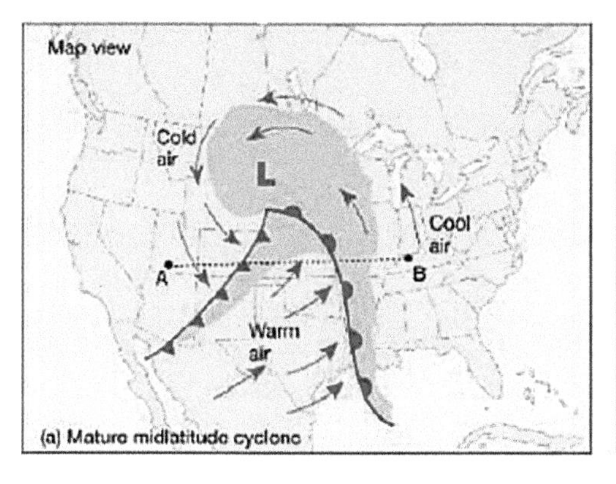

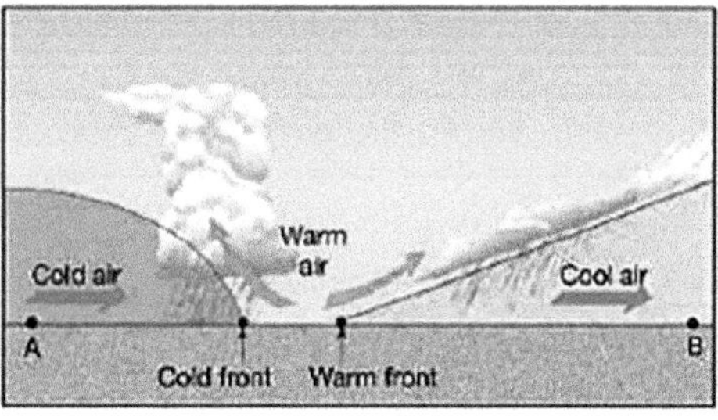

Fig. 2.7 Top (left) and cross sectional (right) view of a cold front, schematized on weather maps as blue lines with triangles, and cold front, red line with half-circles. Clouds are embedded within these frontal systems, as the rising of warm air encountering colder heavier air, leads to cloud formation. From Lutgens *et al.*, *The Atmosphere*, 2001, ©Pearson Education, Inc. 2010. Reproduced by permission of the publisher.

as its density is not only a function of temperature, but also of pressure $\rho(T,p)$. The three are related through the ideal gas law

$$p = \rho RT$$

where R denotes the specific constant of the gas. This specific form of the ideal gas law is readily deduced from its molecular form $pV = Nk_BT$, where V denotes the volume of gas, N the number of molecules in V, and k_B the Boltzmann constant, by introducing the molecular mass m: $p = (Nm/V)(k_B/m)T = \rho RT$ with

$$R \stackrel{\text{def}}{=} \frac{k_B}{m}. \tag{2.4}$$

Note that, due to its dependence on the molecular mass of the gas, the specific constant depends on the gas considered.

To determine the stability of air, we thus need to account for changes in T and p with height. We use the so-called "parcel method" to assess whether a parcel of air is unstable to upward motion. We consider a hypothetical parcel of air near the surface displaced vertically adiabatically, and ask the following question: if this parcel of air is displaced upwards, will it return to its original position, or will it keep rising? If the displaced parcel has lower density than the environment, it is lighter and will keep rising: the atmosphere is unstable to dry convection. If instead its density is larger, it is heavier and will accelerate back down: the atmosphere is stable to dry convection. The displacement is supposed to be slow enough that the pressure of the parcel is always in equilibrium with the pressure of the environment ("quasi-static" displacement; see e.g., (Bohren and Albrecht, 2000) for a discussion of this assumption).

Conservation of potential temperature

We now show that during the quasi-static adiabatic parcel displacement, there is an invariant called *potential temperature*,

$$\theta \stackrel{\text{def}}{=} T(p/p_0)^{-R/c_p}, \tag{2.5}$$

where T denotes temperature, p pressure, p_0 a reference pressure (typically 1000 hPa), and c_p heat capacity at constant pressure. Then we will use this invariant to determine the condition under which the atmosphere is unstable to dry convection.

Applying the first law of thermodynamics to an infinitesimal displacement, the change in internal energy $c_v dT$ is equal to the heat added, which is zero in this adiabatic displacement, plus the work done on the parcel, in that case due to pressure forces $\delta W = -pd(1/\rho)$:

$$c_v dT = -pd\left(\frac{1}{\rho}\right). \tag{2.6}$$

Using the ideal gas law $p = \rho RT$ and recalling that $c_v + R = c_p$, we obtain

$$c_v dT = -p\; d\left(\frac{RT}{p}\right) = -RdT + RT\frac{dp}{p} \Leftrightarrow c_p dT + RT\frac{dp}{p} = 0 \tag{2.7}$$

implying,

$$\frac{dT}{T} - \frac{R}{c_p}\frac{dp}{p} = d\ln(Tp^{-R/c_p}) = 0. \tag{2.8}$$

This shows that Tp^{-R/c_p} is constant, hence $\theta = T(p/p_0)^{-R/c_p}$ is conserved during the displacement.

Before assessing the stability of the parcel, we note that in the special case of a hydrostatic atmosphere, i.e., assuming $dp = -\rho g dz$, the variable

$$h_{dry} \stackrel{\text{def}}{=} c_p T + gz \tag{2.9}$$

is conserved. It is called the *dry static energy*. Indeed, if we make this hydrostatic approximation, Equation (2.8) becomes

$$c_p dT + RT\rho g\frac{dz}{p} = d(c_p T + gz) = dh_{dry} = 0, \tag{2.10}$$

where we have again used the ideal gas law $p = \rho RT$. Thus, the dry static energy $c_p T + gz$ is conserved in an adiabatic quasi-static displacement under the hydrostatic approximation. Furthermore, in that case, it is readily seen from Equation (2.10) that the dry adiabatic lapse rate Γ_d, defined as the decrease of temperature with height, is given by

$$\Gamma_d \stackrel{\text{def}}{=} -\frac{dT}{dz} = -\frac{g}{c_p} \approx 10^\circ \text{ K / km}. \tag{2.11}$$

How can we assess the stability of dry air?

We now return to the general case (relaxing the hydrostatic approximation) and to our original question, namely: is the displaced parcel lighter or heavier than its environment? Recall that the pressure of the parcel is equal to that of the environment, so that during the displacement its pressure changes following the environmental

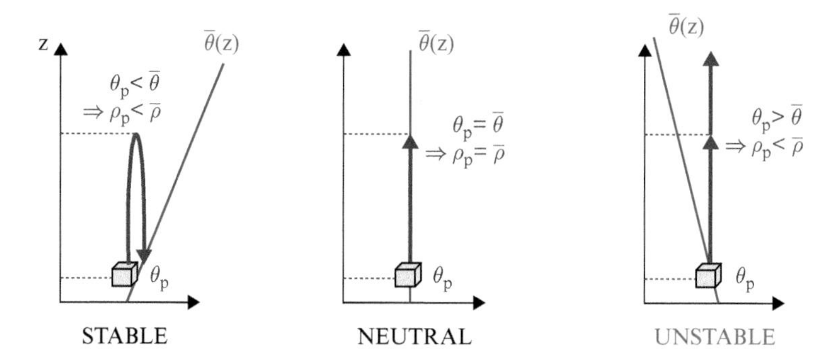

Fig. 2.8 Schematic representation of the parcel method.

pressure, while its temperature changes such that the potential temperature is conserved. To fix ideas, let's raise a parcel upwards (a similar argument can be made for downward displacements). Figure 2.8 schematically describes the three possible cases, depending on the environmental potential temperature profile $\bar{\theta}$, shown in red as a function of height.

The displaced parcel starts with the near-surface environmental value $\theta_p = \bar{\theta}$, and conserves its potential temperature θ_p during its adiabatic ascent (blue). Once displaced, comparing θ_p with $\bar{\theta}$ at the displaced pressure level determines whether the parcel is heavier or lighter than the environment. If $\bar{\theta}$ increases with height (left panel), the displaced parcel has colder potential temperature than the environment $\theta_p < \bar{\theta}$, and thus is heavier and accelerates back down: the atmosphere is stable to dry convection. On the other hand, if $\bar{\theta}$ decreases with height (right panel), the displaced parcel has warmer potential temperature than the environment $\theta_p > \bar{\theta}$, and thus is lighter and keeps rising: the atmosphere is unstable to dry convection. If $\bar{\theta}$ is constant with height (middle panel), the displaced parcel is neither accelerated downwards nor upwards: the atmosphere is neutral to dry convection.

In the stable case, the displaced parcel will accelerate back towards and past its original equilibrium altitude. It will then be lighter than the environment and accelerate back up towards its equilibrium altitude. Thus, the displaced parcel oscillates around its equilibrium height. The frequency of oscillation is known as the buoyancy frequency, or Brunt Väisälä frequency, and can easily be shown to be given by:

$$N = \sqrt{\frac{g}{\bar{\theta}} \frac{\partial \bar{\theta}}{\partial z}}.$$

In the unstable case, convection is very efficient at removing the instability. Indeed, in the planetary subcloud layer (first kilometer of the atmosphere or so), the convective adjustment time scale is very fast (minutes for dry convection) compared to destabilizing factors (surface warming, atmospheric radiative cooling ...). Thus, the observed state is very close to convective neutrality $\bar{\theta}$ =constant, see for instance the review (Stevens, 2005) and references therein.

But above this thin boundary layer, this observation does not hold anymore and $\bar{\theta}$ is observed to increase with height. This is because above the subcloud layer, atmospheric convection involves phase change of water vapor. We need to revisit the previous calculations to account for the significant latent heat released during the phase changes of water. But let's first introduce the most common variables used to quantify the amount of water (vapor, liquid, or ice) in the atmosphere.

2.3.2 Atmospheric thermodynamics: Moist variables

Commonly used moist variables (Emanuel, 1994) are:

- Water vapor density (where M_v denotes the mass in kg of water vapor in the volume V in m^3):

$$\rho_v \stackrel{\text{def}}{=} \frac{M_v}{V}.$$

- Dry air density (where M_d denotes the mass in kg of dry air in the volume V in m^3):

$$\rho_d \stackrel{\text{def}}{=} \frac{M_d}{V}.$$

- Total air density:

$$\rho = \rho_v + \rho_d.$$

- Specific humidity:

$$q_v \stackrel{\text{def}}{=} \frac{\rho_v}{\rho}.$$

- Mixing ratio:

$$r \stackrel{\text{def}}{=} \frac{\rho_v}{\rho_d}.$$

- Partial pressure of water vapor e, satisfying the ideal gas law (where R_v denotes specific constant of water vapor; recall from Equation (2.4) that its value depends on the gas considered; here $R_v = k_B/m_v$ with m_v molecular mass of water):

$$e = \rho_v R_v T.$$

- Partial pressure of dry air p_d, satisfying the ideal gas law (where $R_d = k_B/m_d$ denotes specific constant of dry air):

$$p_d = \rho_d R_d T$$

- The total pressure is then given by Dalton's law:

$$p = p_d + e.$$

- Dew point temperature T_d: Temperature at which a parcel must be cooled at constant pressure to reach saturation (see Section 2.3.3 for a discussion of saturation).
- Virtual temperature T_v: Temperature that dry air would have in order to have the same density as moist air at same pressure.

Let's derive the formula for the virtual temperature T_v, as a function of T, r and the ratio of molecular mass of water vapor to dry air ϵ:

$$\epsilon \stackrel{\text{def}}{=} \frac{m_v}{m_d} = \frac{R_d}{R_v} \approx 0.622.$$

By definition, T_v satisfies

$$p = \rho R_d T_v.$$

On the other hand, Dalton's law for partial pressures yields

$$p = \rho_v R_v T + \rho_d R_d T.$$

Therefore,

$$T_v = T\left(\frac{\rho_v}{\rho_v + \rho_d}\frac{R_v}{R_d} + \frac{\rho_d}{\rho_v + \rho_d}\right) = T\left(\frac{1 + r/\epsilon}{1 + r}\right).$$

Note that since $\epsilon < 1$, $T_v > T$, i.e., the virtual temperature is warmer than the actual temperature. This is expected since moist air is lighter than dry air, as the molecular mass of water vapor is smaller than the molecular mass of dry air. Therefore, in order to have the same lighter density as moist air, dry air needs to be warmer.

2.3.3 Atmospheric thermodynamics: Moist convective instability

What is the effect of moisture on convection? Beyond the virtual effect just discussed, i.e., water vapor making air lighter, an important impact of moisture on convection is the condensation and concomitant latent heat released (we will focus on vapor–liquid phase transition, though all the results to follow can be extended to the ice phase).

When does water vapor condense into liquid water?

The water vapor contained in air will condense when its partial pressure e exceeds a certain value, called the saturation partial pressure e_s. The latter is governed by the Clausius–Clapeyron equation, which can be derived using the thermodynamic equilibrium between liquid water and water vapor:

$$\frac{de_s}{dT} = \frac{L_v e_s}{R_v T^2}, \tag{2.12}$$

where e_s is the saturation vapor pressure, T the absolute temperature, L_v the latent heat of vaporization of water vapor, and R_v the water vapor gas constant. There is net condensation when $e > e_s(T)$.

This law predicts that the saturation water vapor pressure strongly increases with temperature. A physical interpretation of this increase can be obtained by considering liquid water with a flat interface, above which water vapor is found with partial pressure e. Saturation corresponds to an equilibrium between evaporation from the liquid water below and condensation of the water vapor above.

- $e < e_s$ means that there is more evaporation than condensation,
- $e > e_s$ means that there is more condensation than evaporation,
- $e = e_s$ means there is as much condensation as there is evaporation.

Molecularly, e_s increases with temperature because the evaporation from the liquid phase increases with temperature, i.e., with the mean square velocity of the molecules. Thus, the amount of water vapor required to equilibrate the evaporation is larger at larger temperatures.

We note here in passing that this is often phrased "warm air can hold more water vapor than cold air." This is a useful shortcut to remember that the maximum amount of water vapor e_s, attainable by a volume of air before it starts to condense, is an increasing function of temperature. But it gives the wrong impression that air is a "sponge" with holes in it, with the number of holes increasing with temperature. The saturation and condensation have nothing to do with "holes" in air, it simply has to do with equilibrium between evaporation and condensation. For a more in-depth discussion of the "sponge theory," see e.g., (Bohren and Albrecht, 2000).

Can we derive a conserved quantity for moist air?

We saw that to determine the stability of dry air, it was important to derive a conserved quantity under adiabatic displacements, namely the potential temperature θ in Equation (2.5). Can we derive a similar conserved quantity for moist air? The answer is yes, as we will now show, though this quantity, called equivalent potential temperature, is *approximately* conserved under adiabatic displacements.

For simplicity, we neglect the temperature dependence of the specific constant of air R, of the latent heat of vaporization L_v, and of the heat capacity at constant pressure c_p, which in the following denote constants for dry air. We also neglect the virtual effect discussed previously. For more details the reader is referred to (Emanuel, 1994).

As before, we apply the first law of thermodynamics to an infinitesimal displacement of a parcel of air. We first suppose that the parcel is saturated, i.e., $q = q_s$ where q is the specific humidity and q_s the specific humidity at saturation. The only difference with our earlier dry case Equation (2.7) is that we need to take into account the latent heat released during the condensation of water vapor—$L_v dq$, where dq denotes the change in water vapor specific humidity:

$$c_v dT = \delta W + \delta Q_{\text{cond}} = -p d\left(\frac{1}{\rho}\right) - L_v dq \tag{2.13}$$

$$\Leftrightarrow \; c_p dT - RT\frac{dp}{p} = -L_v dq \tag{2.14}$$

$$\Leftrightarrow \; d\ln\left(Tp^{-R/c_p}\right) = -L_v\frac{dq}{c_p T} \approx d\left(\frac{L_v q}{c_p T}\right). \tag{2.15}$$

The latter approximation holds as long as

$$\frac{dq}{q} \gg \frac{dT}{T},$$

which is typically the case in the troposphere. We thus obtain

$$Tp^{-R/c_p} \exp\left(\frac{L_v q}{c_p T}\right) = \text{constant},$$

leading to the introduction of a new variable approximately conserved for saturated adiabatic motion, the equivalent potential temperature:

$$\theta_e \stackrel{\text{def}}{=} \theta \exp\left(\frac{L_v q}{c_p T}\right),$$

where θ is the dry potential temperature. Now note that in the case where the parcel is not saturated, there is no condensation of water vapor and q is conserved, so that θ_e is also conserved. Thus, θ_e is (approximately) conserved under adiabatic motion, saturated or not.

Before investigating implications for the stability of air to moist convection, we first note that under the hydrostatic approximation, we can define the moist equivalent of the dry static energy in Equation (2.9). It is called the moist static energy:

$$h \stackrel{\text{def}}{=} c_p T + gz + L_v q.$$

With the hydrostatic approximation, h is conserved under adiabatic displacements. Indeed, from Equation (2.14) and the ideal gas law,

$$dh = c_p dT + g dz + L_v dq \stackrel{\text{hydrostasy}}{=} c_p dT - \frac{dp}{\rho} + L_v dq \stackrel{(2.14)}{=} 0.$$

How can we assess the stability of moist air?

Traditionally, skew-T diagrams are used in meteorology (Figure 2.9), which allow to easily compare a measured temperature profile (red curve) to theoretical dry and moist adiabatic profiles (constant θ and θ_e respectively). Such diagrams have iso-temperature lines slanted at 45° to the right (slanted thin brown lines on the figure, hence the name "skew-T"; for more details on those diagrams, see the online MetEd module on Skew-T Mastery (COMET program, 2018)). Since temperature typically decreases with height, observed temperature profiles are largely vertical when reported on those diagrams. The green curve shows the observed dewpoint temperature, which is the temperature at which a parcel must be cooled at constant pressure to reach saturation. This dewpoint temperature curve depends on the environmental humidity (the more humid the air, the closer the dewpoint temperature is to the environmental temperature).

We use the parcel method to evaluate the stability of this environmental temperature profile, by lifting a hypothetical parcel of air from the ground. Comparing, at a given pressure, the temperature of the parcel (shown in black) with the environmental temperature gives us information on its upward (warmer) or downward (colder) acceleration, and thus, of its stability to vertical displacement.

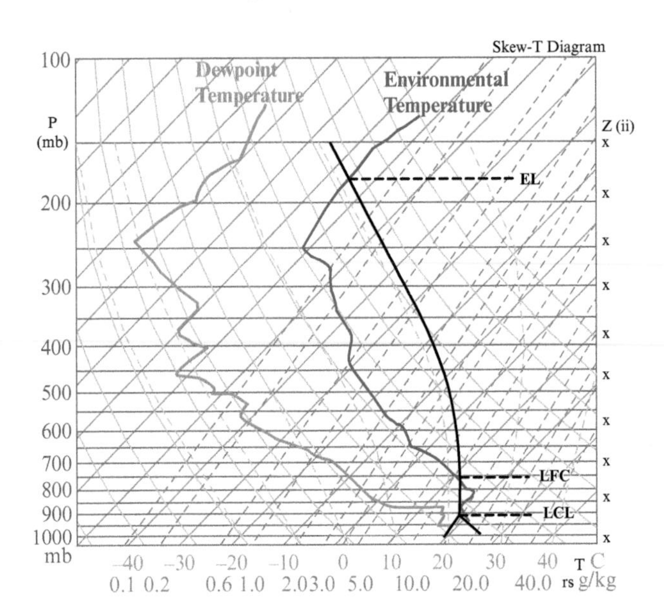

Fig. 2.9 Skew-T diagram, showing observed temperature profile in red, observed dewpoint temperature in green. The parcel method consists of assessing the stability of a near-surface parcel to an upward displacement (parcel temperature shown in black). Adapted from the weathertogether.netblog.

- At first, the near-surface parcel is unsaturated. It thus follows a dry adiabatic curve (line of constant θ, thin green lines on the figure), until the lifted condensation level (LCL) is reached, where the parcel reaches saturation.
- Above the lifted condensation level, θ_e will be conserved for the parcel which is undergoing moist adiabatic ascent (line of constant θ_e, thin dashed green lines). Note that its temperature decreases with height slower than the dry adiabatic curve, due to the latent heat released as water vapor condenses.
- At a certain height, called level of free convection (LFC), the parcel becomes warmer than the environment. As long as this moist adiabatic curve is warmer than the environmental temperature profile, as "warm air rises," the parcel is convectively unstable and keeps ascending.
- This ends when the parcel reaches its equilibrium level (EL), where the parcel's temperature is equal to the environmental temperature.

In order to find the lifted condensation level, the dew point temperature is used, as well as lines of constant saturation mixing ratio iso-r_s (thin dashed purple lines on the skew-T diagram). By definition of the dewpoint temperature, at the surface, $r_s(T_{d,\mathrm{sfc}}, p_{\mathrm{sfc}}) = r_{\mathrm{sfc}}$ where r_{sfc} is the water vapor mixing ratio of the parcel at the surface. The lifted condensation level is thus located where the iso-r_s line passing through the surface dewpoint temperature intersects the parcel temperature.

Convective Available Potential Energy (CAPE)

During the ascent, we just saw that the upward acceleration is related to the difference between the parcel temperature and the environmental temperature. This can be quantified further, in fact the area between the parcel and the environmental temperature is directly related to the potential energy of convection.

This can be clarified by considering the vertical momentum equation

$$\frac{\partial w}{\partial t}+u\frac{\partial w}{\partial x}+v\frac{\partial w}{\partial y}+w\frac{\partial w}{\partial z}=-g\frac{\rho'}{\rho}-\frac{1}{\rho}\frac{\partial p}{\partial z}+\nu\Delta w, \quad (2.16)$$

where ρ denotes the density of the environment, ρ' the density of the parcel minus that of the environment, and the last term is the viscous force. In strong vertical ascent, we can expect the leading order balance to be between the vertical advection and the buoyancy force

$$w\frac{\partial w}{\partial z}=-g\frac{\rho'}{\rho}\Leftrightarrow\frac{w^2(z)}{2}=\int_0^z-\frac{\rho'}{\rho}gdz. \quad (2.17)$$

The right-hand side has units of a specific energy. It represents an upper bound (as it neglects forces opposing the motion including viscosity and pressure gradients, as well as turbulent entrainment of less buoyant air at the edge of the rising plume) for the kinetic energy of the rising parcel. It is called the Convective Available Potential Energy, or CAPE.

CAPE can be rewritten as a function of temperature using the ideal gaz law $p=\rho RT$ and assuming that pressure perturbations between the parcel and the environment are small:

$$\frac{\rho'}{\rho}=-\frac{T'}{T}.$$

If we further make the hydrostatic approximation,

$$\text{CAPE}=\int_{p(z)}^{p(0)}\frac{T'}{T}\frac{dp}{\rho}=R\int_{p(z)}^{p(0)}T'd\ln p.$$

This expression shows that this convective potential energy is proportional to the area between the parcel and the environmental temperature on the skew-T diagram shown in Figure 2.9.

CAPE can be used to derive an upper bound for vertical velocities of buoyant parcels

$$w_{max}=2\sqrt{\text{CAPE}}.$$

As mentioned earlier, for simplicity, we neglected virtual effects. We note though, that it is straightforward to include them in the previous computation, yielding the more general formula:

$$\text{CAPE}=R\int_{p(z)}^{p(0)}T_v'd\ln p.$$

Thus, during the ascent, the area between the parcel temperature and the environment temperature on the skew-T diagram is a measure of atmospheric instability. The larger the CAPE, the stronger the upward motion during the ascent. If enough atmospheric instability is present, cumulus clouds are capable of producing severe convection and storms. In the following, we give a brief overview of the life cycle of such severe convective clouds. We also use the fundamental knowledge gained throughout this section to clarify the physical processes leading to cloud formation, for the different cloud types listed in Section 2.2.2.

2.3.4 What are the processes leading to cloud formation?

We saw that condensation of water vapor, and thus, cloud formation occurs when the atmosphere becomes saturated. Saturation can occur through increased water vapor, but given the strong sensitivity of saturation water vapor pressure to temperature (governed by the Clausius–Clapeyron Equation (2.12)), saturation very often occurs through cooling, for instance by the lifting of air to higher altitudes and thus, colder temperatures, by contact with a cold surface or by radiative cooling.

What are the leading physical mechanisms governing the formation and life cycle of deep convective clouds?

In this section we describe the formation of deep clouds, i.e., cumulonimbus on Figure 2.3 (and to some extent deep nimbostratus). Such clouds occur when the atmosphere is unstable, i.e., in the presence of CAPE.

The formation of a typical single-cell storm (Figure 2.10a) involves three stages (the interested reader is also referred to the MetEd module on Principles of Convection And Buoyancy (COMET program, 2018) for more details). The developing stage, as parcels ascend above the lifted condensation level, cool and saturate, thus forming a cloud. When the atmosphere is unstable (high CAPE), the ascent will continue during the mature stage to a high altitude until the equilibrium level is reached. Then, in the dissipating stage, the cloud will spread horizontally at high levels and form an anvil cloud at high altitudes.

During this last stage, the falling precipitation partially evaporates at low levels, cooling the air and forming downdrafts (descending pockets of cold air formed by evaporative cooling). These downdrafts of cold, heavy air eventually hit the ground and spread horizontally as gravity currents. These are known as cold pools. Cold pools can help initiate other clouds by mechanically lifting moist air above the cold pool's boundary. Other lifting mechanism include orographic lifting (mechanical lifting above a mountain), or large-scale convergence and fronts (sharp temperature gradients). More generally, all forced ascent can lead to deep convection if the atmosphere above is unstable (i.e., high CAPE).

The isolated single-cell cumulus cloud just described is the most common form of cumulonimbus. However, this single-cell storm can sometimes serve as the building block of a larger multi-cell storm (Figure 2.10b), composed of multiple cells each being at a different stage in the life cycle of a thunderstorm. In the presence of strong vertical mean wind shear, supercells can form (Figure 2.10c). These are characterized by the presence of a deep rotating updraft, and are associated with extreme weather, potentially causing significant damage. More generally, if enough

Note that thunderstorms can be:

(a) single cell (typically with weak wind shear)

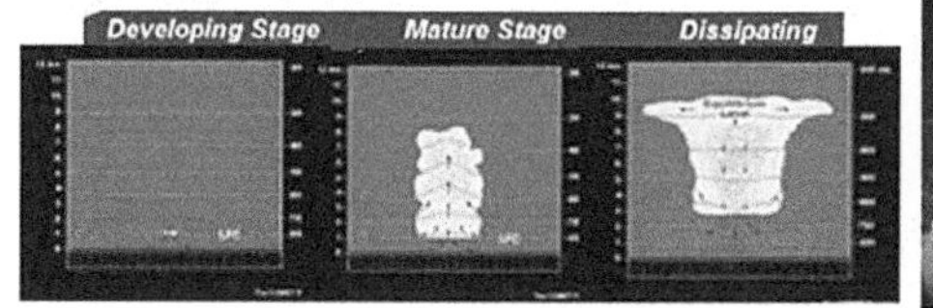

(b) multi cell (composed of multiple cells, each being at a different stage in the life cycle of a thunderstorm)

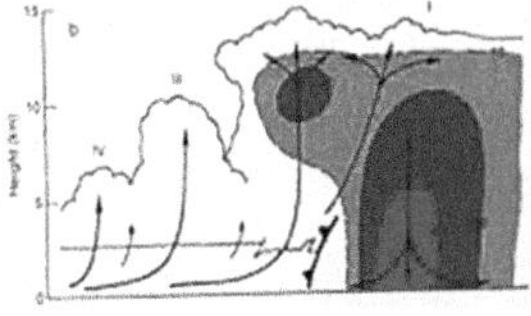

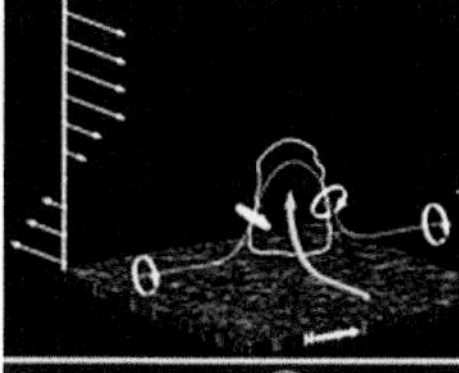

(c) or super cell, characterized by the presence of a deep, rotating updraft

Typically occur in a significant vertically sheared environment

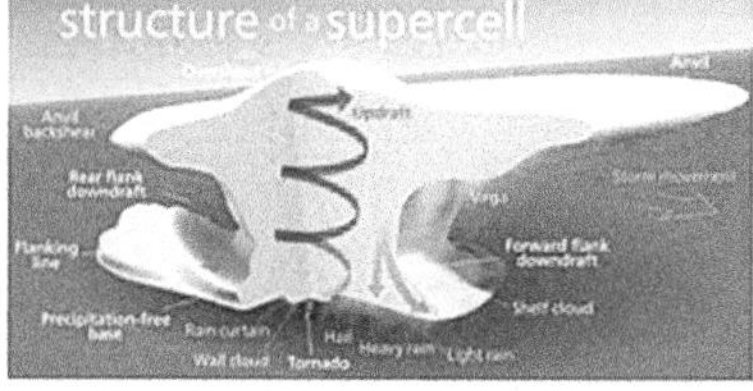

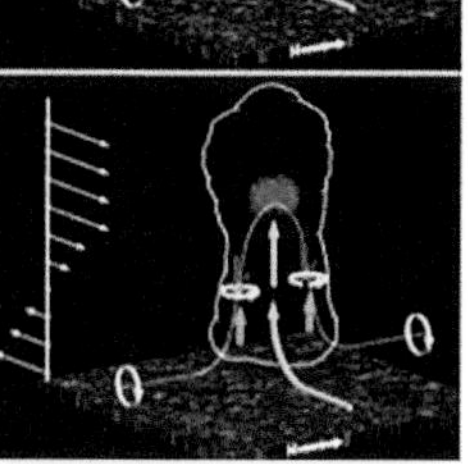

Fig. 2.10 Life cycle of deep convective clouds. (a) single cell, (b) multi cell or (c) super cell storms. Adapted from the COMET® website at http://meted.ucar.edu/ of the University Corporation for Atmospheric Research (UCAR), sponsored in part through cooperative agreement(s) with the National Oceanic and Atmospheric Administration (NOAA), U.S. Department of Commerce (DOC). © 1997–2017 University Corporation for Atmospheric Research.

atmospheric instability is present, i.e., in the presence of high CAPE, cumulus clouds are capable of producing severe storms.

What are the leading physical mechanisms governing the formation of shallow clouds?

We now discuss the formation of clouds in shallow layers at low, middle, and high levels (all but the cumulonimbus and nimbostratus on Figure 2.3). Such clouds typically occur in a stable layer cooled from below, or in an unstable layer bounded above and below by a surface and/or a stable layer. For a more in-depth discussion of the dynamics of those different clouds, the interested reader is referred to (Houze Jr, 2014).

At low levels, we can distinguish two types of dynamics:

- Fog and stratus; these form in the planetary boundary layer when it is cooled from below, by radiation or/and conduction from a cold surface. In that case, the boundary layer is stable, and the air reaches saturation by cooling.

- Stratus or stratocumulus or shallow cumulus; these form in an unstable boundary layer heated from below, with a stable atmosphere above. The stable atmosphere aloft limits the convective motion to the bottom boundary layer. The radiative cooling at the top of the cloud layer can further destabilize the cloud layer and contribute to the convection.

In the latter case, there is an unstable layer capped by a stable layer. This is the case, for instance, when there is a so-called temperature inversion, i.e., when warm air is found above cold air. An inversion can develop aloft as the result of a frontal system advecting warm air above cold air, or in a high-pressure system with upper-level air gradually sinking over a wide area and being warmed by adiabatic compression. This is often the case in subtropical high-pressure systems associated with the descending branch of the Hadley cell. This explains why shallow clouds (e.g., stratocumulus, stratus) are very common in the subtropics (as we saw in e.g., Figure 2.5). These shallow clouds at low levels can organize at the mesoscales, into open and closed cells. Not all is known about the organizational processes, but several mechanisms are believed to play a role, including background shear, thermal instability of the boundary layer, cloud-top entrainment, and precipitation-driven cold pools.

At middle and high levels, shallow layer clouds also include:

- Cirriform clouds; these most often form by detrainment from deep convective clouds, consistent with the largest cirrus cloud cover in the tropics and in the extratropics where deep convection occurs. But they can also form away from generating sources, when an unstable layer is found aloft. These clouds are mainly composed of ice and are found in an unstable layer between two stable layers. There is not much water vapor at those high altitudes, thus cirriform clouds are largely radiatively driven. The solar shortwave radiation heats throughout the cloud, while there is longwave cooling above and warming below the cloud layer.
- Altostratus and altocumulus clouds; these can be remnants of other clouds, in particular protruding layers at mid-levels due to horizontal winds. Altocumulus are sometimes high-based convective clouds, with the same dynamics as deep convective clouds. Altostratus or shallow layers of altocumulus can also resemble a radiatively driven "mixed layer" aloft, leading to a cloud-filled layer radiatively cooled at its top.

2.4 Organization of deep convection at mesoscales in the tropics

In the previous section, we reviewed the physics behind the formation of individual clouds. But from Section 2.2, we know that clouds often organize at large scales, in particular at planetary and synoptic scales, where they are tightly coupled to the large-scale circulation. It was also apparent from Figure 2.6 that clouds often organize at mesoscales (hundreds of kilometers), into what are called mesoscale convective systems. The formation of such systems is still an active area of research, with important societal impacts, as it is associated with extreme weather and strong precipitation (see Section 2.5). It also has strong climatic impacts, as it affects the large-scale atmospheric radiation budget, by affecting cloud cover and the large-scale thermodynamic profiles (temperature and humidity, (Bony Stevens, Frierson, Jakob, Kageyama, Pincus, Shepherd, Sherwood, Siebesma, Sobel, *et al.*, 2015)). In this section, we focus on deep convective clouds in the tropics, and review the basics of mesoscale convective organization and the physical processes involved. We then discuss in more detail a recently discovered phenomenon in idealized simulations of the tropical atmosphere, namely the self-aggregation of convection.

2.4.1 Basics of convective organization

Organized convection refers to convection that is long-lived, i.e., that lasts longer than an individual convective cell (which typically lasts a few hours, < 3 hours), and that grows upscale, i.e., that covers an area larger than an individual convective cell (which typically is < 10 km across). The organization can arise from large-scale forcing, such a sea-surface temperature gradient or the presence of land. It can also arise from the interaction with a large-scale flow, for instance the interaction of cold pools below precipitating clouds with a background vertical wind shear (see following). Or it can arise from internal feedbacks, leading to upscale growth in the absence of large-scale forcing, for instance self-organization of deep clouds by propagating waves or by "self-aggregation" feedbacks (see following).

Organized convection at mesoscales takes the form of mesoscale convective systems, or MCS. The American Meteorological Society (AMS) glossary defines an MCS as a "cloud system that occurs in connection with an ensemble of thunderstorms and produces a contiguous precipitation area on the order of 100 km or more in horizontal scale in at least one direction." Mesoscale convective systems include squall lines, mesoscale convective complexes, or tropical cyclones (Figure 2.11). Mesoscale convective complexes, or MCC, are a subset of MCS that exhibit a large, circular (eccentricity > 0.7), long-lived (> 6 hours), cold cloud shield. The cloud shield must have an area $> 100\ 000$ km^2 with infrared temperature colder than $-32°$C, and an area $> 50\ 000$ km^2 with infrared temperature colder than $-52°$C. Note that these are not mutually exclusive, in fact tropical cyclones can evolve from mesoscale convective complexes, and squall lines can be emitted from tropical cyclones and their outward spiraling bands of precipitation.

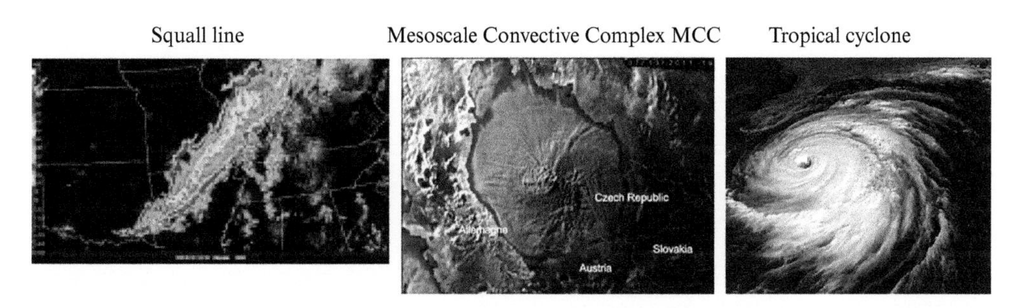

Fig. 2.11 Mesoscale convective systems (MCS) include squall lines (radar image), mesoscale convective complexes or MCCs (from EUMETSAT Meteosat-8 satellite), or tropical cyclones (from NOAA GOES satellite).

The leading physical processes for convective organization are an active area of research, with a lot of recent progress arising from the ability to simulate mesoscale systems, requiring large hundreds of kilometers domains, while resolving deep convection, requiring fine kilometric resolution. These physical processes include:

- Vertical shear;
- Waves;
- Wind-induced surface heat exchange feedbacks;
- Convective self-aggregation feedbacks.

We describe each process in more detail later.

2.4.2 Vertical shear

The presence of background vertical wind shear is known to favor the formation of squall lines. More precisely, the interaction of the shear with cold pools below precipitating clouds, is believed to be key in the formation of squall lines.

One possible explanation (Figure 2.12a) is the advection of cold pools away from the convective updraft. Recall from the life cycle of convective clouds in Section 2.3.4 (see also Figure 2.10a) that in the dissipating stage, the partial evaporation of the falling rain cools the air, creating cold heavy downdrafts, which hit the surface and spread horizontally. These pockets of cold air below clouds are known as cold pools and inhibit further convection. In the case where the region with downdrafts and cold pools is advected away from the updrafts, as represented schematically in

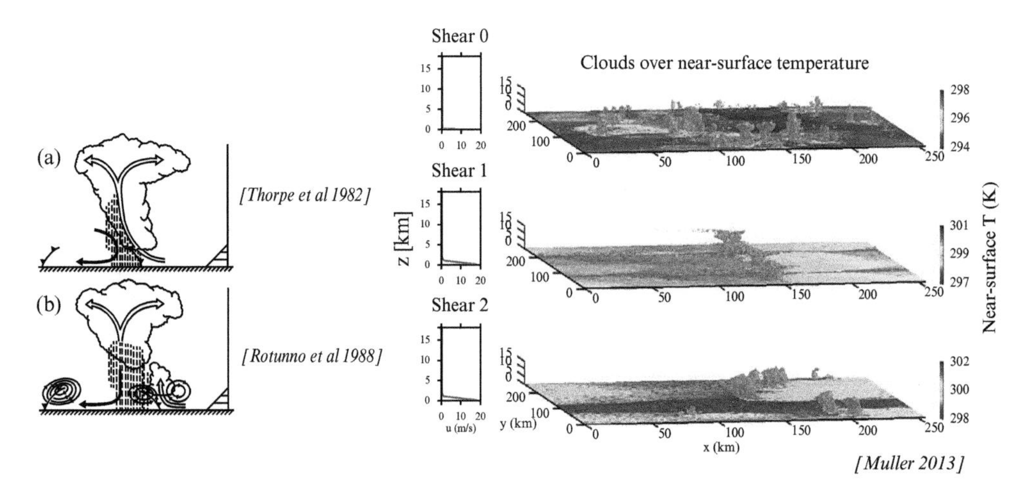

Fig. 2.12 Left: Schematic interaction of a vertical wind shear with cold pools below precipitating clouds, adapted from (Rotunno, Klemp and Weisman, 1988); © 1988 American Meteorological Society (AMS). Right: 3D view of cloud-resolving simulations with different wind shear, in which convection organizes into arcs, adapted from (Muller, 2013); © 2013 American Meteorological Society (AMS).

Figure 2.12a, the updraft can persist on the upwind side of the cold pool, leading to long-lived convective clouds (Garner and Thorpe, 1992).

Another possible explanation is the interaction of the vorticity of the background shear with the vorticity of the spreading cold pool, which favors the formation of new updrafts and convective cells upshear (Figure 2.12b). Note that in the previous theoretical explanation, the squall line is a system of long-lived convective cells, while in this case the squall line is a long-lived system of ordinary cells. (Rotunno, Klemp, and Weisman, 1988) argue that the latter is more consistent with observations, though squall lines can occasionally be composed of long-lived supercell thunderstorms.

Consistently, in cloud-resolving simulations (right panels of Figure 2.12), imposing a vertical wind shear, at low levels where cold pools are, yields the organization of clouds into arcs. The top panel shows a simulation without shear, in which the convection is somewhat randomly distributed, resembling "pop-corn" convection. The middle panel shows a simulation with critical shear, defined as the shear yielding squall lines perpendicular to the mean wind (in the x direction in these simulations from left to right). This critical shear was empirically determined in these simulations, decreasing from 10 m s^{-1} at the surface to zero at 1 km. The last panel shows a simulation with supercritical shear (20 m s^{-1} at the surface), in which the squall line orients itself at an angle with the background wind, so that the projection of the shear on the squall line is critical (Muller, 2013).

2.4.3 Waves

Unlike in mid-latitudes, shear is often weak in the tropics. Thus, shear alone cannot explain all organized convective systems in the tropics. Additionally, in the tropics, upscale growth is ubiquitous and sometimes rapid, occuring beyond the extent of cold pools, and convective inhibition is small so that small perturbations can easily initiate new convection. Internal feedbacks, independently of a large-scale forcing or a large-scale circulation, are natural candidates to explain the observed organization of tropical clouds.

(Mapes, 1993) proposed that gravity waves, generated by the convection and propagating horizontally away from the convection (located at $x = 0$ on Figure 2.13), can destabilize the near-cloud environment and promote new convection nearby. Indeed, the deepest wave which warms and thus stabilizes the atmosphere, propagates the fastest. It is associated with subsidence throughout the troposphere (Figure 2.13 $l = 1$ bore). The second mode ($l = 2$ bore on the figure) is a baroclinic mode which propagates slower, and with cooling (through adiabatic ascent) at low levels. This lifting in the lower troposphere encourages convection close to the original cloud, allowing for convection to be "gregarious" (Mapes, 1993).

2.4.4 Wind-induced surface heat exchange (WISHE)

The so-called "wind-induced surface heat exchange," or WISHE (Emanuel, 1986), is a positive feedback of convection on itself, related to enhanced surface fluxes in the moist convecting region. This feedback is particularly crucial for tropical cyclones, whose extremely strong surface winds in the eyewall yield enhanced surface fluxes there (mainly in the form of evaporation from the ocean). Thus, the eyewall, which is the most energetic region where moisture and clouds are found, is the place where the surface fluxes of energy are strongest. In other words, surface fluxes enhance energy in the high-energy region, thus reinforcing energy gradients and yielding a positive feedback on the convective organization.

2.4.5 Convective self-aggregation

An active area of research is linked to the spontaneous self-aggregation of convection. Self-aggregation refers to the spectacular ability of deep clouds to spontaneously cluster in space (see Figure 2.14) despite spatially homogeneous conditions and no

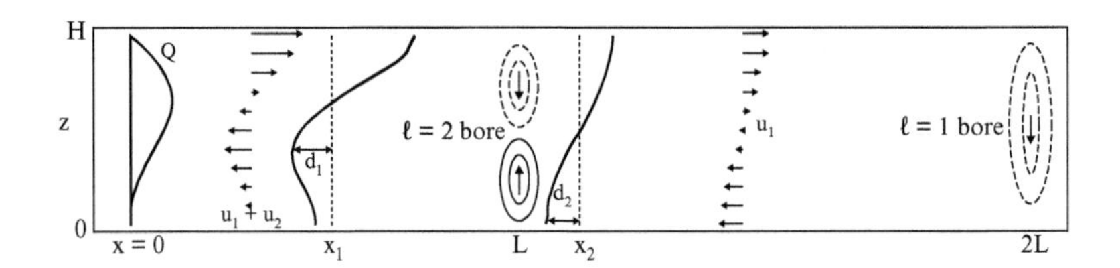

Fig. 2.13 Schematic response to the heating associated with convection and clouds occuring at $x = 0$. The heating profile $Q(z)$ is the sum of a deep mode with heating at all heights and a maximum at mid-level, and of a baroclinic mode with cooling at low levels and heating at upper levels (Mapes, 1993). This distribution of heat excites waves that then propagate away from the convection, yielding adiabatic subsidence warming ($l = 1$ bore and $l = 2$ bore at upper levels) and adiabatic cooling through ascent ($l = 2$ bore at lower levels); © 1993 American Meteorological Society (AMS).

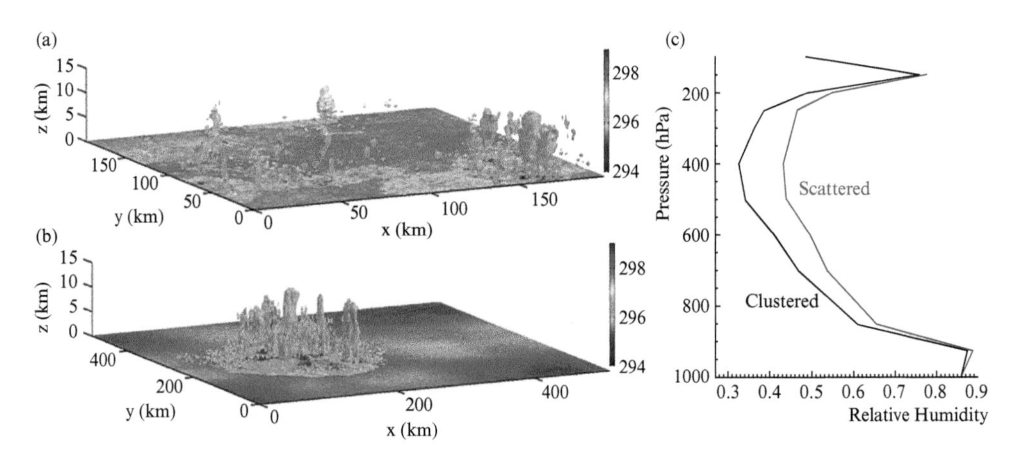

Fig. 2.14 In models, convective organization (panel b) emerges spontaneously, increasingly so with increasing temperatures. It is associated with a large-scale drying of the atmosphere and enhance large-scale outgoing radiative cooling to space. In observations (panel c, relative humidity profiles from AIRS satellite measurements) the middle troposphere is drier in an atmosphere in which the same amount of precipitation is concentrated in a smaller number of convective clusters (adapted from Bony *et al.*, 2015), consistent with modeled aggregation; © 2015, Springer Nature.

large-scale forcing, in high-resolution cloud-resolving models (CRMs) of the tropical atmosphere. These are models with fine, kilometer-scale resolution, i.e., simulations with sufficiently high spatial resolution to explicitly resolve the deep convection and deep clouds, instead of parameterizing them. Since its discovery in CRMs, the rapidly growing body of literature on self-aggregation confirmed its occurrence in a hierarchy of models, from two- and three-dimensional CRMs, to regional models and global climate models with parameterized convection, with super-parameterizations or without convective parameterization (Wing, Emanuel, Holloway, and Muller, 2017).

This phenomenon was first discovered in idealized settings, namely non-rotating (Coriolis parameter $f = 0$) radiative-convective equilibrium (RCE). This equilibrium is introduced next, followed by a more detailed discussion of the physical processes responsible for the self-aggregation of convection in non-rotating RCE simulations.

Radiative-convective equilibrium

Non-rotating RCE is an idealization of the tropical atmosphere, in which the rotation of the Earth is neglected (a reasonable approximation in the tropics where the Coriolis parameter f is small), and in which the large-scale motion (larger than the domain) is neglected. Thus, there is no import or export of moist-static energy into or out of the domain, and the net atmospheric radiative cooling (top of atmosphere minus surface) must balance the input of energy into the atmosphere at the surface, namely latent and sensible heat fluxes. Over oceans, surface fluxes are largely dominated by the latent heat flux, so that in RCE over oceans, the net atmospheric radiative cooling is approximately equal to surface evaporation. From water conservation, the latter is equal to precipitation. In other words, in RCE, the net atmospheric radiative cooling is in balance with the latent heating associated with the condensation of water vapor into precipitation by convection.

RCE is most easily understood by first looking at radiative equilibrium. Radiative equilibrium is the equilibrium state of the atmosphere and surface in the absence of non-radiative fluxes. In that case, radiative cooling and heating drive the atmosphere towards a state of radiative equilibrium. At radiative equilibrium, the incoming shortwave solar heating $\pi R^2 S_0(1-a)$, where R denotes the Earth's radius, S_0 incoming solar flux, and a albedo, exactly balances the outgoing longwave radiation $4\pi R^2 \sigma T_e^4$ where σ is the Stefan–Boltzmann constant, and T_e the emission temperature (temperature with which a planet needs to emit in order to achieve energy balance), yielding:

$$\sigma T_e^4 = S_0 \frac{1-a}{4}. \tag{2.18}$$

In the absence of atmosphere (left panel Figure 2.15), the surface energy balance implies

$$\sigma T_e^4 = \sigma T_s^4 = S_0 \frac{1-a}{4} \Rightarrow T_s = T_e = 255 \text{ K } = -18° \text{ C},$$

which is much colder that the observed mean surface temperature $\approx$ 288 K = 15° C. This warmer surface temperature is due to the presence of the atmosphere and can be understood by adding a level to our simple conceptual model Figure 2.15. We assume that the atmosphere is transparent to solar radiation, opaque to infrared radiation, and we assume black-body emission from the surface and each level (though the computation can easily be extended to account for emissivities smaller than 1). Energy balance at the surface and level 1 implies:

$$\text{Level 1: } 2\sigma T_1^4 = \sigma T_s^4 \tag{2.19}$$

$$\text{SFC: } \sigma T_s^4 = \sigma T_e^4 + \sigma T_1^4, \tag{2.20}$$

yielding $T_s = 2^{1/4} T_e = 303$ K, warmer than before.

If we add an additional atmospheric level (Figure 2.15),

$$\text{Level 2: } 2\sigma T_2^4 = \sigma T_1^4 \tag{2.21}$$

$$\text{Level 1: } 2\sigma T_1^4 = \sigma T_s^4 + \sigma T_2^4 \tag{2.22}$$

$$\text{SFC: } \sigma T_s^4 = \sigma T_e^4 + \sigma T_1^4, \tag{2.23}$$

yielding $T_s = 3^{1/4} T_e$, even warmer.

The full calculation of radiative equilibrium was done by (Manabe and Strickler, 1964) and yields the temperature profile shown on the right panel of Figure 2.15. Compared with observations, this profile is too hot near the surface, too cold near the tropopause, yielding a lapse rate of temperature which is too large in the troposphere (but the stratosphere temperature is close to the observed). In other words, the radiative equilibrium profile is unstable to moist convection.

The observed temperature profile in the troposphere is closer to a radiative-convective equilibrium profile. Physically, what happens is that radiation destabilizes the atmosphere by cooling the interior of the troposphere, thus making the lapse rate steeper. But the radiation time scale ≈ 40 days is much slower than the convective adjustment time scale $\approx$ minutes for dry and hours for moist convection. Thus, in the competition between radiation and convection, convection "wins," and the observed state is much closer to convective neutrality than to radiative equilibrium. Convection has a stabilizing effect by bringing moist and hot air from the surface to the free-

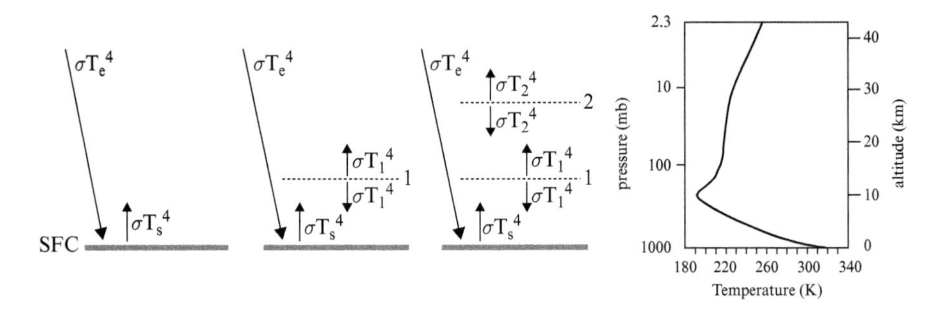

Fig. 2.15 Radiative equilibrium without, with one or with two atmospheric levels (three left panels). The last panel shows the full calculation of radiative equilibrium (after Manabe and Strickler, 1964); © 1964 American Meteorological Society (AMS).

troposphere (updrafts) and by bringing cold and dry air from the interior to the surface (downdrafts), thus reducing the lapse rate towards convective neutrality. More precisely, the vertical temperature profile is close to neutral to dry convection below the condensation level (dry adiabat θ =constant), and close to neutral to moist convection above (moist adiabat θ_e =constant, see Section 2.3.3). It is this equilibrium between radiative cooling and convective heating which is referred to as RCE.

Physical mechanisms of self-aggregation

In simulations of RCE, illustrated in Figure 2.14a, convection is somewhat randomly distributed, resembling "pop-corn" convection. Self-aggregation (Figure 2.14b) can be seen as an instability of radiative-convective equilibrium, in which random pop-corn convection is replaced by a highly organized climate. Convection is confined to a subregion of the domain and is surrounded by extremely dry air. In this section, we investigate in more detail the physical processes involved.

Most of the simulations described here are performed with the cloud-resolving model System for Atmospheric Modeling, or SAM (Khairoutdinov and Randall, 2003). Briefly, this model solves the anelastic momentum, continuity, and scalar conservation equations. It is run here with fixed sea-surface temperature (close to current tropical values, 300 K), on a square domain with doubly periodic geometry. The horizontal resolution is on the order of one or a few kilometers, in order to resolve deep cloud processes. The domain size is a few hundreds of kilometers to allow mesoscale organization of convection. The vertical resolution is finer, tens of meters in the low troposphere increasing to 500 m in the mid-troposphere. A sponge layer is added in the upper third of the domain (18 km to 27 km altitude) in order to absorb gravity waves which would otherwise unrealistically fill the domain (see (Muller and Held, 2012) for more details).

From sensitivity experiments, i.e., simulations where the various feedbacks are turned on and off (e.g., surface flux feedbacks, radiative feedbacks ...), we now know that longwave radiative feedbacks are crucial for self-aggregation (Figure 2.16), at least at current tropical temperatures (Muller and Held, 2012). More precisely, the longwave radiative cooling from low clouds in dry regions is found to be necessary for the spontaneous onset of self-aggregation from homogeneous initial conditions. When simulations are initiated from aggregated conditions though, the clear-sky radiative feedback from dry regions and the high-cloud radiative feedback from moist regions are also found to be sufficient to maintain the aggregation.

The importance of longwave radiative feedbacks for convective aggregation can be understood by considering the moist static energy transport between the dry and the moist regions. Note that in the tropics, horizontal temperature gradients are small, so that the variability in moist static energy is largely dominated by the variability of water vapor. Thus, high energy regions correspond to moist regions and vice versa.

Figure 2.17 shows the circulation (black streamfunctions) in height and moisture space (Bretherton, Blossey, and Khairoutdinov, 2005; Muller and Bony, 2015). The top panels show the circulation along with radiative cooling rates (left) and moist static energy (right). The arrows show the direction of the circulation. The strong radiative cooling in dry regions at low levels, which is largely due to the presence of

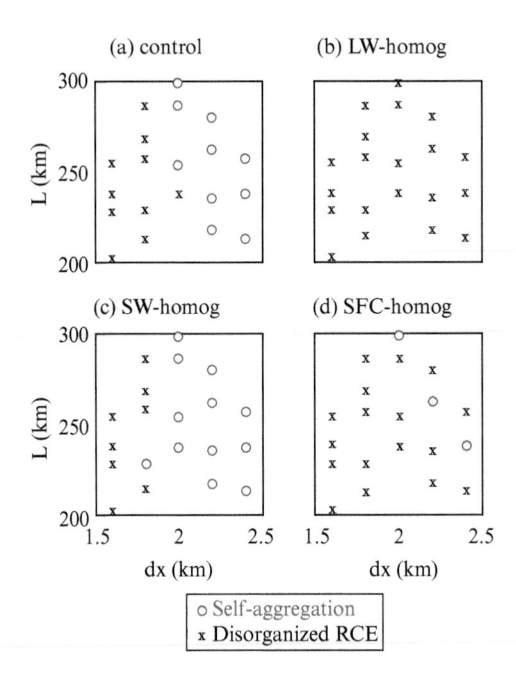

Fig. 2.16 Results from sensitivity numerical simulations started from homogeneous initial conditions, in which various feedbacks are turned on and off. Simulations are shown as a function of domain size and resolution, and simulations that self-aggregate are shown as red circles. Although shortwave radiation feedbacks and surface flux feedbacks impact the range of parameters for which self-aggregation occurs, it is the longwave feedback which is found to be crucial for self-aggregation. Indeed, there is no spontaneous self-aggregation of convection when longwave radiative feedbacks are removed (after Muller and Held, 2012); © 2012 American Meteorological Society (AMS).

low clouds (pink contours), generates subsidence (blue arrow) in the lowest kilometers of the dry columns. This forces a near-surface flow (black arrow) from dry to moist columns. The high moist static energy near the surface is thus exported from the dry regions into the moist regions, yielding an upgradient energy transport. This is the positive feedback believed to be responsible for the strengthening energy gradients and concomitant self-aggregation of convection.

As mentioned previously, even without the longwave radiative feedbacks from low clouds, convective aggregation can be maintained from aggregated initial conditions. The bottom panels show the same circulation, but in a simulation without low cloud longwave radiative contributions. The clear-sky low-level cooling in dry regions along with radiative warming from high clouds in the moist columns again yield subsidence in dry (blue arrow) and upward motion (red arrow) in moist regions. The near-surface flow associated with this dynamical response to the radiative cooling distribution (black arrow) again exports energy from dry regions to moist regions, yielding an upgradient energy transport.

In all cases, it is the low-level circulation, forced by differential radiative cooling rates between dry and moist regions, which is responsible for the upgradient energy

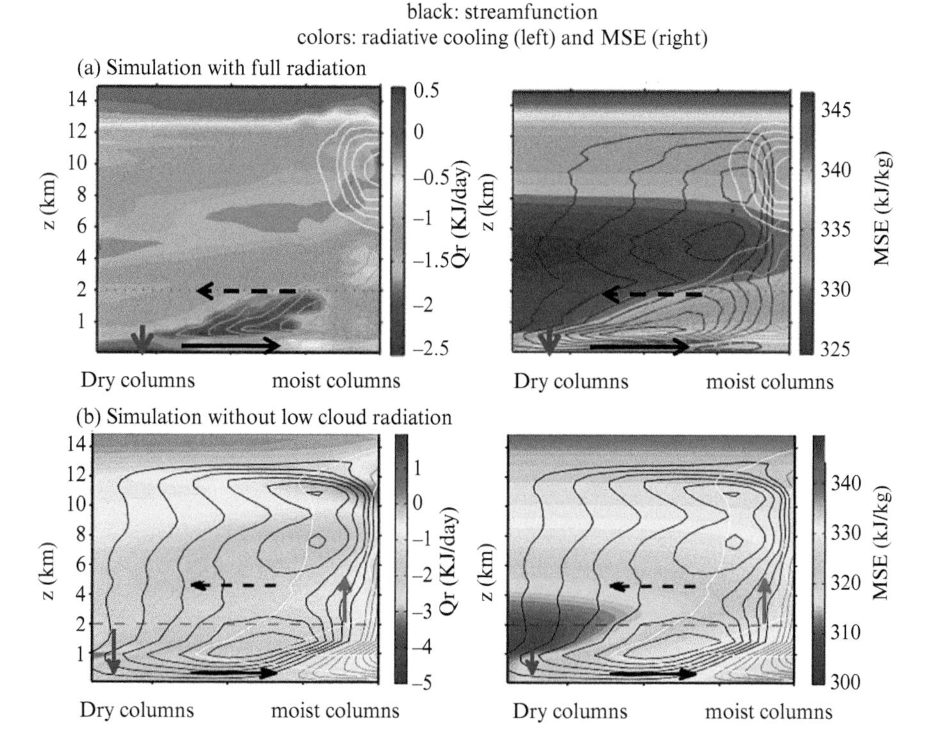

Fig. 2.17 Circulation in height and moisture space (black streamfunction) in simulations that aggregate. The top panels show a simulation with full radiation, while the bottom panels show a simulation where the low-cloud longwave radiative feedback is removed (after Muller and Bony, 2015); © 2015, John Wiley and Sons.

transport yielding convective aggregation. Note that moist static energy is a strong function of height, thus the altitude of the radiative cooling and heating is important. In fact, (Muller and Bony, 2015) show that imposing enhanced radiative cooling in dry regions in radiative-convective equilibrium simulations can lead to the self-aggregation of convection, if the cooling is applied at low altitudes.

A recent study has also been able to simulate self-aggregation even while suppressing radiation and other diabatic feedbacks (Muller and Bony, 2015), a result later confirmed in other models. The process leading to self-aggregation seen in these simulations has been called "moisture-memory" feedback, since it relies only on intrinsic interactions between clouds and the water vapor around them to spontaneously organize into clusters. It occurs when the evaporation of the falling rain is suppressed (i.e., at unrealistically high precipitation efficiency). The physical process leading to aggregation in that case is still unclear, but the absence of downdrafts below deep clouds when the evaporation of rain is suppressed is hypothesized to be important.

In standard conditions, the cooling associated with the evaporation of rain below deep convecting clouds generates downdrafts, which through their thermodynamical effect oppose the upward motion that generated the cloud. This negative feedback on upward convection suppresses the deep cloud in a few hours. Without the evaporation of rain and the effect of the associated downdrafts, moist areas remain moist (or even get moister by convergence) and thus become even more favorable to convection. This tends to "localize" the convection, as observed in these simulations.

This spontaneous self-aggregation of deep convection could have numerous implications. In particular, we saw that the longwave cooling from the dry subsiding region surrounding clouds is key. Most studies of deep convection focus on the moist region where clouds and convection occur. The discovery of self-aggregation thus highlighted the need to investigate the dry regions devoid of deep clouds as well. It could also help shed new light into challenging geophysical open questions, notably the Madden–Julian Oscillation (Kerry Emanuel and Marat Khairoutdinov, personal communication) and tropical cyclogenesis (Muller and Romps, 2018).

2.5 Response of the hydrological cycle to climate change

2.5.1 Context

In this section, we address the important question of the response of precipitation extremes to global warming. As in the previous section, we focus on tropical convection. Indeed, tropical precipitation extremes are particularly challenging for climate models. The "pop-corn" small-scale nature of convection there (compared the mid-latitudes where clouds and convection are embedded in large-scale low- and high-pressure frontal systems) implies that coarse-resolution global climate models have to rely on convective parameterizations to represent convective processes in the tropics.

Despite uncertainties in those parameterizations, global climate models robustly predict a pattern of mean precipitation changes with warming now known as the "rich-get-richet" pattern. Rainy regions (tropics and extratropics Figure 2.18) become rainier, and regions with little precipitation (subtropics Figure 2.18) receive even less rain. This can be understood via simple thermodynamics (Held and Soden, 2006; Muller and O'Gorman, 2011). If changes in relative humidity are small, as is the case in

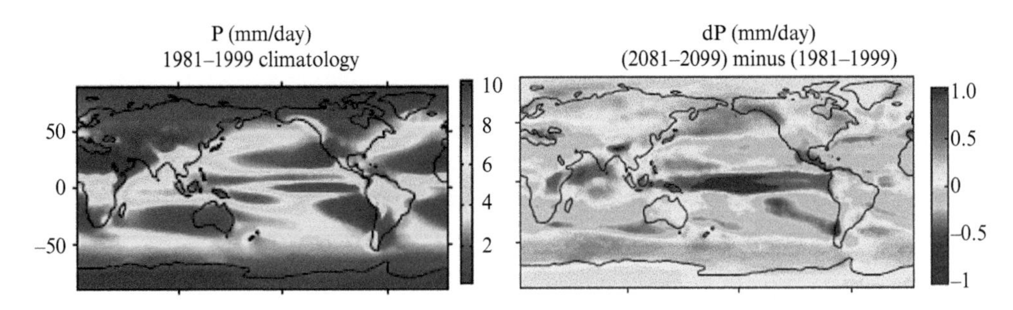

Fig. 2.18 Mean precipitation climatology (left) and change in mean precipitation with global warming (right), illustrating the "rich-get-richer" pattern. High-precipitation regions (tropics and extratropics) have enhanced precipitation, and low-precipitation regions (subtropics) have decreased precipitation (after Muller and O'Gorman, 2011); © 2011, Springer Nature.

climate models, we expect atmospheric water vapor to increase with warming following the Clausius–Clapeyron Equation (Section 2.3.3, Equation (2.12)). Furthermore, if the atmospheric circulation does not change significantly to leading order we expect regions with moisture convergence (and thus, precipitation) to have increased moisture convergence due to the increased moisture. Similarly, regions with moisture divergence are expected to have stronger moisture divergence, and hence decreased precipitation. (Actually moisture divergence and convergence are linked to precipitation minus evaporation; but the changes in precipitation have considerably more structure than the changes in evaporation, so that the previous results on patterns of precipitation changes hold. Note also that the large-scale tropical circulation does change, it weakens slightly, see (Held and Soden, 2006) for more details.)

The global mean precipitation does not follow the Clausius–Clapeyron increase, as it is constrained by global energetics. Atmospheric energy balance implies that the global mean precipitation must balance the global mean radiative cooling (neglecting changes in the Bowen ratio), which increases at a slower rate of about 2% K^{-1} (Held and Soden, 2006).

These results for mean precipitation are extremely robust between climate models, and well understood. But large-scale constraints have little direct relevance to precipitation extremes in tropical storms, and there is a large uncertainty of precipitation extremes in climate models (Figure 2.19, (Kharin, Zwiers, Zhang, and Hegerl, 2007)). This uncertainty is largest in the tropics due to uncertainties in convective parameterizations. Since simulations of tropical precipitation extremes with current global climate models are unreliable, progress on the problem of changing

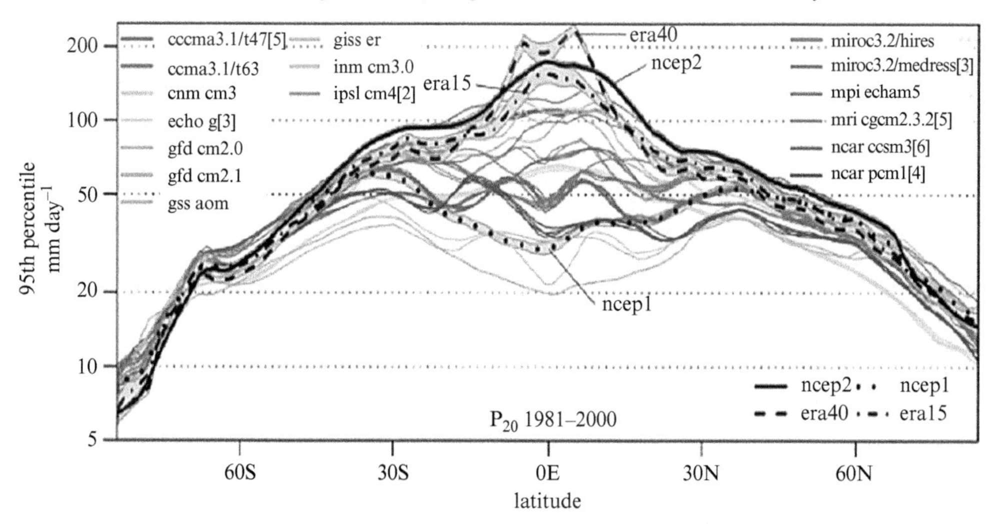

Fig. 2.19 Precipitation extremes (95th percentile) in the different IPCC climate models (after Kharin *et al.*, 2007). There is a large uncertainty in tropical precipitation extremes, due to uncertainties in convective parameterizations; © 2007 American Meteorological Society (AMS).

tropical precipitation extremes must rely on either theory, observations, or simulations that resolve the convective-scale processes. Here we will use theory and cloud-resolving simulations to address this question, in disorganized "pop-corn" convection at first, and then assessing the impact of convective organization on the results.

2.5.2 Amplification of precipitation extremes with warming: Disorganized convection

What can we expect from theoretical considerations? If the dynamics do not change with warming, precipitation extremes can be expected to scale with the moisture convergence into deep convective updrafts, which would then scale with water vapor following the Clausius–Clapeyron equation. In the tropics, this equation predicts an increase of water vapor $> 8\%\ \mathrm{K}^{-1}$ (O'Gorman and Muller, 2010). We will assess the accuracy of this thermodynamic expectation for precipitation extremes in cloud-resolving simulations, addressing the following questions:

- By how much do precipitation extremes increase with warming?
- How does it compare with the change in water vapor?
- How do vertical velocities in updrafts change, and how does it impact precipitation extremes?
- Can we derive a scaling that relates changes in precipitation extremes to mean quantities?

The cloud-resolving model used here is System for Atmospheric Modeling, or SAM, see Section 2.4.5 and (Khairoutdinov and Randall, 2003) for more details. Two simulations are performed, one with a sea-surface temperature of 300 K and another warmer simulation with a sea-surface temperature of 305 K. The radiative cooling profiles are imposed but are different for the two sea-surface temperatures, computed from short small-domain runs with the corresponding sea-surface temperatures (see (Muller, O'Gorman, and Back, 2011) for more details). A weak background vertical shear is added, with horizontal wind decreasing from 5 m s^{-1} at low levels to zero at upper levels in the x direction. Note that this shear is too deep and too weak to generate a squall line, so that convection resembles somewhat randomly distributed "pop-corn" convections in these simulations.

Figure 2.20 shows composites around the location of extreme precipitation. We see that, as expected, precipitation is strongest in the dissipating stage of a cloud life cycle, as indicated by the downdrafts seen below the cloud (consistent with the schematic life cycle in Figure 2.10). Also, as expected, there is preferred upward motion and cloud formation in the direction upshear (Section 2.4.2). The extremes, i.e., high percentiles, of daily precipitation are shown in the left panel of Figure 2.21. We see that for a given percentile, the corresponding rainfall rate is always larger in the warmer simulation. Consistently, the ratio between the precipitation in the warm and in the cold runs is above 1. This ratio is shown in the middle panel for daily precipitation, and in the right panel for hourly precipitation. Although the values of precipitation extremes are sensitive to the temporal average, the *ratio* is not. In other words, the fractional increase in precipitation extremes is robust to the time scale used.

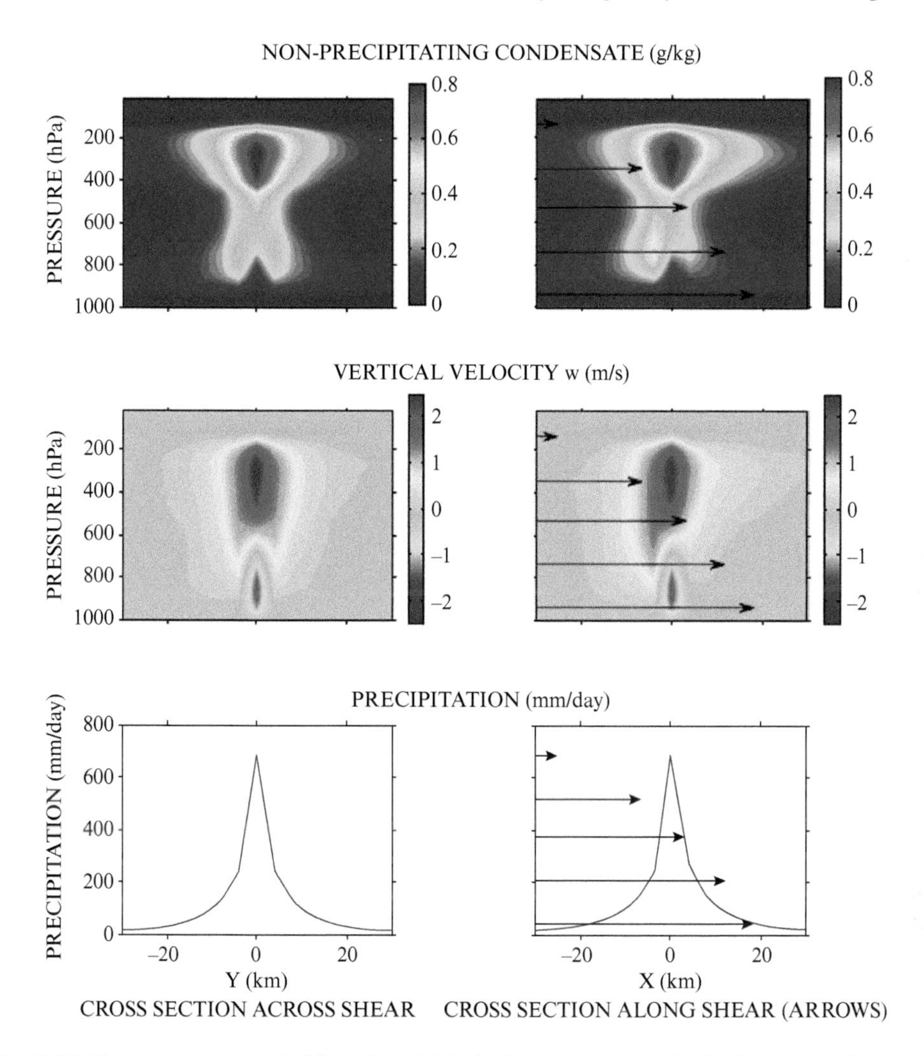

Fig. 2.20 Composites in y (left) and x (right) directions around the location of extreme precipitation (placed at the origin). The top panels show non-precipitating condensates, the middle panels vertical velocity, and the bottom panels precipitation (after Muller *et al.*, 2011); © 2011 American Meteorological Society (AMS).

The fractional increase in precipitation extremes is found to asymptote at the highest percentiles, to $\approx 7\ \%\ \mathrm{K}^{-1}$. In order to clarify the physical origin of this value, we derive a scaling for extreme rainfall rates. From the equations of the model (Khairoutdinov and Randall, 2003), neglecting subgrid scale fluxes, and radiation which is expected to be a small contribution in locations of extreme precipitation (largely dominated by the latent heat term), (Muller, O'Gorman, and Back, 2011) use the vertically integrated dry static energy budget to derive the following scaling for extreme precipitation rates P_e:

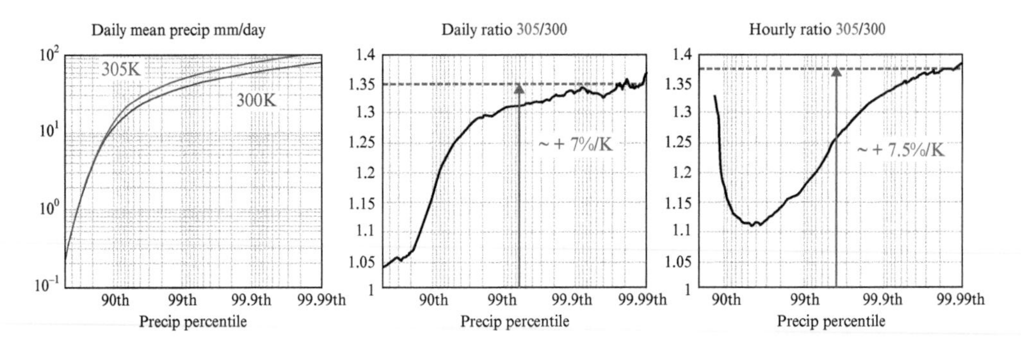

Fig. 2.21 Values of daily precipitation extremes (i.e., high percentiles, left panel) in the cold (blue) and warm (red) simulations. The ratio between the warm and cold rainfall rates is shown in the middle panel. Similar results are obtained at hourly time scales (right panel, after Muller *et al.*, 2011); © 2011 American Meteorological Society (AMS).

$$P_e \approx \int w \frac{-\partial q_s}{\partial z} \overline{\rho} dz - \int \frac{D(L_v q_l + L_s q_i)}{L_v Dt} \overline{\rho} dz \tag{2.24}$$

$$\approx \epsilon_P \int w \frac{-\partial q_s}{\partial z} \overline{\rho} dz, \tag{2.25}$$

where $\overline{\rho}$ denotes the reference density profile of the anelastic model SAM, q_s specific humidity at saturation, q_l liquid condensate amount, q_i solid condensate amount, and ϵ_P the precipitation efficiency. Although this scaling was derived from the dry static energy equation, it resembles a water budget and can be interpreted as such: the first term on the right-hand side of Equation (2.24) represents the total net condensation (and deposition) in the atmospheric column, including condensation from upward motion as well as evaporation of condensates maintaining a moist adiabatic lapse rate in downdraft regions. The second term on the right-hand side accounts for an additional sink of water vapor, namely water vapor detrained as cloud condensates (liquid or ice). This sink can be included in a precipitation efficiency, where only a fraction of the net condensation precipitates out at the surface. In the limit $\epsilon_P = 1$, all the condensates precipitate out; in the limit $\epsilon_P = 0$, all condensates are advected from the column or build up in the column over the time scale in question.

Assuming that changes in precipitation efficiency are small with warming, the change in precipitation can thus be decomposed into a dynamic and a thermodynamic contribution:

$$\delta P_e \approx \underbrace{\delta\left(\int -\frac{\partial q_s}{\partial z} w\overline{\rho} dz\right)}_{\text{scaling}} \approx \underbrace{\int \delta\left(-\frac{\partial q_s}{\partial z}\right) w\overline{\rho} dz}_{\text{thermodynamic}} + \underbrace{\int -\frac{\partial q_s}{\partial z} \delta\left(w\overline{\rho}\right) dz}_{\text{dynamic}}. \tag{2.26}$$

This simple scaling is found to be in very good agreement with numerical results (Figure 2.22). Interestingly, the scaling predicts an increase in extreme precipitation which is smaller than the atmospheric water vapor increase, and closer to the increase in low-tropospheric moisture (Figure 2.22). We will come back to this important

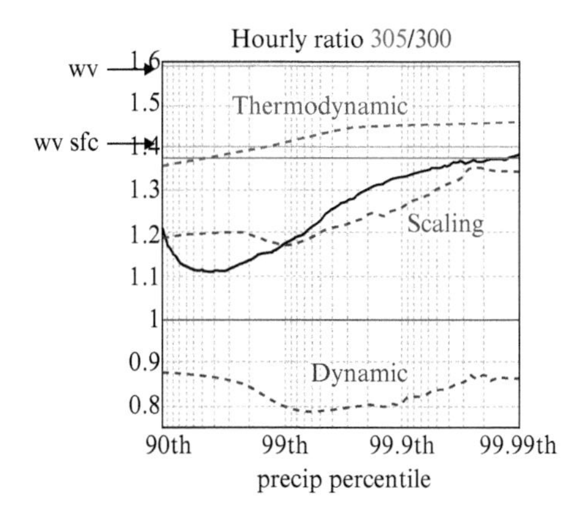

Fig. 2.22 Increase in high percentiles of hourly mean precipitation (repeated from right panel of Figure 2.21), and comparison with a theoretical scaling involving a dynamic and a thermodynamic contribution. The increase in atmospheric water vapor (wv) and low-tropospheric water vapor (wv sfc) are also shown (after Muller *et al.*, 2011); © 2011 American Meteorological Society (AMS).

result in Section 2.5.3 (see e.g., Equation (2.29)). These results suggest that we can thus expect tropical precipitation extremes to increase following the low-level water vapor increase ($< 6\%\ K^{-1}$ in global climate models) instead of atmospheric humidity ($> 8\%\ K^{-1}$, (O'Gorman and Muller, 2010)).

From Figure 2.22, to first order, the amplification of precipitation extremes is well captured by the thermodynamic scaling. The dynamics play a secondary role and tend to oppose the amplification of extreme rainfall rates with warming. We will come back to this point in Section 2.5.3 (see e.g., Figure 2.25). We note also that these results seem to be robust to the model used, as similar increases in precipitation extremes, close to low-tropospheric moisture, have been found in another study using a different cloud-resolving model (Romps, 2011).

2.5.3 Impact of convective organization

As we saw in Section 2.4, convective organization is ubiquitous in the tropics, and is associated with extreme weather and strong rainfall rates. A key question is thus to determine how precipitation extremes in organized convection can be expected to change with warming. In this section, we assess the impact of organization on the results of the previous section, addressing the following questions:

- How do precipitation extremes in organized systems respond to warming?
- How sensitive is the amplification of precipitation extremes to the degree of organization?

To that end, we use vertical wind shear to organize the convection into squall lines, using the three simulations illustrated in Figure 2.12: no shear, critical shear, and supercritical shear. We perform simulations at a control sea-surface temperature value of 300 K, and a warmer simulation at 302 K (see (Muller, 2013) for details). Figure 2.23

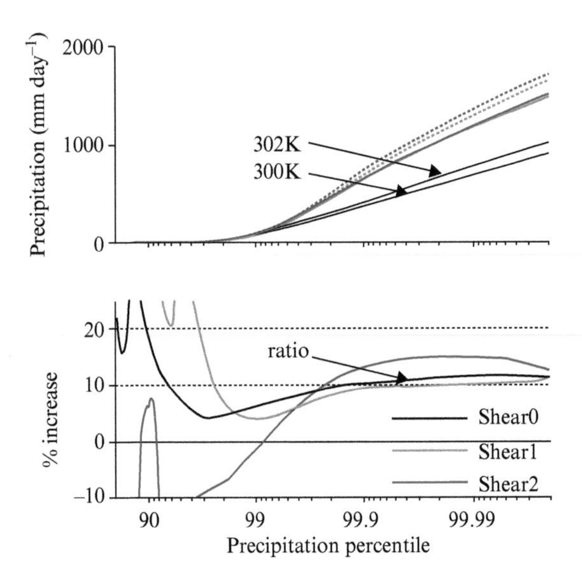

Fig. 2.23 Increase in high percentiles of precipitation, in simulations with different shear strengths (after Muller, 2013); © 2013 American Meteorological Society (AMS).

shows the high percentiles of precipitation in the various simulations, at cold and warm temperatures. As before, precipitation extremes are found to increase with warming, by about 6–7% K^{-1}. We also see that for a given temperature, precipitation extremes are sensitive to vertical shear and almost double in the presence of shear, but increasing the shear from critical to supercritical shear has very little effect on the rainfall rates. This may not be too surprising since, in the supercritical case, the squall lines orient themselves so that the line-perpendicular component of the shear is critical. Therefore, one would expect rainfall rates similar to the ones obtained with critical shear as long as the shear is above critical.

What is perhaps more surprising is that despite very different organization, the amplification of precipitation extremes with warming is similar for all shears, though it is slightly larger in the supercritical shear simulation. This behavior is again well captured by the scaling in Equation (2.26) (Figure 2.24). As before, to leading order, the increase in precipitation extremes is determined by the thermodynamic contribution, and dynamics play a secondary role. But interestingly, the dynamic contribution is not robust to the shear: no shear or critical shear yield a negative contribution, opposing the amplification of precipitation extremes with warming. But supercritical shear yields a positive dynamic contribution, which explains the slightly stronger increase of precipitation extremes in that case. As in the previous section, the amplification of precipitation extremes is found to be closer to low-tropospheric humidity increase than to atmospheric humidity increase (not shown). These results thus confirm the conclusions of the previous section, the only difference being the dynamic contribution which can become positive in the presence of strong shear.

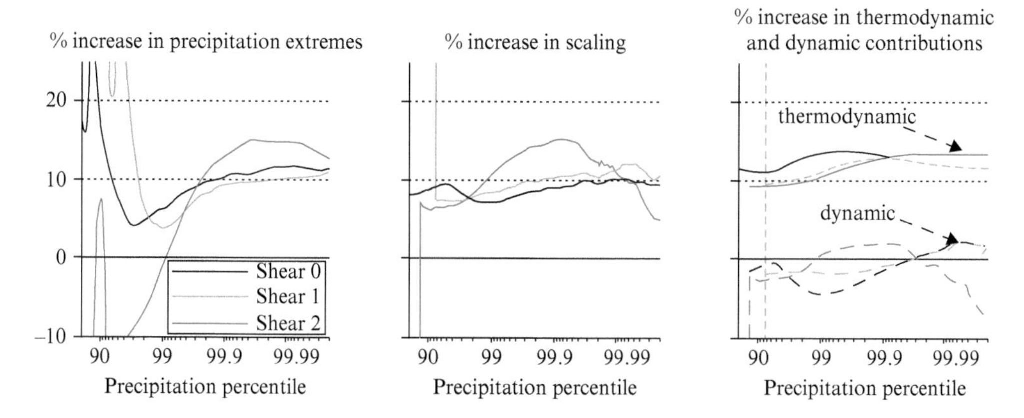

Fig. 2.24 Increase in high percentiles of precipitation, and comparison with the theoretical scaling involving a dynamic and a thermodynamic contribution, in simulations with different shear strengths (after Muller, 2013); © 2013 American Meteorological Society (AMS).

The fact that precipitation extremes follow low-tropospheric humidity, and not atmospheric humidity, can be understood using a simplified scaling, if we assume that ρw at 500 hPa is a representative value for ρw in Equation (2.26):

$$\delta P_e \approx \delta\left(\int -\frac{\partial q_s}{\partial z} w\overline{\rho} dz\right) \tag{2.27}$$

$$\approx \delta\left((w\overline{\rho})_{500hPa} \int -\frac{\partial q_s}{\partial z} dz\right) \tag{2.28}$$

$$\approx \underbrace{\delta\left((w\overline{\rho})_{500hPa}\, q_{s,BL}\right)}_{\text{simplified scaling}}, \tag{2.29}$$

where $q_{s,BL}$ denotes the saturation specific humidity in the boundary layer. If changes in relative humidity are small, precipitation extremes are thus expected to follow low-tropospheric water vapor.

The dynamic contribution deserves further investigation, as it is the contribution which is sensitive to the shear and thus, the organization. Figure 2.25 shows the vertical profiles of ρw and of w in the various simulations. We see that the decrease in vertical mass fluxes with warming at critical and zero shear, is not observed with supercritical shear. Figure 2.25 also shows that the decrease in convective mass flux occurs despite an increase in the maximum updraft velocity (bottom panels). The former is more relevant to precipitation extremes.

2.5.4 Discussion

Cloud-resolving simulations show that precipitation extremes increase with warming at a rate of about 6–7% K^{-1} following the low-tropospheric humidity, yielding a smaller increase than atmospheric humidity. This behavior can be understood using

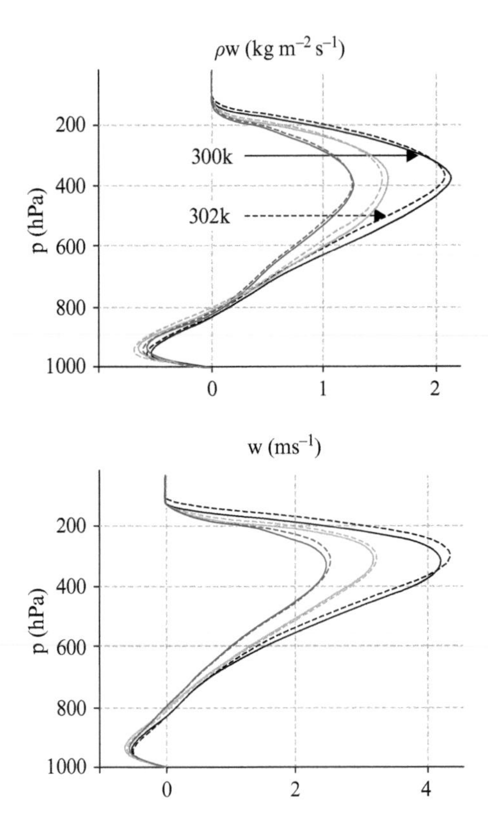

Fig. 2.25 Change in vertical velocity and vertical mass flux with warming for the different shears. Despite an increase in vertical velocity, the mass flux decreases with warming (except for the supercritical shear in red). The latter is more relevant to precipitation extremes, explaining the negative dynamic contribution except with the strongest shear (Figure 2.24, after Muller, 2013); © 2013 American Meteorological Society (AMS).

simple scalings, which relate precipitation extremes to thermodynamic and dynamic contributions. To leading order, precipitation extremes follow the thermodynamic scaling, even in the presence of convective organization. In fact, despite very different organizations, the amplification of precipitation extremes with warming is surprisingly robust in all the simulations shown on Figure 2.12, closely following the increase in lower-tropospheric humidity.

Note that a large uncertainty regarding tropical precipitation extremes and their response to warming, is related to convective organization and its response to warming. Indeed, here we investigated the increase of precipitation extremes with warming *for a given degree of organization.* But Figure 2.23 implies that a change in the degree of organization can lead to up to a doubling of extreme rainfall rates, while, for a given degree of organization precipitation extremes increase at about 7% K^{-1} of warming. Thus, the increase of precipitation extremes from a change in convective organization is larger than that associated with warming.

A recent observational study (Tan, Jakob, Rossow, and Tselioudis, 2015) finds that recent trends in tropical precipitation can be linked to changes in the frequency of occurrence of organized mesoscale cloud systems. Improved fundamental understanding of convective organization and its sensitivity to warming is hence an area of priority for climate model development to achieve accurate rainfall projections in a warming climate.

2.6 Clouds in a changing climate

2.6.1 Climate sensitivity

Climate sensitivity refers to the temperature change at equilibrium in response to a doubling of CO_2. In 1979, Charney published an early assessment of the impact of carbon dioxide on long-term climate, known as the "Charney Report" (Charney and Coauthors, 1979). In his report, Charney concluded that climate sensitivity ranged from 1.5 to 4.5 K, with a likely value of 3 K. He added that the key uncertainties in these estimates came from cloud feedbacks, the role of the ocean in carbon and heat uptake, and the prediction of regional precipitation changes. Since Charney's report, several state-of-the-art IPCC reports have been published, summarizing the scientific knowledge on climate change, with increasing theoretical understanding and improved numerical tools. Despite almost 40 years of research in climate science, his aforementioned results remain largely true. Given the strong radiative impact of clouds, more work is desirable to reduce the large uncertainty in climate sensitivity associated with clouds and their response to climate change.

2.6.2 Clouds and radiation

In this section, we discuss the impact of clouds on the Earth energy budget, i.e., on the top-of-atmosphere incoming radiation. The radiative impact of a cloud depends on its height and thickness. Low thick clouds have a high albedo, i.e., they reflect a significant amount of sunlight (Figure 2.26a). But their temperature is close to the surface temperature, thus, their thermal emission is close to the surface emission. So low clouds have little longwave (LW) effect, but are associated with strong shortwave (SW) cooling.

High thin clouds on the other hand, are nearly transparent to the incoming solar shortwave radiation, with thus a low albedo (Figure 2.26b). But their emission temperature is much lower than the surface temperature, implying a strong longwave signature. High clouds emit less to space due to their cold temperatures. So high clouds have little shortwave effect, but are associated with strong longwave warming.

Note that deep clouds (cumulonimbus) have both a strong albedo and a cold top emission temperature, so that the shortwave cooling is largely balanced by the longwave warming. Their radiative impact at the top of the atmosphere is nearly neutral.

Quantitatively, the *cloud radiative effect* is a measure of the cloud impact on the Earth energy budget (i.e., incoming radiation at the top of the atmosphere). It is defined as the difference between the all-sky and the clear-sky flux (defined positive for warming):

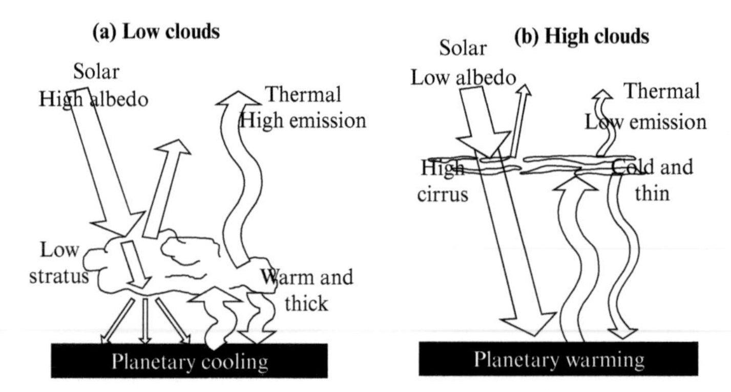

Fig. 2.26 Schematic of the top-of-atmosphere radiative impact of low clouds (left) and high clouds (right). Figure from Turco 1997 © 2002 Oxford University Press, Inc.

- shortwave radiative effect = $\mathrm{SW}_{\text{in all sky}}$ - $\mathrm{SW}_{\text{in clear sky}}$ (typically < 0 because of low clouds cooling)
- longwave radiative effect = $\mathrm{LW}_{\text{in all sky}}$ - $\mathrm{LW}_{\text{in clear sky}}$ (typically > 0 because of high clouds warming).

The annual mean globally averaged LW cloud radiative effect is about +30 W m^{-2}, and the SW cloud radiative effect -50 W m^{-2}. In the net, the annual mean cloud radiative effect is thus negative and ≈ -20 W m^{-2}. This value can be compared to the radiative forcing associated with a doubling of CO_2 +4 W m^{-2}. Clarifying how clouds respond to climate change is thus crucial to accurately estimate climate sensitivity.

The *cloud radiative forcing* quantifies the difference between all-sky and clear-sky flux changes, providing a measure of the contribution of clouds to climate sensitivity. The net cloud radiative forcing is the sum of the longwave and the shortwave forcings, by convention < 0 if clouds oppose warming, and > 0 if clouds strengthen warming. Key questions are thus:

- How will clouds respond to increased CO_2?
- Can we formalize the link between clouds and climate sensitivity?

The latter question will be addressed first, in Section 2.6.3, where we introduce a classical framework widely used to quantify climate feedbacks and their contribution to climate sensitivity. The former question is still an active area of research, and the Section 2.6.3 will present a brief overview of the physical processes believed to contribute significantly to the cloud feedback and its spread in climate models.

2.6.3 Quantifying climate feedbacks

As discussed in Section 2.4.5 (see e.g., Equation (2.18)), the net incoming radiation at the top of the atmosphere is proportional to

$$R = \frac{S_0(1-a)}{4} - OLR,$$

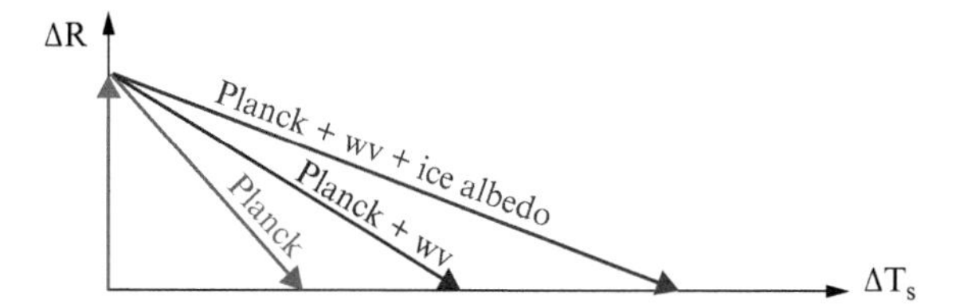

Fig. 2.27 Global mean surface temperature response ΔT_s to a radiative forcing ΔR due to the Planck response (light blue), including the water vapor feedback as well (dark blue), and including the ice albedo feedback (purple). Each additional positive feedback implies that the surface temperature needs to increase more in order to reach equilibrium $\Delta R = 0$.

where OLR denotes the outgoing longwave radiation σT_e^4. There is equilibrium when $R = 0$. Now let's imagine a forcing, such that $\Delta R > 0$. The dependence of OLR on temperature constitutes the main restoring force towards Earth's energy balance. Thus, temperatures need to warm to reach the new equilibrium such that $\Delta R = 0$. It has been found from model experiments that to leading order, the radiative response can be assumed proportional to the global average surface air temperature change.

We can suppose that

$$OLR = f(CO_2, wv, cld)\sigma T_s^4,$$

where T_s denotes surface temperature, wv water vapor and cld cloud. If CO_2 abruptly increases, the emission level goes up, thus the emission temperature goes down and OLR is smaller, so that $\Delta R = F > 0$ (red arrow Figure 2.27). If only T_s responds to the perturbation, a positive $\Delta T_s > 0$ is needed to reach a new equilibrium $\Delta R = 0$ (Planck response on Figure 2.27).

Now if water vapor also increases as T_s increases, as can be expected from the Clausius–Clapeyron Equation (2.12), the greenhouse effect of water vapor implies that a larger ΔT_s is needed to reach equilibrium (Planck+wv on Figure 2.27). If additionally the ice cover decreases with warming, the associated albedo decrease implies than an even larger ΔT_s is needed (Planck+wv+ice albedo on Figure 2.27).

These physical considerations can be formalized by assuming $R = R(CO_2, T_s)$ and writing the radiative imbalance as

$$\Delta R = \left(\frac{\partial R}{\partial CO_2}\right)_{T_s} \Delta CO_2 + \left(\frac{\partial R}{\partial T_s}\right)_{CO_2} \Delta T_s \tag{2.30}$$

$$\Leftrightarrow \Delta R = F + \lambda \Delta T_s, \tag{2.31}$$

where F is the instantaneous radiative forcing due to increased CO_2 (in W m^{-2}), and $\lambda = (\partial R/\partial T_s)_{CO_2}$ is the so-called feedback parameter (in W m^{-2} K^{-1}). If $\lambda < 0$, the feedback is stabilizing, if $\lambda > 0$, the feedback is destabilizing the warming.

Note that $\Delta R = 0$ yields

$$\Delta T_{eq} = -\frac{F}{\lambda}. \tag{2.32}$$

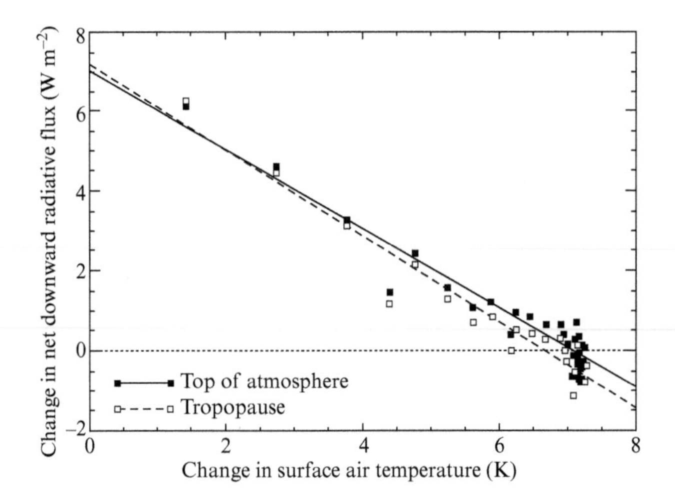

Fig. 2.28 Gregory plot showing the time evolution of net downward radiative imbalance at the top of atmosphere (and tropopause) in response to a quadrupling of CO_2 in a climate model (HadSM3), as a function of surface air temperature anomaly (1.5 m height). The dotted line represents radiative equilibrium $\Delta R = 0$ (from Gregory *et al.*, 2004); © 2004, John Wiley and Sons.

For a doubling of CO_2, this is the equilibrium climate sensitivity. Figures such as Figure 2.27 are known as Gregory plots (Gregory, Ingram, Palmer, Jones, Stott, Thorpe, Lowe, Johns, and Williams, 2004). Its application to a $4 \times CO_2$ simulation is shown in Figure 2.28 (Gregory, Ingram, Palmer, Jones, Stott, Thorpe, Lowe, Johns, and Williams, 2004). The increased $4 \times CO_2$ yields a positive anomalous net incoming radiative flux, which decreases in time as the surface air temperature increases, until a new equilibrium $\Delta R = 0$ is reached. The slope of the line is the feedback parameter λ.

We can extend the previous analysis to include the contribution of the various feedbacks to the feedback parameter:

$$\frac{\partial R}{\partial T_s} = \sum_x \frac{\partial R}{\partial x}\frac{\partial x}{\partial T_s} \Leftrightarrow \lambda = \lambda_{Planck} + \underbrace{\lambda_{wv} + \lambda_{ice} + \lambda_{cld} + \ldots}_{\text{influence of each feedback } x \text{ on climate sensitivity}} \tag{2.33}$$

This framework helps interpret inter-model differences in climate sensitivity (Figure 2.29, (Dufresne and Bony, 2008)). Based on global climate model simulations, clouds are found to be the largest source of uncertainty between models. Explaining this spread remains an active area of research, and various physical processes involved are discussed in Section 2.6.4. For more information on how to compute those feedback parameters, notably on the Kernel approach, the interested reader is referred to (Soden, Held, Colman, Shell, Kiehl, and Shields, 2008).

2.6.4 Cloud feedback processes

How do different cloud types contribute to global cloud feedbacks? Figure 2.30 shows the cloud feedbacks in several climate models (from (Zelinka, Klein, Taylor, Andrews,

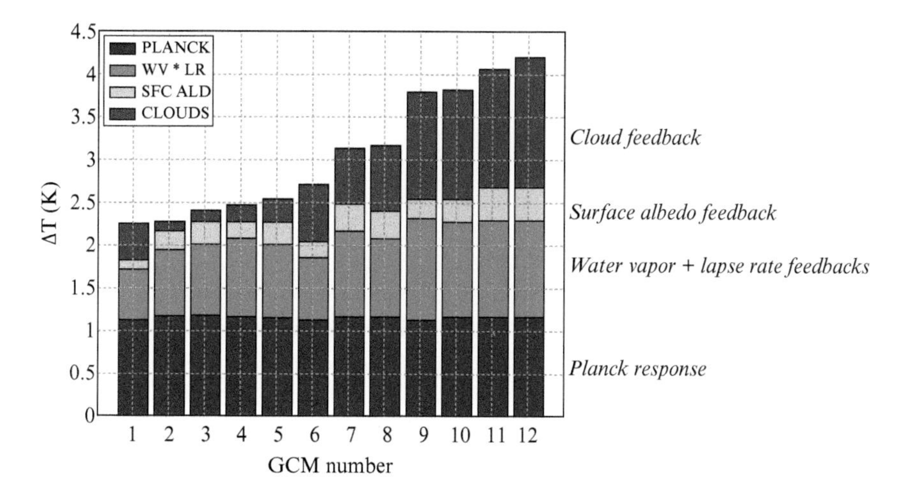

Fig. 2.29 Contributions of various feedbacks to equilibrium climate sensitivity in global climate models (GCMs) (from Dufresnes and Bony, 2008). The cloud feedback is responsible for the largest spread between models; © 2008 American Meteorological Society (AMS).

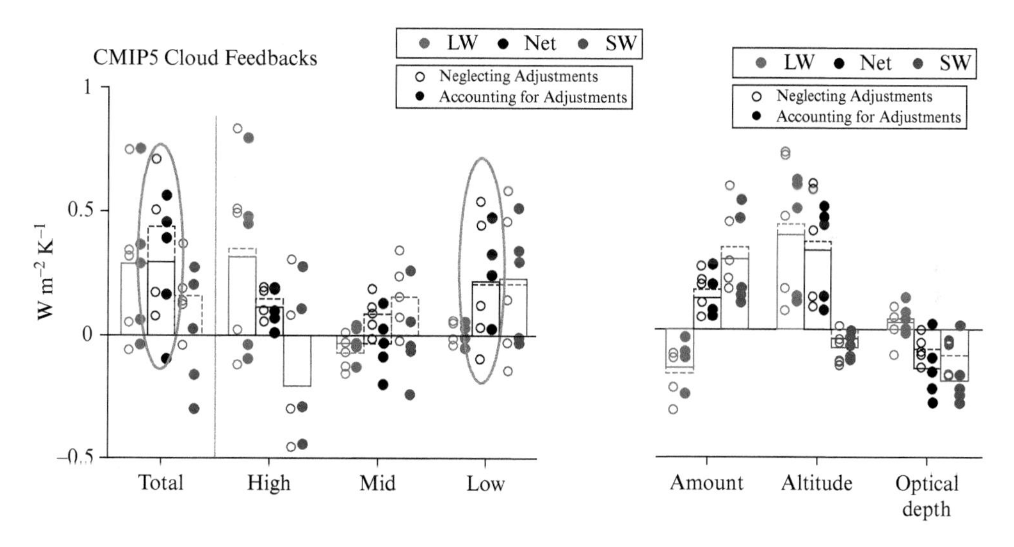

Fig. 2.30 Total cloud feeedback in several CMIP5 models (left), contributions from high, middle, and low clouds (middle), and contributions split into amount, altitude, and optical depth (right) (adapted from Zelinka *et al.*, 2013; the interested reader is also referred to Zelinka *et al.*, 2016 for a larger ensemble of models). The low-cloud feedback dominates the spread between models. © 2013 American Meteorological Society (AMS).

Webb, Gregory, and Forster, 2013)). The spread between models largely comes from low clouds. Note that high clouds have a large spread in longwave and shortwave separately, but these tend to cancel, since as mentioned previously, high deep clouds have both a strong albedo and a cold top emission temperature. So the shortwave cooling is largely balanced by the longwave warming.

Alternatively, we can split the cloud feedback into cloud amount, altitude and optical depth (Figure 2.30, right). The latter yields a negative cloud feedback, associated with increased cloud optical depth. This negative cloud optical depth feedback arises mostly from the extratropics, with a robust increase in cloud optical depth at latitudes poleward of about 40°. This high-latitude cloud optical thickness response is likely related to changes in the phase and/or total water content of clouds (Zelinka, Klein, Taylor, Andrews, Webb, Gregory, and Forster, 2013).

Cloud altitudes yield a positive cloud feedback contribution, associated with higher clouds. In a warmer climate, climate models robustly predict a rise in upper-level clouds. So do cloud-resolving models. A theoretical explanation for this behavior was proposed by (Hartmann and Larson, 2002), using the radiative-convective equilibrium framework (Section 2.4.5). It is known as the FAT hypothesis, or fixed anvil temperature hypothesis. This hypothesis implies that tropical anvil clouds detrain at a fixed temperature independent of surface warming. This behavior is closely related to the shape of the radiative cooling profile.

More precisely, in radiative-convective equilibrium, the depth of the convection layer is determined by the depth of the atmospheric layer destabilized by radiation (Figure 2.31). In clear skies, the radiative cooling is balanced by adiabatic heating through subsidence

$$\omega = \frac{Q}{\sigma},$$

where ω denotes vertical velocity, Q radiative cooling and σ static stability. The strong decline of radiative cooling with altitude around 200 hPa (Figure 2.31) must thus be accompanied by a strong horizontal convergence of mass in clear skies at that level

$$-\nabla.V = \frac{\partial \omega}{\partial p}.$$

This convergence in subsidence regions must in turn be balanced by a strong divergence of mass from the convective regions. The divergence of mass is associated with the frequent occurrence of convective anvil clouds at this level.

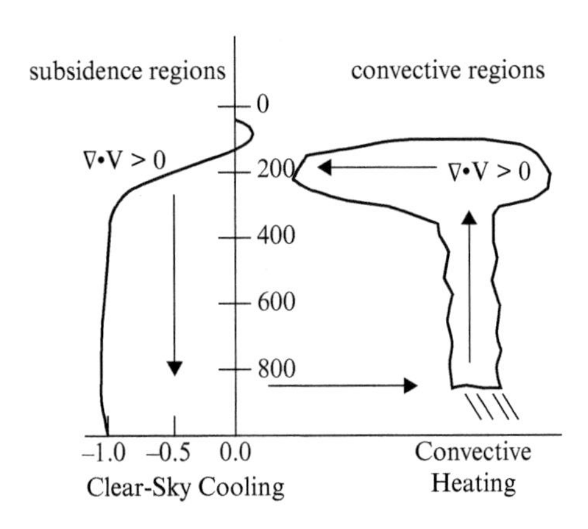

Fig. 2.31 Two box schematic representation of convection, with radiative cooling in clear sky subsidence regions balanced by convective heating in convective regions (from Hartmann and Larson, 2002); © 2002, John Wiley and Sons.

The height of anvils is thus closely related to the region of strong decline of radiative cooling. Water vapor is responsible for most of the cooling of the tropical upper troposphere. The height at which the cooling has a strong vertical gradient is thus determined by the amount of water above it. Since the saturation vapor pressure is a function of temperature only (Equation (2.12)), if the relative humidity is fixed, the profile of water vapor pressure in the vertical is determined by the temperature, and the temperature at which this gradient occurs will be roughly constant, including in climate change scenarios. The implication of the FAT hypothesis for climate is that cloud tops do not warm in step with surface and atmospheric temperatures. In other words, the tropics become less efficient at radiating away heat, yielding a positive longwave cloud feedback.

Finally, cloud amounts yield a positive feedback, associated with decreased cloud fraction. In many regions, the feedback from cloud amounts is not robust between models, particularly in the tropics. Several mechanisms have been proposed for the decreased low cloud amount, including the role of enhanced surface fluxes deepening the boundary layer, and hence, the mixing of dry and warm air to the surface, leading to decreased cloudiness as climate warms (Rieck, Nuijens, and Stevens, 2012). Radiative effects of clouds have also been suggested to be important. Low-level clouds contribute to their own maintenance through their radiative effect, which could explain the large spread of low cloud feedbacks (Brient and Bony, 2012).

For deep clouds, the FAT theory does not predict the change in cloud amount. How the deep cloud cover will change with warming remains an open question. Notably, convective organization can impact cloud cover, and as we saw in Section 2.4 convective organization is still an active area of research. More work is desirable to clarify the response of convective organization and cloud cover, both low and high clouds, to warming, as well as implications for the hydrological cycle, including mean and extreme precipitation.

References

Bohron, C. F. and Albrecht, B. A. (1998). *Atmospheric Thermodynamics.* Oxford University Press, New York, pp 402.

Bony, S., Stevens, B., Frierson, D., Jakob, C., Kageyama, M., Pincus, R., Shepherd, T. G., Sherwood, S. C., Siebesma, A. P., Sobel, A. H. *et al.* (2015). Clouds, circulation and climate sensitivity. *Nature Geoscience*, **8**(4), 261.

Bretherton, C. S., Blossey, P. N., and Khairoutdinov, M. (2005). An energy-balance analysis of deep convective self-aggregation above uniform sst. *Journal of the atmospheric sciences*, **62**(12), 4273–92.

Brient, F. and Bony, S. (2012). How may low-cloud radiative properties simulated in the current climate influence low-cloud feedbacks under global warming? *Geophysical Research Letters*, **39**(20).

Charney, J. G. and Coauthors (1979). *Carbon Dioxide and Climate: A Scientific Assesment.* National Academy of Science, Washington, DC.

COMET program (2007–2018). *MetEd.* Website of the University Corporation for Atmospheric Research (UCAR). https://www.meted.ucar.edu/index.php.

Dufresne, J-.L. and Bony, S. (2008). An assessment of the primary sources of spread of global warming estimates from coupled atmosphere–ocean models. *Journal of Climate*, **21**(19), 5135–44.

Emanuel, K. A. (1986). An air-sea interaction theory for tropical cyclones. Part 1: Steady-state maintenance. *Journal of the Atmospheric Sciences*, **43**(6), 585–605.

Emanuel, K. A. (1994). *Atmospheric convection.* Oxford University Press on Demand.

EUMETSAT (2017). Year of Weather. Website.https://www.youtube.com/watch?v=9YAXEHLNphY.

Garner, S. T. and Thorpe, A. J. (1992). The development of organized convection in a simplified squall-line model. *Quarterly Journal of the Royal Meteorological Society*, **118**(503), 101–24.

Gregory, J. M., Ingram, W. J., Palmer, M. A., Jones, G. S., Stott, P. A., Thorpe, R. B., Lowe, J. A., Johns, T. C., and Williams, K. D. (2004). A new method for diagnosing radiative forcing and climate sensitivity. *Geophysical Research Letters*, **31**(3).

Hartmann, D. L. and Larson, K. (2002). An important constraint on tropical cloud-climate feedback. *Geophysical Research Letters*, **29**(20), 12–1.

Held, I. M. and Soden, B J (2006). Robust responses of the hydrological cycle to global warming. *Journal of climate*, **19**(21), 5686–99.

Houze Jr, R. A. (2014). *Cloud dynamics.* Volume 104. Elsevier, USA.

ISCCP (2009). International Satellite Cloud Climatology Project. Website. https://isccp.giss.nasa.gov/climanal2.html.

Khairoutdinov, M. F. and Randall, D. A. (2003). Cloud resolving modeling of the arm summer 1997 iop: Model formulation, results, uncertainties, and sensitivities. *Journal of the Atmospheric Sciences*, **60**(4), 607–25.

Kharin, V. V., Zwiers, F. W., Zhang, X., and Hegerl, G. C. (2007). Changes in temperature and precipitation extremes in the ipcc ensemble of global coupled model simulations. *Journal of Climate*, **20**(8), 1419–44.

Kiladis, G. N., Wheeler, M. C., Haertel, P. T., Straub, K. H., and Roundy, P. E. (2009). Convectively coupled equatorial waves. *Reviews of Geophysics*, **47**(2).

Manabe, S. and Strickler, R. F. (1964). Thermal equilibrium of the atmosphere with a convective adjustment. *Journal of the Atmospheric Sciences*, **21**(4), 361–85.

Mapes, B. E. (1993). Gregarious tropical convection. *Journal of the atmospheric sciences*, **50**(13), 2026–37.

Matsuno, T. (1966). Quasi-geostrophic motions in the equatorial area. *Journal of the Meteorological Society of Japan. Ser. II*, **44**(1), 25–43.

Muller, C. J. (2013). Impact of convective organization on the response of tropical precipitation extremes to warming. *Journal of Climate*, **26**(14), 5028–43.

Muller, C. J. and Bony, S. (2015). What favors convective aggregation and why? *Geophysical Research Letters*, **42**(13), 5626–34.

Muller, C. J. and Held, I. M. (2012). Detailed investigation of the self-aggregation of convection in cloud-resolving simulations. *Journal of the Atmospheric Sciences*, **69**(8), 2551–65.

Muller, C. J. and O'Gorman, P. A. (2011). An energetic perspective on the regional response of precipitation to climate change. *Nature Climate Change*, **1**(5), 266.

Muller, C. J., O'Gorman, P. A., and Back, L. E. (2011). Intensification of precipitation extremes with warming in a cloud-resolving model. *Journal of Climate*, **24**(11), 2784–800.

Muller, C. J. and Romps, D. M. (2018). Acceleration of tropical cyclogenesis by self-aggregation feedbacks. *Proceedings of the National Academy of Sciences*, 201719967.

O'Gorman, P. A. and Muller, C. J. (2010). How closely do changes in surface and column water vapor follow clausius–clapeyron scaling in climate change simulations? *Environmental Research Letters*, **5**(2), 025207.

Rieck, M., Nuijens, L., and Stevens, B. (2012). Marine boundary layer cloud feedbacks in a constant relative humidity atmosphere. *Journal of the Atmospheric Sciences*, **69**(8), 2538–50.

Romps, D. M. (2011). Response of tropical precipitation to global warming. *Journal of the Atmospheric Sciences*, **68**(1), 123–38.

Rossow, W. B. and Schiffer, R. A. (1999). Advances in understanding clouds from isccp., **80**(11), 2261–88.

Rotunno, R., Klemp, J. B., and Weisman, M. L. (1988). A theory for strong, long-lived squall lines. *Journal of the Atmospheric Sciences*, **45**(3), 463–85.

Soden, B. J., Held, I. M., Colman, R., Shell, K. M., Kiehl, J. T., and Shields, C. A. (2008). Quantifying climate feedbacks using radiative kernels. *Journal of Climate*, **21**(14), 3504–20.

SSEC (2018). Space Science and Engineering Center. Website. https://www.ssec.wisc.edu/data/geo-list/.

Stevens, B. (2005). Atmospheric moist convection. *Annu. Rev. Earth Planet. Sci.*, **33**, 605–43.

Tan, J., Jakob, C., Rossow, W. B., and Tselioudis, G. (2015). Increases in tropical rainfall driven by changes in frequency of organized deep convection. *Nature*, **519**(7544), 451.

Wheeler, M. and Kiladis, G. N. (1999). Convectively coupled equatorial waves: Analysis of clouds and temperature in the wavenumber–frequency domain. *Journal of the Atmospheric Sciences*, **56**(3), 374–99.

Wing, A. A., Emanuel, K., Holloway, C. E., and Muller, C. (2017). Convective selfaggregation. *Surveys of Geophysics*, 1–25.

Zelinka, M. D., Klein, S. A., Taylor, K. E., Andrews, T., Webb, M. J., Gregory, J. M., and Forster, P. M. (2013). Contributions of different cloud types to feedbacks and rapid adjustments in cmip5. *Journal of Climate*, **26**(14), 5007–27.

3
Dynamical system approaches to climate variability

HENK A. DIJKSTRA

Institute for Marine and Atmospheric research Utrecht, Department of Physics, Utrecht University, Princetonplein 5, 3584 CC Utrecht, The Netherlands

Dijkstra, H. A., *Dynamical system approaches to climate variability* In: *Fundamental Aspects of Turbulent Flows in Climate Dynamics*. Edited by: Freddy Bouchet, Tapio Schneider, Antoine Venaille, Christophe Salomon, Oxford University Press (2020).
DOI. 10.1093/oso/9780198855217.003.0003

Chapter Contents

3.1 Introduction

A tutorial is provided on the application of dynamical systems theory to problems in climate dynamics. We start with the analysis of low-dimensional deterministic dynamical systems using bifurcation theory and provide examples in conceptual climate models. We then proceed to stochastic low-dimensional systems, and eventually end with operator-based techniques within ergodic theory.

In these notes, we start each section from a climate dynamics problem, motivate the choice of the model to study it, and use dynamical systems analysis to understand the behavior of the model solutions. In each of the chapters, a different phenomenon, a different type of model and/or a different dynamical systems tool will be presented. Problems that are addressed are midlatitude SST variability (Section 2), the Pleistocene ice ages (Section 3), the Dansgaard–Oeschger oscillations (Section 4), the El Niño/Southern Oscillation (Section 5), and the midlatitude atmospheric flow transitions (Section 6).

These notes are merged from different sources of material (parts from the book *Nonlinear Climate Dynamics* (Cambridge University Press, 2013), contributions from fellows of the WHOI 2015 Summer School, and material on ergodic theory of climate from the PhD thesis of Dr. Alexis Tantet.[1]

3.1.1 Climate variability

The climate system covers all processes and phenomena in the atmosphere, ocean, ice, and land. It displays variability on many spatial and temporal scales, from weather changes on a day-to-day time scale to climate changes over centuries. Natural climate variability is used to indicate all variability which would occur if human activity were to be absent. Of this natural variability, part is caused by (external) periodic changes in radiative forcing (e.g., diurnal, seasonal). Intrinsic variability is that part of natural variability which arises due to instabilities of e.g., oceanic and atmospheric flows. These instabilities introduce time scales of variability which cannot be anticipated by considering the external forcing frequencies and would even occur if the external forcing were steady. Human activities have introduced a component of climate variability that is usually referred to as anthropogenic climate change. It is associated with changes in the radiation balance mainly due to the emission of greenhouse gases. Because it occurs on a time scale much faster than natural carbon cycle processes, it can be considered as a "forcing." Climate variability as seen in the instrumental record (1870–present) is the result of natural variability and anthropogenic induced climate change.

Unfortunately, the observational record is very limited to determine time scales and patterns of variability in the climate system and the only ocean observable that is available over more than a century long period (1870–2014) is sea surface temperature (SST). In Figure 3.1a, the mean SST over the period 1900–2000 from the HadISST data set, Rayner *et al.* (2003) shows the strong equator-to-pole SST gradient, caused by the net positive (negative) radiation at the equator (poles). There is a strong

[1]Laboratoire de Météorologie Dynamique, École Polytechnique, Paris, France

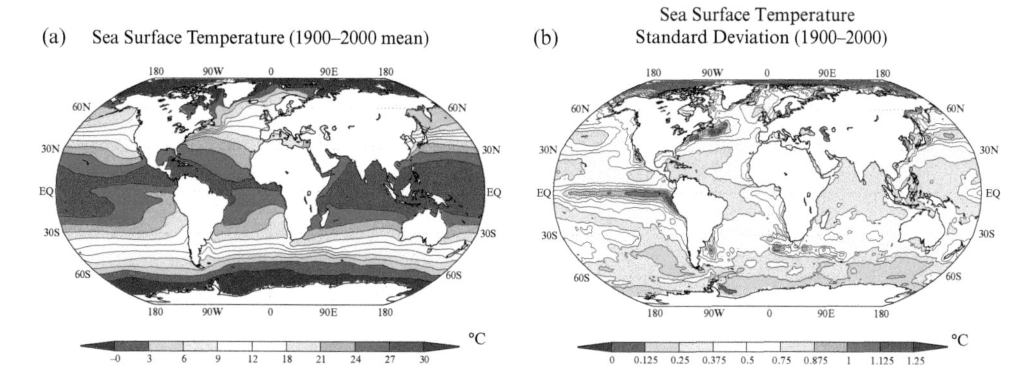

Fig. 3.1 (a) Mean sea surface temperature field (°C) over the years 1900–2000. (from the HadISST data set Rayner *et al.* (2003). (b) Standard deviation of the sea surface temperature field (°C) over the period 1900–2000; the seasonal cycle has been filtered out.

inter-basin asymmetry with much higher SST in the northern North Atlantic than in the northern North Pacific. Another clear asymmetry can be seen in the equatorial Pacific, where the eastern Pacific is a few degrees cooler than the western Pacific. The standard deviation of the SST field (after filtering the seasonal cycle) is plotted in Figure 3.1b. High variability appears in the eastern Pacific, and along the western boundaries of the ocean basins, in the Gulf Stream, Kuroshio (Japan) and Agulhas (South Africa) regions.

Patterns of SST variability can be determined through multivariate statistical analysis of SST variance, Ghil (2002). The most pronounced patterns are associated with El Niño/Southern Oscillation (ENSO), the Pacific Decadal Oscillation (PDO), the Atlantic Multidecadal Oscillation (AMO) and the Indian Ocean Dipole (IOD). These patterns can also be visualized by determining a box-averaged time series and then regressing this time series on the global SST anomaly field.

For the ENSO phenomenon, one can take the so-called NINO3 time series (Figure 3.2a) which is the average SST anomaly (with respect to the seasonal cycle) over the domain 150°W–90°W × 5°S–5°N. The SST anomaly pattern of the ENSO phenomenon is the largest climate variability signal on interannual time scales and restricted to the equatorial Pacific (Figure 3.2b). The AMO time series is the SST anomaly over the domain 75°W–7°W × 25°S–60°N. The AMO has a period of about 20–70 years (Figure 3.2a) and its pattern appears to be a basin wide anomaly localized in the North Atlantic basin (Figure 3.2d). The PDO appears to vary in the range 20–30 years and has dominant amplitudes in the North Pacific with SST anomalies also overlapping with those of ENSO, Deser *et al.* (2010). The IOD is a zonal dipole pattern of SST over the subtropical and tropical Indian Ocean varying on an interannual-to-decadal time scale, Deser *et al.* (2010).

A challenge in climate research is to understand the physical processes controlling the time-mean SST (Figure 3.1a) and the dominant time scales and patterns of SST variability. Of the phenomena mentioned, the physics of ENSO is understood best in Neelin *et al.* (1994, 1998); Neelin (2011), and the mechanisms of the other

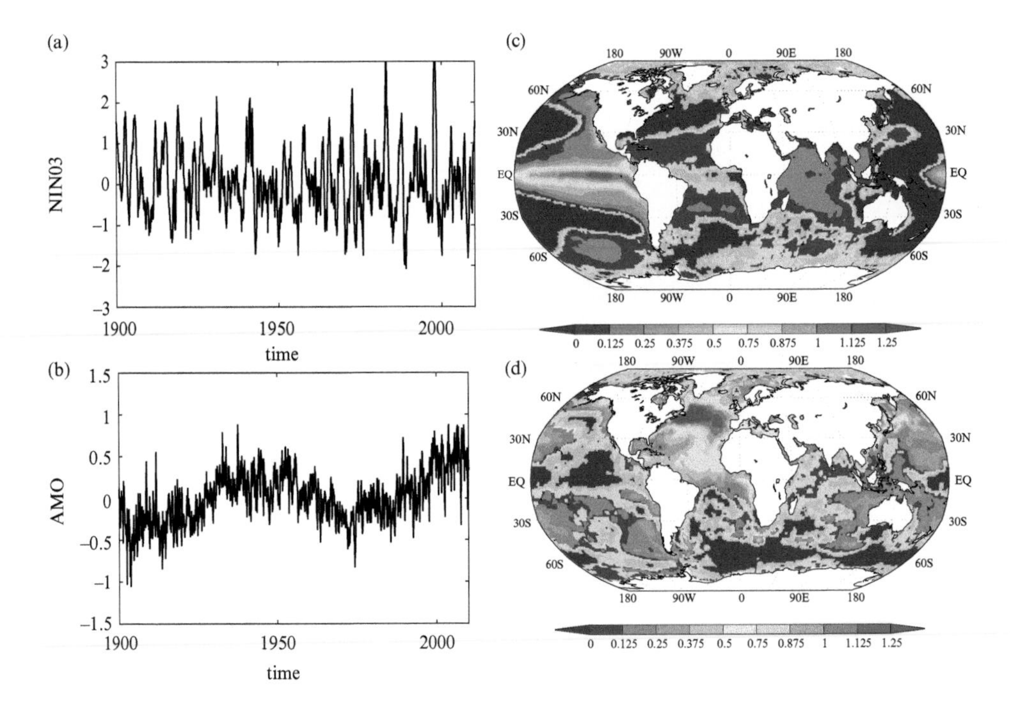

Fig. 3.2 (a) The NINO3 time series (SST anomaly over the domain 150°W–90°W × 5°S–5°N). (b) The AMO time series (SST anomaly over the domain 75°W–7°W × 25°S–60°N) as computed in van Oldenborgh *et al.* (2009). (c) Regression of the NINO3 time series on the global SST anomaly field. (d) Regression of the AMO time series on the global SST anomaly field. All units are in °C.

patterns of variability are relatively unknown. Several different mechanisms have been proposed for AMO, PDO, and IOD variability, but it is difficult to falsify each of these mechanisms with the available observations. The mechanisms of these phenomena are crucial to understanding changes in ocean heat content, and hence in variations of the global mean surface temperature, England *et al.* (2014).

3.1.2 Dynamical systems theory

The aim of these lecture notes is to provide a tutorial on how the concepts of dynamical systems theory can be used to study the behavior of the climate system. Climate scientists aim to understand this behavior with a hierarchy of models and with a very limited observational database. The classical analysis of the models is to integrate them forward in time and then compare properties of the solutions (e.g., statistics) found with observations.

However, there is a complementary way to analyse the behavior of models (and also observations) provided by dynamical systems analysis. This type of analysis uses different mathematical approaches such as bifurcation theory, chaos theory, and ergodic theory. The application of dynamical systems theory also includes the analysis of models described by systems of stochastic differential equations, Arnold (1998).

Some of these approaches also strongly connect to those in statistical physics and thermodynamics. A non-exhaustive summary of the past developments in ergodic theory, bifurcation theory, and chaos will help understand the relevance of such approaches to the study of climate.

An autonomous deterministic system of differential equations containing parameters can be written as

$$\frac{d\mathbf{x}}{dt} = \dot{\mathbf{x}} = \mathbf{f}(\mathbf{x}; \mathbf{p}), \tag{3.1}$$

where $\mathbf{x} \in \mathbb{R}^n$ is the state vector and $\mathbf{p} \in \mathbb{R}^p$ is the parameter vector. The right-hand side $\mathbf{f}$ is a mapping $\mathbb{R}^n \to \mathbb{R}^n$ and usually called a vector field. The advent of dynamical systems analysis started with the early discovery of chaos and pioneering work of Poincaré (1881); Poincaré (1892), who studied the qualitative behavior of solutions of systems such as (3.1). This was followed by results on the stability of these solutions, Bendixson (1899); Lyapunov (1892); Perron (1929).

Meanwhile, inspired by the work of Maxwell (1860), who derived a probability distribution of molecular velocities on heuristic grounds, the young Boltzmann (1909) revolutionized modern physics with his mechanical interpretation of the second law of thermodynamics and the association of an equilibrium state with a probability distribution μ (or, in modern terms, measure) invariant under the dynamics. Such a description proved very well suited for understanding the macroscopic properties of systems with many degrees of freedom, such as an ideal gas, and led to the foundations of equilibrium thermodynamics.

Boltzmann's work was subsequently extended by Gibbs (1902), in his developments of statistical physics. The existence of such a distribution relies on an "ergodic hypothesis" and guaranties that the (macroscopic) average $\bar{g}$ of an observable g, such as the energy, exists independently of almost any initial (microscopic) state $\mathbf{x}$, such that

$$\bar{g} = \lim_{T \to \infty} \frac{1}{T} \int_0^T g(\phi(t)\mathbf{x})dt = \int g(\mathbf{x})\mu(dx), \tag{3.2}$$

where the flow $\phi(t), t \geq 0$ yields the state at time t of a solution of the system (3.1) with initial state $\mathbf{x}$. The last identity is true when μ is ergodic and was proved by Birkhoff (1931), who further developed the link made by Boltzmann and Gibbs between ergodic theory and dynamical systems analysis, Birkhoff (1927); then Doob (1934) made the bridge with stochastic processes. The ergodic theorem was also proved in a different functional context by von Neumann (1932) following the ideas of Stone (1930), who considered groups of unitary operators in Hilbert space, and Koopman (1931), in application to the evolution of observables induced by the flow.

In the footsteps of Poincaré and Bendixson, the "Moscow School" of Andronov started, in the late 30s, to develop bifurcation theory in the plane, Andronov *et al.* (1971), after Andronov and Pontryagin (1937) had introduced the important concept of structural stability of a vector field. Bifurcation theory is a particular branch of dynamical systems theory introduced by Poincaré (1885) and is concerned with the study of qualitative changes in solutions of dynamical systems (3.1). However, the study of chaos took off later, in particular with the seminal work of Kolmogorov (1954) (followed by Moser, 1962; and Arnold, 1963), who showed that the integrability of Hamiltonian systems was robust to small perturbations but that irregular behavior could occur for larger perturbations, and with the early work of Chirikov (1960) on Hamiltonian chaos.

At this time, Kolmogorov (1958) and Sinai (1959) had the great intuition to find that the concepts from thermodynamics could be extended to chaotic systems with the study of the evolution of distributions in phase space rather than that of unpredictable and apparently stochastic trajectories. This led to the definition of the Kolmogorov–Sinai entropy as a measure of the degree of "chaoticity" or predictability of a system. As it became clear that the positive entropy of dynamical systems is related to the exponential divergence of orbits originating at nearby points, Oseledets (1968) extended the definition of Lyapunov exponents to nonlinear systems and proved their existence. It was then Pesin (1977) who proved the relation between the entropy and the sum of the positive Lyapunov exponents (i.e., the total expansion rate of the system) and developed the ergodic theory for non-uniformly hyperbolic systems with notable extensions by Katok (1980); and Ledrappier and Young (1985). The interested reader is redirected to the review by Livi *et al.* (2003) for more details on the role of Kolmogorov in the study of chaos.

The appreciation of the importance of chaos to forced-dissipative systems, such as climate, really started with the work of Lorenz (1963). He not only showed, thanks to extensive numerical integrations, that such systems could have aperiodic, yet bounded, solutions exhibiting sensitive dependence to initial conditions, but also that these solutions are attracted to some complicated set, a strange attractor, which is neither a fixed point nor a periodic orbit or a torus. His study had profound consequences regarding the inherent limitations of numerical weather predictions (a first example of which is the numerical weather prediction by Charney, Fjortoft, and von Neumann (1950) on the ENIAC computer) and the clarity of his exposure and quality of his intuition inspired many subsequent works on chaos.

Bifurcation theory was further developed in higher dimensions by the "Gorky School" (Nizhny Novgorod), led by Shilnikov, who showed that homoclinic orbits play a key role in the route to chaos (as already suspected by Poincaré). In particular, the discovery of spiral chaos near a saddle-node loop, Shilnikov (1965) was a genuinely paradigmatic shift for bifurcation theory, Afraimovich *et al.* (2014). Indeed, it provides one of the simplest routes to chaos for dissipative systems and it was found in many real-world systems, Shilnikov (1984) such as the in the Lorenz model, Shilnikov *et al.* (1995). Another major contribution was due to Smale (1995) who characterized unstable orbits of dissipative systems by dynamics of stretching due to the boundedness of the attractor, and worked on the problem of structural stability of a vector field, Smale (1966). Anosov (1962) showed that even though orbits of chaotic systems are sensitive to perturbations, their statistical properties can be robust, as long as the system is sufficiently chaotic (i.e., hyperbolic). This topological approach also raised the interest of Ruelle and Takens (1971) who demonstrated that strange attractors, such as the famous "butterfly" of Lorenz, are bound to emerge in a forced-dissipative system far from equilibrium, and who suggested that such an attractor could be at the origin of (fluid) turbulence.

After Anosov and Smale had shed light on the relevance of hyperbolic systems to the study of dissipative chaos, the link between the dynamics of such systems and their statistical properties was formalized by Sinai (1972); and Bowen and Ruelle (1975).

They showed that, even though non-conservative forces continually push a dissipative system out of equilibrium (so that classical statistical mechanics does not apply), a unique invariant probability measure with physical relevance exists (the Sinai–Ruelle–Bowen or (SRB) measure), taking the role of the Gibbs measure found in equilibrium thermodynamics. As a consequence, the SRB measure was naturally coined with the term of Non-Equilibrium Steady State (NESS) by Gallavotti and Ruelle (1997) and coworkers. The strong connections between the topological and statistical approaches was summarized in the review by Eckmann and Ruelle (1985).

While the invariant measure μ allows to calculate averaged quantities, the correlation function between two observables f and g, defined as

$$C_{f,g}(t) = \int f(\mathbf{x})g(\phi(t)\mathbf{x})\mu(dx) - \int f(\mathbf{x})\mu(dx) \int g(\mathbf{x})\mu(dx)$$

gives a measure, in time domain, of the variability of a system (where the $\phi(t), t \geq 0$ is the flow). A striking result regarding the statistical properties of chaotic systems is that the correlation function of many such systems, called *mixing*, decays to zero, as in the stochastic case.

While the metric entropy introduced by Kolmogorov and Sinai gives a measure of predictability due to the divergence of nearby trajectories, the rate at which the correlation function decays with time is another particularly important quantity which, roughly speaking, indicates of how fast a mixing system converges to the invariant measure. Pollicott (1985) and Ruelle (1986*a*) related this rate of decay with the spectral properties of the nonequilibrium counterparts of the operators introduced by Koopman and von Neumann half a century before. Ruelle (1997) could then relate this spectrum to the response of hyperbolic systems to forcing (i.e., to the differentiability of the SRB measure). Such results amongst others strongly revived the development of nonequilibrium statistical mechanics (which had been much slower than for equilibrium statistical mechanics). In particular, Ruelle (1997) gave a generalization to systems far from equilibrium of the linear response formula by Kubo (1966). Furthermore, the relevance of hyperbolic systems for the study of more general chaotic systems with a large number of degrees of freedom found in physics was argued by Gallavotti and Cohen (1995), who, inspired by the work of Ruelle (1980) on the statistical properties of turbulence and the role of thermal fluctuations, Ruelle (1979), proposed an extension of the "ergodic hypothesis" to nonequilibrium systems, namely, the "chaotic hypothesis." These successful developments led Ruelle (1999) and Gallavotti (2014) to propose smooth dynamical systems and SRB measures as the appropriate framework for the rigorous study of nonequilibrium statistical mechanics. Along these lines and as a final remark, the late twentieth century was thus marked by a formidable convergence between mathematicians and physicists in the domain of dynamical systems and statistical mechanics, Bolibruch *et al.* (2005).

3.2 The null-hypothesis of climate variability

From observations, a spectrum of midlatitude sea surface temperature (SST) anomalies, Dommenget and Latif (2002) is plotted in Figure 3.3a. To understand this

(a)

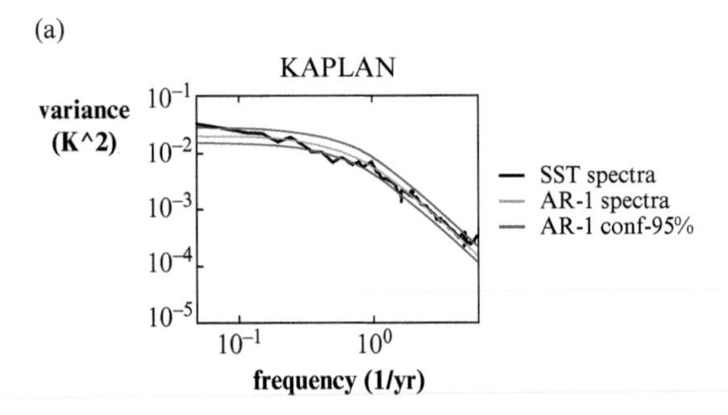

(b)

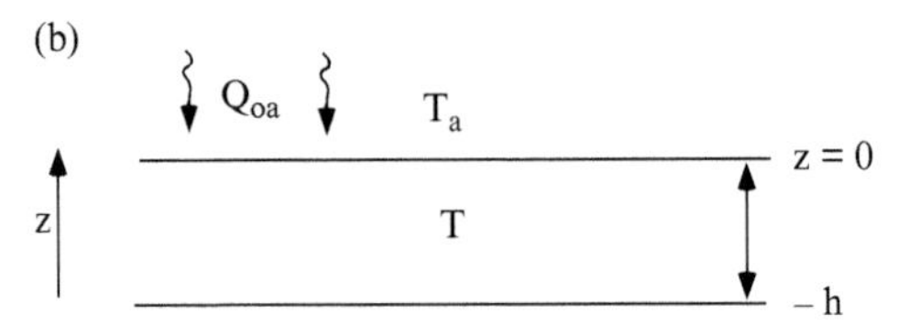

Fig. 3.3 (a) Spectra of midlatitude SST anomalies Dommenget and Latif (2002) with frequency (1/yr) plotted on the x-axis. (b) Sketch of an upper ocean mixed layer forced by a heat flux Q_{oa}; the mixed-layer depth is indicated by h.

variability, a very idealized model was proposed by Hasselmann (1976). An oceanic mixed layer, with temperature T, is forced by an atmospheric heat flux Q_{oa} Figure 3.3a. If we assume that the mixed layer depth h is fixed, the governing equation for T is simply

$$\rho C_p h \frac{dT}{dt} = Q_{oa}, \tag{3.3}$$

where ρ and C_p are the constant density and heat capacity of the ocean water, respectively (Figure 3.3b).

The heat flux can be approximated as

$$Q_{oa} = K_Q(T_a - T), \tag{3.4}$$

where K_Q (Wm^{-2}K^{-1}) is a heat exchange coefficient and T_a the atmospheric temperature just above the ocean surface. Combining (3.3) and (3.4), we obtain (with $\xi = \gamma T_a$)

$$\frac{dT}{dt} = -\gamma T + \xi \ ; \ \gamma = \frac{K_Q}{\rho C_p h}. \tag{3.5}$$

In general, the forcing part of this equation (here represented by ξ) will be very irregular (have energy in a wide range of frequencies) and hence can be represented by a random process. In this section, we will discuss how this is formulated mathematically.

3.2.1 Random processes

The starting point is the concept of a random variable. We are all familiar with examples where random variables play a role, such as throwing a dice and tossing a coin. In this example, we have the only outcomes "head" or "tail." If we attribute 0 to the outcome $\omega =$ "head" and 1 to the outcome $\omega =$ "tail," then we can define a random variable $X : \Omega \to \{0,1\}$, where Ω is the outcome space. In general, a random variable $X(\omega)$ is a real-valued function defined on Ω.

This is easily generalized to a random vector $\mathbf{X} = (X_1,...,X_n)$ where each X_i is a random variable. The distribution function $F_{\mathbf{X}}(\mathbf{x})$ is

$$F_{\mathbf{X}}(\mathbf{x}) = P(X_1 \leq x_1,...,X_n \leq x_n) = \int_{-\infty}^{x_1} \cdots \int_{-\infty}^{x_n} f_{\mathbf{X}}(y_1,...,y_n)dy_1 \dots dy_n, \quad (3.6)$$

where $f_{\mathbf{X}}$ is the corresponding probability density function. As an example, the multidimensional Gaussian distribution has a probability density function

$$f_{\mathbf{X}}(\mathbf{x}) = \frac{1}{(2\pi)^{n/2}(\det \Sigma)^{1/2}} e^{-\frac{1}{2}(\mathbf{x}-\mu_{\mathbf{X}})\Sigma^{-1}(\mathbf{x}-\mu_{\mathbf{X}})^T}, \quad (3.7)$$

where Σ is the covariance matrix with elements

$$\Sigma_{i,j} = cov[X_i, X_j] = E[(X_i - \mu_{X_i})(X_j - \mu_{X_j})]. \quad (3.8)$$

Two random variables X_1 and X_2 are independent if, and only if,

$$F_{X_1,X_2}(x_1,x_2) = F_{X_1}(x_1)F_{X_2}(x_2). \quad (3.9)$$

When two random variables X_i and X_j are independent, then $cov[X_i, X_j] = E[(X_i - \mu_{X_i})(X_j - \mu_{X_j})] = E[(X_i - \mu_{X_i})]E[(X_j - \mu_{X_j})] = 0$. If all components in a random vector are independent, then Σ is a diagonal matrix.

A stochastic process X_t is defined as a collection of random variables

$$(X_t, t \in T) = (X_t(\omega), t \in T, \omega \in \Omega), \quad (3.10)$$

where T denotes the time interval and Ω the outcome space. When t is fixed, then $X_t(\omega)$ is just a random variable. When ω is fixed, then $X_t(\omega)$ is a function of time which is called a trajectory, a realization, or a sample path. The expectation function of X_t is defined by $\mu_X(t) = E[X_t]$ and the covariance function $c_X(t,s)$ is defined as

$$c_X(t,s) = cov(X_t, X_s) = E[(X_t - \mu_X(t))(X_s - \mu_X(s))]. \quad (3.11)$$

In particular, the variance function is given by $\sigma_X^2(t) = c_X(t,t)$.

A stochastic process $(X_t, t \in T)$ is strictly stationary if for all choices of $t_1,...,t_n$ and h such that $t_i + h \in T$ for all i, the finite dimensional distributions satisfy

$$(X_{t_1},...,X_{t_n}) \stackrel{d}{=} (X_{t_1+h},...,X_{t_n+h}), \quad (3.12)$$

where $\stackrel{d}{=}$ indicates equality in distribution sense.

A stochastic process $(X_t, t \in T)$ has stationary increments if

$$X_t - X_s \overset{d}{=} X_{t+h} - X_{s+h}, \tag{3.13}$$

for each t, s. A stochastic process $(X_t, t \in T)$ has independent increments if the random variables $X_{t_2} - X_{t_1}$, ..., $X_{t_n}, -X_{t_{n-1}}$ are independent for every $t_1 < ... < t_n$.

In the following, we associate the indices $1, \ldots, n$ with times $t_1, \ldots, t_n$ and write

$$f_{\mathbf{X}}(x_1, ..., x_n) = p(x_1, t_1; \ldots; x_n, t_n). \tag{3.14}$$

as the joint distribution function. The interpretation of $p(x_1, t_1; x_2; t_2)$ is shown in Figure 3.4, where $p(x_1, t_1; x_2; t_2) dx_1 dx_2$ is the probability that the process X_t passes through windows of size dx_1 and dx_2 at times t_1 and t_2, respectively.

This can be easily generalized to multi-point joint probability density functions, i.e., $p(x_1, t_1; \ldots; x_n, t_n)$.

The conditional probability $P(A|B)$ of two events A and B is defined as

$$P(A|B) = \frac{P(A \cap B)}{P(B)}, \tag{3.15}$$

where $P(A)$ and $P(B)$ are the probabilities of the events A and B, respectively. Hence, the probability $P(A|B)$ concerns events A which are contained in the set B. We need this concept to define a Markov process for which the following property, the Markov property, holds:

$$p(x_n, t_n; \ldots; x_1, t_1 | y_n, \tau_n; \ldots; y_1, \tau_1) = p(x_n, t_n; \ldots; x_1, t_1 | y_n, \tau_n) \tag{3.16}$$

for $t_n \geq \ldots \geq t_1 \geq \tau_n \geq \ldots \geq \tau_1$. Loosely speaking, for a Markov process, one can make future predictions based solely on its present state just as well as one could knowing the process's full history.

A well-known example of a Markov process is the following: suppose that someone is popping many kernels of popcorn, and each kernel will pop at an independent,

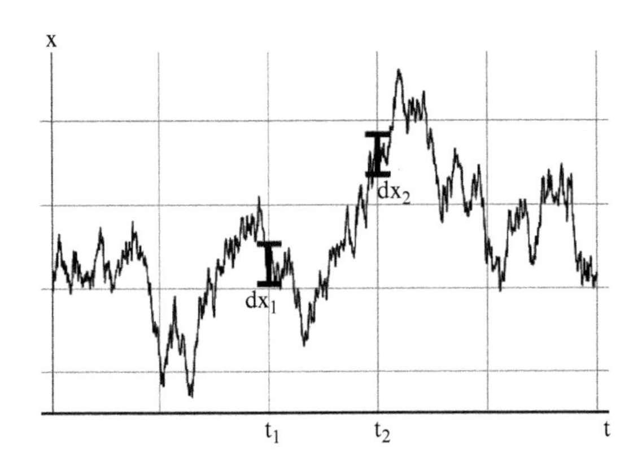

Fig. 3.4 Sketch of the meaning of the joint probability function $p(x_1, t_1; x_2; t_2)$.

uniformly random time within the next time interval. Let X_t denote the number of kernels which have popped up to time t. If, after some amount of time, one wants to guess how many kernels will pop in the next second, one needs only know how many kernels have popped. It will not help me to know when they popped, so knowing X_t for previous times t will not inform the guess any better.

For a Markov process, we find (using 3.15),

$$\begin{aligned} p\ (x_n,t_n;\ldots;x_1,t_1) &= p(x_n,t_n;\ldots;x_2,t_2|x_1,t_1)p(x_1,t_1) = \\ &= p\ (x_n,t_n;\ldots;x_3,t_3|x_2,t_2;x_1,t_1)p(x_2,t_2|x_1,t_n1)p(x_1,t_1) = \\ &= p\ (x_n,t_n;\ldots;x_3,t_3|x_2,t_2)p(x_2,t_2|x_1,t_1)p(x_1,t_1) = \\ &= p\ (x_n,t_n|x_{n-1},t_{n-1})\ldots p(x_2,t_2|x_1,t_1)p(x_1,t_1). \end{aligned}$$

Hence, only the so-called transition probability $p(x_{i-1},t_{i-1}|x_i,t_i)$ is needed to describe the joint probability density function of a Markov process.

3.2.2 Examples of random processes

A Gaussian process (Figure 3.5a) is defined over the interval $T=[0,1]$ with $0 \leq t_1 \leq \ldots \leq t_n \leq 1$ such that all $X_{t_1},\ldots,X_{t_n}$ are independent, standard, and normally distributed, i.e., each X_{t_i} has a distribution function

$$\Phi(x) = \frac{1}{\sqrt{2\pi}}e^{-\frac{x^2}{2}}.$$

The multidimensional distribution function is then given by

$$F_{\mathbf{X}}(\mathbf{x}) = \Phi(x_1)\ldots\Phi(x_n), \tag{3.17}$$

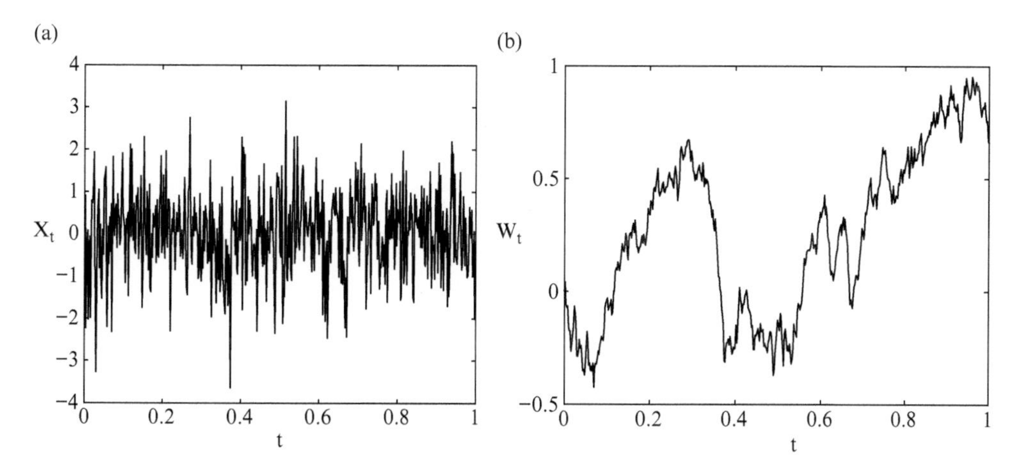

Fig. 3.5 (a) A realization of a Gaussian process. (b) A realization of a Wiener process

and the expectation function and (co)variance functions are given by

$$\mu_X(t) = 0 \; ; \; t \neq s : c_X(t,s) = 0 \; ; \; \sigma_X^2(t) = 1. \tag{3.18}$$

The Wiener process $W_t, t \in [0,\infty)$ is a stochastic process (Figure 3.5b) with the following properties:

(i) $W_0 = 0$,
(ii) W_t has stationary, independent increments,
(iii) $\forall t > 0 : W_t$ has a $N(0,t)$ distribution, and
(iv) W_t has continuous sample paths.

From these properties, it follows immediately that with $0 \leq s < t \leq T$,

$$W_t - W_s \stackrel{d}{=} N(0, t-s) \tag{3.19a}$$
$$\mu_W(t) = 0 \tag{3.19b}$$
$$c_W(t,s) = s. \tag{3.19c}$$

To obtain the result (3.19a), we note that from property (i) and (ii), it follows that $W_t - W_s \stackrel{d}{=} W_{t-s} - W_0 \stackrel{d}{=} W_{t-s}$ and (3.19a) follows then directly from property (iii). Equation (3.19b) follows directly from property (iii) and (3.19c) follows from $c_W(t,s) = E[W_t W_s] = E[(W_t - W_s + W_s)W_s] = E[(W_t - W_s)(W_s - W_0)] + E[W_s^2] = E[W_s^2] = s$, where the last two equalities follow from properties (ii) and (iii).

The Wiener process has transition probability

$$p(x,t|y,s) = \frac{1}{\sqrt{2\pi(t-s)}} e^{-\frac{1}{2}\frac{(x-y)^2}{t-s}} \tag{3.20}$$

for $t > s$ and $p(x,0) = \delta(x)$, and probability density function

$$p(x,t) = \int_{-\infty}^{\infty} p(x,t|y,0)p(y,0)dy = \frac{1}{\sqrt{2\pi t}} e^{-\frac{1}{2}\frac{x^2}{t}}. \tag{3.21}$$

From the probability density functions, it can also be easily shown that

$$E[W_t^{2n}] = \int_{-\infty}^{\infty} w^{2n} p(w,t) dw = \frac{(2n)!}{2^n n!} t^n \tag{3.22}$$

and that odd moments are zero.

To simulate the Wiener process W_t on a computer, we discretize time from t_0 to t_n and start with $W_0 = 0$. Given the current value W_{t_i} at $t = t_i$, we repeatedly draw the next random value $W_{t_{i+1}}$ using the probability distribution $p(W_{t_{i+1}}, t_{i+1} | W_{t_i}, t_i)$. The increment $\Delta W = W_{t_{i+1}} - W_{t_i}$, it follows from (3.22) that $E[\Delta W^2] = \Delta t$, and hence this suggests that $\Delta W = \mathbf{O}(\sqrt{\Delta t})$. Although $\Delta W / \Delta t = \mathbf{O}(1/\sqrt{\Delta t})$ becomes unbounded when $\Delta t \to \infty$, one can always compute this quantity; this is what is called "white noise" and is the quantity appearing as ξ in the mixed layer ocean model (3.5).

Hence, more formally, $E[\xi(t)] = 0$, $E[\xi(t)\xi(s)] = \delta(t-s)$, and $\xi(t) = dW_t/dt$ (the latter has to be interpreted in a distribution sense).

3.2.3 Stochastic calculus

Consider a smooth function $h : [0,T] \to \mathbb{R}$ for which the derivative h' is bounded on $[0,T]$. To define the Riemann integral of h, the interval $[0,T]$ is partitioned into subintervals $0 = t_0 < t_1 < ... < t_{N-1} < t_N = T$. The Riemann integral of h is then given by

$$\int_0^T h(t)dt = \lim_{N\to\infty} \sum_{j=0}^{N-1} h(t_j)(t_{j+1} - t_j). \tag{3.23}$$

The stochastic integral can be defined in a similar way and two forms exist, the Itô form and the Stratonovich form. The Itô integral of h is

$$\int_0^T h(t)dW_t = \lim_{N\to\infty} \sum_{j=0}^{N-1} h(t_j)(W(t_{j+1}) - W(t_j)), \tag{3.24}$$

where $W(t_j)$ indicates the value of the Wiener process W_t at $t = t_j$. The Stratonovich integral of h is

$$\int_0^T h(t) \circ dW_t = \lim_{N\to\infty} \sum_{j=0}^{N-1} h(\frac{t_j + t_{j+1}}{2})(W(t_{j+1}) - W(t_j)). \tag{3.25}$$

Note that the difference between the two forms of the stochastic integral is the time values of h considered with respect to the Wiener process values W. In the Itô integral, only h values at the left endpoint are considered, just as in the Riemann integral. In the Stratonovich integral, values of h at the midpoint of the interval are considered. The Itô and Stratonovich integrals in general lead to different outcomes, but a relation exists between these results and hence both definitions have their use.

We next consider the stochastic version of the main theorem of integral calculus,

$$f(b) - f(a) = \int_a^b f'(t)dt, \tag{3.26}$$

for a smooth function f on the interval $[a,b]$. To proceed, we use the notation $dW_t = W_{t+dt} - W_t$ and consider the Taylor series expansion

$$f(W_x + dW_x) - f(W_x) = f'(W_x)dW_x + \frac{1}{2}f''(W_x)(dW_x)^2 + \ldots. \tag{3.27}$$

With $E[(dW_x)^2] = dx$, we obtain the first Itô Lemma by integration of (3.27) over the interval $[s,t]$, i.e.,

$$f(W_t) - f(W_s) = \int_s^t f'(W_x)dW_x + \int_s^t \frac{1}{2}f''(W_x)dx. \tag{3.28}$$

We see that (3.28) is the generalization of (3.26) to the stochastic case. In addition to the first term on the right-hand side, there is now an additional Riemann integral involving the second derivative of f.

There are two extensions of the first Itô Lemma. Consider a stochastic process $f(t,W_t)$ for which the function $f(t,y)$ is smooth. Again, by Taylor series expansion, we find

$$f(x+dx, W_{x+dx}) - f(x, W_x) = f_1(x, W_x)dx + f_2(x, W_x)dW_x + \frac{1}{2}\left[f_{11}(x, W_x)(dx)^2 + 2f_{12}(x, W_x)dxdW_x + f_{22}(x, W_x)(dW_x)^2\right] + \ldots,$$

where $f_1 = \partial f/\partial t$, $f_2 = \partial f/\partial y$, $f_{11} = \partial^2 f/\partial t^2$, etc. We use again that $E[(dW_x)^2] = dx$, neglect higher order terms dx^2 and $dx\ dW_x$, and integrate over the interval $[s,t]$ to obtain the second Itô Lemma

$$f(t, W_t) - f(s, W_s) = \int_s^t \left[f_1(x, W_x) + \frac{1}{2}f_{22}(x, W_x)\right] dx + \int_s^t f_2(x, W_x)dW_x. \quad (3.29)$$

If $f = f(W_t)$, then $f_1 = 0, f_2 = f', f_{22} = f''$ and the second Itô Lemma (3.29) reduces to the first Itô Lemma (3.28).

A third extension of the main theorem of integral calculus is for stochastic processes of the form $f(t, X_t)$, where X_t is given by

$$X_t = X_0 + \int_0^t A^{(1)}(s, X_s)ds + \int_0^t A^{(2)}(s, X_s)dW_s. \quad (3.30)$$

Here, the $A^{(i)}$ are smooth functions of s and X_s. Using the same procedure as for the first two Itô Lemma's (Taylor series, neglect higher order terms, and $E[(dW_x)^2] = dx$), leads to the third Itô Lemma,

$$f(t, X_t) - f(s, X_s) = \int_s^t \left[f_1(x, X_x) + A_x^{(1)} f_2(x, X_x) + \frac{1}{2}(A_x^{(2)})^2 f_{22}(x, X_x)\right] dx + \int_s^t A_x^{(2)} f_2(x, X_x)dW_x, \quad (3.31)$$

where $A_x^{(i)} = A^{(i)}(x, X_x)$.

3.2.4 Stochastic differential equations

A general, a scalar ordinary differential equation (ODE) is written as

$$\dot{x} = \frac{dx}{dt} = f(t, x) \rightarrow dx = f(t, x)dt. \quad (3.32)$$

With an initial condition $x(0) = x_0$, it has a formal solution

$$x(t) = \int_0^t f(s,x)ds + x_0. \tag{3.33}$$

A general, a stochastic differential equation is written as

$$dX_t = a(t,X_t)dt + b(t,X_t)dW_t, \tag{3.34}$$

for smooth functions a, b and with initial condition X_0. The formal solution of (3.34) is given,

$$X_t - X_0 = \int_0^t a(s,X_s)ds + \int_0^t b(s,X_s)dW_s. \tag{3.35}$$

Either form (3.34) or (3.35) is referred to as the Itô Stochastic Differential Equation (SDE). It can be deduced, see Section 3.2.3 of Mikosch (2000), that for each Itô SDE (3.34), there is an equivalent Stratonovich SDE of the form

$$dX_t = (a(t,X_t) - \frac{1}{2}b(t,X_t)\frac{\partial b}{\partial x}(t,X_t))dt + b(t,X_t) \circ dW_t. \tag{3.36}$$

As an example of the use of the Itô Lemma's, consider the Itô SDE

$$X_t - X_0 = \int_0^t (c_1(s)X_s + c_2(s))ds + \int_0^t \sigma_2(s)dW_s. \tag{3.37}$$

To solve this equation, we use the process $Y_t = f(t,X_t) = \alpha(t)X_t$ where

$$\alpha(t) = e^{-\int_0^t c_1(s)ds}.$$

With $A^{(1)} = c_1X + c_2$ and $A^{(2)} = \sigma_2$, the third Itô Lemma (3.31) is applied to Y_t to give (with $f_1 = \alpha' x$, $f_2 = \alpha$ and $f_{22} = 0$),

$$\begin{aligned}\alpha(t)X_t - \alpha(0)X_0 = & \int_0^t \left[\alpha'(x)X_x + (c_1(x)X_x + c_2(x))\alpha(x)\right] dx + \\ & + \int_0^t \alpha(x)\sigma_2(x)dW_x.\end{aligned}$$

Because $\alpha' = -c_1\alpha$ and $\alpha(0) = 1$, we find

$$X_t = \frac{1}{\alpha(t)}\left[X_0 + \int_0^t \alpha(x)c_2(x)dx + \int_0^t \alpha(x)\sigma_2(x)dW_x\right]. \tag{3.38}$$

A prominent example is the Langevin equation for which $c_1(t) = -\gamma$, $c_2 = 0$, and $\sigma_2 = \sigma$, where γ and σ are constants. We find that in this case

$$\alpha(t) = e^{\int_0^t \gamma ds} = e^{\gamma t},$$

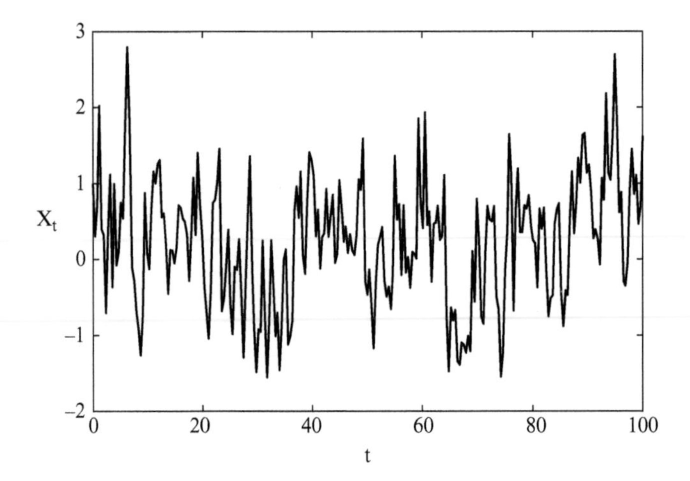

Fig. 3.6 A path of the Ornstein–Uhlenbeck process (3.39) with $\gamma = 1$, $\sigma = 1$, and $X_0 = 1$.

and the solution (3.38) becomes

$$X_t = e^{-\gamma t}\left[X_0 + \sigma \int_0^t e^{\gamma x}\, dW_x\right]. \tag{3.39}$$

The stochastic process associated with this solution is called the Ornstein–Uhlenbeck process (Figure 3.6a).

From this process, the covariance function is calculated (just by working out the integrals) as

$$c_{OU}(t,s) = E[X_t X_{t+s}] = \frac{\sigma^2}{2\gamma}(e^{-\gamma s} - e^{-\gamma(2t+s)}) \tag{3.40}$$

and the spectrum follows from the Fourier transform as

$$P(\omega) = \frac{\sigma^2}{\gamma^2 + \omega^2},$$

which is a Lorentz spectrum. These spectra (indicated there by AR(1) in Figure 3.3a) are called red-noise spectra (the OU process is the red noise process) and they decay for large ω (compared to γ) as ω^{-2}.

3.2.5 The Fokker–Planck equation

We now return to the general Itô SDE (3.34) given by

$$X_t = X_0 + \int_0^t a(X_s, s)ds + \int_0^t b(X_s, s)dW_s \tag{3.41}$$

for smooth functions a and b. With X_0 given, the future time development is uniquely determined by $W_t, t > 0$. As W_t for $t > 0$ is independent of X_t for $t < 0$, we conclude that X_t for $t>0$ is independent of X_t for $t<0$, provided X_0 is known, and hence X_t is a Markov process (for a more extensive discussion, see Gardiner (2002), Section 4.3.2). Let the transition probability be indicated by $p(x,t) = p(x,t|x_0,t_0)$.

Now, by definition of the expectation operator, for any smooth function $f:\mathbb{R}\to\mathbb{R}$, we find

$$E[f(X_t)] = \int_{-\infty}^{\infty} f(x)p(x,t)dx, \tag{3.42}$$

and hence,

$$\frac{d}{dt}E[f(X_t)] = \int_{-\infty}^{\infty} f(x)\frac{\partial p}{\partial t}(x,t)dx. \tag{3.43}$$

On the other hand, when we use the third Itô Lemma for f, we find

$$\begin{aligned} f(X_t) - f(X_0) = &\int_0^t \left[a(X_s,s)\frac{\partial f}{\partial x}(X_s) + \frac{1}{2}b^2(X_s,s)\frac{\partial^2 f}{\partial^2 x}(X_s)\right] ds \\ &+ \int_0^t b(X_s,s)\frac{\partial f}{\partial x}(X_s)dW_s. \end{aligned} \tag{3.44}$$

Taking the expectation operator of (3.44), using (3.42) and differentiating the result to t then gives

$$\frac{d}{dt}E[f(X_t)] = \int_{-\infty}^{\infty} \left[a(x,t)\frac{\partial f}{\partial x}(x) + \frac{1}{2}b^2(x,t)\frac{\partial^2 f}{\partial^2 x}(x)\right] p(x,t;x_0,t_0)dx. \tag{3.45}$$

Combining (3.45) and (3.43), we find

$$\int_{-\infty}^{\infty} \left[(a(x,t)\frac{\partial f}{\partial x}(x) + \frac{1}{2}b^2(x,t)\frac{\partial^2 f}{\partial^2 x}(x))p(x,t) - f(x)\frac{\partial p}{\partial t}(x,t)\right] dx = 0.$$

When furthermore it is assumed that $p, \partial p/\partial x \to 0$ for $x \to \pm\infty$, then partial integration of the terms with a and b finally gives

$$\int_{-\infty}^{\infty} f\ (\frac{\partial p}{\partial t} + \frac{\partial (ap)}{\partial x} - \frac{1}{2}\frac{\partial^2 (pb^2)}{\partial^2 x})\ dx = 0, \tag{3.46}$$

and as f is arbitrary, we find for p the Fokker–Planck equation

$$\frac{\partial p}{\partial t} + \frac{\partial (ap)}{\partial x} - \frac{1}{2}\frac{\partial^2 (pb^2)}{\partial^2 x} = 0. \tag{3.47}$$

Once this Fokker–Planck equation is solved, the probability distribution of the stochastic process X_t is totally determined.

For the Ornstein–Uhlenbeck process we have $a(x,t) = -\gamma x$ and $b(x,t) = \sigma$. The Fokker–Planck equation then becomes

$$\frac{\partial p}{\partial t} = \frac{\partial (\gamma x p)}{\partial x} + \frac{\sigma^2}{2}\frac{\partial^2 p}{\partial^2 x},$$

with $p, \partial p/\partial x \rightarrow 0$ for $x \rightarrow \pm\infty$. In many cases, only the stationary distribution of p is desired. When putting the time-derivative to zero, the resulting equation can be integrated to x to give

$$\gamma x p + \frac{\sigma^2}{2}\frac{\partial p}{\partial x} = C_1,$$

and $C_1 = 0$ through the boundary conditions. Integrating once more, we find

$$p(x) = C_2 e^{-\frac{\gamma}{\sigma^2}x^2} \; ; \; \int_{-\infty}^{\infty} p(x)dx = 1 \Rightarrow C_2 = \sqrt{\frac{\gamma}{\pi}}\frac{1}{\sigma}.$$

We immediately conclude from this normal distribution that $\mu[X] = 0$ and that $Var[X] = \sigma^2/(2\gamma)$. The latter is also the limit for $t \rightarrow \infty$ in the variance $c_{OU}(t,0)$ in (3.40).

The multi-dimensional generalization of the Fokker–Planck equation of the SDE

$$d\mathbf{X}_t = \mathbf{f}(\mathbf{X}_t, t)dt + \mathbf{g}(\mathbf{X}_t, t)d\mathbf{W}_t, \tag{3.48}$$

where $\mathbf{W}$ is a $d \times n$ vector of Wiener processes and $\mathbf{g}$ is usually an $n \times d$ matrix, is (in tensor notation)

$$\frac{\partial p}{\partial t} = -\frac{\partial}{\partial x_i}(f_i p) + \frac{1}{2}\frac{\partial^2}{\partial x_i \partial x_j}(D_{ij}p), \tag{3.49}$$

where $D_{ij} = g_{ik}g_{kj}$.

3.2.6 Backward-Kolmogorov equation

For general stochastic processes, the following relations always holds,

$$p(x_3,t_3;x_1,t_1) = \int p(x_3,t_3;x_2,t_2;x_1,t_1)dx_2 = p(x_3,t_3|x_1,t_1)p(x_1,t_1). \tag{3.50}$$

For a Markov process, we can write $p(x_3,t_3;x_1,t_1) = p(x_3,t_3|x_2,t_2)p(x_2,t_2|x_1,t_1)$ $p(x_1,t_1)$ and hence combing this with (3.50) gives the Chapman–Kolmogorov equation

$$p(x_3,t_3|x_1,t_1) = \int p(x_3,t_3|x_2,t_2)p(x_2,t_2|x_1,t_1)dx_2. \tag{3.51}$$

Using $x = x_3, t = t_3, x_1 = y, t_1 = s$ and $x_2 = x', t_2 = t'$ and differentiating (3.51) to t' gives

$$0 = \int_{-\infty}^{\infty} \frac{\partial p(x,t|x',t')}{\partial t'}p(x',t'|y,s) + p(x,t|x',t')\frac{\partial p(x',t'|y,s)}{\partial t'}dt'. \tag{3.52}$$

Using the Fokker–Planck equation in the second term gives

$$0 = \int_{-\infty}^{\infty} dx' \left[\frac{\partial p(x,t|x',t')}{\partial t'} p(x',t'|y,s) + p(x,t|x',t') \right.$$
$$\left. \left(\frac{\partial}{\partial x'}(-f(x') + \frac{1}{2}\frac{\partial}{\partial x'} g^2(x'))p(x',t'|y,s) \right) \right] = \int_{-\infty}^{\infty} dx' p(x',t'|y,s) \left[\frac{\partial p(x,t|x',t')}{\partial t'} \right.$$
$$\left. + f(x') \frac{\partial p(x,t|x',t')}{\partial x'} + \frac{1}{2} g^2(x') \frac{\partial^2 p(x,t|x',t')}{\partial^2 x'} \right] \tag{3.53}$$

Letting $t' \to s$ gives $p(x',t'|y,s) = \delta(x'-y)$ which gives the Backward–Kolmogorov Equation (BKE)

$$-\frac{\partial p(x,t|y,s)}{\partial s} = f(y) \frac{\partial p(x,t|y,s)}{\partial y} + \frac{1}{2} g^2(y) \frac{\partial^2 p(x,t|y,s)}{\partial^2 s}. \tag{3.54}$$

We will use this equation in Section 3.4 to compute exit times for a particular interval.

The operator in the right-hand side of (3.54) is the formal adjoint of the Fokker–Planck operator and it often referred to as the generator and indicated by $\mathbf{K}$. The multi-dimensional extension of the BKE is in tensor notation given by

$$-\frac{\partial p}{\partial t} = f_i \frac{\partial p}{\partial x_i} + \frac{D_{ij}}{2} \frac{\partial^2 p}{\partial x_i \partial x_j}, \tag{3.55}$$

where again $D_{ij} = g_{ik} g_{kj}$.

3.2.7 Numerical solutions of SDEs

The numerical solution of SDEs is more involved than the solution of the deterministic counterparts. Consider an Itô SDE of the form

$$X(t) = X(0) + \int_0^t f(X(s))ds + \int_0^t g(X(s))dW(s), \tag{3.56}$$

where the notation of the stochastic integral is slightly changed. Let us define a partition $\tau_j = j\Delta t, j = 0, \ldots, n$ on $[0,T]$ with $\Delta t = T/n$ and indicate the numerical solution at τ_j with X_j (which is the reason for changing the notation) and the analytical solution with $X(\tau_j)$.

The order η of strong convergence for fixed k is such that

$$E[|X_k - X(\tau_k)|] \le (\Delta t)^\eta. \tag{3.57}$$

Strong convergence therefore implies that the mean of the error converges to zero. On the contrary, weak convergence indicates only convergence of the expectation (error in the mean) and its order η is determined by

$$|E[X_k] - E[X(\tau_k)]| \leq (\Delta t)^\eta. \tag{3.58}$$

In the following subsections, two much-used schemes and their convergence behavior are presented.

The Euler–Maruyama scheme for (3.56) is

$$X_j - X_{j-1} = f(X_{j-1})\Delta t + g(X_{j-1})(W(\tau_j) - W(\tau_{j-1})). \tag{3.59}$$

It turns out that the order of strong convergence is only $\eta = 1/2$ and of weak convergence is $\eta = 1$. To improve the order of strong convergence, we need higher-order terms to be included into the discretization scheme. One of these schemes is the Milstein scheme which we present now for the Itô SDE (3.56). We first write the discretization as

$$X_{t_j} - X_{t_{j-1}} = \int_{t_{j-1}}^{t_j} f(X_s)ds + \int_{t_{j-1}}^{t_j} g(X_s)dW_s, \tag{3.60}$$

and recover the Euler–Maruyama scheme, with $\Delta_j t = t_j - t_{j-1}$ and $\Delta_j W = W_{t_j} - W_{t_{j-1}}$, as

$$\int_{t_{j-1}}^{t_j} f(X_s)ds = f(X_{t_{j-1}})\Delta_j t \tag{3.61a}$$

$$\int_{t_{j-1}}^{t_j} g(X_s)dW_s = g(X_{t_{j-1}})\Delta_j W. \tag{3.61b}$$

The crucial step in the derivation of higher order schemes is the application of the third Itô Lemma for a function $f(x)$, with $f_1 = 0, f_2 = f', f_{22} = f''$, while $A^{(1)} = f$ and $A^{(2)} = g$, according to (3.60). We then find

$$f(X_s) - f(X_{t_{j-1}}) = \int_{t_{j-1}}^{s} \left[ff' + \frac{1}{2}g^2 f''\right] dy + \int_{t_{j-1}}^{s} gf'dW_y, \tag{3.62}$$

where the integration argument, y has been suppressed for clarity. We do the same for the function g to obtain

$$g(X_s) - g(X_{t_{j-1}}) = \int_{t_{j-1}}^{s} \left[fg' + \frac{1}{2}g^2 g''\right] dy + \int_{t_{j-1}}^{s} gg'dW_y. \tag{3.63}$$

Next, we substitute the last two expressions into (3.60) and obtain

$$X_{t_j} - X_{t_{j-1}} = f(X_{t_{j-1}})\Delta_j t + g(X_{t_{j-1}})\Delta_j W + R_j^1 + R_j^2 \tag{3.64}$$

$$R_j^1 = \int_{t_{j-1}}^{t_j} \int_{t_{j-1}}^{s} gg' dW_y dW_s. \tag{3.65}$$

As R_j^2 can be shown to be of smaller magnitude than R_j^1, Kloeden and Platen (1999), what remains is to evaluate R_j^1 as

$$R_j^1 = \frac{1}{2} g(X_{t_{j-1}}) g'(X_{t_{j-1}})((\Delta_j W)^2 - \Delta_j t), \tag{3.66}$$

to finally give the Milstein scheme

$$X_{t_j} - X_{t_{j-1}} = f(X_{t_{j-1}})\Delta_j t + g(X_{t_{j-1}})\Delta_j W + \frac{1}{2} g(X_{t_{j-1}}) g'(X_{t_{j-1}})((\Delta_j W)^2 - \Delta_j t). \tag{3.67}$$

3.3 The Pleistocene ice ages

3.3.1 Phenomena

Very detailed information on past temperatures on Earth has been obtained from marine benthic records. The ratio δ^{18}O is a proxy of combined temperature and global ice-volume changes. In Figire 3.7a a time series is shown of a composite δ^{18}O ocean sediment (benthic) record over the last 2 myr, Lisiecki and Raymo (2005). High values indicate a colder climate (and hence, the axis is plotted positive downward), as the

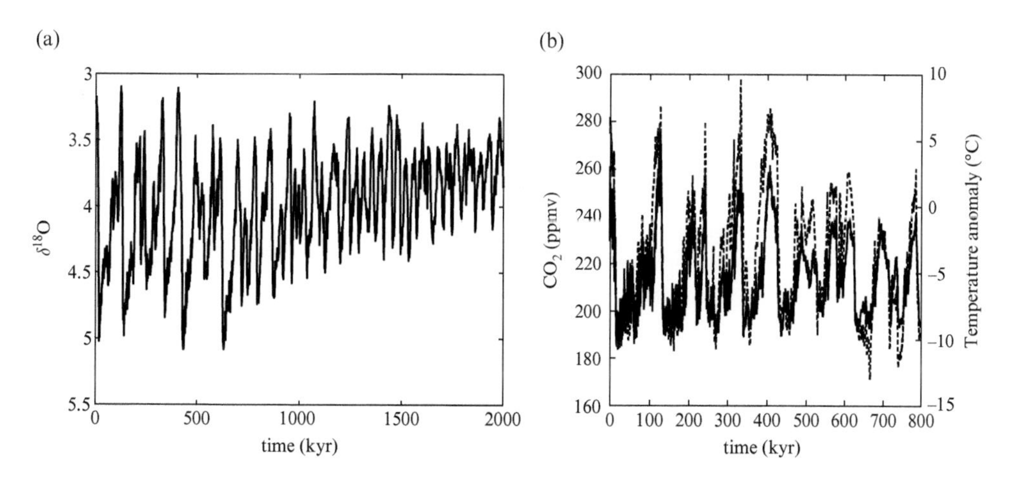

Fig. 3.7 (a) The LR04 benthic $\delta^{18}O$ stack over the Pleistocene, constructed by the graphic correlation of 57 globally distributed benthic $\delta^{18}O$ records (data from Lisiecki and Raymo (2005)). (b) Reconstructed temperature and atmospheric CO_2 concentration ($p^a_{CO_2}$) from ice cores on Antarctica. The drawn curve is the temperature anomaly with respect to the mean temperature over the last 100 years. The dotted curve is a composite CO_2 record.

ocean is enriched with O^{18} during the colder conditions (and ice sheets are enriched with O^{16}). The time series in Figure 3.7a indicates a cooling trend on which variability in ice cover is superposed. Analysis reveals that this variability is first dominated by a 41 kyr period and after the so-called Mid-Pleistocene Transition (MPT) at about 700 kyr, it is dominated by a 100 kyr period.

The European Project for Ice Coring in Antarctica (EPICA) has provided two deep ice cores in East Antarctica from which climate conditions can be reconstructed back to 800 kyr B. P. Jouzel and coauthors (2007). From the reconstructed temperature anomaly time series (Figure 3.7b) on Antarctica, one observes the asymmetry between the slow glaciation and the rapid deglaciations. From the ice-core data, the marine-core records and other evidence, it was found that the glacial-interglacial transitions have a global expression with northern hemispheric temperatures varying approximately in phase with those in the southern hemisphere. One important player in the climate system responsible for the globalization of these transitions is believed to be the atmospheric CO_2 concentration. A composite CO_2 record is shown in Figure 3.7b, created from a combination of records from the Dome C and Vostok ice cores. It is observed that the atmosphere CO_2 concentration varies from about 180 ppm to 280 ppm during a glacial-interglacial transition and that an optimal correlation with the $\delta^{18}O$ time series occurs near lag zero. As CO_2 is well mixed over these large time scales, there is no north–south asymmetry in CO_2 concentration. This record also demonstrates that the atmospheric concentration of CO_2 did not exceed 300 ppmv for at least 800,000 years before the industrial era, Siegenthaler *et al.* (2005).

Glacial-interglacial transitions have affected all components of the climate system and induced relatively large amplitude changes of many variables in these components. The results immediately lead to several fascinating questions: (i) Which processes in the climate system caused the glacial-interglacial changes in global mean temperature, CO_2 concentration, and ice sheet extent? (b) What caused the transition (the MPT) from the 41 kyr world to the 100 kyr world about 700 kyr ago? Any theory of the Pleistocene ice ages should contain a satisfactory answer to each of these main questions.

3.3.2 Conceptual Models

Many conceptual models have been suggested of the Pleistocene ice ages that are basically able to produce the 100 kyr period when forced with orbital variability in insolation, Crucifix (2012). One of such conceptual models is that by Saltzman, and Maasch Saltzman, and Maasch (1991); Saltzmann (2001). It describes the evolution of the ice mass (I), the atmospheric CO_2 concentration (μ), and the bulk ocean temperature (θ). The governing equations are

$$\frac{dI}{dt} = \alpha_1 - \alpha_2 c\mu - \alpha_3 I - \alpha_2 \kappa_\theta \theta \tag{3.68a}$$

$$\frac{d\mu}{dt} = \beta_1 - \beta_2 \mu + \beta_3 \mu^2 - \beta_4 \mu^3 - \beta_5 \theta + F_\mu \tag{3.68b}$$

$$\frac{d\theta}{dt} = \gamma_1 - \gamma_2 I - \gamma_3 \theta \tag{3.68c}$$

where the constants c, κ_R, κ_θ and the α_i, β_i and γ_i are as in Table 3.1.

Table 3.1 Coefficients for the Saltzman and Maasch (1991) model, where Ekg indicates 10^{18}kg.

Parameter	Value	Parameter	Value
α_1	1.67×10^{-2} Ekg/yr	α_2	9.52×10^{-3} Ekg/yr
α_3	1.00×10^{-4} 1/yr	β_1	5.12×10^{-1} ppm/yr
β_2	6.26×10^{-3} 1/yr	β_3	2.64×10^{-5} 1/(ppm yr)
β_4	3.63×10^{-8} 1/(ppm^2 yr)	β_5	5.83×10^{-3} ppm/(yr °C)
γ_1	1.85×10^{-3} °C/yr	γ_2	1.12×10^{-5} 1/(yr Ekg)
γ_3	2.50×10^{-4} 1/yr	c	4.00×10^{-3} 1/ppm
κ_θ	4.44×10^{-2} 1/°C	F_μ	0.00 ppm/yr

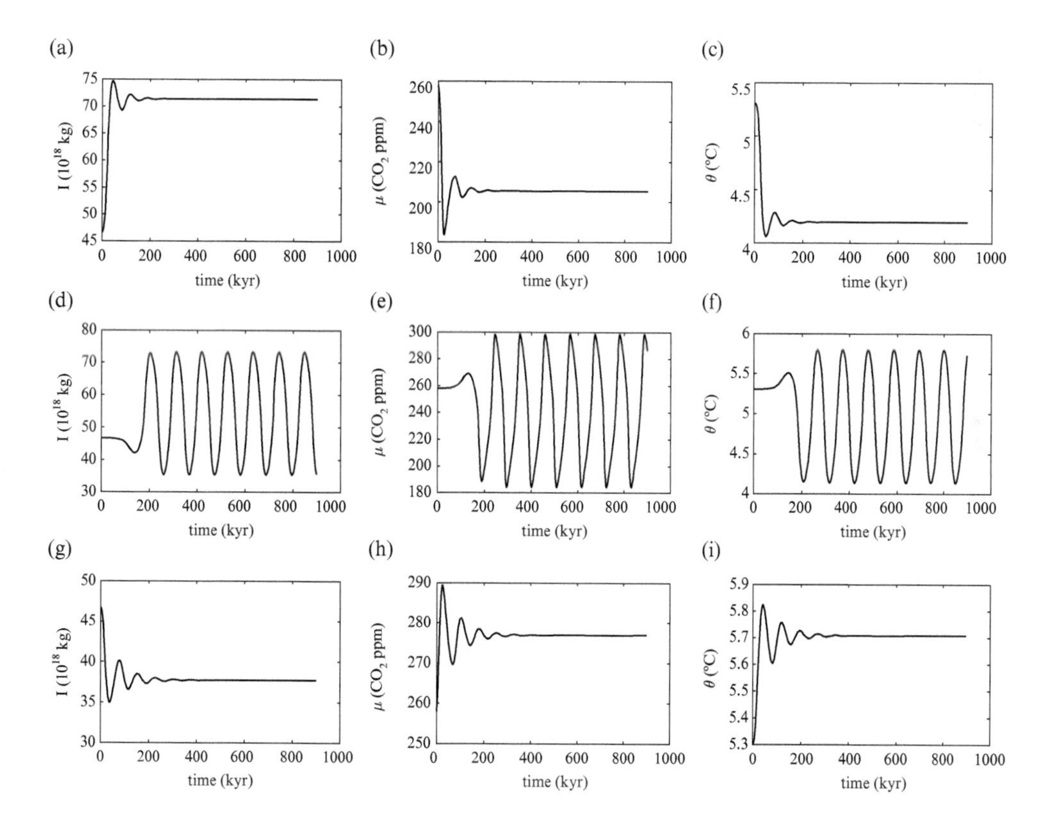

Fig. 3.8 Values of I, μ, and θ, from the Saltzman and Maasch (1991) model for (a-c) $F_\mu = -1.0$ ppm/kyr, (d-f) $F_\mu = 1.0$ ppm/kyr and (g-i) $F_\mu = 1.0$ ppm/kyr.

One of these parameters, i.e., F_μ is of particular interest, as it monitors the strength of the greenhouse gas induced radiative forcing and it can be considered as the control parameter. Several trajectories of this model for three different values of F_μ are plotted in Figure 3.8. For $F_\mu = -10^{-3}$ ppm/yr and $F_\mu = 10^{-3}$ ppm/yr, steady states are found, while for $F_\mu = 0.0$ ppm/yr there is an oscillation with a period of about 100 kyr (even without the orbital insolation variations). Hence, the frequency of this oscillation is internally determined through the interaction of ocean, ice, and atmosphere (greenhouse gas) processes.

3.3.3 Bifurcation theory

The mathematical model (3.68) is an example of an autonomous dynamical system (3.1) with three degrees of freedom (I, μ and θ) and several parameters, i.e., where $\mathbf{x} = (I, \mu, \theta)$ is the state vector the parameter vector $\mathbf{p}$ contains all of those in Table 3.1. Bifurcation theory provides a geometric framework to analyse the behavior of dynamical systems such as (3.1) capturing the whole solution structure in parameter space, Guckenheimer and Holmes (1990); Strogatz (1994). It addresses changes in the qualitative behavior of a dynamical system as one or several of its parameters vary. The results of this theory permit one to follow systematically the behavior from the simplest kind of model solutions to the most complex, from single to multiple equilibria, and from periodic, chaotic, to fully turbulent solutions.

Suppose that the autonomous dynamical system (3.1) has a steady solution (also called a fixed point) $\bar{\mathbf{x}}$ at a certain single parameter value $\bar{p}$. For the linear stability of this fixed point, the transient development of small perturbations $\mathbf{y}$ is considered. Substituting the solutions $\mathbf{x} = \bar{\mathbf{x}} + \mathbf{y}(t)$ with $\mathbf{y}(t) = e^{\sigma t}\hat{\mathbf{y}}$, into (3.1), an eigenvalue problem results:

$$J(\bar{\mathbf{x}}, \bar{p})\ \hat{\mathbf{y}} = \sigma \hat{\mathbf{y}}. \tag{3.69}$$

Here, $J(\bar{\mathbf{x}}, \bar{p})$ is the Jacobian matrix and $\sigma = \sigma_r + i\sigma_i$ is the complex growth factor. Fixed points for which there are eigenvalues of J with $\sigma_r > 0$ are unstable since the associated perturbations are exponentially growing, whereas fixed points for which $\sigma_r < 0$ are linearly stable. In the situation where $\sigma_i \neq 0$ the associated eigenmodes will be oscillatory with frequency σ_i, i.e., with a characteristic period of $2\pi/\sigma_i$.

Bifurcations occur at parameter values for which $\sigma_r = 0$. Normal forms of bifurcations are the simplest dynamical systems in which a particular type of bifurcation occurs. The strength of dynamical systems theory is that there is a classification of bifurcation points when only one parameter is varying. The elementary bifurcations giving rise to multiple equilibria are described in many textbooks, Strogatz (1994). The three relevant ones for which multiple equilibria appear, with the simplest dynamical system in which such a bifurcation occurs, are given in Figure 3.9.

The simplest system in which a saddle-node bifurcation occurs is

$$\frac{dx}{dt} = p \pm x^2. \tag{3.70}$$

The sign characterizes supercriticality ($p - x^2$) or subcriticality ($p + x^2$). In the supercritical case, it is straightforward to check that the branch of solutions $x = \sqrt{p}$ is linearly stable and the branch $x = -\sqrt{p}$ is unstable (see Figure 3.9a,b).

For the transcritical bifurcation, the normal form is given by

$$\frac{dx}{dt} = px \pm x^2. \tag{3.71}$$

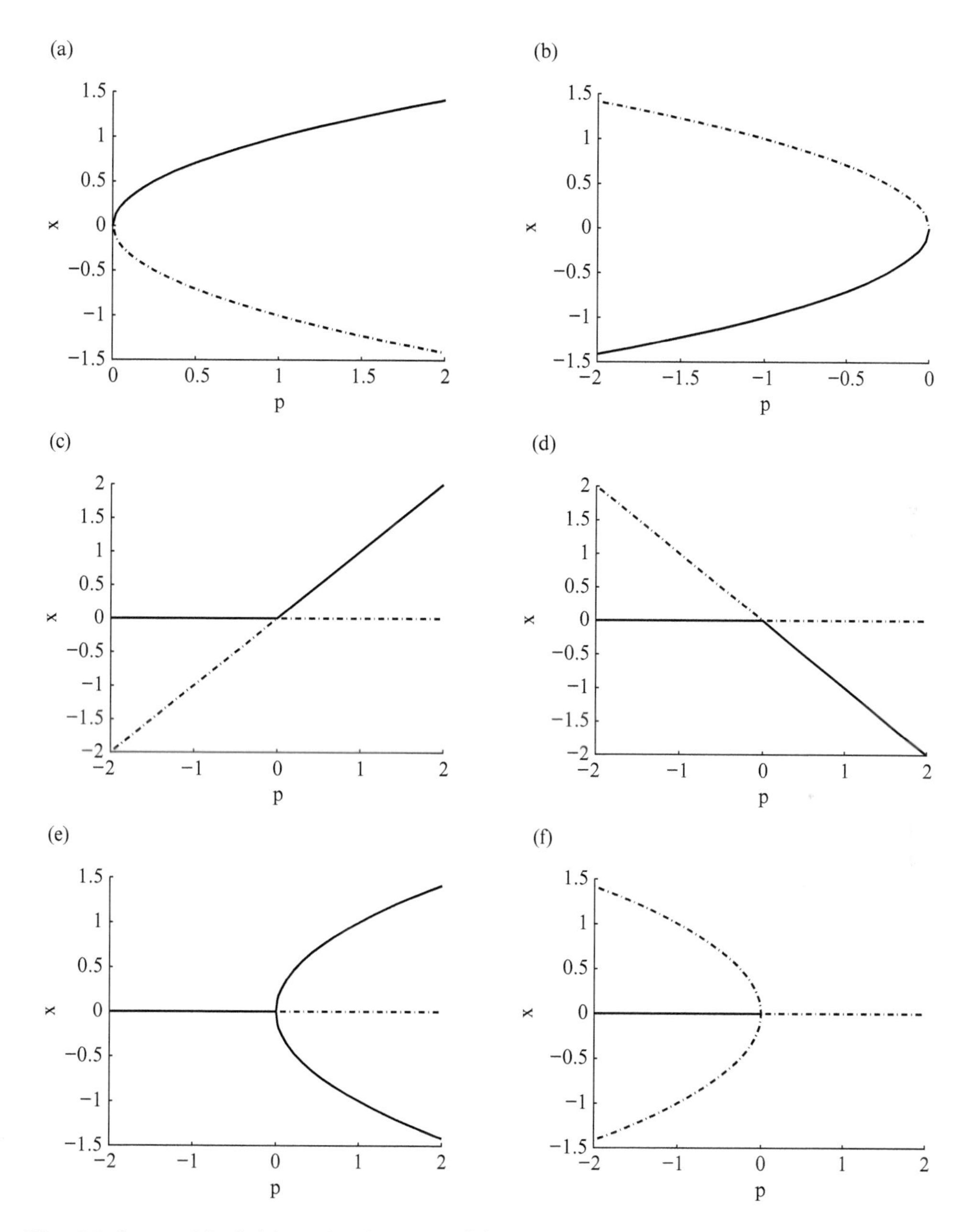

Fig. 3.9 Supercritical (a) and subcritical (b) saddle-node bifurcation with normal form $dx/dt = p \pm x^2$. Supercritical (c) and subcritical (d) of the transcritical bifurcation with normal form $dx/dt = px \pm x^2$. Supercritical (e) and subcritical (f) of the pitchfork bifurcation with normal form $dx/dt = px \pm x^3$. The solid (dash-dotted) branches indicate stable (unstable) solutions.

In both subcritical and supercritical cases, there is an exchange of stability from stable to unstable fixed points and vice versa as the parameter p is varied through the bifurcation at $p = 0$ (see Figure 3.9c,d). The normal form of the pitchfork is

$$\frac{dx}{dt} = px \pm x^3. \tag{3.72}$$

In the supercritical situation ($dx/dt = px - x^3$), there is a transfer of stability from the symmetric solution $x = 0$ to the pair of conjugated solutions $x = \pm\sqrt{p}$ (Figure 3.9f). In the supercritical case, it must be noted that the system remains in a neighborhood of the equilibrium so that one observes a soft or non-catastrophic loss of stability. In the subcritical case ($dx/dt = px + x^3$), the situation is very different as can been seen in Figure 3.9f. The domain of attraction of the fixed point is bounded by the unstable ones and shrinks as the parameter p approaches zero to eventually disappear.

An additional bifurcation occurs (in a system of at least two-dimensions) when varying only one parameter: the Hopf bifurcation. The normal form for a Hopf bifurcation is

$$\dot{x} = px - \omega y - x(x^2 + y^2), \tag{3.73a}$$

$$\dot{y} = py + \omega x - y(x^2 + y^2). \tag{3.73b}$$

It is clear that $(x,y) = (0,0)$ is an equilibrium for this system. The Jacobian at $(0,0)$ is

$$J(0,0) = \begin{pmatrix} p & -\omega \\ \omega & p \end{pmatrix}, \tag{3.74}$$

which has eigenvalues $\sigma = p \pm i\omega$, and so the equilibrium $(x,y) = (0,0)$ is stable for $p < 0$ and unstable for $p > 0$.

To demonstrate that this system has a periodic orbit for $p > 0$ it is convenient to use polar coordinates $(x,y) = r(\cos\theta, \sin\theta)$, in which case (use $\dot{x} = \dot{r}\cos\theta - r\dot{\theta}\sin\theta$ and the same for $\dot{y}$)

$$\dot{r} = p\,r - r^3, \tag{3.75a}$$

$$\dot{\theta} = \omega, \tag{3.75b}$$

and so, provided $\omega \neq 0$, there is a stable periodic orbit solution $r = \sqrt{p}$ and $\theta = \omega t + \theta_0$ when $p > 0$. Since the equation for r is nearly pitchfork-like (we do not allow $r < 0$), changing the signs of terms in the previous equations yields super/subcritical Hopf bifurcations with the same convention as for the pitchfork case.

Inspection of the model equations which represent dominant balances of momentum, heat, freshwater, or maybe other properties in the physical system may already a priori indicate what type of elementary bifurcations can be expected. When symmetry is present in the model equations, a restriction will be put on the type of elementary bifurcations that can occur. For example, consider the presence of a reflection symmetry in a physical model defined by $dx/dt = f(x,p)$, such as $f(-x,p) = -f(x,p)$.

Hence, when a bifurcation that occurs as a parameter p is varied, one expects pitchfork bifurcations rather than transcritical bifurcations, because the normal form of the latter bifurcation does not satisfy the requirement $f(-x,p) = -f(x,p)$. This is only a very elementary example of the constraints put on bifurcation diagrams through symmetry, Golubitsky *et al.* (1988). For systems of equations which have no symmetry, only transcritical and saddle-node bifurcations are expected to cause multiple equilibria.

Of particular importance are solutions which remain a solution for all values of a particular control parameter p. Note that when bifurcations occur from these solutions, the requirement on the dynamical system will be $f(\bar{x},p) = 0$ for the steady state $\bar{x}$ and for every value of p. This excludes the occurrence of saddle node bifurcations on this branch of solutions.

A Hopf bifurcation can be viewed physically as occurring through feedbacks amplifying perturbations to give an oscillatory signal. Many more of these examples exist which demonstrate that a priori information on the solution structure can be derived.

3.4 Dansgaard–Oeschger events

3.4.1 Phenomena

Isotope analyses from ice cores on Greenland provide information on the local temperatures over the last 100 ky. The local oxygen isotope anomalies ($\delta^{18}O$) from the NGRIP ice core are plotted in Figure 3.10. Slow variations are associated with the development of the last ice age of which the extremum occurred around 25 ky. The relatively rapid transitions (for example between 50 ky and 20 ky) with an equivalent peak-to-peak amplitude of about 10°C are called the Dansgaard–Oeschger events, Oeschger *et al.* (1984). There has been an extensive discussion on the dominant time scale of these events, Wunsch (2000). Through careful analysis of the GISP2 Stuiver and Grootes (2000) record, Schultz (2002) concludes that between 46 and 13 ky, the onset of Dansgaard–Oeschger events was paced by a fundamental period of ~1470 years. Before 50 ky, the presence of such a dominant period is unclear, due to dating uncertainties in the ice core record.

The behavior of the climate system on millennial time scales during the last glacial period is highly interesting for an understanding of feedbacks between the ocean, atmosphere and cryosphere. There are many indications from proxy data that there have been large-scale reorganizations of both the atmosphere and ocean associated with Dansgaard–Oeschger events and a review is provided in Clement and Peterson (2008). In the subpolar North Atlantic, Dansgaard–Oeschger events were matched with corresponding sea surface temperature changes of at least 5°C. A theory of Dansgaard–Oeschger events will have to explain at least the processes controlling the dominant ~1500 year time scale of the variability and the asymmetric character of the transition with a rapid warming and a relatively slow cooling phase. As discussed in Clement and Peterson (2008), several different views have been proposed to explain the millennial climate variability during the last glacial period. Leading theories all involve changes in the Atlantic Ocean circulation.

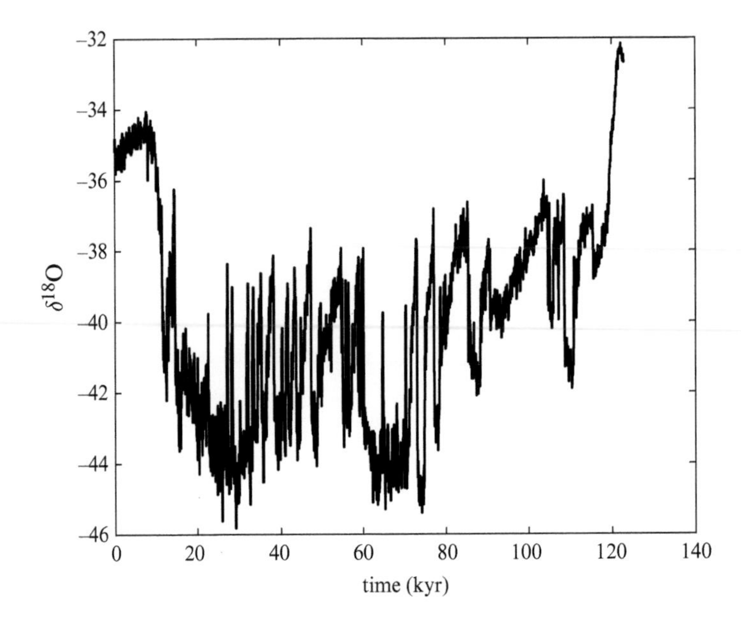

Fig. 3.10 Oxygen isotope anomaly ($\delta^{18}O$) from the NGRIP ice core, Andersen *et al.* (2004). Peak to peak temperature changes between 50 ky and 20 ky are about 10°C.

3.4.2 The Atlantic Meridional Overturning Circulation

On the large scale, the ocean circulation is driven by momentum fluxes (by the wind), the tides, and affected by fluxes of heat and freshwater at the ocean-atmosphere interface. The buoyancy fluxes affect the surface density of the ocean water and through mixing and advection, density differences are propagated horizontally and vertically. In the North Atlantic, the Gulf Stream transports relatively warm and saline waters northwards. Part of the heat is taken up by the atmosphere, making the water denser. In certain areas (e.g., the Labrador Sea), when there is strong cooling in winter, the water column becomes unstably stratified resulting in strong convection, Marshall and Schott (1999). The interaction of this convection with boundary currents, Spall (2003) eventually leads to the formation of deepwater, which overflows the various ridges that are present in the topography and enters the Atlantic basin.

This deepwater is transported southwards at a depth of about 2 km, where it enters the Southern Ocean. Through upwelling in the Atlantic, Pacific, and Indian Oceans, the water is slowly brought back to the surface, Talley (2008). To close the mass balance the water is eventually transported back in the upper ocean to the sinking areas in the North Atlantic. In the Southern Ocean also, bottom water is formed which has a higher density than that from the northern North Atlantic and therefore appears in the abyssal Atlantic and Pacific. In the North Pacific no deep water is formed.

The Atlantic Meridional Overturning Circulation (MOC) is the zonally integrated volume transport, characterized by the meridional overturning stream function. This transport is mainly responsible for the meridional heat transport in the Atlantic. The strength and spatial pattern of the MOC are determined by density differences

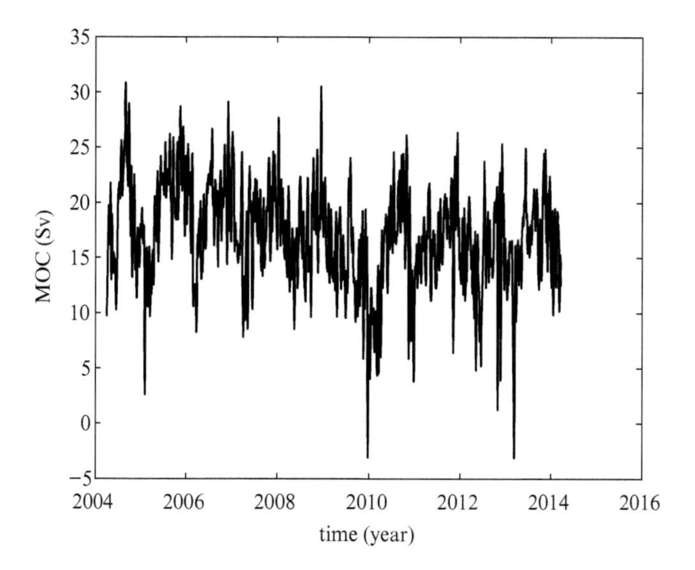

Fig. 3.11 Volume transport of the Atlantic MOC at 26°N as measured by the RAPID-MOCHA array from April 2004 to April 2014, Smeed *et al.* (2014).

which set up pressure differences in the Atlantic. There are no observations available to reconstruct the pattern of the MOC but its strength at 26°N in the Atlantic is now routinely monitored by the RAPID-MOCHA array, Cunningham *et al.* (2007); Srokosz and Bryden (2015). The currently available time series of the MOC strength is shown in Figure 3.11 indicating a mean of about 19 Sv, a standard deviation of 5 Sv, and a decreasing trend of about 1.6 Sv over the last decade, Smeed *et al.* (2014). At 26°N the heat transport associated with the Atlantic MOC is estimated to be 1.2 PW, Johns *et al.* (2011). This heat is transferred to higher latitudes leading to a relatively mild climate over Western Europe, compared to similar latitudes on the eastern Pacific coast.

3.4.3 Stochastic conceptual models

The simplest picture one can imagine that captures the key aspects of the MOC can be traced back to Stommel (1961). It is reasonable to suppose that the transport between equatorial and polar water reservoirs depends upon their mutual density difference $\Delta\rho$. A physical reason for this is that denser polar water is more pre-conditioned to convect to the ocean floor, enhancing meridional overturning. Stommel supposed the existence of two reservoirs of water, one representing the poles and the other the equator, with temperatures and salinities T_p, S_p, and T_e, S_e, respectively (see Figure 3.12).

The density of seawater is approximated following a simple linear dependence upon T and S,

$$\rho = \rho_0 - \alpha_T(T - T_0) + \alpha_s(S - S_0), \tag{3.76}$$

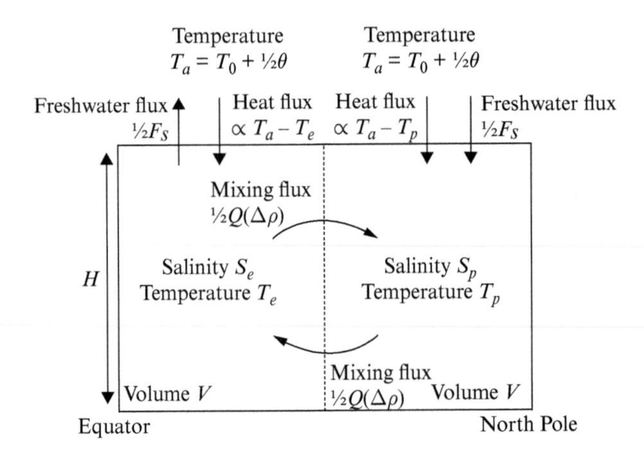

Fig. 3.12 Schematic of the Stommel two-box model of the meridional overturning circulation.

where the thermal expansivity α_T and salinity coefficients α_s are assumed constant. One may then express the density difference between the two reservoirs as

$$\Delta\rho = -\alpha_T(T_p - T_e) + \alpha_s(S_p - S_e), \tag{3.77}$$

which in turn governs the transport rate per unit volume $Q(\Delta\rho)$.

The two reservoirs do not only interact with each other, but are individually forced at their upper surface. The temperature is supposed to relax, over a timescale t_r, to the local atmospheric temperature T_a, which is formulated as $T_a = T_0 - \theta/2$ for the polar box and $T_a = T_0 + \theta/2$ for the equatorial box. Whereas colder water will have greater tendency to draw in heat than warmer water, salty water does not stimulate the atmosphere to rain on it! Consequently, salinity forcing is poorly modelled as a relaxation to some equilibrium values. A more physical form for the forcing is chosen whereby a prescribed flux $F_S/2$ of fresh water enters the polar ocean (in the form of rain, meltwater, etc.), with an equal volume (for simplicity) leaving at the equator by evaporation ($-F_S/2$). As S_0 is the typical value of salinity in the ocean, the result of the freshwater flux is a decrease in salinity in the polar box with rate proportional to $F_S S_0$ and an equivalent increase in the equatorial box.

The equations governing the two-box system are then, Cessi (1994),

$$\dot{T}_e = -\frac{1}{t_r}[T_e - (T_0 + \tfrac{1}{2}\theta)] - \frac{Q(\Delta\rho)}{2}(T_e - T_p), \tag{3.78a}$$

$$\dot{S}_e = +\frac{F_S}{2H}S_0 - \frac{Q(\Delta\rho)}{2}(S_e - S_p) \tag{3.78b}$$

$$\dot{T}_p = -\frac{1}{t_r}[T_p - (T_0 - \tfrac{1}{2}\theta)] - \frac{Q(\Delta\rho)}{2}(T_p - T_e), \tag{3.78c}$$

$$\dot{S}_p = -\frac{F_S}{2H}S_0 - \frac{Q(\Delta\rho)}{2}(S_p - S_e), \tag{3.78d}$$

where H is the ocean depth. We can now see that in the form written previously, $Q(\Delta\rho)$ must be positive. The reason for this is that although Q is physically the advection of water between two reservoirs, this advection is closed, with as much going in as is coming out for each reservoir. If you reverse the direction of circulation the quantity of polar water moving into the equator and vice versa remain unchanged. With this in mind, considering the simplicity of the model, we are free to choose a functional form for Q that depends only on the magnitude of $\Delta\rho$. In Cessi (1994), the form

$$Q(\Delta\rho) = \frac{1}{t_d} + \frac{q}{\rho_0^2 V}(\Delta\rho)^2 \tag{3.79}$$

is chosen, where V is the volume of each reservoir, q is a dimensional transport coefficient, and t_d is the timescale of diffusive mixing between the two reservoirs that would occur in the absence of a density difference.

It is convenient to define the temperature and salinity differences

$$\Delta T \equiv T_e - T_p, \qquad \Delta S \equiv S_e - S_p, \tag{3.80}$$

and work in terms of these variables. From Equations 3.78, we obtain the time evolution of the temperature and salinity differences:

$$\frac{d\Delta T}{dt} = -\frac{1}{t_r}(\Delta T - \theta) - Q(\Delta\rho)\Delta T, \tag{3.81a}$$

$$\frac{d\Delta S}{dt} = \frac{F_s}{H}S_0 - Q(\Delta\rho)\Delta S. \tag{3.81b}$$

Next, appropriate scales are introduced to reduce the dynamical variables ΔT and ΔS, together with time t, to their respective dimensionless forms. Appropriate choices are as follows:

$$x \equiv \frac{\Delta T}{\theta}, \qquad y \equiv \frac{\alpha_s \Delta S}{\alpha_T \theta}, \qquad t' \equiv \frac{t}{t_d}. \tag{3.82}$$

Once scaled, the dynamical equations for $x(t')$ and $y(t')$ read:

$$\dot{x} = -\alpha(x - 1) - x\left[1 + \mu^2(x-y)^2\right], \tag{3.83a}$$

$$\dot{y} = F - y\left[1 + \mu^2(x-y)^2\right], \tag{3.83b}$$

where

$$\alpha = \frac{t_d}{t_r}, \qquad \mu^2 = \frac{q t_d(\alpha_t\theta)^2}{V}, \qquad F = \frac{\alpha_s S_0 t_d}{\alpha_t \theta H} F_S. \tag{3.84}$$

The parameter α is the ratio of the diffusive timescale to the timescale over which temperature would exponentially decay to the local atmospheric value. The parameter μ measures the strength of the buoyancy-driven convection between the two basins relative to the diffusive mixing. The parameter F measures the strength of freshwater forcing. Standard values of the two-box model parameters can be found in Table 3.2.

We may simplify the previous equation by noting that for parameters typical of the real ocean (see Table 3.2) $\alpha \gg 1$, which means that the reservoirs will equilibrate with

Table 3.2 Parameters of the Stommel two-box model.

Parameter	Meaning	Value	Unit
t_r	temperature relaxation timescale	25	days
H	mean ocean depth	4,500	m
t_d	diffusion time scale	180	years
t_a	advection time scale	29	years
q	transport coefficient	1.92×10^{12}	m^3s^{-1}
V	ocean volume	$300 \times 4.5 \times 8,250$	km^3
α_T	thermal expansion coefficient	10^{-4}	K^{-1}
α_S	haline contraction coefficient	7.6×10^{-4}	–
S_0	reference salinity	35	$\text{g}\,\text{kg}^{-1}$
θ	meridional temperature difference	25	K

their local forcing temperatures much more rapidly than they are likely to mix each other's temperatures. Therefore, we may suppose that x remains close to 1, which reduces the problem to an ODE in $y(t)$ alone (where we drop the primes on t' for convenience):

$$\frac{dy}{dt} = F - y\left[1 + \mu^2(1-y)^2\right]. \tag{3.85}$$

If we suppose for now that $F = \bar{F}$ is independent of time, we can represent the time evolution of y using a potential function $V(y)$:

$$\frac{dy}{dt} = -V'(y), \qquad \text{where } V(y) = -\bar{F}y + \frac{1}{2}y^2 + \mu^2\left(\frac{1}{4}y^4 - \frac{2}{3}y^3 + \frac{1}{2}y^2\right), \tag{3.86}$$

and its derivative with respect to y is denoted by the prime. The potential $V(y)$ is a so-called double-well potential with two stable minima and an unstable maximum. In order to transition from one potential well to the other, a finite amplitude "kick" in y is required.

Recalling that y is simply the dimensionless salinity difference, we immediately see that the two reservoirs can remain in a stable state with either a large salinity difference or a small one. Physically, these correspond to the following: the poles are colder and fresher than the equator, and if we freshen the poles, we increase ΔS, but because temperature drives the convection, this freshening reduces $\Delta\rho$ and so the MOC weakens. Therefore, the higher (lower) value of y is usually referred to as the off (on) state of circulation. Another way to look at it is that in order to balance the freshwater forcing at a large ΔS we need less mixing between the reservoirs than if we have a smaller ΔS. Ultimately, the conclusion here is that the meridional overturning circulation can jump between the on and off states impulsively, given a finite-amplitude perturbation, such as a particularly large ice-melt event.

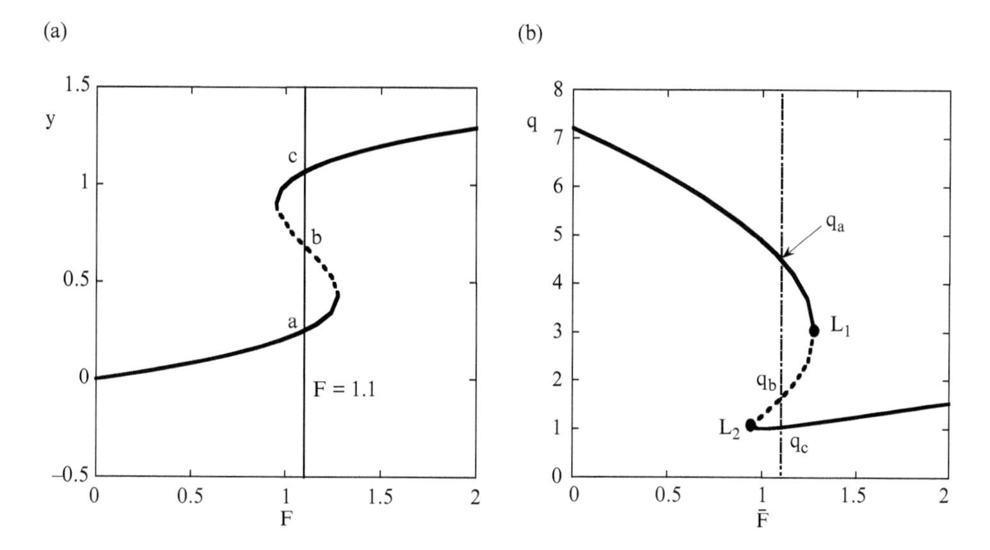

Fig. 3.13 Bifurcation diagram of the model (3.85) for $\mu^2 = 6.2$, showing (a) y and (b) $q = 1 + \mu(1 - y)^2$ versus $\bar{F}$.

As an alternative to the potential $V(y)$, one can also plot the steady solutions $\bar{y}$ of the Equation (3.85), i.e., solutions of

$$\bar{F} - y(1 + \mu^2(1 - y)^2) = 0, \tag{3.87}$$

versus $\bar{F}$. This bifurcation diagram, where both y (Figure 3.13a) and the dimensionless volume transport $q = 1 + \mu(1 - y)^2$ (Figure. 3.13b) are used, indeed shows that there is an interval of values $\bar{F}$ for which there are multiple equilibria. Here, the dashed states are unstable and the drawn states are stable. The interval of multiple states is bounded by two so-called saddle-node bifurcation points L_1 and L_2.

3.4.4 Transitions

Of course, the freshwater forcing F is unlikely to have been constant in reality, and next we consider F to vary stochastically. This component is represented as white noise with amplitude σ such that $F = \bar{F} + \sigma\xi(t)$. This leads to the Itô equation

$$dY_t = -V'(Y_t)\,dt + \sigma\,dW_t. \tag{3.88}$$

Note here that the result of adding fluctuations to F is additive noise in the equation for Y, rather than noise in the potential $V(y)$.

Starting at one fixed point $y_a = 0.24$, two transient solutions of (3.88) for $\bar{F} = 1.1$, $\mu^2 = 6.2$ are plotted in Figure 3.14, one for $\sigma = 0.1$ and one for $\sigma = 0.25$. The transient solution for $\eta = 0.1$ does not make any transition and stays near the equilibrium $y_a = 1.07$ ($q_a = 4.58$). As can be seen, the trajectory for $\sigma = 0.25$ undergoes

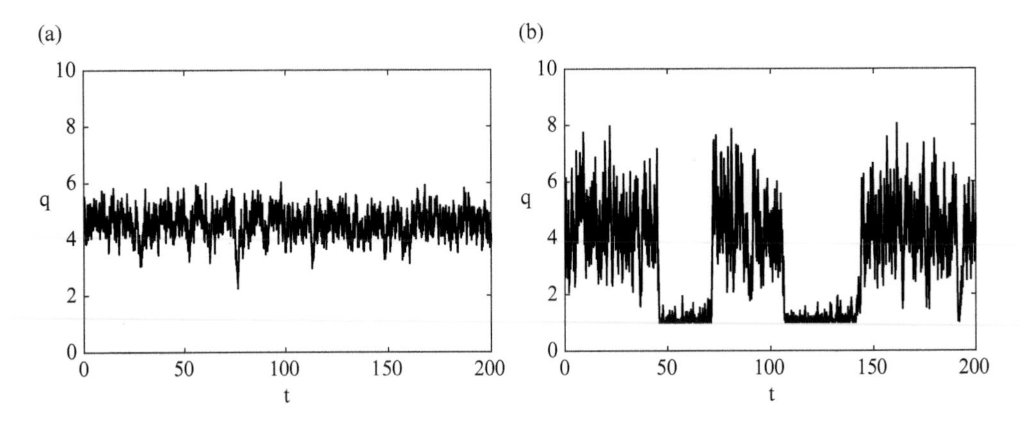

Fig. 3.14 (a) Realization of the box model starting at $y_a = 0.24$ for $\bar{F} = 1.1$, $\mu^2 = 6.2$ and (a) $\sigma = 0.1$ and (b) $\sigma = 0.25$.

transitions between the two stable states (y_c and y_a). Clearly, the transitions in Figure 3.14b are noise induced transitions as the value of $\bar{F}$ is still in the multiple equilibrium regime and smaller than the $\bar{F}$ value at the saddle node bifurcation L_1 (Figure 3.13).

As we have seen in Section 3.3, we can write down the forward Fokker–Planck equation in order to solve for the probability density function $p(y,t)$ of the process Y_t, i.e.,

$$\frac{\partial p}{\partial t} = \frac{\partial}{\partial y}\left(V'(y)p\right) + \frac{1}{2}\sigma^2 \frac{\partial^2 p}{\partial y^2}. \tag{3.89}$$

Now, in the previous deterministic case, we sought time-independent solutions for y. Of course, it makes no sense to look for truly time-independent solutions for the random variable Y_t, but a *statistically steady* solution may be found by setting $\partial p/\partial t = 0$ and solving for the function $p_s(y)$, satisfying stationary statistics. The solution method is similar to that for the Ornstein–Uhlenbeck process and the result is,

$$p_s(y) = Ce^{-\frac{2}{\sigma^2}V(y)}, \text{ where } C = \left(\int_{-\infty}^{\infty} e^{-\frac{2}{\sigma^2}V(y)}\, dy\right)^{-1} \tag{3.90}$$

which is the normalization coefficient, and we have used the boundary condition that $p \to 0$ as $y \to \pm\infty$.

Numerical results for Equations (3.88) and (3.89) are shown in Figure 3.15. The histograms and probability densities are initially peaked at the well near which the system was launched, indicating that the peak at $y = y_b$ is difficult to cross. They do eventually spread out, though, and attain the steady state given by Equation 3.90. In this state, the system typically fluctuates around in one of the two wells and randomly transitions between them, while spending more time overall in the deeper well.

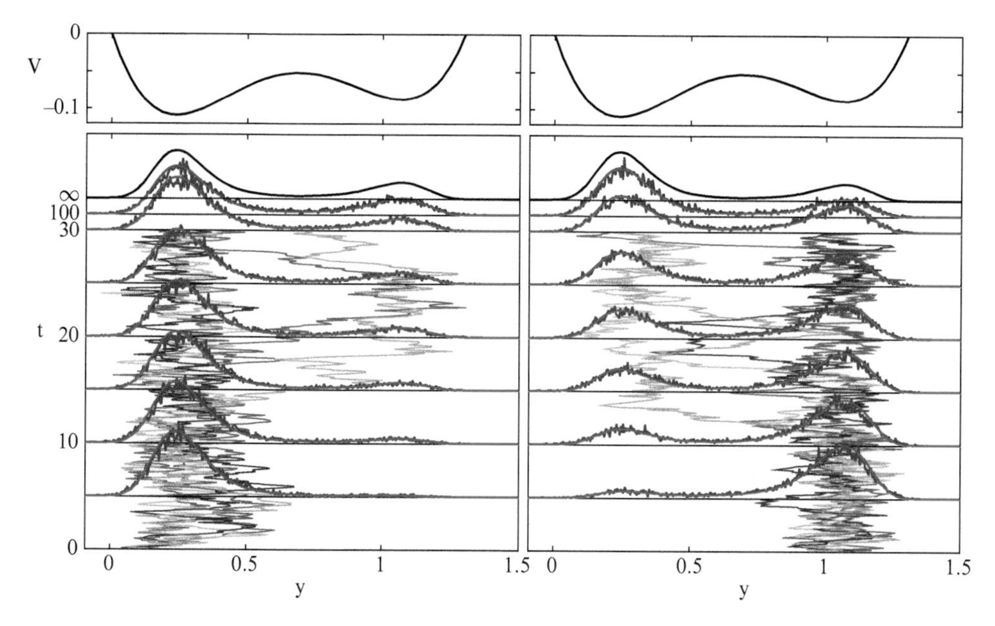

Fig. 3.15 Motion in the double-well potential $V(y)$ from (3.86) with $\bar{F}=1.1$ and $\mu^2=6.2$. Top: Potential $V(y)$. Bottom: Stochastic motion (3.88) with noise amplitude $\sigma=0.2$ starting from $Y_0=0$ (left) or $Y_0=1$ (right). The time evolution of five realizations are shown, as well as histograms (blue) from 10,000 realizations and the probability density (red) obtained from numerical solution of the corresponding Fokker–Planck equation (3.89). The distribution labelled $t=\infty$ is the steady-state distribution $p_s(y)$ from (3.90)

3.4.5 Escape time

Suppose we are in the "on"-state $y=y_a$ of the meridional overturning, but subject the system to given stochastic freshwater forcing. How long is it likely to take for the system to flip into the other ("off") state $y=y_c$? To solve this exit-time problem, let the time when the particle leaves the interval (also referred to as the first exit time) be indicated by $T(y)$. It can be shown that the mean time $\bar{T}(y)$ required to escape to y_c when starting from y satisfies the equation:

$$-1=-V'\bar{T}'+\tfrac{1}{2}\sigma^2\bar{T}'', \qquad \text{with} \qquad \bar{T}(y_c)=0, \qquad \bar{T}'(-\infty)=0, \tag{3.91}$$

where the boundary conditions state that it takes no time to reach y_c when starting from y_c, and that the escape time varies very little for y, far below the potential at y_a, since the restoring deterministic drift is very strong there.

The equation is a linear first-order equation for $\bar{T}'(y)$ which we solve by multiplying by the integrating factor $\exp(-2V(y)/\sigma^2)$:

$$-e^{-\frac{2}{\sigma^2}V}=e^{-\frac{2}{\sigma^2}V}\left(-V'\bar{T}'+\tfrac{\sigma^2}{2}\bar{T}''\right)=\tfrac{\sigma^2}{2}\left(e^{-\frac{2}{\sigma^2}V}\bar{T}'\right)'. \tag{3.92}$$

Integration of both sides and using the boundary condition $\bar{T}'(-\infty)=0$ yields

$$\bar{T}'(y)=e^{\frac{2}{\sigma^2}V(y)}\int_{-\infty}^{y}-\frac{2}{\sigma^2}e^{-\frac{2}{\sigma^2}V(s)}\,ds=-\frac{2}{\sigma^2}\int_{-\infty}^{y}e^{\frac{2}{\sigma^2}[V(y)-V(s)]}\,ds. \tag{3.93}$$

A second integration using $\bar{T}(y_c)=0$ yields

$$\bar{T}(y)=-\frac{2}{\sigma^2}\int_{z=y_c}^{y}\int_{s=-\infty}^{z}e^{\frac{2}{\sigma^2}[V(z)-V(s)]}\,ds\,dz. \tag{3.94}$$

Hence, the mean escape time from the "on" state $y=y_a$ to the "off" state $y=y_c$ is

$$\bar{T}(y_a)=\frac{2}{\sigma^2}\int_{z=y_a}^{y_c}\int_{s=-\infty}^{z}\exp\left(\frac{2}{\sigma^2}[V(z)-V(s)]\right)ds\,dz. \tag{3.95}$$

An asymptotic approximation to the previous integral can be obtained in the limit of small noise, where σ^2 is much smaller than the typical variation $V(y_b)-V(y_a)$ of the potential, so that we can treat $M=2/\sigma^2$ as a large parameter. In this case, the main contribution to the integral in Equation 3.95 comes from the region where the exponent $M[V(z)-V(s)]$ is maximal, i.e., $z\approx y_b$ and $s\approx y_a$. The contributions from any other regions are exponentially small and can be ignored (this technique is called Laplace's method). We can thus approximate the result as

$$\bar{T}(y_a)\approx M\int_{y_b-\epsilon}^{y_b+\epsilon}e^{MV(z)}\,dz\int_{y_a-\epsilon}^{y_a+\epsilon}e^{-MV(s)}\,ds, \tag{3.96}$$

where $\epsilon>0$ is small.

After a change of variables $z=y_b+x$ or $s=y_a+x$, the two integral factors in Equation (3.96) have the form

$$I\equiv\int_{-\epsilon}^{\epsilon}e^{Mf(x)}\,dx, \tag{3.97}$$

where $M\gg 1$ and $f(x)=V(y_b+x)$ or $f(x)=-V(y_a+x)$ has a maximum at $x=0$. We have argued that almost all of the contribution to the integral I comes from the region near this maximum, so we may Taylor expand $f(x)$ as $f(x)\approx f(0)+f''(0)x^2/2$, where no linear term is present, and $f''(0)<0$ since $x=0$ is a maximum. After the expansion, we can extend the limits to infinity, again because the contributions from regions away from the exponential maximum near $x=0$ are negligible, and hence

$$\int_{-\epsilon}^{\epsilon}e^{Mf(x)}\,dx\approx e^{Mf(0)}\int_{-\epsilon}^{\epsilon}e^{-\frac{1}{2}M|f''(0)|x^2}\,dx \tag{3.98a}$$

$$\approx e^{Mf(0)}\int_{-\infty}^{\infty}e^{-\frac{1}{2}M|f''(0)|x^2}\,dx \tag{3.98b}$$

$$\approx e^{Mf(0)}\sqrt{\frac{2\pi}{M|f''(0)|}}, \tag{3.98c}$$

where we have made use of the standard result $\int_{-\infty}^{\infty} e^{-\alpha x^2}\,dx = \sqrt{\pi/\alpha}$.

The two integral factors in Equation 3.96 are thus,

$$\int_{y_b-\epsilon}^{y_b+\epsilon} e^{MV(z)}\,dz \approx \sqrt{\frac{2\pi}{M|V''(y_b)|}}e^{MV(y_b)}, \tag{3.99a}$$

$$\int_{y_a-\epsilon}^{y_a+\epsilon} e^{-MV(s)}\,ds \approx \sqrt{\frac{2\pi}{M|V''(y_a)|}}e^{-MV(y_a)}, \tag{3.99b}$$

and hence, the mean escape time from the "on" state $y = y_a$ to the "off" state $y = y_c$ is approximately

$$\bar{T}(y_a) = 2\pi\sqrt{\frac{1}{|V''(y_a)||V''(y_b)|}}\exp\left(\frac{2}{\sigma^2}\left[V(y_b) - V(y_a)\right]\right). \tag{3.100}$$

From the calculations, we can see that this escape time is the same from any state in the well near $y = y_a$, over the peak $y = y_b$, to any state in the well near $y = y_c$. This is in line with our intuition that, for weak noise, the deterministic drift quickly drives the system to the bottom of the well $y = y_a$, where it fluctuates until eventually a large enough random perturbation kicks the system over the crest $y = y_b$ and it falls into the other well $y = y_c$.

3.4.6 Periodic forcing and noise

Within this autonomous framework, the system will jump between on and off states stochastically, but will not display any dominant time scale (e.g., periodic behavior), as is observed for Dansgaard–Oeschger events. We therefore augment the previous model with a periodic modulation to the deterministic part of the freshwater forcing, so that

$$F = \bar{F} + \sigma\xi(t) + A\sin\left(2\pi\frac{t}{T}\right), \tag{3.101}$$

where A is the amplitude of periodic forcing and T is the dimensionless period of forcing (as we are still working with dimensionless variables). The governing equation is thus $dy/dt = -dV/dy + \sigma\xi(t)$, where the potential $V(y,t)$ is chosen as

$$V(y,t) = -\bar{F}y + \frac{1}{2}y^2 + \mu^2\left(\frac{1}{4}y^4 - \frac{2}{3}y^3 + \frac{1}{2}y^2\right) - A\sin\left(2\pi\frac{t}{T}\right)(y - 0.7). \tag{3.102}$$

In Figure 3.16, we show what happens for a small periodic forcing ($A = 0.05$) to the mean forcing $\bar{F}$ for various values of the noise amplitude σ. For small noise, the

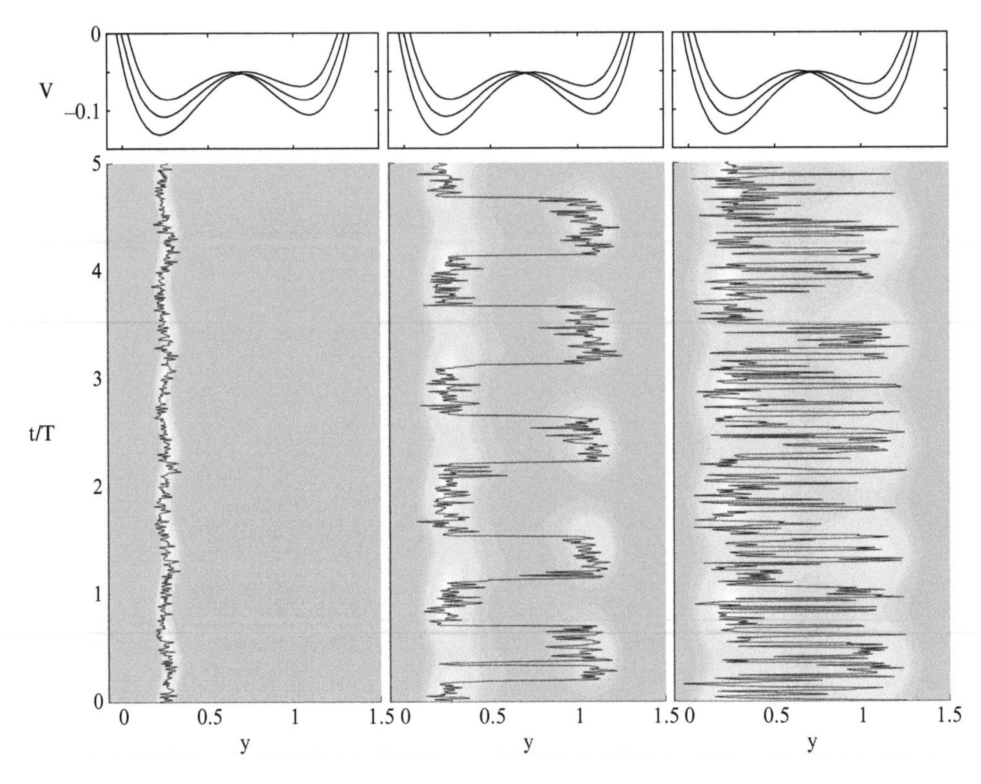

Fig. 3.16 Motion in a time-periodic double-well potential (Equation 3.102 with $\bar{F}=1.1$, $\mu^2=6.2$ and $A=0.05$). Top: The potential V at $t=-T/2$, 0, $T/2$. Bottom: Stochastic motion with noise amplitude $\sigma=0.05$ (left), $\sigma=0.15$ (middle), $\sigma=0.25$ (right). The time evolution of one realization is shown (black curve), as well as the probability density (heat map) obtained from evolving the corresponding Fokker–Planck equation forward until a time-periodic state is reached. The period T chosen corresponds to 100000 years.

system remains in the deeper well most of the time as expected. For large noise, the probability density system frequently transitions between the two wells, almost as if the middle peak at $y=y_b$ did not exist, and the periodicity is quite weak. However, for an intermediate value of noise strength, we recover periodic behavior on the timescale T. The response is not a small perturbation, but a jump between on and off states every cycle. We have ended up with a system exhibiting so-called "stochastic resonance," whereby the noise is just large enough to switch between states almost every time the background forcing oscillates, see Figure 3.17.

To explain this mechanism in more detail, consider the slightly simplified system with potential (Fig. 3.17),

$$V(y) = -\frac{y^2}{2} + \frac{y^4}{4} - \epsilon y \cos(\Omega\tau).$$

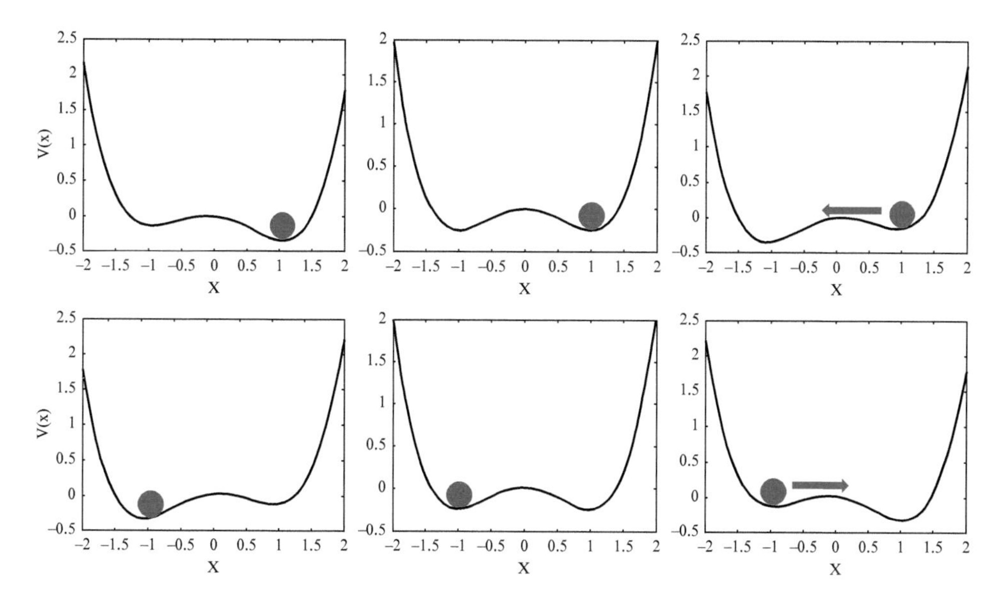

Fig. 3.17 Upper: $V(y)$ vs y for $\tau = 0$ (left), $\tau = \frac{\pi}{2\Omega}$ (middle), and $\tau = \frac{\pi}{\Omega}$ (right). Lower: $V(y)$ vs y for $\tau = \frac{\pi}{\Omega}$ (left), $\tau = \frac{3\pi}{2\Omega}$ (middle), and $\tau = \frac{2\pi}{\Omega}$ (right). The state of the system is represented by the red dot.

Note that, the fixed points location (defined by $V'(y) = 0$ and $V''(y) > 0$) does not strongly vary with τ if the amplitude ϵ is small (in which case the fixed points are given by $y_\pm \approx \pm 1$), unlike the value of the potential V at these fixed points. For $\epsilon \ll 1$, these two values are approximately given by:

$$V(y_\pm) \approx V(\pm 1) = -[\frac{1}{4} \pm \epsilon \cos(\Omega\tau)].$$

Using the Laplace approximation, the transition times are approximately given by:

$$< t_{-1\to 1} > \approx 2\pi \sqrt{\frac{1}{-V''(0)V''(-1)}} \exp\{\frac{2[V(0) - V(-1)]}{\sigma^2}\} \approx \sqrt{2}\pi \exp[\frac{1 - 4\epsilon\cos(\Omega\tau)}{2\sigma^2}]$$

$$< t_{1\to -1} > \approx 2\pi \sqrt{\frac{1}{-V''(0)V''(1)}} \exp\{\frac{2[V(0) - V(1)]}{\sigma^2}\} \approx \sqrt{2}\pi \exp[\frac{1 + 4\epsilon\cos(\Omega\tau)}{2\sigma^2}].$$

The transition times vary with τ as the potential changes shape. Because the variance in the transition time is very small compared to the transition time itself, the transition occurs over a small time interval. As a consequence, the Fourier spectrum has a strong peak at the forcing frequency Ω. In the case of a small periodic forcing, ϵ, the synchronization can occur for moderate values of σ.

For example, if we take the small amplitude to be $\epsilon = 0.1$, the shape of the potential is very close to a double well. If we suppose that at $\tau = 0$, the state of the system is near $y_+ \approx 1$, the transition time $< t_{1\to-1} >$ at this τ is maximal, as the potential well is deepest. If $\frac{\pi}{\Omega} \ll < t_{1\to-1} > (\tau = 0)$, then the well will change shape and the system will almost surely exit the well at $\tau = \frac{\pi}{\Omega}$ where the mean escape time $< t_{1\to-1} >$ is minimal: the same reasoning can be applied when the system starts near $y_- \approx -1$ at $\tau = \frac{\pi}{\Omega}$. Thus, for a small amplitude, the transitions of the system approximately occur when τ is a multiple of $\frac{\pi}{\Omega}$, and the system stochastically resonates with the forcing of angular frequency Ω.

It is unclear whether the Dansgaard–Oeschger events are in fact generated by such a mechanism (the addition of a ~1500 year periodicity in freshwater forcing is *ad hoc*—we know of no such forcing in reality), but it nonetheless constitutes a fascinating result that ordered behavior may come out of the addition of white noise.

3.5 El Niño/Southern Oscillation

3.5.1 Phenomena

About once every four years, the sea surface temperature in the equatorial eastern Pacific is a few degrees higher than normal, Philander (1990). Near the South American coast, this warming of the ocean water is usually at its maximum around Christmas. Long ago, Peruvian fishermen called it El Niño—the Spanish phrase for the "Christ Child."

During the last decades, El Niño has been observed in unprecedented detail, thanks to the implementation of the TAO/TRITON array and the launch of satellite-borne instruments, McPhaden and coauthors (1998). The relevant quantities to characterize the state in the equatorial ocean and atmosphere are sea level pressure, sea surface temperature (SST), sea level height, surface wind, and ocean sub-surface temperature.

The annual mean state of the equatorial Pacific sea-surface temperature is characterized by the zonal contrast between the western Pacific "warm pool" and the "cold tongue" in the eastern Pacific. The mean temperature in the eastern Pacific is approximately 23°C, with seasonal variability of about 3°C. What makes El Niño unique among other interesting phenomena of natural climate variability is that it has both a well-defined spatial pattern and a relatively well-defined time scale. The pattern of the sea-surface temperature anomaly for December 1997 is plotted in Figure 3.18a and shows a large area where the SST is larger than average. Changes in the tropical atmospheric circulation are strongly connected to changes in sea-surface temperature. Hence, there are strong correlations between surface pressure anomalies, as shown in Figure 3.18b.

An index of this sea-surface temperature anomaly pattern is the NINO3 index, defined as the sea-surface temperature anomaly averaged over the region 5°S –5°N, 150°W–90°W. In the time series (blue curve in Figure 3.19a), the high NINO3 periods are known as El Niños and the low NINO3 periods as La Niñas. There is no clear-cut distinction between El Niños, La Niñas, and normal periods, rather the system exhibits continuous fluctuations of varying strengths and durations with an average period of about 4 years (blue curve in Figure 3.19b).

The red curve in Figure 3.19a is the normalized pressure difference between Tahiti (Eastern Pacific region) and Darwin; this index is referred to as the Southern

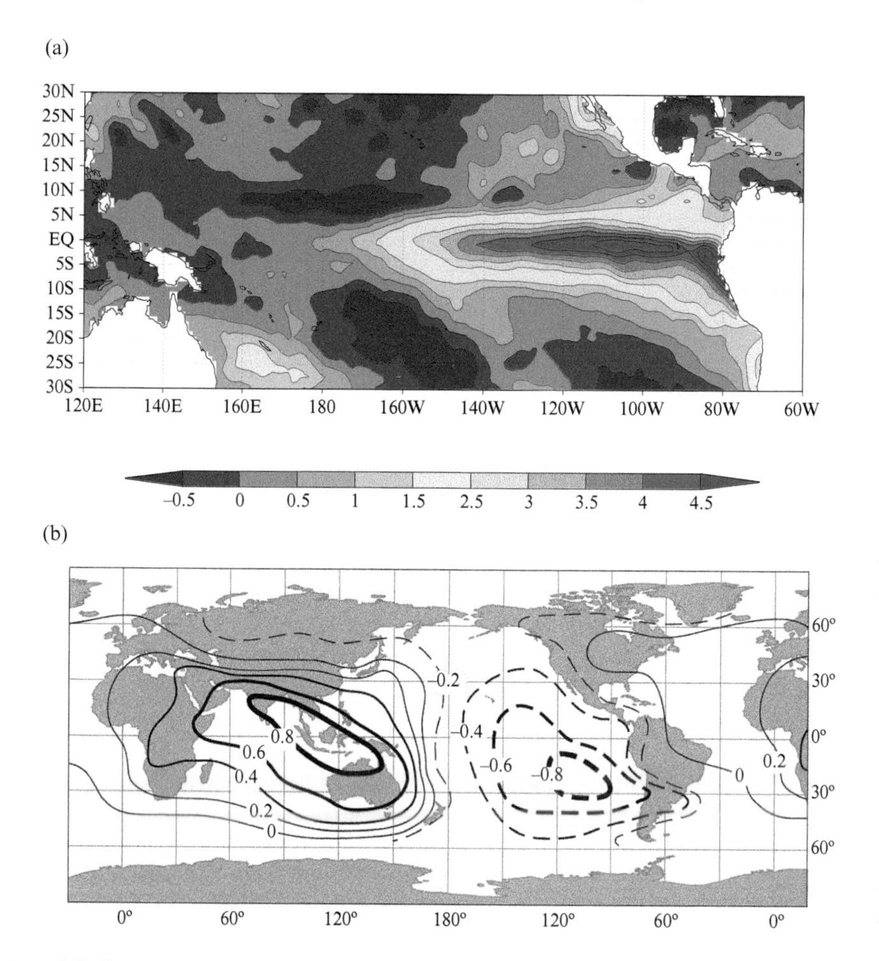

Fig. 3.18 (a) Sea-surface temperature anomaly field (with respect to the 1982–2010 mean) of December, 1997, at the height of the 1997/1998 El Niño. Data from NOAA, see http://www.emc.ncep.noaa.gov/research/cmb/sst_analysis/. (b) Correlations of sea level pressure anomalies over the Tropic Pacific, illustrating the Southern Oscillation.

Oscillation Index (SOI). It measures the variations in the tropical surface winds, dominated by the trade winds. When the SOI is negative (positive), the pressure in Tahiti is relatively low (high) with respect to that in Darwin, and hence the trade winds are weakened (strengthened). The anti-correlation of the NINO3 index and the SOI is obvious from Figure 3.19a and the spectrum of the SOI in Figure 3.19b also shows a similar broad peak as the NINO3 index (centered at about 4 years). As El Niño and the Southern Oscillation are one phenomenon, it is referred to as the ENSO phenomenon.

There are relations between the seasonal cycle, the spatial sea-surface temperature pattern of the annual-mean state, and the El Niño variability. Large sea-surface temperature anomalies often occur within the cold tongue region. In addition, El Niño is to some extent phase-locked to the seasonal cycle as most El Niños and La

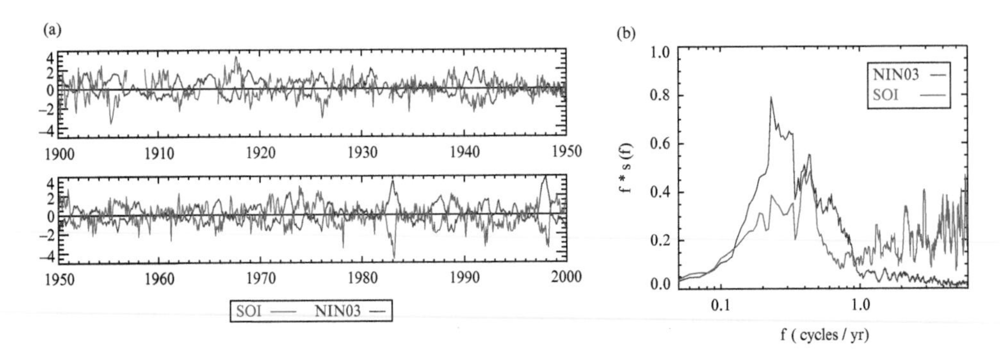

Fig. 3.19 (a) Time series of the NINO3 index (dark) and SOI (light) over the years 1900–2000. (b) Spectrum of the NINO3 index (dark) and SOI (light) in (a), where on the vertical axis the product of frequency f and the spectral power $S(f)$ is plotted. (figure based on Dijkstra and Burgers (2002)).

Niñas peak around December. The root mean square of the NINO3 index is almost twice as large in December than in April.

When one considers the spectrum of the NINO3 index (Figure 3.19b), energy is also found at lower frequencies, in particular in the decadal-to-interdecadal range, Jiang *et al.* (1995); Zhang *et al.* (1997); Fedorov and Philander (2000). The strength of El Niño before the mid-1970s appears to be smaller than that after this period; this transition is sometimes referred to as the "Pacific climate shift," Trenberth (1997). According to NCEP data, the standard deviation of the SOI (NINO3) for 1951–1975 is 1.64 (0.81), to be compared for 1976–2000 where it is 1.84 (1.00). The spatial pattern of these (multi)decadal changes is fairly similar to that of the interannual variability, but the sea-surface temperature anomalies at the eastern side of the basin extend from the equator to midlatitudes, Zhang *et al.* (1997).

3.5.2 The Zebiak & Cane model

To capture the oscillatory behavior of ENSO dynamically, a coupled atmosphere-ocean model is required, which admits feedback between perturbations to the equatorial easterlies, the thermocline depth, and equatorial SSTs, and as such allows the spontaneous growth of anomalies. We shall also see that oceanic wave dynamics are important to the development and decay of El Niños, and so necessary in a minimal model of ENSO.

Model formulation

Zebiak & Cane (1987), hereon (ZC), consider a $1\frac{1}{2}$-layer reduced gravity ocean (depicted in Figure 3.20) below a constant-depth mixed layer of temperature T, which feels a temperature-dependent wind stress

$$\tau^x = \tau^x_{\text{ext}} + \mu \mathcal{A}(T - T_0), \tag{3.103}$$

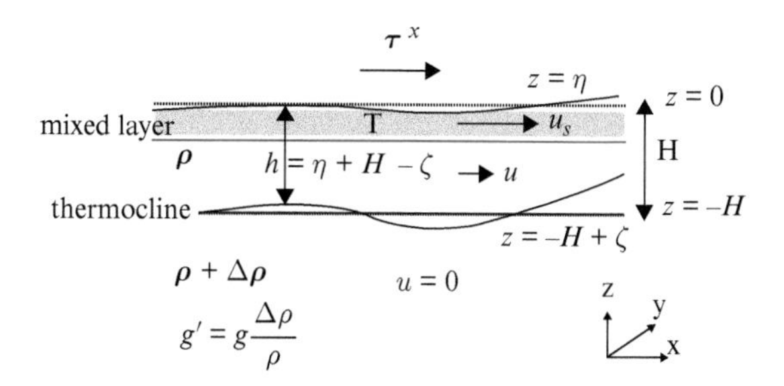

Fig. 3.20 The ocean component of the ZC model. A thermocline of density ρ overlies a denser stationary layer of density $\rho + \Delta\rho$. The ocean feels atmospheric wind stress and temperature through a constant depth mixed layer of temperature T.

for some atmospheric operator $\mathcal{A}$, and coupling parameter μ (with $\mu = 0$ corresponding to the entirely uncoupled case, and $\mu = 1$ describing "normal" coupling).

The reduced-gravity ocean model equations for the horizontal velocities (u, v) and thermocline depth h are

$$\frac{\partial u_1}{\partial t} - \beta_0 y v_1 = -g' \frac{\partial h}{\partial x} + \frac{\tau^x}{\rho H}, \tag{3.104a}$$

$$\beta_0 y u_1 = -g' \frac{\partial h}{\partial y}, \tag{3.104b}$$

$$\frac{\partial h}{\partial t} = -H\left(\frac{\partial u_1}{\partial x} + \frac{\partial v_1}{\partial y}\right), \tag{3.104c}$$

with boundary conditions

$$x = 0 : \int_{-\infty}^{\infty} u_1(y)dy = 0, \tag{3.105a}$$

$$x = L : u_1 = 0, \tag{3.105b}$$

$$y \to \pm\infty : u_1, v_1, h, \text{bounded}. \tag{3.105c}$$

The evolution of the mixed layer temperature T is governed by an advection-diffusion equation with relaxation back to the radiation equilibrium temperature T_0 as follows;

$$\frac{\partial T}{\partial t} + u_1 \frac{\partial T}{\partial x} + v_1 \frac{\partial T}{\partial y} + w_1 \mathcal{H}(w_1) \frac{T - T_s(h)}{H} + \alpha_T (T - T_0) - \kappa_H \nabla^2 T = 0, \tag{3.106}$$

where $\mathcal{H}$ is the Heaviside function (needed because the mixed layer temperature is only affected by net upwelling). In addition, the subsurface temperature $T_s(h)$ is a monotonically increased function of h and κ_H is a horizontal diffusion coefficient. The boundary conditions for the mixed layer temperature are:

$$x = 0, L : \frac{\partial T}{\partial x} = 0, \tag{3.107a}$$

$$y \to \pm\infty : T \, \text{bounded}. \tag{3.107b}$$

Equatorial wave dynamics in the ZC model

Consider free waves with $\tau^x = 0$, corresponding to no wind stress input, and no coupling with the mixed layer temperature field T. Let $u = \hat{u}(y)e^{i(kx-\sigma t)}$ and define $v = \hat{v}(y)e^{i(kx-\sigma t)}$ and $h = H + \hat{h}(y)e^{i(kx-\sigma t)}$ similarly. Then,

$$-i\sigma\hat{u} - \beta_0 y\hat{v} = -ikg'\hat{h}, \tag{3.108a}$$

$$\beta_0 y\hat{u} = -g'\hat{h}', \tag{3.108b}$$

$$-i\sigma\hat{h} + H(ik\hat{u} + \hat{v}') = 0. \tag{3.108c}$$

Solutions with $\hat{v} = 0$ are determined from

$$-\sigma\hat{u} \quad = -g'k\hat{h}, \tag{3.109a}$$

$$-\sigma\hat{h} + Hk\hat{u} \quad = 0, \tag{3.109b}$$

$$\tag{3.109c}$$

which has a non-zero solution only if

$$\sigma^2 = k^2 g' H, \tag{3.110}$$

and so,

$$\frac{\sigma}{k} = \pm\sqrt{g'H} \equiv \pm c_0. \tag{3.111}$$

We can also solve for $\hat{h}$ and $\hat{u}$, since

$$\beta_0 y\hat{u} = \frac{\beta_0 y g' k\hat{h}}{\sigma} = -g'\hat{h}', \tag{3.112}$$

and so

$$\hat{h}(y) = \hat{h}(0)\exp\left[-\frac{\beta_0 k}{2\sigma}y^2\right] \equiv \hat{h}(0)\exp\left[-\frac{1}{2}\left(\frac{y}{\lambda_0}\right)^2\right], \tag{3.113}$$

where $\lambda_0 = \sqrt{c_0/\beta_0}$ is the Rossby deformation radius. Note that, for $\hat{h}(y)$ to be bounded as $y \to \pm\infty$, we have to set $\sigma/k = +c_0$. These eastward propagating waves are called equatorial Kelvin waves.

The general case $\hat{v} \neq 0$ can also be solved by using the Hermite polynomials H_n, giving

$$\hat{u}_j(y) = \frac{1}{2\sqrt{2}}\left(\frac{\psi_{j+1}(y)}{\sqrt{j+1}} - \frac{\psi_{j-1}(y)}{\sqrt{j}}\right), \tag{3.114a}$$

$$\hat{h}_j(y) = \frac{1}{2\sqrt{2}}\left(\frac{\psi_{j+1}(y)}{\sqrt{j+1}} + \frac{\psi_{j-1}(y)}{\sqrt{j}}\right), \tag{3.114b}$$

$$\hat{v}_j(y) = \psi_j(y), \tag{3.114c}$$

where

$$\psi_j(y) = \frac{H_j(y/\lambda_0)\exp[-(y/\lambda_0)^2/2]}{(2^j j!\pi^{1/2})^{1/2}}, \tag{3.115}$$

and the corresponding phase speeds are

$$c_j = -\frac{c_0}{2j+1}. \tag{3.116}$$

These westward propagating waves are called equatorial Rossby waves.

Coupled feedbacks in the ZC model

To explore the feedbacks possible in the full model, consider a perturbation (denoted by hats) to some steady state (denoted by overbars) of the simplified temperature equation

$$\frac{\partial T}{\partial t} = -w\frac{T - T_s(h)}{H}. \tag{3.117}$$

Linearizing about the steady state, this becomes

$$\frac{\partial \hat{T}}{\partial t} = -\hat{w}\frac{\bar{T} - T_s(\bar{h})}{H} - \bar{w}\frac{\hat{T} - T_s'(\bar{h})\hat{h}}{H}. \tag{3.118}$$

Now it can be seen that if there is a warm anomaly in the mixed layer (i.e., $\hat{T} > 0$) giving rise to a deepening of the thermocline (i.e., $\hat{h} > 0$), the second term on the right of Equation 3.118 will be positive, leading to more warming. This positive feedback is known as the *thermocline feedback*.

Similarly, from the first term on the right of Equation 3.118, it can be deduced that a positive temperature anomaly, associated with a reduction in upwelling ($\hat{w} < 0$), will likewise enhance the positive temperature anomaly, acting as a positive feedback. This is called the *upwelling feedback*. An analogous treatment of the zonal advection terms of the temperature equation

$$\frac{\partial T}{\partial t} = -u\frac{\partial T}{\partial x} \tag{3.119}$$

yields linearized equation

$$\frac{\partial \hat{T}}{\partial t} = -\bar{u}\frac{\partial \hat{T}}{\partial x} - \hat{u}\frac{\partial \bar{T}}{\partial x}. \tag{3.120}$$

Now, a positive temperature anomaly will produce a zonal velocity anomaly $\hat{u}$, that acts to enhance this anomaly by the advection of the mean temperature field $\bar{T}$. This is the *zonal advection feedback*.

3.5.3 Hopf bifurcation in the ZC model

The zonal wind stress τ^x is decomposed into an external and a coupled contribution Van der Vaart *et al.* (2000):

$$\tau^x = \tau^x_{ext} + \tau^x_c. \tag{3.121}$$

The coupled part of the wind stress is assumed to be proportional to the zonal wind field u_a, i.e., $\tau^x_c = \rho H \gamma_\tau U$, with γ_τ a constant coefficient. The velocity field U is determined from an equivalent barotropic atmospheric model given by Matsuno (1966); Gill (1980):

$$\frac{\partial U}{\partial t} - \beta_0 y V - \frac{\partial \Theta}{\partial x} + a_M U = 0 \tag{3.122a}$$

$$\frac{\partial V}{\partial t} + \beta_0 y U - \frac{\partial \Theta}{\partial y} + a_M V = 0 \tag{3.122b}$$

$$\frac{\partial \Theta}{\partial t} - c_a^2\left(\frac{\partial U}{\partial x} + \frac{\partial V}{\partial y}\right) + a_M \Theta = Q, \tag{3.122c}$$

where (U, V) are the low-level winds, Θ the geopotential height (with dimension m^2/s^2), a_M is a damping coefficient, and c_a is the phase speed of the first baroclinic Kelvin wave in the atmosphere. The flow is forced by a representation of the adiabatic heating term Q (having dimension m^2/s^3) given by

$$Q = \alpha_T (T - T_0). \tag{3.123}$$

The external wind stress τ^x_{ext} does not depend on the coupled feedbacks within the basin and can be thought of to represent the easterly stress component due the Hadley circulation and it is assumed constant in the zonal direction, Dijkstra and Neelin (1995). In the meridional direction the external wind stress is assumed to be symmetric with respect to the equator, having the form, (Van der Vaart *et al.* (2000))

$$\tau^x_{ext} = -\tau_0 e^{[-\frac{1}{2}(\frac{y}{L_a})^2]}, \tag{3.124}$$

where τ_0 is a typical amplitude of the external wind stress and L_a is the atmospheric Rossby deformation radius.

In order to obtain the proper climatology of the present-day Pacific together with realistic ENSO variability, the standard parameter values as in Table 3.3 are used. The coupling parameter μ_0 is a dimensionless product of the dimensional parameters and is given by

$$\mu_0 = \mu \frac{\alpha_T \gamma_\tau \Delta T L^2}{c_o^2 c_a^2}, \tag{3.125}$$

where ΔT is a typical SST difference over the basin, here taken as $\Delta T = 1°\text{C}$. The dimensionless parameter μ is used below to control the strength of the coupling.

To solve the model equations numerically, variables are expanded into spectral basis functions, with Chebychev polynomials in zonal direction and Hermite functions

Table 3.3 *Values of dimensional parameters used in the ZC model.*

L	$=1.5\times10^{7}$	[m]	c_0	$=2$	[m/s]
c_a	$=30$	[m/s]	H	$=200$	[m]
H_1	$=50$	[m]	H_2	$=150$	[m]
τ_0	$=0.01$	[Pa]	T_{s0}	$=23.0$	[°C]
a_m	$=1.3\times10^{-8}$	[s^{-1}]	T_0	$=30.0$	[°C]
a_s	$=5.0\times10^{-6}$	[s^{-1}]	$\hat{H}$	$=40$	[m]
a_T	$=9.25\times10^{-8}$	[s^{-1}]	h_0	$=20$	[m]
A_m	$=2.5\times10^{-6}$	[s^{-1}]	β_0	$=2.2\times10^{-11}$	[(ms)$^{-1}$]
g'	$=0.02$	[ms^{-2}]	L_a	$=1.5\times10^{6}$	[m]
α_T	$=5.4\times10^{-3}$	[m^{2}s^{-3}K^{-1}]	γ_τ	$=6.5\times10^{-6}$	[s^{-1}]

in meridional direction, Van der Vaart *et al.* (2000). The solutions are then obtained by a collocation method with N_x collocation point in the zonal direction and N_y in the meridional direction. In the deterministic ZC model, with the parameters as in Table 3.3, a Hopf bifurcation occurs at $\mu=\mu_c=3.0$ Van der Vaart *et al.* (2000). When the coupling strength is smaller than μ_c, for example $\mu=2.7$, the system is in the subcritical regime where it exhibits a damped ENSO oscillation when no noise is present. This is shown in the behavior of the NINO3.4 index (red curve) in Figure 3.21a. When the coupling strength is increased to just above the critical value ($\mu=3.02>\mu_c$), the system will enter the supercritical regime where the NINO3.4 index displays an interannual oscillation (red curve in Figure 3.21c) and the spectrum shows a peak at about 4 years (red curve in Figure 3.21d). When an additive (white) noise forcing is added to the deterministic zonal wind stress (Equation 3.124), the response of the ZC model is shown as the black curves in Figure 3.21a,b (subcritical) and Figure 3.21c,d (supercritical). In the subcritical regime, the noise forcing is necessary to excite the ENSO variability, while in the supercritical regime, the noise forcing simply causes a higher amplitude of ENSO variability, Roulston and Neelin (2000).

3.5.4 Physical mechanisms for ENSO

We have seen from the ZC model that with idealized ocean-atmosphere coupling and oceanic wave dynamics it is possible to find oscillatory solutions in certain parts of parameter space that resemble ENSO in amplitude and period. Next, we heuristically describe two mechanisms that might give rise to such oscillatory behavior.

Consider a positive temperature anomaly at the equator in the Pacific Ocean, which corresponds to a positive SSH anomaly on-equator, with compensatory negative SSH anomalies off-equator to the north and south. We have seen that such a signal may propagate eastwards as an equatorial Kelvin wave on the equator, which may be interpreted as the eastward propagating and growth of an El Niño. Meanwhile,

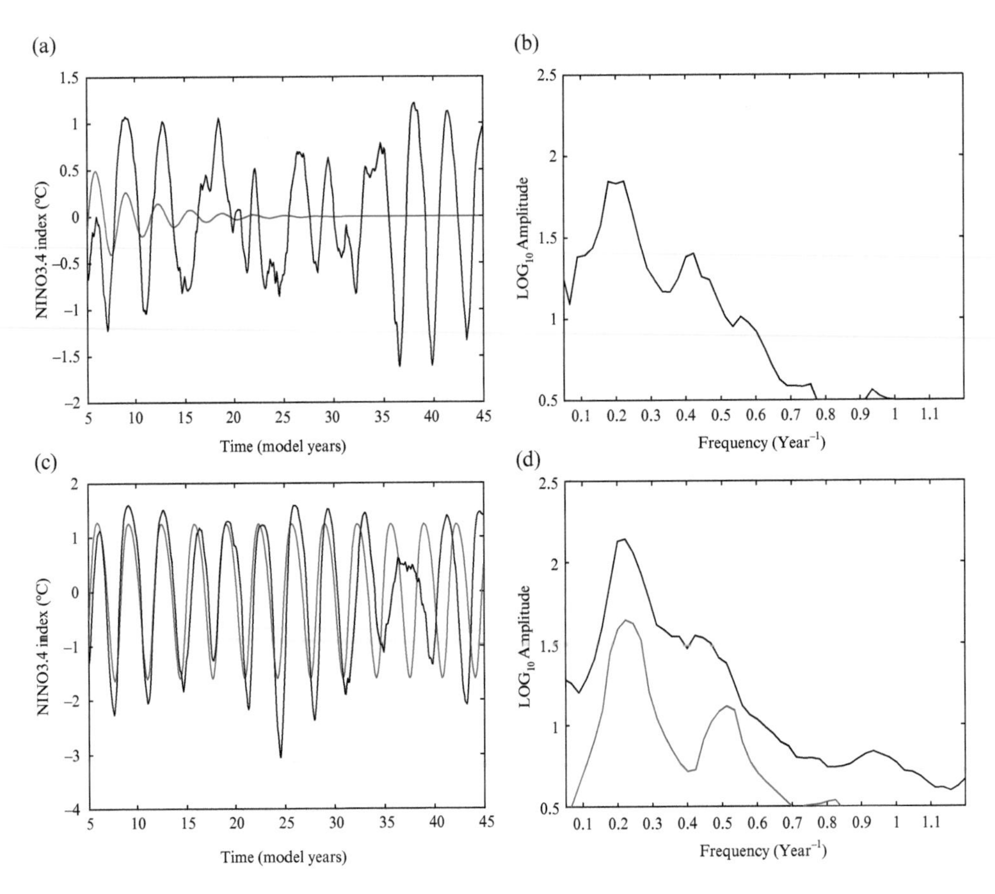

Fig. 3.21 The response of the Zebiak and Cane (ZC) model. Red curves are for the deterministic model and black curves are for the stochastic model with red noise wind-stress forcing. (a) The NINO3.4 index at a coupling strength $\mu = 2.7$, (b) the amplitude spectrum for (a), (c) same as (a) but at $\mu = 3.02$, (d) the amplitude spectrum for (c).

the off-equator signal will propagate westward as a Rossby wave and, on reaching the westerward basin boundary, may be reflected as an equatorial Kelvin wave. This reflected wave signal has the possibility of interfering with and killing the original positive temperature anomaly, ending the El Niño. Whilst this delayed oscillator mechanism of El Niño undoubtedly influences ENSO dynamics, a consideration of the timescales involved (from the Kelvin and Rossby wave speeds) does not explain the observed ENSO period of 4–7 years, Schopf and Suarez (1988); Battisti (1988).

An alternative mechanism that produces longer timescale variability comes from considering the overall basin adjustment. A positive SST anomaly in the eastern Pacific will produce a westerly wind stress anomaly. The wind stress acts to change the thermocline slope, piling up water and so depressing the thermocline in the east, whilst shoaling the thermocline in the west. Such a perturbation to the thermocline slope will enhance the SST perturbation, acting as a positive feedback. As the positive temperature anomaly strengthens, there is a divergent transport of heat off-equator by

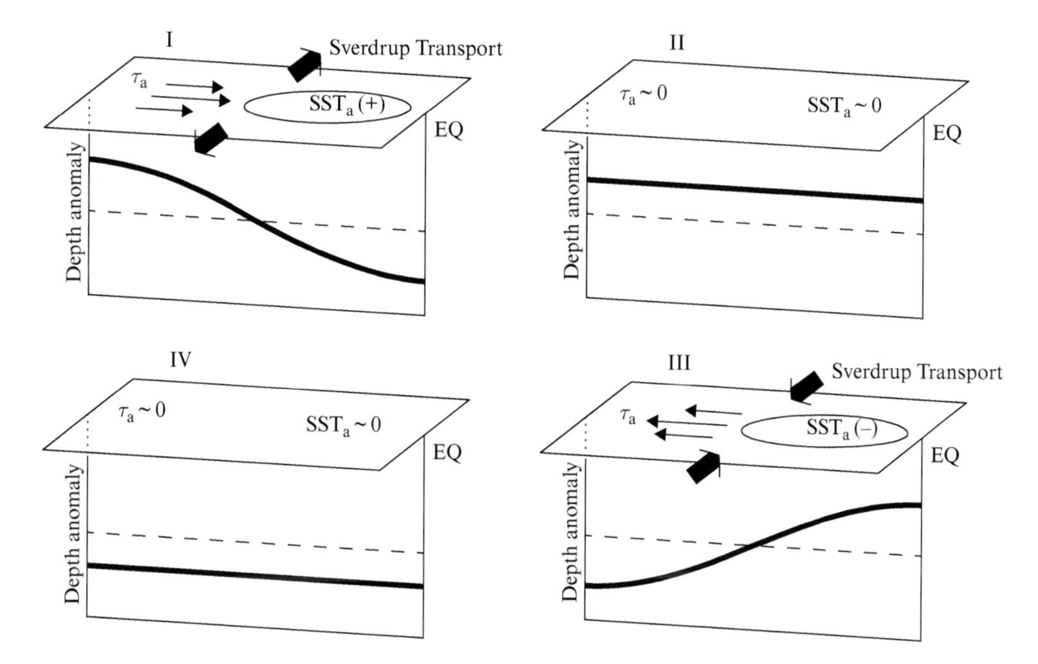

Fig. 3.22 A schematic of the stages of the recharge oscillator mechanism for ENSO.

the ocean, which shoals the thermocline suppressing the SST anomaly, and so reducing the westerly wind anomaly. The shoaling of the thermocline eventually carries the system into the opposite phase, with a negative SST anomaly in the East, and so an easterly wind stress anomaly. This causes the convergent transport of heat to the equator, resulting in the "recharge" of the ocean heat content there. As such, this mechanism is known as the *recharge oscillator* view of ENSO Jin (1997). This process is shown schematically in Figure 3.22.

3.5.5 The irregularity of ENSO

So far, we have seen that the oscillatory behavior of El Niño Southern Oscillation (ENSO) mechanism was related to the saturation of an unstable mode above the threshold of a Hopf bifurcation, corresponding to a given critical coupling strength between the atmosphere and the ocean. However, this does not explain the irregularity, for example, in the NINO3 time series. Two views exist on this irregularity: in one view it arises through nonlinear interactions between ENSO and the seasonal cycle, in the another it arises solely through atmospheric noise.

Deterministic chaos

An interesting point in the record of the ENSO signal is the signature of some mean seasonal cycle. For the western tropical Pacific Ocean, negative anomalies in the records of zonal winds occur around April, whereas positive anomalies occur around December. Furthermore, sea surface temperature (SST) anomalies are observed at the same periods: positive SST anomalies are associated with negative zonal wind anomalies, and negative SST anomalies are associated with positive zonal wind anomalies. It is important to note that ENSO events and the seasonal cycle are sensitive to the same environmental factors such as wind forcing and the ocean circulation. ENSO's non-linear interaction with the seasonal cycle is characterized by a tendency to synchrony in periodic, subharmonic oscillation.

An idealized model to understand the interaction of an external and internal frequency is the circle map

$$x_{n+1} = x_n + \Omega - \frac{K}{2\pi}\sin(2\pi x) \ \ (mod\ 1) \tag{3.126}$$

In order to illustrate the tendency for phase-locking we pick up a constant driving frequency Ω and a starting point x_0. The result of the iterations displaying the interaction between anomalies and the driving cycle is obtained by displaying the computed winding number W, given by

$$W = \lim_{n\to\infty} \frac{x_n - x_0}{n}, \tag{3.127}$$

in the (Ω, x) plane, for all the described Ω. As we increase the parameter K in the non-linear forcing, an increasing number of "windows" are opening and widening in the (Ω, x) space, the so-called Arnold tongues. These windows are the orbital periods (Figure 3.23) of limit circles encountered in the iterative process, and correspond to rational multiples of the driving frequency Ω onto which the system is locking. The frequency ratio of the model to the driving frequency describes a "Devil's staircase"

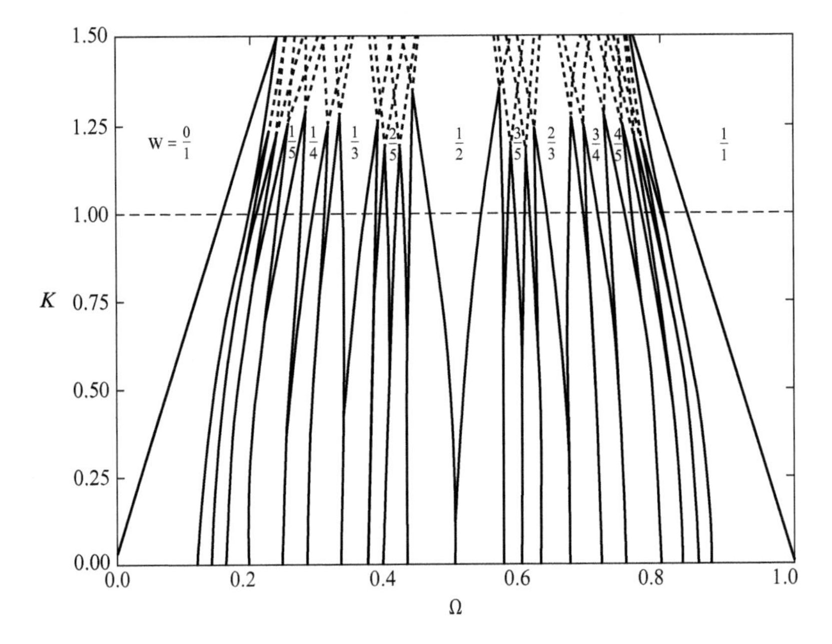

Fig. 3.23 Plot of regions of rational rotation number in the $\Omega - K$ plane displaying the Arnold tongues (Bak *et al.* (1985)) for the circle map.

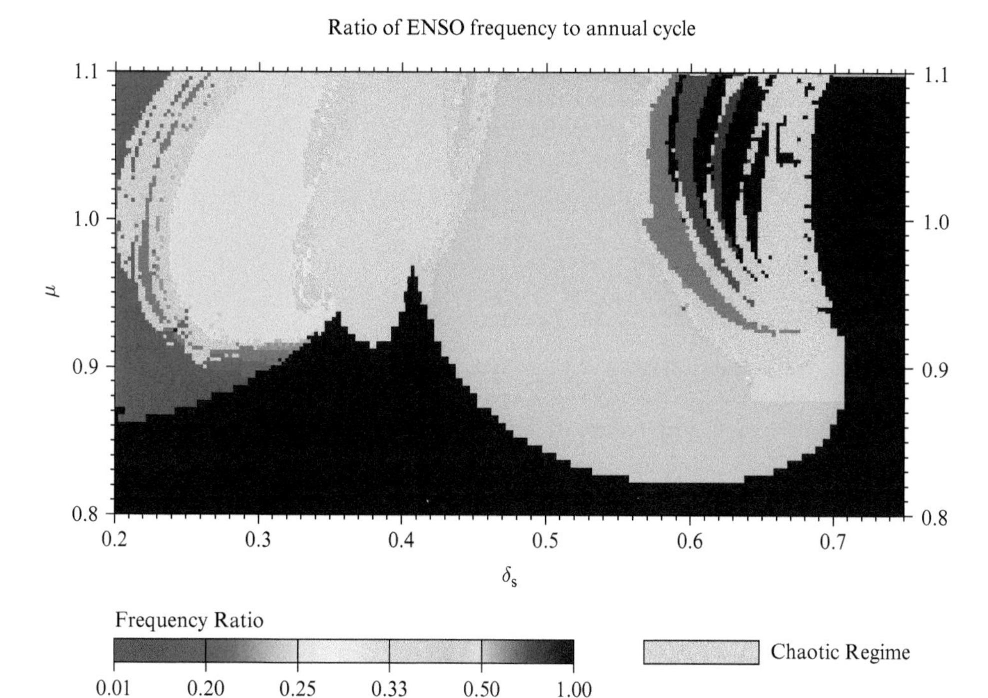

Fig. 3.24 The Devil's terrace as computed in Jin *et al.* (1996). Colors indicate the frequency locked regimes, with chaotic regimes in between. Along a section for fixed μ, a Devil's staircase appears.

as the number and width of frequency-locked steps (corresponding to the windows) increases infinitely. Above $K = 1$, chaotic behavior (sensitive dependence on initial conditions) is found due to the overlap of Arnold's tongues. This route to chaotic behavior is called the quasi-periodicity route.

In the Zebiak–Cane model, the interaction between the seasonal cycle and the Hopf bifurcation oscillatory frequency has been studied in the parameter plane spanned by the atmospheric/oceanic coupling strength parameter μ and the upwelling feedback parameter δ leading to a so-called "Devil's terrace" (Figure 3.24). As the coupling strength is increased, both the amplitude and the time scale of the oscillations are enhanced. By varying the parameters μ and δ, the Zebiak–Cane model predicts frequency locked ENSO events (e.g., 3 ENSOs in 10 years) in some regions in parameters space and chaotic behavior in others.

Effects of noise

Unresolved fast and short scales can be integrated into ENSO models by adding noise. As an example, the westerly wind bursts (WWB) events are characterized by velocities above 7 m s^{-1}, with a typical duration of a few days. These unresolved processes are known to trigger the propagation of perturbations in the form of equatorial Kelvin and Rossby waves. The correlation between these events can be verified in using a singular value decomposition analysis of the SST-Wind covariance matrix. The response of Zebiak–Cane model to white noise was shown in Figure 3.21 for both subcritical and supercritical regimes. A remarkable result is that wind-stress noise can trigger a response even before the critical point for the Hopf bifurcation is reached, that is, while still in the subcritical regime.

To study the effect of noise in more detail, we consider the following SDE system:

$$dX_t = (\lambda X_t - \omega Y_t - X_t(X_t^2 + Y_t^2))dt + \sigma dW_1, \tag{3.128a}$$
$$dY_t = (\lambda Y_t + \omega X_t - Y_t(X_t^2 + Y_t^2))dt + \sigma dW_2, \tag{3.128b}$$

where dW_1 and dW_2 are independent Wiener processes.

In polar coordinates ($r = \sqrt{X^2 + Y^2}$ and $\theta = \arctan \frac{X}{Y}$), we get for the stochastic part (using Ito's formula for change of variables and omitting the subscript t):

$$\begin{aligned} dR =& \frac{\partial r}{\partial x} dX + \frac{\partial r}{\partial y} dY + \frac{1}{2}\left(\frac{\partial^2 r}{\partial x^2}(dX)^2 + \frac{\partial^2 r}{\partial y^2}(dY)^2\right) + \ldots \\ =& \frac{X}{r}\sigma dW_1 + \frac{Y}{r}\sigma dW_2 + \frac{1}{2}\left(\frac{Y^2}{r^3}(\sigma)^2 + \frac{X^2}{r^3}(\sigma)^2\right)dt + \ldots \\ =& \underbrace{\sigma(\cos\theta dW_1 + \sin\theta dW_2)}_{\text{noise term}} + \underbrace{\frac{\sigma^2}{2r}dt}_{\text{additional drift term}}, \\ d\theta =& -\frac{y}{r^2}\sigma dW_1 + \frac{x}{r^2}\sigma dW_2 + \frac{1}{2}\left(\frac{2XY}{r^4}(\sigma)^2 - \frac{2XY}{r^4}(\sigma)^2\right)dt + \ldots \\ =& \underbrace{\sigma\left(\frac{\cos\theta}{r}dW_2 - \frac{\sin\theta}{r}dW_1\right)}_{\text{additional drift term}}, \end{aligned}$$

and hence, (3.128a) is transformed into

$$dR = \left(\lambda r - r^3 + \frac{\sigma^2}{2r}\right)dt + \sigma(\cos\theta dW_1 + \sin\theta dW_2), \tag{3.129a}$$
$$d\theta = \sigma\left(\frac{\cos\theta}{r}dW_2 - \frac{\sin\theta}{r}dW_1\right) + \omega dt. \tag{3.129b}$$

The stationary probability density function is determined from the Fokker–Planck equation associated with the stochastic system previously given. We obtain for the drift

$$\mathbf{f} = \begin{pmatrix} \lambda r - r^3 + \frac{\sigma^2}{2r} \\ \omega \end{pmatrix},$$

and for the diffusion matrix

$$\mathbf{g} = \sigma \begin{pmatrix} \cos\theta & \sin\theta \\ -\frac{\sin\theta}{r} & \frac{\cos\theta}{r} \end{pmatrix}.$$

The diffusion operator $\mathbf{D}$ is then

$$\mathbf{D} = \mathbf{g}\mathbf{g}^T = \sigma^2 \begin{pmatrix} 1 & 0 \\ 0 & \frac{1}{r^2} \end{pmatrix},$$

and the Fokker–Planck equation

$$\frac{\partial p}{\partial t} = -\frac{\partial[(\lambda r - r^3 + \frac{\sigma^2}{2r})p]}{\partial r} - \frac{\partial(\omega p)}{\partial \theta} + \frac{\sigma^2}{2}(\frac{\partial^2 p}{\partial^2 r} + \frac{1}{r^2}\frac{\partial^2 p}{\partial^2 \theta}). \tag{3.130}$$

We look for a stationary radially symmetric density function $p_s(r)$ which satisfies, then

$$0 = -\big((\lambda r - r^3 + \frac{\sigma^2}{2r})p_s\big)' + \frac{\sigma^2}{2}p_s'',$$

which can be easily solved through

$$\frac{p_s'}{p_s} = -\frac{2}{\sigma^2}\lambda r - 2\frac{r^3}{\sigma^2} + \frac{1}{r}$$

$$\ln p_s = -\frac{\lambda}{\sigma^2}r^2 - \frac{r^4}{2\sigma^2} + \ln r,$$

and finally, we obtain

$$p_s(r) = N\exp\big(\frac{\lambda r^2}{\sigma^2} - \frac{r^4}{2\sigma^2}\big), \tag{3.131}$$

where N is again a normalization constant.

3.6 Midlatitude flow transitions

3.6.1 Phenomena

The midlatitude atmospheric flow is considered to be a chaotic dynamical system for which predictability is limited, Lorenz (1963); Palmer (1993). Although the behavior of this flow is dominated by weather systems on short time scales caused by baroclinic instability, strong variability on time scales longer than 5–10 days, with a predominantly barotropic structure, is also observed, James (1994). It has been argued that at least part of the observed low-frequency variability can be explained by recurrent and persistent atmospheric regimes, Mo and Ghil (1988); Kimoto and Ghil (1993); Smyth *et al.* (1999), such as the North Atlantic Oscillation (NAO) and blocking events, Plaut and Vautard (1994); Ghil *et al.* (2002).

Many studies identifying atmospheric regimes use algorithms relying on the recurrence property of these regimes such as the k-means, Mo and Ghil (1988); Kondrashov *et al.* (2004) and the Gaussian mixture algorithms, Smyth *et al.* (1999); Smyth (1999). Other studies make use of persistence properties, for example leading to Hidden Markov Models, Majda *et al.* (2006); Franzke *et al.* (2008). Most of these techniques rely on the reduction of the high-dimensional phase space to a few dimensions.

The existence of weather regimes in General Circulation Models (GCM) and in reanalysis has been questioned for some time, Stephenson *et al.* (2004); Christiansen (2007); Fereday *et al.* (2008). Using the Integrated Forecast System (IFS) of the European Centre for Medium-Range Weather Forecasts (ECMWF), it was shown, Dawson *et al.* (2014*b*); Jung *et al.* (2005); Dawson *et al.* (2014*a*) that it was necessary to use a spatial resolution of T1279 (16 km), or to include stochastic parametrizations, in order for the atmospheric regime behavior to occur. This suggests that although the atmospheric regimes are large-scale low-frequency motions, the faster small-scale motions (either explicitly resolved or included as random perturbations) are important to simulate them.

The barotropic structure of midlatitude low-frequency variability has motivated early studies using low-order barotropic models. Charney and DeVore (1979) have shown that such regimes could manifest themselves in highly truncated spectral barotropic models as stable fixed points representative of different solutions of a standing Rossby wave over topography. Flow regimes and spontaneous transitions have been observed in laboratory experiments using rotating annulus experiments for a barotropic fluid with topography, Weeks *et al.* (1997) and for a two-layer shear flow, Williams (2003); Williams *et al.* (2004; 2005; 2008). In Weeks *et al.* (1997), a zonal flow and blocked flow were found for different values of the Rossby number, and spontaneous transitions between the two were observed for intermediate values of the Rossby number. They suggested that these transitions were associated with the existence of two basins of attraction connected by heteroclinic orbits.

A scenario of chaotic itinerancy, Kaneko (1991); Itoh and Kimoto (1996) permitted by heteroclinic connections is supported by the study of Crommelin *et al.* (2004) using a 6-mode barotropic model. For specific values of the forcing parameter, the two stable fixed points of the zonal and blocked regimes merge with a periodic orbit (due to barotropic instability), yielding a heteroclinic connection. Although such a specific situation is unlikely to exist in the real atmosphere, Crommelin (2003) found evidence of ruins of such a heteroclinic connection in a hemispheric barotropic model with realistic topography and forcing, Selten (1995) manifested by the presence of preferred transition paths. Regime behavior was also found in more realistic barotropic, Legras and Ghil (1985); Branstator and Opsteegh (1989); Crommelin (2003) and multilayer quasi-geostrophic models, Itoh and Kimoto (1996); Kondrashov *et al.* (2004). Because these models exhibit chaotic behavior, the regimes are no longer identified by stable fixed points but rather as neighborhoods in the phase space where trajectories tend to persist, motivating their denomination as meta-stable regimes.

When randomness is present in a dynamical system, whether it is because of uncertainty in the initial state of chaotic systems or because of a stochastic forcing, it is of interest to study the evolution of densities in phase space by the flow rather than that of individual trajectories, Lasota and Mackey (1994); Froyland and Padberg-gehle (2014). This evolution is given by the transfer operator whose point spectrum, the Ruelle–Policott resonances, Pollicott (1985); Ruelle (1986*b*, *a*); Butterley and Liverani (2007); Chekroun (2014) give valuable information on the slow dynamics of the system. For mixing dissipative systems, these resonances are associated with a slow correlation decay and the manifestation of meta stability, Froyland and Padberg-gehle (2014).

In this section, we consider the evolution of densities with respect to meta-stable regimes in a reduced phase space of the barotropic model used in Crommelin (2003). To study the slow dynamics in this phase space and to evaluate the effect of memory induced by the reduction, the spectrum of transfer operators estimated for different lags is analyzed. Meta-stable regimes are subsequently detected from the transfer operator at a carefully chosen lag. Finally, a study of the energy budget of the barotropic model is performed, where particular attention is given to the conversion of mean kinetic energy to eddy kinetic energy by Reynolds' stresses.

3.6.2 Intermediate complexity model

Transitions between zonal and blocked regimes of the northern hemisphere atmospheric circulation are here investigated using a barotropic model, Selten (1995); Crommelin (2003); Franzke *et al.* (2005). The dimensionless equation of the model, expressed in terms of the streamfunction ψ (representing the non-divergent flow) and using the mean radius of the Earth and the inverse of its rotation rate as horizontal and temporal scale, is given by the barotropic vorticity equation (BVE),

$$\frac{\partial \nabla^2 \psi}{\partial t} = -\mathcal{J}(\psi, \nabla^2 \psi + f + h_b) - k_1 \nabla^2 \psi + k_2 \nabla^8 \psi + \nabla^2 \psi^*, \tag{3.132}$$

where $\mathcal{J}$ denotes the Jacobian operator, f the Coriolis parameter, h the scaled orography, k_1 the Ekman damping coefficient, k_2 the coefficient of scale-selective damping, and $\nabla^2 \psi^*$ the prescribed vorticity forcing. The non-dimensional orography h_b is related to the one of the real Northern Hemisphere h_b' by

$$h_b = 2A_0 \frac{h_b'}{H} \sin \phi_0, \tag{3.133}$$

where $\phi_0 = 45°\text{N}$, $A_0 = 0.2$ is a factor determining the strength of the surface winds that blow across the topography, and H is a scale height of 10 km.

The BVE is projected onto spherical harmonics, triangularly truncated at the 21st mode (T21). The spherical harmonic coefficients are chosen such that the model is hemispheric with no flow across the equator, resulting in a system of 231 Ordinary Differential Equations (ODE), which are integrated using a fourth order Runge–Kutta numerical scheme. Following Selten (1995), the Ekman damping time scale and the scale-selective damping time scale were chosen as 15 days and 3 days (for wavenumber 21), respectively, so as to adequately reproduce the observed mean and variance of the 500hPa Northern-Hemisphere 10-day mean relative vorticity. The vorticity forcing $\nabla^2 \psi^*$ is calculated from ECMWF reanalysis data of wintertime 500hPa relative vorticity from 1981 to 1991, in order for the first two moments of the simulated relative vorticity to be as close as possible to the observed relative vorticity. The term $\nabla^2 \psi^*$ is calculated, Roads (1987); Selten (1995) according to

$$\nabla^2 \psi^* = \mathcal{J}(\psi_{cl}, \nabla^2 \psi_{cl} + f + h_b) + k_1 \nabla^2 \psi_{cl} - k_2 \nabla^8 \psi_{cl} + \overline{\mathcal{J}(\psi', \nabla^2 \psi')}, \tag{3.134}$$

where ψ_{cl} is the mean of the observed streamfunction. The quantity ψ' is the deviation of the 10-day running mean observed streamfunction from ψ_{cl}.

3.6.3 Ergodic theory

In the previous sections, focus was on individual trajectories and their asymptotic behavior (e.g., to fixed points or periodic orbits). However, the climate system displays chaotic behavior in many of its subsystems, e.g., in its midlatitude atmospheric flow. One is then interested in statistical properties of trajectories, or ergodic properties, of a model. For example, a common approach to improve the skill of weather forecasts and quantify their uncertainty is to use an ensemble of trajectories with slightly different initial conditions, Slingo and Palmer (2011).

Mathematically, let the model satisfy a system of well-posed ordinary differential equations

$$\dot{\mathbf{x}} = \Phi(\mathbf{x}), \quad \mathbf{x} \in X \; ; \; \mathbf{x}(0) = x_0, \tag{3.135}$$

where $X = \mathbb{R}^d$ is the Euclidean state space of dimension d and $\Phi : X \to X$ a smooth vector field with flow S_t. The flow associates to an initial state $\mathbf{x}_0$ the solution of (3.135) at some time $t \geq 0$. An initial ensemble is then represented by the initial distribution $\rho_0 : X \to \mathbb{R}$ with

$$\rho_0(\mathbf{x}) = \frac{1}{m} \sum_{i=1}^{m} \delta(\mathbf{x} - \mathbf{x}_0^{(i)}), \tag{3.136}$$

where the $\mathbf{x}_0^{(i)}$ in X are the initial states of the members of the ensemble and δ is the Dirac distribution. The average of any smooth observable $g : X \to \mathbb{R}$, such as the sea surface temperature at some location, over the initial ensemble ρ_0 is then given by

$$\int_X \rho_0(\mathbf{x}) g(\mathbf{x}) \mathrm{d}x = \frac{1}{m} \sum_{i=1}^{m} g(\mathbf{x}_0^{(i)}), \tag{3.137}$$

where the right-hand side is the usual formula for numerical applications. Similarly, the ensemble average of g after a given time $t \geq 0$, i.e., after propagating the ensemble members by the flow $S_t : \mathbf{x}_0^{(i)} \to \mathbf{x}^{(i)}(t)$, is

$$\int_X \rho_0 g(S_t \mathbf{x}) \mathrm{d}x = \frac{1}{m} \sum_{i=1}^{m} g(\mathbf{x}^{(i)}(t)). \tag{3.138}$$

The latter can then be used to define an ensemble $\rho(x,t)$ at time t such that

$$\int_X \rho(x,t) g(\mathbf{x}) \mathrm{d}x := \int_X \rho_0 g(S_t \mathbf{x}) \mathrm{d}x, \tag{3.139}$$

which, for ρ_0 defined by (3.136), gives

$$\rho(\mathbf{x},t) = \frac{1}{m}\sum_{i=1}^{m}\delta(\mathbf{x}-\mathbf{x}^{(i)}(t)). \tag{3.140}$$

As an example, consider the dynamical system

$$\dot{\mathbf{x}} = A\mathbf{x}, \tag{3.141}$$

where A is a $n \times n$ real matrix. The solution of this system, with initial condition $\mathbf{x}(0) = \mathbf{x}_0$ is

$$\mathbf{x}(t) = e^{tA}\mathbf{x}_0 \rightarrow S_t\mathbf{x} = e^{tA}\mathbf{x}. \tag{3.142}$$

More generally, there exists, Lasota and Mackey (1994) a linear operator $\mathbf{P}_t : L^1(X) \rightarrow L^1(X)$ such that (3.139) holds with $\rho(x,t) = \mathbf{P}_t\rho_0(\mathbf{x})$, for any density ρ_0 (our initial ensemble) in $L^1(X)$ and observable g in $L^\infty(X)$ (Figure 3.25). In particular, taking g in (3.139) to be the characteristic function χ_A of some Borel set A, i.e., $\chi_A(\mathbf{x}) = 1$ if $\mathbf{x}$ is in A, 0 otherwise, one has that

$$\int_A \mathbf{P}_t\rho_0(\mathbf{x})\, dx = \int_{S_t^{-1}A} \rho_0(\mathbf{x})\, dx. \tag{3.143}$$

In other words, the density $\mathbf{P}_t\rho_0$ gives the probability to find a member $\mathbf{x}$ sampled from an initial ensemble ρ_0 in any given set A after some time t.

The family $\mathbf{P}_t, t \geq 0$ inherits from the semigroup property of the flow, i.e.,

$$\mathbf{P}_{s+t} = \mathbf{P}_t\mathbf{P}_s, \quad t \geq s \geq 0 \tag{3.144a}$$

$$\mathbf{P}_0 = I, \tag{3.144b}$$

and satisfies the Liouville equation

$$\frac{d}{dt}\mathbf{P}_t\rho_0 = -\nabla\cdot(\Phi\mathbf{P}_t\rho_0), \quad \rho_0 \in L^1(X). \tag{3.145}$$

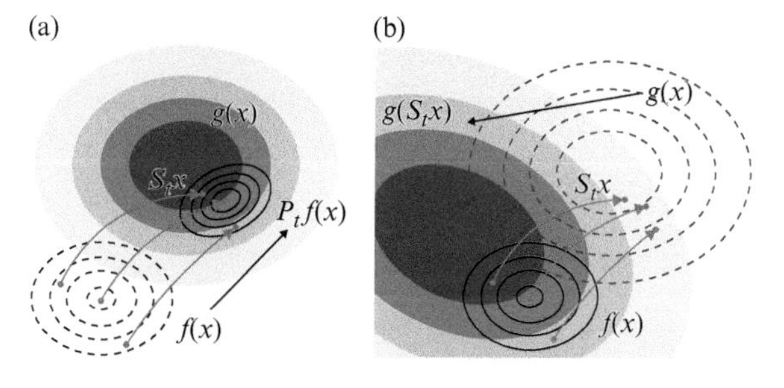

Fig. 3.25 Illustration of the definition (3.139) of the transferred density $\rho(x,t) = \mathbf{P}_t\rho_0(\mathbf{x})$. The average with respect to the initial ensemble ρ_0 of the observable g applied to the propagated states $S_t\mathbf{x}$ coincides with the average of g with respect to the transferred density $\mathbf{P}_t\rho_0(\mathbf{x})$.

This equation expresses the fact that probabilities are conserved in phase space, and thus plays the role of the continuity equation for hydrodynamic flows in physical space.

An explicit representation of the solution of the Liouville equation can be obtained by using $\mathbf{x}(t) = S_t\mathbf{x}_0$ as a formal solution to the dynamical system. Each trajectory starting at $\mathbf{x}_0 \in M$ will be transported to the region $S_t(M)$ after a time t but no trajectory is created or destroyed, hence

$$\int_{S_t(M)} d\mathbf{x}\rho(\mathbf{x},t) = \int_M d\mathbf{x}_0\rho(\mathbf{x}_0,0). \tag{3.146}$$

Switching integration variables $\mathbf{x}_0 = S_{-t}\mathbf{x}$, we can write the integral in the left-hand side as

$$\int_M d\mathbf{x}_0\rho(S_t\mathbf{x}_0,t)|\det J^t(\mathbf{x}_0)| = \int_M d\mathbf{x}_0\rho(\mathbf{x}_0,0), \tag{3.147}$$

where $J^t(\mathbf{x}_0)$ is the Jacobian of S_t. Hence, the density changes with time as the inverse of the volume occupied by the trajectories, i.e.,

$$\rho(\mathbf{x},t) = \frac{\rho(\mathbf{x}_0,0)}{|\det J^t(\mathbf{x}_0)|}. \tag{3.148}$$

This can be written more compactly using delta functions. It is well-known that in one-dimension the delta function $\delta(x)$ is defined as

$$\int_{-\infty}^{\infty} f(x)\delta(x-a)dx = f(a). \tag{3.149}$$

Suppose now that the function $g(x)$ has a simple zero at $x = x_1$ and that the derivative $g'(x_1) > 0$, then the integral (with y = g(x)),

$$\int_{-\infty}^{\infty} f(x)\delta(g(x))dx = \int_{-\infty}^{\infty} \frac{f(g^{-1}(y))}{g'(x_1)}\delta(y)dy = \frac{f(x_1)}{g'(x_1)} = \int_{-\infty}^{\infty} f(x)\frac{\delta(x-x_1)}{g'(x_1)}dx. \tag{3.150}$$

For $g'(x_1) < 0$, the sign reverses and hence we can write

$$\delta(g(x)) = \sum_{m=1}^{n} \frac{\delta(x-x_m)}{|g'(x_m)|}, \tag{3.151}$$

where the x_m are the zeroes of the function g. In multi-dimensions, this result is generalized as

$$\int dx\delta(\mathbf{g}(\mathbf{x})) = \sum_{m=1}^{n} \frac{1}{|\det J(\mathbf{x}_m)|}, \tag{3.152}$$

where J is the Jacobian of $\mathbf{g}$. Using these results, it can be written as

$$\rho(\mathbf{x},t) = \mathbf{P}_t\rho_0 = \int_M d\mathbf{x}_0\delta(\mathbf{x} - S_t(\mathbf{x}_0))\rho(\mathbf{x}_0,0), \tag{3.153}$$

which is formally often written as (with L being the Liouville operator)

$$\rho(t) = e^{tL}\rho_0. \tag{3.154}$$

This results also gives an explicit expression for the Perron–Frobenius operator as

$$\mathbf{P}_t(\mathbf{y},\mathbf{x}) = \delta(\mathbf{y} - S_t(\mathbf{x})), \tag{3.155}$$

and hence it assembles the density at time t by going back in time to the density ρ_0 at time $t = 0$.

A key concept in ergodic theory is that of an invariant measure for the non-singular flow S_t, that is, a probability measure μ such that $\mu(S_t^{-1}A) = \mu(A)$, for any Borel set A. In other words, a measure is invariant if the probability of a state to be in some set does not change as this state is propagated by the flow. It follows then that the average $\bar{g}$ with respect to the invariant measure μ of any integrable observable g is also invariant with time, i.e.,

$$\int_X g(S_t\mathbf{x})\mu(\mathrm{d}x) = \int_X g(\mathbf{x})\mu(\mathrm{d}x). \tag{3.156}$$

A flow S_t with an invariant measure μ has interesting statistical properties when μ is ergodic, that is, when the sets A which are invariant, i.e., $S_t^{-1}A = A$, are either of measure 0 or 1. Then, by the celebrated individual ergodic theorem of Birkhoff, the average of any integrable observable g is such that

$$\int_X g(\mathbf{x})\mu(\mathrm{d}x) = \lim_{T\to\infty} \frac{1}{T}\int_0^T g(S_t\mathbf{x})dt, \quad \text{for almost every } \mathbf{x}, \tag{3.157}$$

where the right-hand side is none other than the infinitely long version of the time mean used in numerical applications, for which the ergodic theorem is in fact implicitly invoked. When μ is ergodic, the time mean thus depends on the initial state $\mathbf{x}$ only for a set of measure 0.

Unfortunately, there may exist many ergodic measures. For example, multi-stable dissipative systems, i.e., with more than one attractor, such as climate models with both a warm and a snow-ball steady state, may have several ergodic measures supported by different attractors. In this case, the equality (3.157) between ensemble averages and time averages only holds for initial states belonging to the attractor supporting the measure. On the other hand, time averages for two initial conditions in different basins of attractions would not coincide in general. This leads to the definition of a physical measure for which the equality (3.157) between ensemble averages and time averages holds almost everywhere with respect to the Lebesgue measure dx. When several physical measures exist, as may be the case when several attractors coexist, one may choose to restrict the phase space to the basin of attraction of only one of the attractors, e.g., by discarding all initial data converging to the snow-ball attractor, in the case of multi-stable climate models. Let us then assume for convenience that μ is the unique physical measure of the flow S_t and denotes the time mean of g in the right-hand side of (3.157) by $\bar{g}$.

In climate studies, one is not only interested in the mean but also in the variability of observables. This can be done by looking at the correlation function $C_{f,g}$ between two observables f and g, defined as

$$C_{f,g}(t) = \int_X f(\mathbf{x})g(S_t\mathbf{x})\mu(\mathrm{d}x) - \int_X g(\mathbf{x})\mu(\mathrm{d}x)\int_X f(\mathbf{x})\mu(\mathrm{d}x). \tag{3.158}$$

For the physical measure μ, the correlation function can be evaluated as the cross-correlation function

$$\hat{C}_{f,g}(t) = \lim_{T\to\infty}\frac{1}{T}\int_0^T (f(S_s\mathbf{x}) - \bar{f})(g(S_{t+s}\mathbf{x}) - \bar{g})\,\mathrm{d}s, \tag{3.159}$$

which is much used in practice, Von Storch and Zwiers (1999). Furthermore, in the definition of the correlation function, only information about the dynamics on the support of the measure μ is required. In particular, one says that the invariant measure μ is mixing for the flow S_t if the correlation function $C_{f,g}(t)$ converges to zero with time for any pair of observables f and g in $L^2_\mu(X)$.

A family of transfer operators $\mathcal{L}_t, t \geq 0$ can be defined on $L^2_\mu(X)$ such that it satisfies the duality relation

$$\int_X \mathcal{L}_t f(\mathbf{x})g(\mathbf{x})\mu(\mathrm{d}x) = \int_X f(\mathbf{x})g(S_t\mathbf{x})\mu(\mathrm{d}x), \qquad t\geq 0, \quad f,g\in L^2_\mu(X) \tag{3.160}$$

$$= C_{f,g}(t) \qquad \text{when } \mu(f) = \mu(g) = 0. \tag{3.161}$$

Note that, compared to the semigroup $\mathcal{P}_t, t \geq 0$ defined by (3.139) with respect to the Lebesgue measure $\mathrm{d}x$, the semigroup of transfer operators $\mathcal{L}_t, t\geq 0$ is defined with respect to μ. As will become clear, this comes as a restriction of the method presented here. In particular, when μ is supported by an attractor, no information on the dynamics away from the attractor is carried by $\mathcal{L}_t$. On the other hand, when μ has a density $\rho_\infty(\mathbf{x}, t)$ with respect to the Lebesgue measure, then both semigroups are related by

$$\rho_\infty \mathbf{L}_t f = \mathbf{P}_t(\rho_\infty f). \tag{3.162}$$

Particularly important are the eigenfunctions of the transfer operators $\mathcal{L}_t$ and their adjoints, the Koopman operators $\mathcal{U}_t : g \to g\circ S_t$. A function ψ_k is an eigenfunction of $\mathbf{L}_t$ if

$$\mathbf{L}_t\psi_k = \zeta_k(t)\psi_k, \tag{3.163}$$

where the complex number $\zeta_k(t)$ is the associated eigenvalue. To each ψ_k corresponds an eigenfunction ψ_k^* of $\mathbf{U}_t$ associated with the complex conjugate of the eigenvalue $\zeta_k(t)$ and such that

$$\int_X \psi_k\psi_l^*\mu(\mathrm{d}x) = \delta_{kl}. \tag{3.164}$$

It follows from the semigroup property that the eigenfunctions ψ_k^* and ψ_k are independent of time. Moreover, under sufficient continuity conditions for the spectral mapping theorem to hold, Engel and Nagel (2001), the eigenvalues $\zeta_k(t)$ of the semigroup $\mathcal{L}_t, t \geq 0$ are also related to the eigenvalues λ_k of its infinitesimal generator $\mathbf{K}$ (right-hand side of the backward–Kolmogorov equation) by (for all k)

$$\zeta_k(t) = \mathrm{e}^{\lambda_k t}, \quad t \geq 0 \tag{3.165}$$

and $\mathrm{Re}(\lambda_k) \leq 0$, since $|\zeta_k(t)| \leq 1$. In particular, one can see from (3.156) that the invariance of μ implies that constant functions on the support of μ are eigenvectors of $\mathbf{L}_t$ and $\mathbf{U}_t$ associated with the eigenvalue 1.

The mixing spectrum, denoting the set eigenvalues λ_k and eigenvectors ψ_k and ψ_k^* of the generator and its adjoint, provides deep insight into the statistical properties of the trajectories of the dynamical system. In particular, when the eigenvectors form a bi-orthonormal family, i.e., when the eigenvalues are all semi-simple, the correlation function $C_{f,g}$ can be decomposed as

$$C_{f,g}(t) = \sum_{k=2}^{\infty} w_k(f,g) e^{\lambda_k t} \tag{3.166a}$$

$$w_k(f,g) = \left(\int f \psi_k^* d\mu \right) \left(\int \psi_k g d\mu \right), \tag{3.166b}$$

so that mixing eigenvalues close to the imaginary axis are responsible for a slow decay of correlations, at a rate given by the real part $-\mathrm{Re}(\lambda_k)$ and with oscillations at an angular frequency given by the imaginary part $\mathrm{Im}(\lambda_k)$.

In addition, the correlation spectrum, given by the Fourier transform of the correlation function, decomposes as

$$\mathbf{S}_{f,g}(\omega) = -\frac{1}{\pi} \sum_{k=2}^{\infty} w_k(f,g) \frac{\mathrm{Re}(\lambda_k)}{(\omega - \mathrm{Im}(\lambda_k))^2 + (\mathrm{Re}(\lambda_k))^2}. \tag{3.167}$$

The largest peaks in the spectrum are thus related to the subset of eigenvalues λ_k closest to the imaginary axis. The position of each peak is located at $\omega = \mathrm{Im}(\lambda_k)$ and the half width of the amplitude is given by $-\mathrm{Re}(\lambda_k)$.

3.6.4 Examples of mixing spectra

Fixed point

Consider first the deterministic dynamical system (3.135), having a fixed point $\mathbf{x}_s$; the $d \times d$ Jacobian matrix at $\mathbf{x} = \mathbf{x}_s$ is indicated by J. The eigenvalues $\xi_1, \ldots, \xi_d$ determining the linear stability of $\mathbf{x}_s$ are the roots of

$$\det(J - \xi I) = 0. \tag{3.168}$$

In case the steady state is not a bifurcation point, these roots fall in two sets: d_s eigenvalues with $\mathrm{Re}(\xi_i) < 0$ and d_u other eigenvalues with $\mathrm{Re}(\xi_i) > 0$.

From (3.154), we deduce that

$$Tr\ e^{Lt} = \sum_l m_l e^{\lambda_l t}, \tag{3.169}$$

where Tr indicates the trace and m_l is the algebraic multiplicity of the eigenvalue λ_l of L. By taking the Laplace transform, we find that

$$\int_0^\infty Tr\ e^{Lt} e^{-st} dt = Tr\ \frac{1}{s-L} = \sum_l \frac{m_l}{s-\lambda_l}, \tag{3.170}$$

and hence, the eigenvalues are determined from the poles of this trace function.

It can be shown (through quite a long derivation Gaspard (2002) that for a fixed point

$$Tr\ e^{Lt} = \frac{1}{|\det(I - e^{Jt})|} = \prod_{i=1}^{d} \frac{1}{|1 - e^{\xi_i t}|}, \tag{3.171}$$

which can be used to evaluate the eigenvalues λ_l in terms of the ξ_i. Assume that all eigenvalues are simple ($m_l = 1$), then we can write (3.171) as

$$\prod_{i=1}^{d} \frac{1}{|1 - e^{\xi_i t}|} = \prod_{i=1}^{d_s} \frac{1}{|1 - e^{\xi_i t}|} \prod_{i=d_s+1}^{d} \frac{e^{-\xi_j t}}{|1 - e^{-\xi_i t}|}. \tag{3.172}$$

Next, using $1/(1-x) = \sum_k x^k$ in both products we find

$$Tr\ e^{Lt} = \sum_{l,m=0}^{\infty} exp \left[\sum_{Re(\xi_i<0)} (m_i + 1) l_i \xi_i t - \sum_{Re(\xi_j>0)} (m_j + 1) \xi_j t \right], \tag{3.173}$$

which provides the eigenvalues λ as

$$\lambda_{l,m} = \sum_{Re(\xi_i<0)} l_i \xi_i - \sum_{Re(\xi_j>0)} (m_j + 1) \xi_j \tag{3.174}$$

for $l_i, m_j = 0, 1, 2, 3, \ldots$. If the stationary state is unstable, then the leading eigenvalue is given by $\lambda_{0,0} = -\sum_{Re(\xi_j>0)} \xi_j < 0$. It follows that the closer the mixing eigenvalues $\lambda_{l,m}$ to the imaginary axis, the closer the stationary point to a loss of hyperbolicity.

Deterministic Hopf bifurcation

The reduced dynamics close to a Hopf bifurcation is captured by the following normal form, Guckenheimer and Holmes (1990); Arnold (2012), in polar coordinates (r, θ):

$$\dot{r} = \delta r - r^3 \tag{3.175a}$$
$$\dot{\theta} = \gamma - \beta r^2, \tag{3.175b}$$

which is slightly more general than that used in the previous section, by including the term with β. The parameter δ associated with the Hopf bifurcation controls the stability of the fixed point x_* (for $\delta < 0$) or of the limit cycle Γ (for $\delta > 0$). The parameter γ controls the period of the oscillations, while β regulates their dependence on the radius. Such a dependence may for example arise in systems conserving angular momentum, Arnold (2012). As a result, the limit cycle Γ has a period $T = 2\pi/\omega_f$ where ω_f is the angular frequency $\omega_f = \gamma - \beta\delta$. That is, denoting by $(S_t)_{t\in\mathbb{R}}$ the deterministic flow generated by (3.175), one has that $S_T p = p$ for any point p on the limit cycle Γ. The parameter β in Equation (3.175) will be referred to as the *twist factor*.

The mixing eigenvalues of system (3.175) have been calculated analytically using trace formulas in Gaspard and Tasaki (2001), using the same methodology as in the previous section. Below the bifurcation point, i.e., for δ smaller than its critical value $\delta_c = 0$, the mixing eigenvalues $\lambda_k, k \geq 0$ are given by integer linear combinations of the complex pair of eigenvalues $\lambda^{\pm} = \delta \pm i\gamma$ of the tangent map of the vector field at the fixed point. As a result, the mixing eigenvalues are organized in a triangular array of eigenvalues, (Gaspard and Tasaki, 2001, Equation (43))

$$\lambda_{ln} = (l+n)\delta + i(n-l)\gamma, \quad l, n \in \mathbb{N}. \tag{3.176}$$

Above the bifurcation point, i.e., for $\delta > \delta_c$, the mixing eigenvalues are composed of two families of eigenvalues associated with the limit cycle and the unstable fixed point respectively. The family associated with the limit cycle is organized in an array of equally spaced eigenvalues (Gaspard and Tasaki, 2001, Equation (44))

$$\lambda_{ln} = -2l\delta + in(\gamma - \beta\delta), \quad l \in \mathbb{N}, n \in \mathbb{Z}. \tag{3.177}$$

The spectrum given by (3.177) contain pure imaginary eigenvalues λ_{0n}, n in $\mathbb{Z}$, showing in particular that the deterministic system (3.175) is not mixing. This can be intuitively understood by the neutral dynamics along Γ, i.e., the dynamics are neither contracting nor expanding. Indeed, due to those dynamics, a density with support contained in Γ is simply rotated without mixing along Γ. On the other hand, there is also a family of eigenvalues (Gaspard and Tasaki, 2001, Equation (44)) forming a triangular array

$$\lambda_{ln} = -(l+n+2)\delta - i(l-n)\gamma, \quad l, n \in \mathbb{N}, \tag{3.178}$$

associated with the unstable fixed point. All these eigenvalues are located to the left of the imaginary axis, in agreement with the fact that the unstable fixed point is a repeller. To this repeller can then be associated an escape rate of densities given by the real part $|\Re(\lambda_{00})| = 2\delta$ of the leading eigenvalue. Finally, exactly at the critical value δ_c, the spectrum is continuous, resulting in an algebraic decay of correlations, at a rate $t^{-1/2}$ (Gaspard and Tasaki (2001), Equation (82)), known as *critical slowing down*.

The stochastic Hopf bifurcation

As a minimal model of nonlinear oscillator perturbed by noise, we analyze the Hopf normal form (3.175) subject to white noise disturbances added to its Cartesian coordinates, as in Deville *et al.* (2011). This stochastic process is thus governed by the SDE

$$\begin{aligned} \mathrm{d}x &= \underbrace{\left[(\delta-(x^2+y^2))x-(\gamma-\beta(x^2+y^2))y\right]}_{F_x(x,y)}\mathrm{d}t+\epsilon\,\mathrm{d}W_x, \\ \mathrm{d}y &= \underbrace{\left[(\gamma-\beta(x^2+y^2))x+(\delta-(x^2+y^2))y\right]}_{F_y(x,y)}\mathrm{d}t+\epsilon\,\mathrm{d}W_y, \end{aligned} \tag{3.179}$$

where W_x and W_y are two independent Wiener processes with differentials interpreted in the Itô sense, Gardiner (2009); Pavliotis (2014) and ϵ is a parameter controlling the level of noise. In the following, Equation (3.179) will be referred to as the *Stochastic Hopf Equation (SHE)* in Cartesian coordinates. The BKE corresponding to (3.179) is then given by

$$\partial_t u = F_x\partial_x u + F_y\partial_y u + \frac{\epsilon^2}{2}\partial^2_{xx}u + \frac{\epsilon^2}{2}\partial^2_{yy}u. \tag{3.180}$$

For $\delta > 0$, deterministic solutions converge (i.e., when $\epsilon = 0$) to the limit cycle Γ with radius $r_* = \sqrt{\delta}$ so that it will be more convenient to work in polar coordinates (r,θ) with $x = r\cos\theta$ and $y = r\sin\theta$. Applying Itô's formula, Gardiner (2009); Pavliotis (2014) allows one to transform the equations to polar coordinates, as follows:

$$dr = (\delta r - r^3 + \frac{\epsilon^2}{2r})dt + \epsilon\,\mathrm{d}W_r \tag{3.181}$$

$$d\theta = (\gamma - \beta r^2)\,\mathrm{d}t + \frac{\epsilon}{r}dW_\theta, \tag{3.182}$$

where W_r and W_θ are two Wiener processes satisfying the SDE system

$$\mathrm{d}W_r = \cos\theta\,\mathrm{d}W_x + \sin\theta\,\mathrm{d}W_y, \tag{3.183a}$$

$$\mathrm{d}W_\theta = -\sin\theta\,\mathrm{d}W_x + \cos\theta\,\mathrm{d}W_y. \tag{3.183b}$$

The BKE in polar coordinates corresponding to the SDE (3.182) has a diffusion matrix

$$D = \epsilon^2\begin{pmatrix}1 & 0\\ 0 & 1/r^2\end{pmatrix},$$

and is thus given by

$$\partial_t u = \left(\delta r - r^3 + \tfrac{\epsilon^2}{2r}\right)\partial_r u + (\gamma - \beta r^2)\partial_\theta u + \tfrac{\epsilon^2}{2}\partial^2_{rr}u + \tfrac{\epsilon^2}{2r^2}\partial^2_{\theta\theta}u \tag{3.184}$$

$$= \mathcal{K}u. \tag{3.185}$$

One can see that the nonlinear drift term $\gamma - \beta r^2$ in the θ-direction hinders the separation of the BKE (3.185) in r and θ.

To learn more about the mixing spectrum of the SHE (3.179) for $\delta \approx \delta_c$, we proceed to a numerical approximation of the generator $\mathcal{K}$ associated with the BKE (3.180). This numerical problem is tractable without any preliminary reduction and is presented in Chekroun *et al.* (2016), since the state space here is only two-dimensional. For this relatively simple numerical problem, the standard finite-difference scheme proposed by Chang and Cooper (1970) is chosen for the adjoint $\mathcal{K}^*$ in the Fokker–Planck equation, since it satisfies the conservation of probabilities and of positivity and is straightforward to implement. The numerical approximation of $\mathcal{K}$ is then simply given by the transpose of that of $\mathcal{K}^*$. Here, we impose no-flux boundary conditions for convenience (instead of vanishing at infinity), but with a sufficiently large domain to avoid boundary effects. The square $[-5\hat{\sigma}, 5\hat{\sigma}]^2$ is discretized into 200-by-200 boxes, where $\hat{\sigma}$ is an approximation of the standard deviation of the x and y coordinates. The spectrum of the finite-difference approximation of the generator $\mathcal{K}$ is then calculated numerically using the implicitly restarted Arnoldi iterative algorithm implemented in ARPACK Lehoucq *et al.* (1997). The domain and resolution of the grid have been chosen for the approximation of at least the second eigenvalue to converge.

Different experiments for varying δ, β, and ϵ will be analyzed, while γ is kept fixed to 1. We start by analyzing the numerical results for a fixed value of the noise level $\epsilon = 1$ and a vanishing twist factor $\beta = 0$, but different values of the control parameter δ. In Figure 3.26, the leading eigenvalues of the finite-difference approximation of the generator $\mathcal{K}$ are represented as black dots on the left panels for (a) $\delta = -5$, (c) $\delta = 0$, (e) $\delta = 3$, and (g) $\delta = 7$. In addition, the small noise predictions, for the mixing eigenvalues of the stable fixed point, are also represented as black crosses (see Tantet *et al.* (2015), but not discussed here) in panel Figure 3.26a. In Figure 3.26g small noise predictions for the eigenvalues of the unstable fixed point and of the limit cycle are also represented, Tantet *et al.* (2015) as blue crosses and black pluses, respectively. On the same panels, to the right, the power spectra between the three monomials x, x^2, and x^3 of the $x = r\cos\theta$ coordinate are also represented as blue, green, and red lines, respectively. These power spectra were calculated from the numerical approximations of the eigenvalues, eigenfunctions, and adjoint eigenfunctions (i.e., the eigenvectors of the transpose of the finite-difference approximation of $\mathcal{K}$). Finally, on the right panels, the corresponding eigenvector associated with the second eigenvalue with positive imaginary part are represented

For a small value of δ, panel (a) of Figure 3.25, a triangular structure of eigenvalues is found and, because of the large gap between the eigenvalues and the imaginary axis, the power spectra are broad, with no distinct resonance. As the control parameter δ is increased (from panel (a) to (c) in Figure 3.26) the eigenvalues get closer to the imaginary axis, as expected from the weaker stability of the limit cycle. One can also see from the larger gaps between the contour lines in Figure 3.26d compared to those of Figure 3.26b that the amplitude of the second eigenvector flattens. As δ is further increased (panels (c–d) to (g–h) of Figure 3.26) and the bifurcation point is crossed, a rather smooth transition from the small-noise expansions for $\delta > \delta_c$ and then $\delta < \delta_c$ occurs, in which the first line of eigenvalues gets closer and closer to the imaginary axis. As a result, strong resonant behavior occurs for all three observables, as can

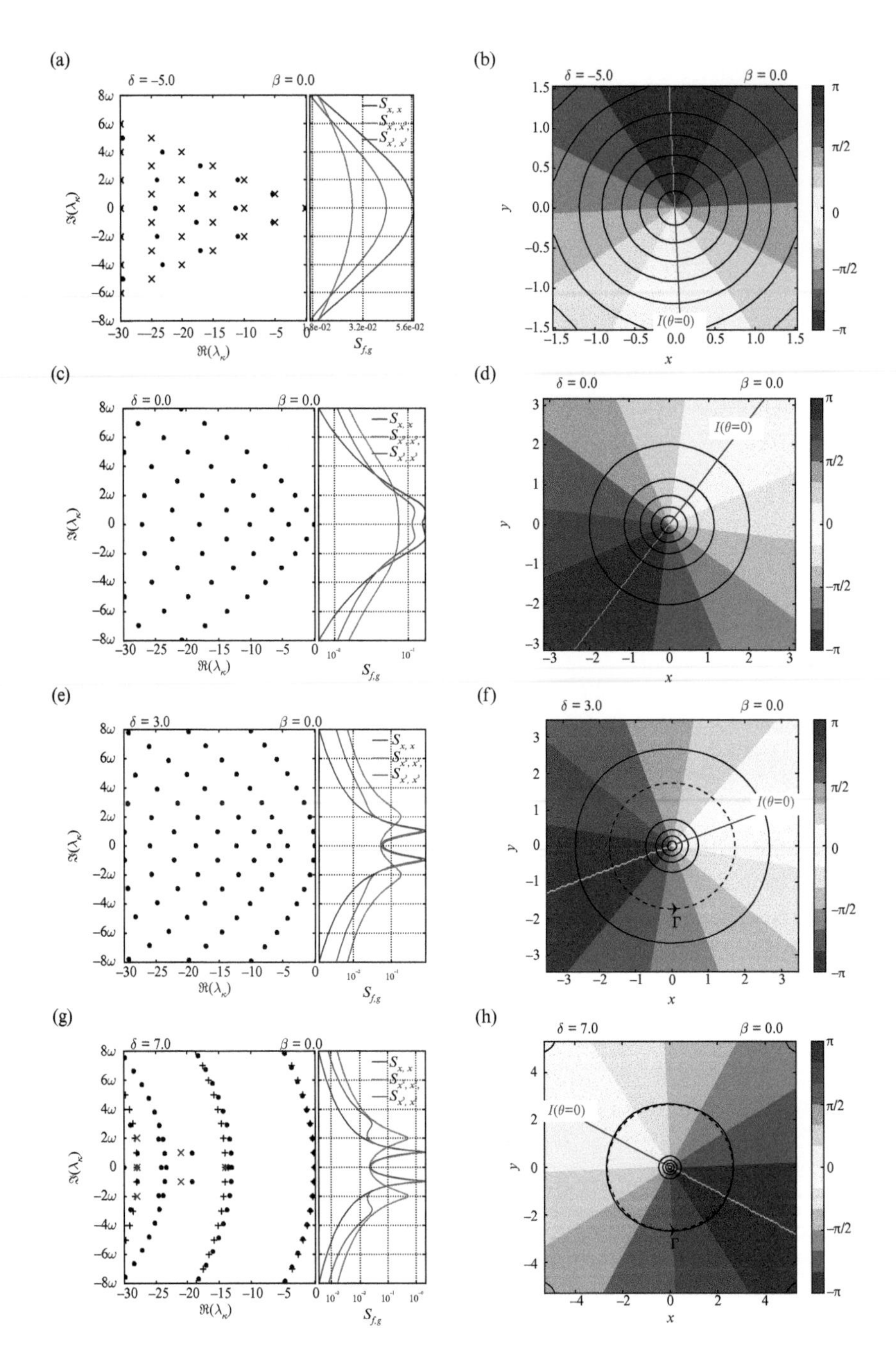

Fig. 3.26 Left: Numerical approximation of the leading eigenvalues (black dots) of the generator $\mathcal{K}$ for (a) $\delta = -5$, (c) $\delta = 0$, (e) $\delta = 3$, and (g) $\delta = 7$. In addition, the small noise prediction for the mixing eigenvalues of the stable fixed point, is also represented as black crosses in panel (a). In (g), the small noise predictions for the eigenvalues of the unstable fixed point and of the limit cycle are also represented as blue crosses and black pluses, respectively. On the same panels, to the right, the power spectra between the three monomials x, x^2, and x^3 of the x coordinate are also represented as blue, green and red lines, respectively (end of caption on next page). Right: Eigenvector associated with the second eigenvalue with positive imaginary part. The phase of the eigenvector is represented by filled contours and its amplitude by contour lines.

be seen from the sharpening of the spectral peaks at the position of the first three harmonics. The peaks remain finite, however, since a spectral gap persists between the eigenvalues and the imaginary axis, due to the noise. Finally, for $\delta = 7$ in panel Figure 3.26, one finds the superposition of a family of parabolas and of a triangular family of eigenvalues.

The spectrum remains discrete during the transition, as opposed to the deterministic case (c.f., Gaspard and Tasaki (2001)). On the other hand, precisely how the transition occurs could not be calculated analytically from the geometric properties of the deterministic flow. In particular, eigenvalues farther away from the real axis tend to approach the imaginary axis at a faster rate than the others, resulting in a curving of the triangle array of eigenvalues, while the second eigenvector continues to flatten away from the origin. Eventually (from panel Figure 3.26e to Figure 3.26g), parabolas of eigenvalues detach one after the other, while other eigenvalues persist as a triangular family.

3.6.5 Reduction methods

The barotropic model in Section 3.6.2 has too large a dimension to solve the eigenvalue problem for the generator $\mathbf{K}$ or to apply trace methods. In order to get information on the mixing spectrum for high-dimensional systems, projections of the transfer operators on a reduced space Y (a subset of the phase space X) will be approximated from time series. The present study relies on a 500,000-day-long simulation using an integration time-step of 30 minutes, with daily output and a spin-up of 5000 days removed.

After defining an observation operator $h: Y \to X$, Ulam's method is applied which relies on a Galerkin approximation of the infinite-dimensional transfer operators by finite-dimensional transition matrices, Ulam (1964); Froyland (1998); Dellnitz and Junge (1999). For this purpose, the reduced space is discretized into a family $G = \{B_i\}_{1 \le i \le m_b}$ of m_b grid boxes corresponding to the orthogonal basis $\{\chi_{B_1}, \ldots, \chi_{B_{m_b}}\}$ of characteristic functions. The transfer operator $\mathcal{L}_\tau$ is then approximated by a time-homogenous Markov chain with transition matrix P_τ, whose elements are the transition probabilities

$$(P_\tau)_{ij} = \mathbb{P}(h(\mathbf{x}_{t+\tau}) \in B_j | h(\mathbf{x}_t) \in B_i). \tag{3.186}$$

These probabilities can be estimated from a long time-series $\{\mathbf{x}_t\}_{1 \le t \le N}$ of $\mathbf{x}$ using the Maximum Likelihood Estimator,

$$(\hat{P}_\tau)_{ij} = \hat{\mathbb{P}}(h\mathbf{x}_{t+\tau}) \in B_j | h(\mathbf{x}_t) \in B_i) = \frac{\#\{(h(\mathbf{x}_t) \in B_i) \wedge (h(\mathbf{x}_{t+\tau}) \in B_j)\}}{\#\{h(\mathbf{x}_t) \in B_i\}}, \tag{3.187}$$

where $\#\{(h(\mathbf{x}_t) \in B_i) \wedge (h(\mathbf{x}_{t+\tau}) \in B_j)\}$ is the number of observations $h(\mathbf{x})$ in box B_i such that the observation $h(\mathbf{x}_{t+\tau})$ (a time τ later) is in box B_j, and $\#\{h(\mathbf{x}_t) \in B_i\}$ is the total number of observations $h(\mathbf{x})$ in B_i.

From the eigenvalues $\hat{\zeta}_k(\tau)$ of the matrix $\hat{P}_\tau$, for a chosen delay time τ, eventually the $\hat{\lambda}_k$ are determined through

$$\hat{\lambda}_k = \frac{1}{\tau} \ln \hat{\zeta}_k(\tau). \tag{3.188}$$

There are all kind of technical issues in this approximation of the transfer operator and the ergodicity eigenvalues. One important issue is that the semigroup property of $\mathbf{L}_t$ may no longer hold in the reduced space because memory enters the reduced system due to projection into the low-dimensional subspace. If the projection does not introduce any non-Markovian effects, the family of reduced transfer operators should inherit from the semigroup property and the $\hat{\lambda}_k$ should be constant. If this is not the case, however, one can choose the lag τ in a range in which at least the leading eigenvalues $\hat{\lambda}_k$ vary as little as possible, so that the latter behave as Markovian. Another issue is the choice of the delay time τ. Apart from this, the reduced subspace should be quite small as otherwise the computation of the transition probabilities becomes intractable. Hence, in each application, the robustness of the mixing spectrum has to be addressed carefully, Tantet *et al.* (2015).

3.6.6 Spectral properties and slow dynamics

In order to approximate the mixing spectrum, as filtered by the observable h, we solve for each estimated transition matrix in $\{\hat{P}_\tau\}$, the eigenvalue problem

$$\hat{P}_\tau \vec{e}_i(\tau) = \lambda_i(\tau)\vec{e}_i(\tau) \quad \text{for } i \in \{1, ..., m\}, \tag{3.189}$$

where $\vec{e}_i(\tau)$ is the eigenvector associated with the ith eigenvalue $\lambda_i(\tau)$ of $\hat{P}_\tau$. The spectrum of $\hat{P}_\tau$ changes with the lag τ. However, if $\{\hat{P}_\tau\}_{\tau \geq 0}$ was a semigroup with generator $\mathcal{K}_m$, the spectrum $\{\alpha_i\}_{i \in \{1,...,m\}}$ of $\mathcal{K}_m$ would not depend on τ and applying the SMT would give

$$r_i = -Re(\alpha_i) = -\frac{1}{\tau} \log|\lambda_i(\tau)| \quad \forall \tau \geq 0, \text{ and for } i \in \{1, ..., m\}, \tag{3.190}$$

where r_i corresponds to the rate at which the autocorrelation of the eigenvector associated with λ_i would decay if $\{\hat{P}_\tau\}_{\tau \geq 0}$ would be the semigroup of transfer operators.

As noted previously, the transition matrices $\{\hat{P}_\tau\}_{\tau \geq 0}$ do not necessarily inherit from the semigroup property of the transfer operators $\{\mathcal{L}_\tau\}_{\tau \geq 0}$. Thus, no generator may exist for $\{\hat{P}_\tau\}_{\tau \geq 0}$ and the rates r_i in (3.190) may depend on the lag τ. However, calculating the rates $r_i(\tau)$ for each lag allows (i) to give an approximation of the dominant RP resonances with a control on the lag and (ii) to test the semigroup property.

For this purpose, we calculated the rates $r_i(\tau)$ by solving the eigenvalue problem (3.189) and applying (3.190) for τ in $\{1, ..., 39\}$ (days). The leading rate equals 0, since it is associated to the unit-eigenvalue. The rates corresponding to the 10 leading eigenvalues different from unity of each $\hat{P}_\tau$ are represented Figure 3.27 with the lag τ as abscissa and the (cyclic) coloring distinguishing the rank of the rate. A complex pair of conjugate eigenvalues is represented by one square for the two conjugates. The

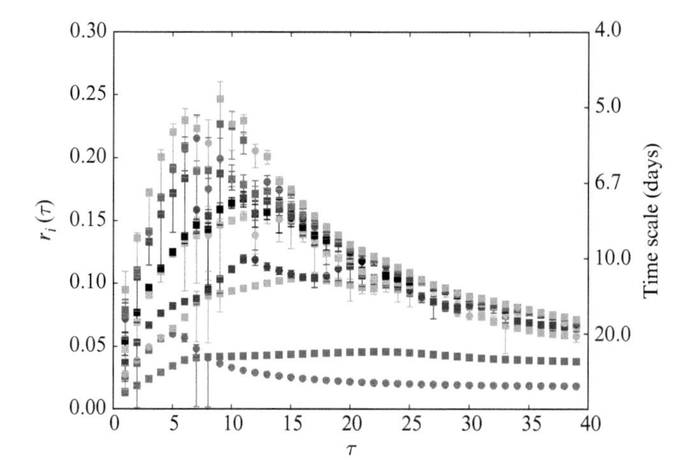

Fig. 3.27 Rates $r_i(\tau)$ corresponding to the 10 leading eigenvalues different from unity of each $\hat{P}_\tau$, with the lag τ as abscissa and the (cyclic) coloring giving the rank of the rate. A complex pair of eigenvalues is represented by one square for the two conjugates.

error bars represent 99% confidence intervals estimated from a thousand surrogate transition matrices by applying the bootstrap method.

There is a small width in the confidence intervals (some are even hidden by the marker size). These intervals evaluate the robustness of the estimates to the limited length of the time series. The largest intervals occur when two rates almost overlap, so that one of them may appear or disappear in the surrogates, resulting in a change of rank for all higher-rank rates. Here, large confidence intervals are thus usually indicative of an uncertainty in the existence of two close but distinct rates or of only one (as for the leading rates at $\tau = 7$ or 8, for example). The two rates closest to zero, the leading rates in red and green, are well separated from the rest of the spectrum after a lag of between 5 and 10 days. One of these rates derives from a real eigenvalue (the circle), the other represents a pair of complex conjugate eigenvalues (the square); they exchange rank at a lag of 8 days. We can calculate an indicative time scale associated with each rate as the inverse of the rate. Whether this time scale corresponds to a good approximation of a decorrelation time is not the matter of this study. For a lag of 15 days, the first rate (in green) and the second rate (in red) correspond to a time scale of 40 and 23 days, respectively. Furthermore, the second rate is separated from the third (in cyan) by a gap of 13 days. This time-scale separation suggests that the reduced dynamics are slowly mixing due to the presence of meta-stable regimes responsible for low-frequency variability, Dellnitz and Junge (1997); Froyland and Dellnitz (2003); Chekroun (2014). This confirms the work on meta-stable atmospheric regimes in this model by Crommelin (2003).

An important feature is the relative constance of the two leading rates for lags larger than 8 days. We can say that the slow dynamics associated with these rates "behave as Markovian," by which we mean that looking only at these rates, one cannot disprove the semigroup property, even though the dependence on the lag of the other rates is clearly indicative that $\{\hat{P}_\tau\}_{\tau\geq 0}$ cannot constitute a semigroup. Thus, the two leading rates do not seem to be affected by memory effects due to the partial observation of the system or by estimate errors, since one would not expect them to be constant otherwise. From the separation of the two leading rates from the other rates, as well as their relative independence on the lag τ for lags larger than 8 days, we expect 8 days to be the minimum lag for which the transition matrix $\hat{P}_{\tau=8}$ is likely to resolve the dynamics associated with the meta-stable regimes and to satisfy, to a good approximation, the semigroup property. Such strategy for the choice of the lag is similar to the one of DelSole (2000) and Berner (2005), who look directly at the decorrelation rate of their time series to infer for which lag they should estimate the drift and diffusion coefficients of the Fokker–Planck equation they want to approximate. However, considering the decorrelation rate alone would correspond to looking only at the first rate different from zero of the Markov operators, leaving behind the information conveyed by the secondary rates.

3.6.7 Meta-stable regimes as almost-invariant sets of the transfer operator

We have seen in the previous section, the two leading rates of Figure 3.27 are close to zero and that a large spectral gap separates them from the rest of the rates, a configuration indicative of the presence of meta-stable regimes. This characteristic of meta-stability or persistence allows to formally define these regimes as almost-invariant sets, Dellnitz and Junge (1997); Froyland and Dellnitz (2003). We now give an extension of the definition of almost-invariant sets to sets in the reduced phase space and present an algorithm to detect them from the estimation of the Markov operator $\mathcal{M}_\tau$.

A set A of the phase space X is almost invariant if $S_\tau^{-1}(A) \approx A$, which implies, for the invariant measure μ, that

$$\mathfrak{p}(A,A) = \frac{\mu(A \cap S_\tau^{-1}(A))}{\mu(A)} \approx 1. \tag{3.191}$$

Reformulating, the probability for a trajectory starting in a set A to leave this set after a lag τ is almost zero. These sets are thus associated with persistent or meta-stable regimes.

In the case of almost-invariant sets in the reduced phase space, we are interested in sets E of Y-, almost-invariant with respect to the transition probabilities of the Markov process defined by $\mathcal{M}_\tau$, such that

$$\mathbb{P}(y_{t+\tau} \in E | y_t \in E) \approx 1. \tag{3.192}$$

Furthermore, using Theorem A in Chekroun (2014), we have that

$$\mathbb{P}(y_{t+\tau} \in E | y_t \in E) = \mathfrak{p}(h^{-1}(E), h^{-1}(E)), \tag{3.193}$$

so that

$$\mathbb{P}(y_{t+\tau} \in E | y_t \in E) \approx 1 \quad \Longleftrightarrow \quad \mathfrak{p}(h^{-1}(E), h^{-1}(E)) \approx 1. \tag{3.194}$$

This important result states that if a set E is almost-invariant in the reduced space Y, its pre-image $h^{-1}(E)$ in X is almost-invariant to the flow S_τ. In other words, almost-invariant sets in the reduced phase space are images of almost-invariant, yet coarser, sets in the full phase space. Of course, these coarse-grained almost-invariant sets may not be optimal, in the sense that other, more strongly almost-invariant sets (see (3.192)) may exist but are filtered out by the observable h in the same way RP resonances can be filtered out by h.

Based on these considerations, the transition matrix $\hat{P}_{\tau=8}$ was used to define the meta-stable regimes objectively. For the detection of almost-invariant sets (see also, Dellnitz and Junge, 1997; Froyland and Dellnitz, 2003; Froyland and Padberg, 2009) we use an optimal Markov chain reduction, Deng *et al.* (2011); Rosvall and Bergstrom (2008) with respect to the relative entropy rate, Cover and Thomas (1991). This type of Markov chain reduction is particularly well suited for the detection of almost-invariant sets of large measure (recurrent), since it attempts to minimize the distance between a density transferred by the reduced Markov operator (giving the transition probabilities between the almost-invariants) and the same density transferred by the original Markov operator. The optimization was implemented using a greedy algorithm from network theory, Clauset *et al.* (2004).

Two invariant sets are plotted in Figure 3.28, such that all grid boxes in green belong to the first almost-invariant set and all grid boxes in blue belong to the second one. For the family of almost-invariant sets $\{E_\beta\}_{1 \le \beta \le p=2}$, the 2-by-2 reduced transition matrix $\hat{Q}_{\tau=8,p=2}$, such that $(\hat{Q}_{\tau=8,p=2})_{\beta\gamma} = \hat{\mathbb{P}}(y_{t+\tau} \in E_\gamma | y_t \in E_\beta)$, and its stationary density $\eta_{p=2}$, such that $(\eta_{p=2})_\beta = \hat{m}(E_\beta)$, are found to be

$$\hat{Q}_{\tau=8,p=2} = \begin{pmatrix} 0.79 & 0.21 \\ 0.14 & 0.86 \end{pmatrix} \quad \eta_{p=2} = \begin{pmatrix} 0.27 \\ 0.73 \end{pmatrix}, \tag{3.195}$$

the second almost-invariant set (in blue) being almost three times as dense as the first one (in green).

The algorithm is designed to find almost-invariant sets whose union covers the entire grid. However, in view of the early warning problem discussed in the next section, we need to find a restriction of the definition of the regimes $\{R_\beta\}_{1 \le \beta \le p=2}$ to smaller regions of the grid so that the likelihood $\hat{\mathbb{P}}(y_t \in R_\beta)$ to be in any regime R_β becomes smaller than one, Kharin and Zwiers (2003). To do so, we selected, for each almost-invariant set E_β, their grid-boxes B_i maximizing the likelihood $\hat{\mathbb{P}}(y_t \in B_i, y_{t+\tau} \in E_\beta, y_{t-\tau} \in E_\beta)$ of a realization of $\mathbf{y}$ to be in B_i and to come from and go to the same almost-invariant set E_β, until a sufficiently large number of boxes have been attributed to the regime R_β to have $\hat{\mathbb{P}}(y_t \in R_\beta) = \hat{\mathbb{P}}(y_t \in E_\beta)/2$ (until half of the almost-invariant set has been selected in terms of measure $\hat{\mathfrak{m}}$). These restrictions are plotted in dark green and dark blue (Figure 3.28) and define the blocked and zonal regimes, respectively. The probabilities to stay in the so-defined blocked and zonal regimes after 8 days are 66% and 70%, respectively.

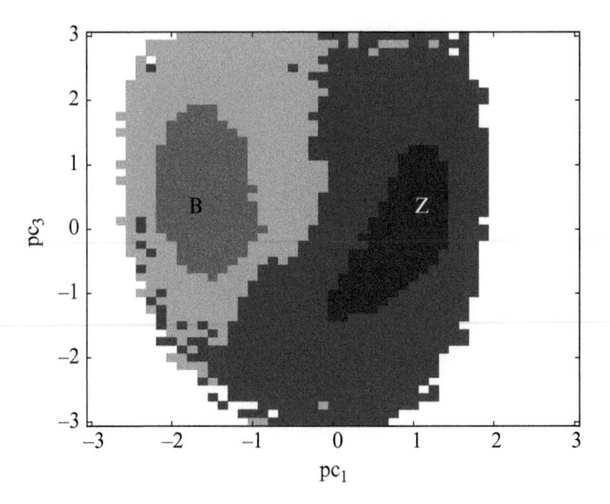

Fig. 3.28 Two almost-invariants sets and their restrictions to the denser half of each regime in dark green and dark blue, corresponding to the blocked regime and the zonal regime, respectively.

3.6.8 Preferred transition paths

Having defined the regimes, we now study the transitions between them. Following Branstator and Berner (2005), we first plot the mean tendencies of the normalized principal components pc_1 and pc_3. The tendencies were calculated for each principal component using a finite difference scheme such that $\Delta \mathrm{pc}_i(t) = (\mathrm{pc}_i(t+\tau) - \mathrm{pc}_i(t))/\Delta t$, where $\Delta \mathrm{pc}_i$ is the approximate tendency of the ith principal component and Δt is the time step. An estimate of the mean tendency for each grid box was then calculated by averaging over all the realizations of $\mathbf{y}$ in this grid box.

The mean tendency for a time-step Δt of 8 days is plotted Figure 3.29. It can be seen as a composition of a clockwise rotation and two sinks. This result corroborates both the meta stability of the regimes and the existence of preferred transition paths between them, reminiscent of a pseudo-periodic orbit, Plaut and Vautard (1994); Crommelin (2003). Indeed, the rotation is such that typical trajectories leaving the zonal regime (blocked regime) to go to the blocked regime (zonal regime) transit through negative values (positive values) of pc_3. Furthermore, the correspondence between the sinks with low values of mean tendency and the regimes is striking, in particular for the zonal regime. We have seen previously that the memory effects are relatively weak in the region of the regimes. At the limit, when these effects can be neglected, the reduced dynamics can be modeled by an SDE and the mean tendency gives an approximation of the drift term involved in the Fokker–Planck equation (together with diffusion, not calculated here, Berner, 2005; Gardiner, 2009) which generates the semigroup of transfer operators associated with the SDE. As a consequence, a weak tendency should coincide with almost invariance.

To further support the existence of preferred transition paths from one regime to the other, we have calculated, for each grid box, the likelihood $\hat{P}_{ZB}$ ($\hat{P}_{BZ}$) that a trajectory starting in the zonal regime (blocked regime) and passing through this

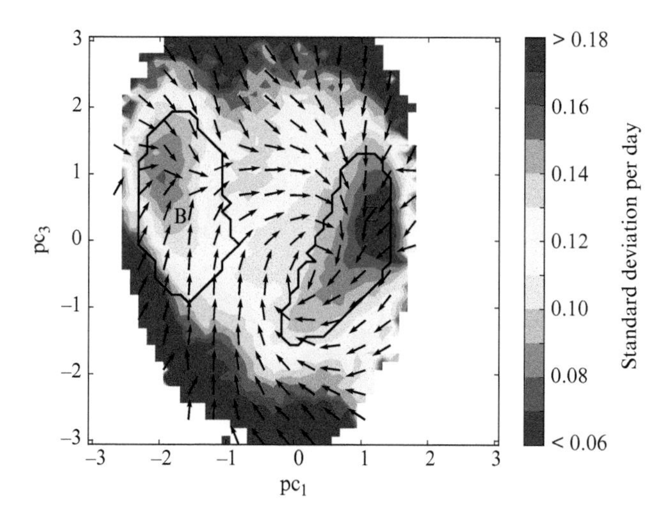

Fig. 3.29 Mean tendency of the normalized principal components calculated using centered differences for $\Delta t = 8$ days. Arrows represent the direction and the colors represent the magnitude (in standard deviation per day).

grid box reaches the blocked regime (zonal regime) before the zonal regime (blocked regime). The resulting probabilities are plotted in Figure 3.30. In agreement with the tendency, the trajectories going from the zonal to the blocked regime are more likely to do so through low values of the 3rd principal component while trajectories going from the blocked to the zonal regime favor high values of the 3rd principal component. Such a scenario can be put in perspective with the work of Froyland and Padberg (2009), where it is demonstrated that almost-invariant sets are often bounded by segments of invariant manifolds. Indeed, one could think of the exit region of the zonal regime (for negative values of pc_3) as part of an unstable invariant manifold of the zonal regime which would go to the blocked regime along its stable manifold. A similar view holds for the invariant manifold linking the blocked regime to the zonal regime and passing through large values of pc_3.

3.6.9 Energetics of the transitions

We next focus on the remaining question of how the dynamics of the barotropic model can explain (i) the persistence of each regime and (ii) the preferred transition paths from the zonal to the blocked regime through high values or pc_3.

To help clarifying these issues the hemispheric energy budget of the model is studied. First, the fields are decomposed in a $\overline{\tau} = 8$ days running mean and a deviation from it. This decomposition yields for the streamfunction

$$\psi = \overline{\psi} + \psi' \quad \text{with} \quad \overline{\psi} = \frac{1}{\overline{\tau}} \int_{t-\overline{\tau}/2}^{t+\overline{\tau}/2} \psi \, dt'. \tag{3.196}$$

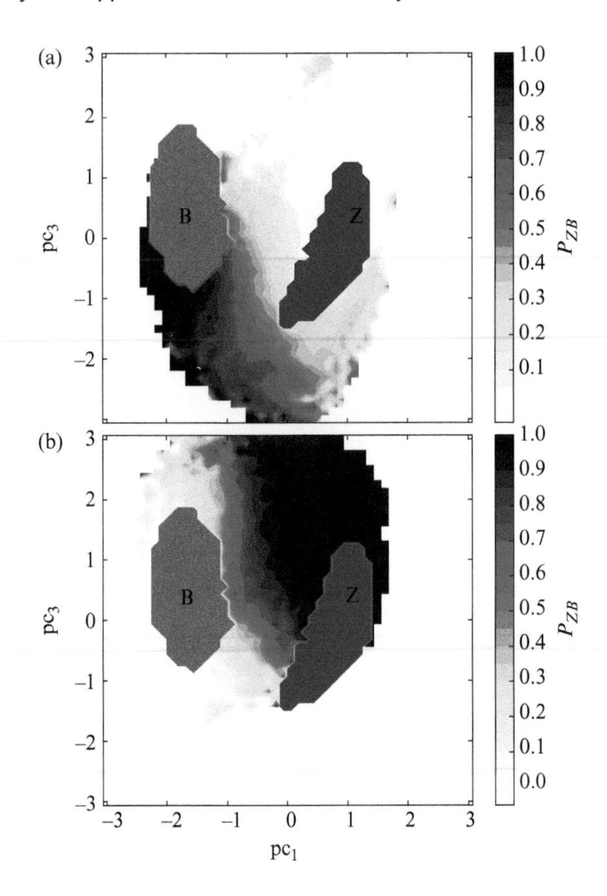

Fig. 3.30 (a) Likelihood to reach the blocked regime before the zonal regime for each grid box. (b) Likelihood to reach the zonal regime before the blocked regime for each grid box.

Inserting (3.196) into Equation (3.132) and applying the running mean gives the equation of mean relative vorticity

$$\frac{\partial \nabla^2 \overline{\psi}}{\partial t} + \mathcal{J}(\overline{\psi}, \nabla^2 \overline{\psi} + f + h) + \overline{\mathcal{J}(\psi', \nabla^2 \psi')} = -k_1 \nabla^2 \overline{\psi} + k_2 \nabla^8 \overline{\psi} + \nabla^2 \psi^*. \quad (3.197)$$

Subtracting (3.197) from (3.132) gives the equation of the deviation from the running mean as

$$\begin{aligned} &\frac{\partial \nabla^2 \psi'}{\partial t} + \mathcal{J}(\overline{\psi}, \nabla^2 \psi') + \mathcal{J}(\psi', \nabla^2 \overline{\psi} + f + h) \\ +&\mathcal{J}(\psi', \nabla^2 \psi') - \overline{\mathcal{J}(\psi', \nabla^2 \psi')} = -k_1 \nabla^2 \psi' + k_2 \nabla^8 \psi'. \end{aligned} \quad (3.198)$$

In order to obtain the equation of the hemispheric average of the mean kinetic energy $\overline{E} = < \frac{\overline{u}^2 + \overline{v}^2}{2} >$, with $< \cdot >$ denoting the hemispheric average $\frac{1}{2\pi} \int_0^{2\pi} \int_0^{\pi/2} \cdot \cos\phi \mathrm{d}\phi \mathrm{d}\lambda$, Equation (3.197) is multiplied by $\overline{\psi}$ and averaged hemispherically, giving

$$\frac{\partial \overline{E}}{\partial t} = < \overline{\psi}\ \overline{\mathcal{J}(\psi', \nabla^2 \psi')} > -2k_1 \overline{E} - k_2 < \overline{\psi} \nabla^8 \overline{\psi} > - < \overline{\psi} \nabla^2 \psi * >. \quad (3.199)$$

The first term on the right-hand side is equal to the opposite of the sum of the Reynold's stress terms which represent a conversion of mean to eddy kinetic energy. Finally, multiplying (3.198) by ψ', applying the running mean and averaging over the hemisphere gives the equation of the global eddy kinetic energy $E' =< \frac{\overline{u'^2 + v'^2}}{2} >$

$$\frac{\partial E'}{\partial t} = - < \overline{\psi \mathcal{J}(\psi', \nabla^2 \psi')} > -2k_1 E' - k_2 < \psi' \nabla^8 \psi' >. \quad (3.200)$$

The terms in the Equations (3.199) and (3.200) were calculated from the model simulation results and we could verify that the calculated tendencies equated the sum of the right-hand side terms but for a small error of up to 13% of the standard deviation of the tendencies due to the running average of a deviation not being exactly zero.

The energetics of the transitions can be studied by plotting the kinetic energies (Figure 3.31) and the terms in the energy budget (Figure 3.32) averaged for each grid box of the reduced phase space. To these plots is added a 200 days long trajectory transiting smoothly from the zonal to the blocked regime is added in green, starting with a black square and ending with a black triangle. It is first interesting to notice that low values of E' coincide rather well with our definition of the regimes (Figure 3.31b). That the eddies are weak in the neighborhood of the regimes is mostly explained by low values of conversion to eddy kinetic energy (Figure 3.32c), in particular for the zonal regime, and additionally by a negative forcing for the blocked regime (Figure 3.32c,d). This stabilization of the flow in the region of the regimes is a good candidate to explain their persistence.

As we have seen, typical trajectories from the zonal to the blocked regime transit through the region of negative pc_3. Figures 3.31 and 3.32 allow us to give a typical

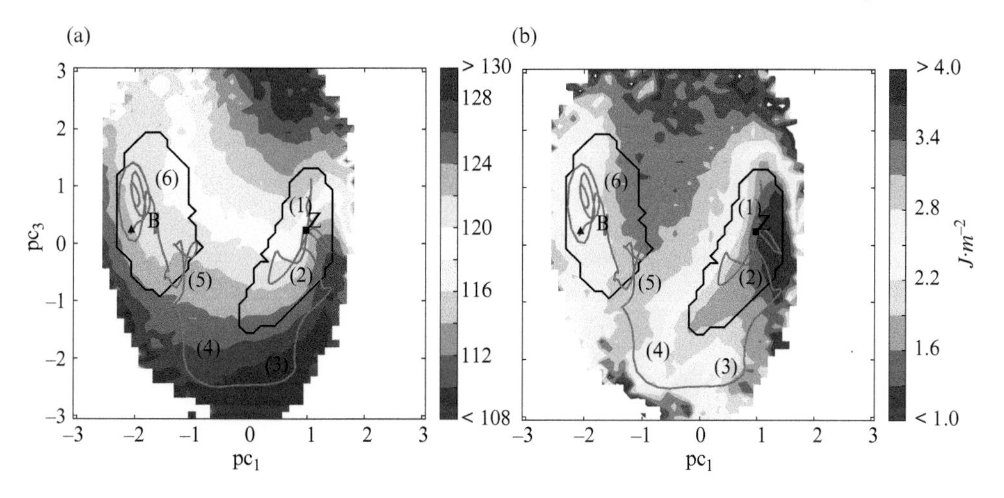

Fig. 3.31 (a) Hemispheric mean kinetic energy $\overline{E}$ in Jm^{-2}. (b) Hemispheric eddy kinetic energy E' in Jm^{-2}.

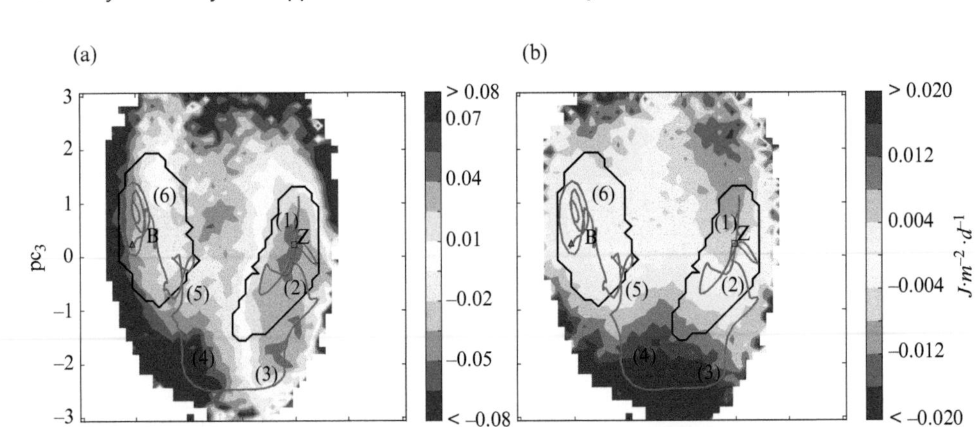

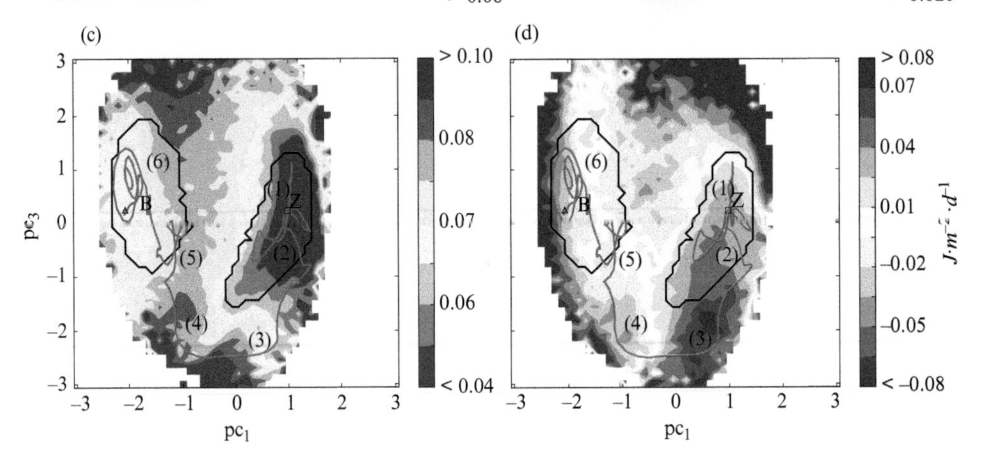

Fig. 3.32 (a) Tendency of the hemispheric mean kinetic energy in Jm^{-2}day^{-1}, (b) tendency of the hemispheric eddy kinetic energy in Jm^{-2}day^{-1}, (c) hemispheric Reynold's stresses (conversion from mean to eddy kinetic energy when positive) in Jm^{-2}day^{-1}, (d) sum of hemispheric forcing and dissipation in Jm^{-2}day^{-1}.

scenario for such a transition. Each step of the following scenario is marked in Figures 3.31 and 3.32 by the corresponding number.

1. Starting in the zonal regime, the Reynold's stress terms are small and the mean flow is stable. However, the positive forcing induces an increase of the mean kinetic energy $\overline{E}$.
2. As $\overline{E}$ increases and the forcing persists, the trajectory evolves to lower value of pc_3 and eventually leaves the zonal regime.
3. The trajectory then reaches a region of pc_1 close to zero and low pc_3. The forcing is still strong but the Reynold's stress terms begin to increase because the strongly sheared flow becomes barotropically unstable for lower values of pc_3, so that the total eddy kinetic energy E' continues to increase.
4. As the trajectory reaches lower values of pc_1, the forcing reverses but the Reynold's stress terms continue to increase as the barotropic eddies which

emanated at the previous step develop, so that $\overline{E}$ is converted to E' which continues to increase.

5. The trajectory then goes to larger values of pc_3 where the forcing is negative and energy is removed both from the mean flow and from the eddies so that the barotropic eddies decay.
6. The trajectory eventually reaches the blocked regime for lower values of pc_1 where E' decreases due to the negative forcing coincident with relatively small Reynold's stress terms. The mean flow is once again relatively stable, although not as much as for the zonal regime, as can be seen for the relatively large Reynold's stress terms in the region of largest pc_1 inside the blocked regime.

This scenario is consistent with the mechanisms of chaotic itinerancy, Itoh and Kimoto (1996), heteroclinic connections, Weeks *et al.* (1997); Crommelin (2003) and almost-invariant sets bounded by invariant manifolds, Froyland and Padberg (2009). Indeed, when the reduced state is in the zonal regime, the flow is relatively stable as it belongs to what would be the basin of attraction of the zonal regime. However, as it moves towards the neighborhood of positive forcing, energy is given to the mean flow, the horizontal shear increases and the flow becomes unstable to small perturbations. The increasing Reynold's stress term indicates that the perturbation grows, starts to interact with the mean flow, and enables the state to leave the basin of attraction of the zonal regime. Thus, we can say that the neighborhood of positive forcing where the flow becomes unstable constitutes the exit region of the meta-stable regime, as described by Froyland and Padberg (2009), where the unstable invariant manifold is located. As the state transits along this manifold (or near ruins of it) through large values of principal component pc_3, it eventually reaches a region where the forcing becomes negative and where the Reynold's stresses are still strong (steps 4 and 5). The region bounding the blocked regime where the forcing is negative and the Reynold's stress positive would constitute the bounding stable manifold of the almost-invariant set as in Froyland and Padberg (2009).

Acknowledgments

I would like to thank the students of both the (2015) Woods Hole Summerschool, in particular Chris Spalding, Gunnar Peng and Tom Beucler, and those of the (2017) Les Houches Summerschool for their excellent comments and for providing some of the figures. Dr. Alexis Tantet is also thanked for his PhD work of which some is included in lecture 6.

References

Afraimovich, Valentin S., Gonchenko, Sergey V., Lerman, Lev M., Shilnikov, Andrey L., and Turaev, Dmitry V. (2014). Scientific heritage of L. P. Shilnikov. *Regul. Chaotic Dyn.*, **19**(4), 435–60.

Andersen, K. and *et al.* (2004). High-resolution record of Northern Hemisphere climate extending into the last interglacial period. *Nature*, **431**, 147–51.

Andronov, Aleksandr A., Leontovich, E. A., Gordon, I. I., and Maier, A. G. (1971). *Theory of Bifurcations of Dynamic Systems on a Plane.* Israel Program for Scientific Translations, Jerusalem.

Andronov, Aleksandr A. and Pontryagin, L. (1937). Systemes grossiers. *Dokl. Akad. Nauk. SSSR*, **14**(5), 247–50.

Anosov, D. V. (1962). Roughness of geodesic flows on compact Riemannian manifolds of negative curvature. *Sov. Math.*, **3**, 1068–70.

Arnold, L. (1998, January). *Random Dynamical Systems.* Springer, Verlag, Berlin.

Arnold, Vladimir Igorevich (1963). Proof of a theorem of A. N. Kolmogorov on the preservation of conditionally periodic motions under a small perturbation of the Hamiltonian. *Russ. Math. Surv.*, **18**(5), 9–36.

Arnold, V. I. (2012). *Geometrical Methods in the Theory of Ordinary Differential Equations.* Volume 250. Springer, Cambridge.

Bak, P., Bohr, T., and Høgh Jensen, M. (1985). Mode-locking and the transition to chaos in dissipative systems. *Physica Scripta*, **T9**, 50–8.

Battisti, D. (1988). The dynamics and thermodynamics of a warming event in a coupled tropical ocean/atmosphere model. *J. Atmos. Sci.*, **45**, 2889–919.

Bendixson, Ivar (1899). Sur les courbes définies par des équations differentielles. *Journal de Mathématiques*, **24**, 1–88.

Berner, Judith (2005, July). Linking nonlinearity and non-Gaussianity of planetary wave behavior by the Fokker–Planck equation. *Journal of the Atmospheric Sciences*, **62**(7), 2098–117.

Birkhoff, George D. (1927). *Dynamical Systems.* American Mathematical Society, New York.

Birkhoff, George D. (1931). Proof of the Ergodic Theorem. *Proceedings of the National Academy of Sciences of the United States of America*, **17**(3), 656–60.

Bolibruch, A. A., Osipov Y. S., and Sinai, Yakov G. (2005). *Mathematical Events of the Twentieth Century.* Springer, Berlin.

Boltzmann, Ludwig (1909). *Wissenschaftliche Abhandlungen I. Band (1865–1874).* Barth, Leipzig.

Bowen, Rufus and Ruelle, David (1975). The ergodic theory of Axiom A flows. *Invent. Math.*, **29**(3), 181–202.

Branstator, Grant and Berner, Judith (2005). Linear and nonlinear signatures in the planetary wave dynamics of an AGCM: Phase space tendencies. *Journal of the Atmospheric Sciences*, **62**, 1792.

Branstator, G. and Opsteegh, J. D. (1989). Free solutions of the barotropic vorticity equation. *Journal of the Atmospheric Sciences*, **46**, 1799.

Butterley, Oliver and Liverani, Carlangelo (2007). Smooth Anosov flows: Correlation spectra and stability. *J. Modern Dynamics* (Prin 2004028108), 1–21.

Cessi, P. (1994). A simple box model of stochastically forced thermohaline flow. *Journal of Physical Oceanography*, **24**, 1911–20.

Chang, J. S. and Cooper, G. (1970). A practical difference scheme for Fokker–Planck equations. *J. Comput. Phys.*, **6**(1), 1–16.

Charney, J. G. and DeVore, J. G. (1979). Multiple flow equilibria in the atmosphere and blocking. *Journal of the Atmospheric Sciences*, **36**(7), 1205.

Charney, Jule G., Fjortoft, R., and von Neumann, John (1950). Numerical integration of the barotropic vorticity equation. *Tellus A*, **2**(4), 238–54.

Chekroun, Mickaël David (2014). Rough parameter dependence in climate models and the role of Ruelle–Pollicott resonances SI. *Proceedings of the National Academy of Sciences of the United States of America*, **111**, 1.

Chekroun, M. D., Tantet, A., Dijkstra, H. A., and Neelin, J. D. (2016). Mixing Spectrum in reduced phase spaces of stochastic differential equations. Part I: Theory. submitted.

Chirikov, B. V. (1960). Resonance processes in magnetic traps. *J. Nucl. Energy, Part C Plasma Phys.*, **1**, 253–60.

Christiansen, Bo (2007, May). Atmospheric circulation regimes: Can cluster analysis provide the number? *Journal of Climate*, **20**(10), 2229.

Clauset, Aaron, Newman, M., and Moore, Cristopher (2004, December). Finding community structure in very large networks. *Physical Review E*, **70**(6), 1.

Clement, A. C. and Peterson, L. C. (2008). Mechanisms of abrupt climate change of the last glacial period. *Reviews of Geophysics*, **46**, RG4002.

Cover, Thomas M. and Thomas, Joy A. (1991). Entropy, relative entropy and mutualiInformation. In *Elements of Information Theory*, Chapter 2, pp. 13–55. John Wiley & Sons, New Jersey.

Crommelin, D. T. (2003). Regime transitions and heteroclinic connections in a barotropic atmosphere. *Journal of the Atmospheric Sciences*, **60**(2), 229–46.

Crommelin, Daan, Opsteegh, J. D., and Verhulst, F. (2004, June). A mechanism for atmospheric regime behavior. *Journal of the Atmospheric Sciences*, **61**(12), 1406–19.

Crucifix, M. (2012, January). Oscillators and relaxation phenomena in Pleistocene climate theory. *Philosophical Transactions of the Royal Society A-Mathematical Physical and Engineering Sciences*, **370**(1962), 1140–65.

Cunningham, S. A., Kanzow, T., Rayner, D., Baringer, M. O., Johns, W. E., Marotzke, J., Longworth, H. R., Grant, E. M., Hirschi, J. J-M., Beal, L. M., Meinen, C. S., and Bryden, H. L. (2007, August). Temporal variability of the Atlantic Meridional overturning circulation at 26.5 N. *Science*, **317**(5840), 935–38.

Dawson, A, Palmer, T. N., and Corti, S. (2014*a*, November). Simulating regime structures in weather and climate prediction models. *Geophysical Research Letters*, **39**(21).

Dawson, A., Palmer, T. N., and Corti, S. (2014*b*, November). Simulating weather regimes: Impact of model resolution and stochastic parametrization. *Climate Dynamics*, 1–17.

Dellnitz, Michael and Junge, Oliver (1997). Almost invariant sets in Chua's circuit. *International Journal of Bifurcation and Chaos*, **7**(11), 2475–85.

Dellnitz, Michael and Junge, Oliver (1999, January). On the approximation of complicated dynamical behavior. *SIAM Journal on Numerical Analysis*, **36**(2), 491–515.

DelSole, T (2000). A fundamental limitation of Markov models. *Journal of the Atmospheric Sciences*, **57**, 2158–68.

Deng, Kun, Mehta, P. G., and Meyn, S. P. (2011). Optimal Kullback–Leibler aggregation via spectral theory of Markov chains. *Automatic Control, IEEE*, **56**(12), 2793–808.

Deser, Clara, Alexander, Michael A., Xie, Shang-Ping, and Phillips, Adam S. (2010, January). Sea Surface surface temperature variability: Patterns and mechanisms. *Annual Review of Marine Science*, **2**(1), 115–43.

Deville, R. E. Lee, Sri Namachchivaya, N., and Rapti, Zoi (2011). Stability of a Stochastic two-dimensional non-Hamiltonian system. *Siam J. Appl. Math.*, **71**(4), 1458–75.

Dijkstra, H. A. and Burgers, G. (2002). Fluid dynamics of El Niño variability. *Annual Review of Fluid Mechanics*, **34**, 531–58.

Dijkstra, H. A. and Neelin, J. D. (1995). Coupled ocean-atmosphere models and the tropical climatology. II: Why the cold tongue is in the East. *J. Climate*, **8**, 1343–59.

Dommenget, D. and Latif, M. (2002). Analysis of observed and simulated SST spectra in the midlatitude. *Clim. Dyn.*, **19**, 277–88.

Doob, J. L. (1934). Stochastic Processes and Statistics. *Proceedings of the National Academy of Sciences of the United States of America*, **20**, 376–9.

Eckmann, J. and Ruelle, D. (1985). Ergodic theory of chaos and strange attractors. *Reviews of Modern Physics*, **57**, 617–58.

Engel, Klaus-Jochen and Nagel, Rainer (2001, June). One-parameter semigroups for linear evolution equations. *Semigroup Forum*, **63**(2), 278–80.

England, Matthew H., McGregor, Shayne, Spence, Paul, Meehl, Gerald A., Timmermann, Axel, Cai, Wenju, Gupta, Alex Sen, McPhaden, Michael J., Purich, Ariaan, and Santoso, Agus (2014, February). Recent intensification of wind-driven circulation in the Pacific and the ongoing warming hiatus. *Nature Climate Change*, **4**(3), 222–7.

Fedorov, A. V. and Philander, S. G. (2000). Is El Niño changing? *Science*, **288**, 1997–2002.

Fereday, D. R., Knight, J. R., Scaife, A. A., Folland, C. K., and Philipp, A. (2008, August). Cluster analysis of North Atlantic–European circulation types and links with tropical Pacific sea surface temperatures. *Journal of Climate*, **21**(15), 3687–703.

Franzke, Christian L., Crommelin, Daan, Fischer, Alexander, and Majda, A. J. (2008, April). A hidden Markov model perspective on regimes and metastability in atmospheric flows. *Journal of Climate*, **21**(8), 1740–757.

Franzke, Christian L., Majda, Andrew J., and Vanden-Eijnden, Eric (2005). Low-order stochastic mode reduction for a realistic barotropic model climate. *Journal of the Atmospheric Sciences*, **62**(6), 1722–45.

Froyland, Gary (1998). Approximating physical invariant measures of mixing dynamical systems in higher dimensions. *Nonlinear Analysis: Theory, Methods & Applications*, **32**(7), 831.

Froyland, Gary and Dellnitz, Michael (2003). Detecting and locating near-optimal almost-invariant sets and cycles. *SIAM Journal on Scientific Computing*, **24**(6), 1839–63.

Froyland, Gary and Padberg, Kathrin (2009, August). Almost-invariant sets and invariant manifolds—Connecting probabilistic and geometric descriptions of coherent structures in flows. *Physica D: Nonlinear Phenomena*, **238**(16), 1507–23.

Froyland, Gary and Padberg-gehle, Kathrin (2014). *Ergodic Theory, Open Dynamics, and Coherent Structures.* Volume 70, Springer Proceedings in Mathematics & Statistics. Springer, New York, NY.

Gallavotti, Giovanni (2014). *Nonequilibrium and irreversibility.* Springer, Cham.

Gallavotti, G. and Cohen, E. G. D. (1995, September). Dynamical ensembles in stationary states. *Journal of Statistical Physics*, **80**(5-6), 931–70.

Gallavotti, Giovanni and Ruelle, David (1997). SRB states and nonequilibrium statistical mechanics close to equilibrium. *Commun. Math. Phys.*, **190**, 279–85.

Gardiner, C. W. (2002). *Handbook of Stochastic Methods, 2nd edition.* Springer.

Gardiner, C. W. (2009). Handbook of Stochastic Methods. *Berichte der Bunsengesellschaft für physikalische Chemie*, **102**(10).

Gaspard, Pierre (2002). Trace formula for noisy flows. *J. Stat. Phys.*, **106**(1-2), 57–96.

Gaspard, P. and Tasaki, S. (2001, October). Liouvillian dynamics of the Hopf bifurcation. *Physical Review E*, **64**(5), 056232.

Ghil, Michael (2002). Natural climate variability. In *Encyclopedia of Global Environmental Change, volume 1* (ed. T. Munn, M. C. MacCracken, and J. S. Perry). Wiley, Hoboken, NJ.

Ghil, M, Feliks, Y., and Sushama, L. (2002). Baroclinic and barotropic aspects of the wind-driven ocean circulation. *Physica D-Nonlinear Phenomena.* in press.

Gibbs, J. Willard (1902). *Elementary Principles in Statistical Mechanics.* Scribner, New York.

Gill, A. E. (1980). Some simple solutions for heat induced tropical circulation. *Quart. J. Roy. Meteor. Soc.*, **106**, 447–62.

Golubitsky, M., Stewart, I., and Schaeffer, D. G. (1988). *Singularities and Groups in Bifurcation Theory, Vol. II.* Springer-Verlag, New York, U.S.A.

Guckenheimer, J. and Holmes, P. (1990). *Nonlinear Oscillations, Dynamical Systems and Bifurcations of Vector Fields, 2e edition.* Springer-Verlag, Berlin/Heidelberg.

Hasselmann, K. (1976). Stochastic climate models. I: Theory. *Tellus*, **28**, 473–85.

Itoh, H. and Kimoto, M. (1996). Multiple attractors and chaotic itinerancy in a quasigeostrophic model with realistic topography: Implications for weather regimes and low-frequency variability. *Journal of Atmospheric Sciences*, **53**(15), 2217–31.

James, I. N. (1994). *Introduction to Circulating Atmospheres.* Cambridge University Press, Cambridge.

Jiang, N., Neelin, J. D., and Ghil, M (1995). Quasi-quadrennial and quasi-biennial varibility in the equatorial Pacific. *Clim. Dyn.*, **12**, 101–12.

Jin, F.-F (1997). An equatorial recharge paradigm for ENSO. II: A stripped-down coupled model. *J. Atmos. Sci.*, **54**, 830–47.

Jin, F.-F, Neelin, J. D., and Ghil, M. (1996). El Niño/Southern Oscillation and the annual cycle: Subharmonic frequency-locking and aperiodicity. *Physica D-Nonlinear Phenomena*, **98**, 442–65.

Johns, W. E., Baringer, M. O., and Beal, L. M. (2011). Continuous, array-based estimates of Atlantic Ocean heat transport at 26.5 N. *Journal Of Climate*, **24**, 2429–49.

Jouzel, J. and coauthors (2007, August). Orbital and Millennial Antarctic climate variability over the past 800,000 years. *Science*, **317**(5839), 793–96.

Jung, T., Palmer, T. N., and Shutts, G. J. (2005). Influence of a stochastic parameterization on the frequency of occurrence of North Pacific weather regimes in the ECMWF model. *Geophysical Research Letters*, **32**(23), L23811.

Kaneko, Kunihiko (1991). Globally coupled circle maps. *Physica D: Nonlinear Phenomena*, **54**, 5.

Katok, A. (1980). Lyapunov exponents, entropy and periodic orbits for diffeomorphisms. *Institut des Hautes Etudes Scientifiques. Publications Mathématiques*, **51**(1), 137–73.

Kharin, V. V. and Zwiers, F. W. (2003). On the ROC Score of probability forecasts. *Journal of Climate*, **16**(1), 4145–50.

Kimoto, M. and Ghil, M. (1993). Multiple Flow Regimes in the northern hemisphere winter. Part 1: Methodology and Hemispheric Regimes. *Journal of the Atmospheric Sciences*, **50**, 2625.

Kloeden, P. E. and Platen, E. (1999). *Numerical Solution of Stochastic Differential Equations*. Springer, Berlin.

Kolmogorov, Andrey N. (1954). On conservation of conditionally periodic motions for a small change in Hamilton's function. *Dokl. Akad. Nauk SSSR*, **98**, 525–30.

Kolmogorov, Andrey N. (1958). New Metric invariant of transitive dynamical systems and endomorphisms of Lebesgue space. *Dokl. Russ. Acad. Sci.*, **119**(N5), 861–4.

Kondrashov, D., Ide, K., and Ghil, M. (2004). Weather regimes and preferred transition paths in a three-level quasigeostrophic model. *Journal of the Atmospheric Sciences*, **61**, 568–87.

Koopman, Bernard O. (1931). Hamiltonian Systems and Transformations in Hilbert Space. *Proc. Natl. Acad. Sci. U. S. A.*, **17**(5), 315–18.

Kubo, Ryogo (1966). The fluctuation-dissipation theorem. *Reports Prog. Phys.*, **29**(1), 255.

Lasota, A. and Mackey, M. C. (1994). *Chaos, Fractals and Noise, 2e edition*. Springer-Verlag, Berlin/Heidelberg.

Ledrappier, François and Young, Lai-Sang (1985). The metric entropy of diffeomorphisms. I. Characterization of measures satisfying Pesin's entropy formula. *Ann. Math.*, **122**(3), 509–39.

Legras, B. and Ghil, M. (1985). Persistent anomalies, blocking and variations in atmospheric predictability. *Journal of the Atmospheric Sciences*, **42**, 433–71.

Lehoucq, Richard B., Sorensen, D. C., and Yang, C. (1997). ARPACK Users' Guide: Solution of Large Scale Eigenvalue Problems with Implicitly Restarted Arnoldi Methods. Technical Report from http://www.caam.rice.edu/software/ARP ACK/, Computational and Applied Mathematics, Rice University.

Lisiecki, Lorraine E. and Raymo, M. (2005). A Pliocene-Pleistocene stack of 57 globally distributed benthic $\delta^{18}O$ records. *Paleoceanography*, **20**(1), PA1003.

Livi, Roberto, Ruffo, Stefano, and Shepelyansky, Dima (2003). Kolmogorov pathways from integrability to chaos and beyond. *Lect. Notes Phys.*, **636**, 3–32.

Lorenz, E. N. (1963). Deterministic nonperiodic flow. *J. Atmos. Sci.*, **20**, 130–41.

Lyapunov, A. M. (1892). The general problem of motion stability. Published by Kharkov Mathematical Society, 250 pp. (in Russian); *Coli. Works*, II, 7 (in Russian). Republished in French in 1908 and in Russian in 1935.

Majda, A. J., Franzke, Christian L., Fischer, Alexander, and Crommelin, Daan (2006, May). Distinct metastable atmospheric regimes despite nearly Gaussian statistics: A paradigm model. *Proceedings of the National Academy of Sciences of the United States of America*, **103**(22), 8309.

Marshall, J. and Schott, F. (1999). Open-ocean convection: Observations, theory and models. *Rev. Geophysics*, **37**, 1–64.

Matsuno, T. (1966). Quasi-geostrophic motions in equatorial areas. *J. Meteorol. Soc. Jpn*, **2**, 25–43.

Maxwell, J. C. (1860, Jan). V. Illustrations of the dynamical theory of gases. Part I. On the motions and collisions of perfectly elastic spheres. *Philos. Mag. Ser. 4*, **19**(124), 19–32.

McPhaden, M. J. and coauthors (1998). The tropical ocean-global atmosphere observing system: A decade of progress. *Journal of Geophysical Research*, **103**, 14,169–240.

Mikosch, T. (2000). *Elementary stochastic calculus.* World Scientific. Singapore

Mo, K. T. and Ghil, M. (1988). Cluster-analysis of multiple planetary flow regimes. *Journal of Geophysical Research-Atmospheres*, **93**, 10927–952.

Moser, Jurgen (1962). On invariant curves of area-preserving mappings of an annulus. *Nachr. Akad. Wiss. Gottingen, Math.-Phys. Kl. II.*, **1**, 1–20.

Neelin, J. D. (2011, October). *Climate Change and Climate Modeling.* Cambridge University Press, Cambridge.

Neelin, J. D., Battisti, D. S., Hirst, A. C., Jin, F.-F, Wakata, Y., Yamagata, T., and Zebiak, S. E. (1998). ENSO theory. *Journal of Geophysical Research*, **103**, 14, 261–290.

Neelin, J. D., Latif, M., and Jin, F.-F (1994). Dynamics of coupled ocean-atmosphere models: The tropical problem. *Ann. Rev. Fluid Mech.*, **26**, 617–59.

Oeschger, H., Beer, J., Siegenthaler, U., Stauffer, B., Dansgaard, W., and Langway, C. C. (1984). Late glacial climate history from ice cores. In *Climate Processes and Climate Sensitivity* (ed. J. Hansen and T. Takahashi), pp. 299–306. Geophys. Monogr. Ser., vol. 29, p. 368, AGU.

Oseledets, V. I. (1968). A multiplicative ergodic theorem. Characteisitic Lyapunov, exponents of dynamical systems. *Tr. Mosk. Mat. Obs.*, **19**, 179–210.

Palmer, T. N. (1993). A nonlinear dynamical perspective on climate change. *Weather*, **48**(1), 314–26.

Pavliotis, Grigorios A. (2014). *Stochastic Processes and Applications.* Springer, New York.

Perron, O. (1929). Über stabilität und asymptotisches verhalten der integrale von Gewöhnlichen differentialgleichungen und differenzengleichungen. *J. Reine Angew. Math.*, **161**, 41–64.

Pesin, Yakov B. (1977). Characteristic Lyapunov exponents and smooth ergodic theory. *Russ. Math. Surv.*, **32**(4), 55–114.

Philander, S. G. H. (1990). *El Niño and the Southern Oscillation.* Academic Press, New York.

Plaut, G. and Vautard, R. (1994). Spells of low-frequency oscillations and weather regimes in the Northern Hemisphere. *Journal of Atmospheric Sciences*, **51**, 210–36.

Poincaré, Henri (1881). Memoire sur les courbes definies par une equation differentielle. *J. Math. Pures Appl.*, **7**(I), 375–422.

Poincaré, H (1885). Sur l'equilibre d'une masse fluide animee d'un mouvement de rotation. *Acta Math.*, **7**, 259–380.

Poincaré, H. (1892). *Les Methodes Nouvelles de la Mecanique Celeste.* Gauthier-Villars, Paris.

Pollicott, Mark (1985, October). On the rate of mixing of Axiom A flows. *Inventiones Mathematicae*, **81**(3), 413–26.

Rayner, N. A., Parker, D. E., Horton, E. B., Folland, C. K., Alexander, L. V., Rowell, D. P., Kent, E. C., and Kaplan, A. (2003). Global analyses of sea surface temperature, sea ice, and night marine air temperature since the late nineteenth century. *Journal of Geophysical Research*, **108**(D14), 10.1029/2002JD002670.

Roads, J. O. (1987). Predictability in the extended range. *Journal of the atmospheric sciences*, **44**(23), 3495.

Rosvall, Martin and Bergstrom, Carl T. (2008, February). Maps of random walks on complex networks reveal community structure. *Proceedings of the National Academy of Sciences of the United States of America*, **105**(4), 1118.

Roulston, M. and Neelin, J. D. (2000). The response of an ENSO model to climate noise, weather noise and intraseasonal forcing. *Geophys. Res. Letters*, **27**, 3723–6.

Ruelle, David (1979). Microscopic fluctuations and turbulence. *Physics Letters A*, **72**(2), 81–2.

Ruelle, David (1980). Measures describing a turbulent flow. *Ann. N. Y. Acad. Sci.*, **357**(1), 1–9.

Ruelle, David (1986*a*). Locating resonances for AxiomA dynamical systems. *Journal of Statistical Physics*, **44**, 281–92.

Ruelle, David (1986*b*). Resonances of chaotic dynamical systems. *Physical Review Letters* (February), 5–7.

Ruelle, David (1997). Differentiation of SRB states. *Commun. Math. Phys.*, **1887**, 227–41.

Ruelle, David (1999). Smooth dynamics and new theoretical ideas in nonequilibrium statistical mechanics. *J. Stat. Phys.*, **95**(1-2), 393–468.

Ruelle, David and Takens, Floris (1971). On the nature of turbulence. *Communications in Mathematical Physics*, **20**(1948), 303–22.

Saltzman, Barry and Maasch, Kirk A. (1991). A first-order global model of late Cenozoic climatic change II. Further analysis based on a simplification of CO2 dynamics. *Climate Dynamics*, **5**(4), 201–10.

Saltzmann, B. (2001, October). *Dynamical Paleoclimatology.* Academic Press.

Schopf, P. and Suarez, M. (1988). Vacillations in a coupled ocean-atmosphere model. *J. Atmos. Sci.*, **45**, 549–66.

Schultz, M. (2002, November). On the 1470-year pacing of Dansgaard–Oeschger warm events. *Paleoceanography*, **17**(2), 4.1–4.9.

Selten, F. M. (1995). An efficient description of the dynamics of barotropic flow. *Journal of the Atmospheric Sciences*, **52**(7), 915–36.

Shilnikov, L. P. (1965). A case of the existence of a denumerable set of periodic motions. *Sov. Math. Dokl.*, **6**, 163–6.

Shilnikov, Leonid P. (1984). Bifurcation theory and turbulence. In *Nonlinear Turbul. Process. Phys.* (ed. R. Sagdeev), pp. 1627–35.

Shilnikov, Leonid P., Nicolis, G., and Nicolis, C. (1995). Bifurcation and predictability analysis of a low-order atmospheric circulation model. *Int. J. Bifurc. Chaos*, **05**(06), 1701–11.

Siegenthaler, U., Stocker, T. F., Monnin, E., and Lüthi, D. (2005). Stable carbon cycle–climate relationship during the late Pleistocene. *Science*, **310**, 1313–17.

Sinai, Yakov G. (1959). On the notion of entropy of a dynamical system. *Dokl. Russ. Acad. Sci.*, **124**, 250.

Sinai, Yakov G. (1972). Gibbs measures in ergodic theory. *Russ. Math. Surv.*, **27**(4), 21–69.

Slingo, J. and Palmer, T. (2011, October). Uncertainty in weather and climate prediction. *Philosophical Transactions Of The Royal Society A-Mathematical Physical And Engineering Sciences*, **369**(1956), 4751–67.

Smale, Stephen (1966). Structurally stable systems are not dense. *Am. J. Math.*, **88**(2), 491–6.

Smale, S. (1995). Differentiable dynamical systems. *Bull. Amer. Math. Soc.*, **73**, 747–817.

Smeed, D. A., McCarthy, G. D., Cunningham, S. A., Frajka-Williams, E., Rayner, D., Johns, W. E., Meinen, C. S., Baringer, M. O., Moat, B. I., Duchez, A., and Bryden, H. L. (2014). Observed decline of the Atlantic meridional overturning circulation 2004 & 2012. *Ocean Science*, **10**(1), 29–38.

Smyth, Padhraic (1999). Model selection for probabilistic clustering using cross-validated likelihood. *Statistics and Computing*, **3425**, 63–72.

Smyth, P., Ide, K., and Ghil, M. (1999). Multiple regimes in Northern Hemisphere height fields via mixture model clustering. *J. Atmos. Sci.*, **56**, 3704–23.

Spall, Michael A. (2003). On the thermohaline circulation in flat bottom marginal seas. *Journal Of Marine Research*, **61**(1), 1–25.

Srokosz, M. A. and Bryden, H. L. (2015, June). Observing the Atlantic Meridional Overturning Circulation yields a decade of inevitable surprises. *Science*, **348**(6241), 1255575:1-5.

Stephenson, D. B., Hannachi, A., and O'Neill, A. (2004, January). On the existence of multiple climate regimes. *Quarterly Journal Of The Royal Meteorological Society*, **130**(597), 583–605.

Stommel, H. (1961). Thermohaline convection with two stable regimes of flow. *Tellus*, **2**, 244–30.

Stone, M. H. (1930). Linear Transformations in Hilbert Space: III. Operational Methods and Group Theory. *Proceedings of the National Academy of Sciences of the United States of America*, **16**(2), 172–5.

Strogatz, S. H. (1994). *Nonlinear Dynamics and Chaos: With Applications to Physics, Biology, Chemistry, and Engineering.* Perseus Books, Reading, MA.

Stuiver, Minze and Grootes, Pieter M (2000, May). GISP2 oxygen isotope ratios. *Quaternary Research*, **53**(3), 277–84.

Talley, L. D. (2008). Freshwater transport estimates and the global overturning circulation: Shallow, deep and throughflow components. *Prog. Oceanogr.*, **78**, 257–303.

Tantet, Alexis, van der Burgt, Fiona R., and Dijkstra, Henk A. (2015). An early warning indicator for atmospheric blocking events using transfer operators. *Chaos: An Interdisciplinary Journal of Nonlinear Science*, **25**(3), 036406, doi:10.1063/1.4908174.

Trenberth, K. E. (1997). El Niño and climate change. *Geophysical Research Letters*, **24**, 3057–60.

Ulam, S. M. (1964). Problems in modern mathematics. In *A Collection of Mathematical Problems*, Interscience Publ. New York, 1961. *Problems in Modern Mathematics.*

Van der Vaart, P. C. F., Dijkstra, H. A., and Jin, F.-F. (2000). The Pacific cold tongue and the ENSO mode: Unified theory within the Zebiak–Cane model. *J. Atmos. Sci.*, **57**, 967–988.

van Oldenborgh, Geert Jan, te Raa, Lianke A., Dijkstra, Henk A., and Philip, Sjoukje Y (2009). Frequency- or amplitude-dependent effects of the Atlantic meridional overturning on the tropical Pacific Ocean. *Ocean Science*, **5**, 293–301.

von Neumann, John (1932). Proof of the quasi-ergodic hypothesis. *Proc. Natl. Acad. Sci. U. S. A.*, **18**(2), 70–82.

Von Storch, H. and Zwiers, F. W. (1999). *Statistical Analysis in Climate Research.* Cambridge University Press, Cambridge, UK.

Weeks, Eric R., Swinney, Harry L., and Ghil, Michael (1997). Transitions between blocked and zonal flows in a rotating annulus with topography. *Science*, **278**(1997), 1601.

Williams, P. D. (2003). Spontaneous generation and impact of inertia-gravity waves in a stratified, two-layer shear flow. *Geophysical Research Letters*, **30**(24), 2255.

Williams, P. D., Haine, Thomas W. N., and Read, Peter L. (2004). Stochastic resonance in a nonlinear model of a rotating, stratified shear flow, with a simple stochastic inertia-gravity wave parameterization. *Nonlinear Processes in Geophysics*, **11**, 127.

Williams, Paul D., Haine, Thomas W. N., and Read, Peter L. (2005, April). On the generation mechanisms of short-scale unbalanced modes in rotating two-layer flows with vertical shear. *Journal of Fluid Mechanics*, **528**, 1.

Williams, Paul D., Haine, Thomas W. N., and Read, Peter L. (2008, November). Inertia–gravity waves emitted from balanced flow: Observations, properties, and consequences. *Journal of the atmospheric sciences*, **65**(11), 3543.

Wunsch, C (2000). On sharp spectral lines in the climate record and the millenial peak. *Paleoceanography*, **15**, 417–24.

Zhang, Y., Wallace, J. M., and Battisti, D. S. (1997). ENSO-like interdecadal variability: 1900–1993. *J. Climate*, **10**, 1004–20.

4
Barotropic aspects of large-scale atmospheric turbulence

THEODORE G. SHEPHERD

Department of Meteorology, University of Reading

Shepherd, T. G., *Barotropic aspects of large-scale atmospheric turbulence* In: *Fundamental Aspects of Turbulent Flows in Climate Dynamics.* Edited by: Freddy Bouchet, Tapio Schneider, Antoine Venaille, Christophe Salomon, Oxford University Press (2020).
DOI: 10.1093/oso/9780198855217.003.0004

Chapter Contents

4.1 Introduction

Although the large-scale atmosphere is baroclinic and driven by the temperature contrasts associated with the spatial distribution of solar heating and infrared cooling, much of large-scale atmospheric turbulence can be understood within the context of barotropic dynamics, with baroclinic processes represented as a stirring or excitation process. In this respect, the barotropic model represents the starting point in the hierarchy of models used to study large-scale atmospheric turbulence.

To provide the context for the use of the barotropic model, the chapter begins with a phenomenological treatment of the observed atmospheric circulation. It then goes on to discuss how the barotropic model arises as a so-called "balanced" model of the slow, vorticity-driven dynamics, from the more general shallow-water model which also admits inertia-gravity waves. This is important because large-scale atmospheric turbulence exhibits aspects of both balanced and unbalanced dynamics.

Because of the first-order importance of zonal flows in the atmospheric general circulation, the large-scale turbulence is highly inhomogeneous, and is shaped by the nature of the interaction between zonal flows and Rossby waves — described eloquently by Michael McIntyre as a "wave-turbulence jigsaw puzzle." This motivates a review of the barotropic theory of wave, mean-flow interaction, which is underpinned by the Hamiltonian structure of geophysical fluid dynamics.

Finally, the pieces are brought together. The structure of these lectures is represented in Figure 4.1.

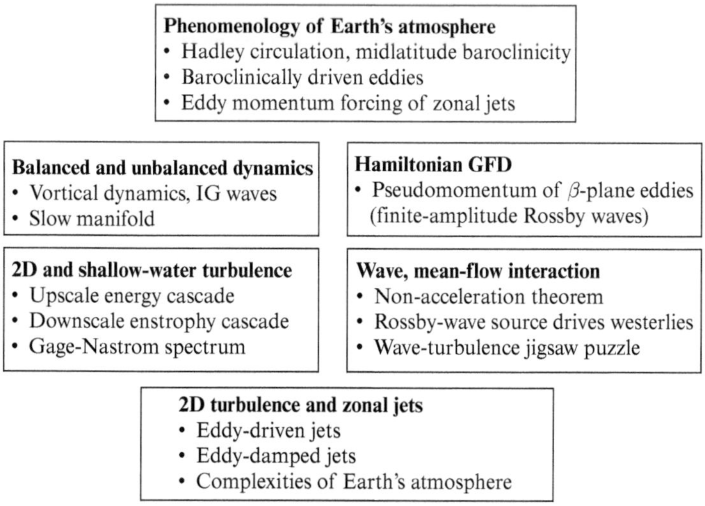

Phenomenology of Earth's atmosphere
- Hadley circulation, midlatitude baroclinicity
- Baroclinically driven eddies
- Eddy momentum forcing of zonal jets

Balanced and unbalanced dynamics
- Vortical dynamics, IG waves
- Slow manifold

Hamiltonian GFD
- Pseudomomentum of β-plane eddies (finite-amplitude Rossby waves)

2D and shallow-water turbulence
- Upscale energy cascade
- Downscale enstrophy cascade
- Gage-Nastrom spectrum

Wave, mean-flow interaction
- Non-acceleration theorem
- Rossby-wave source drives westerlies
- Wave-turbulence jigsaw puzzle

2D turbulence and zonal jets
- Eddy-driven jets
- Eddy-damped jets
- Complexities of Earth's atmosphere

Fig. 4.1 The structure of these lectures.

4.2 Phenomenology of the atmospheric general circulation

4.2.1 Temperature and humidity

The potential temperature distribution in the atmosphere is horizontally uniform in the tropics and has a strong meridional gradient in the extratropics (Figure 4.2). This region of "baroclinicity," or strong horizontal temperature gradients, indicates the presence of available potential energy in the atmosphere, which can be released through baroclinic instability. Such a situation is unsustainable in general, but is possible in the presence of rotation, where meridional temperature gradients can be balanced by the Coriolis force associated with zonal winds. Near the equator, horizontal gradients of temperature generate a force that is orthogonal to the force due to rotation, and therefore cannot be balanced. In fact, the planetary contribution to vorticity goes to zero at the equator, so the tropical atmosphere should behave almost like a non-rotating fluid. This implies that the horizontal temperature gradients near the equator should be small.

Now let's look at the moisture transport. The map of evaporation (E) minus precipitation (P) (Figure 4.3) implies a net transport of moisture from the subtropics both to the tropics and to the extratropics. The water vapor in the atmosphere maximizes in the tropics (Figure 4.4), which implies that water vapor transport is up-gradient in the tropics and down-gradient in the extratropics. Up-gradient transport is unusual, and cannot happen with a random advecting field. Hence, it suggests the presence of a coherent structure that transports the moisture up-gradient. This coherent structure is the Hadley circulation.

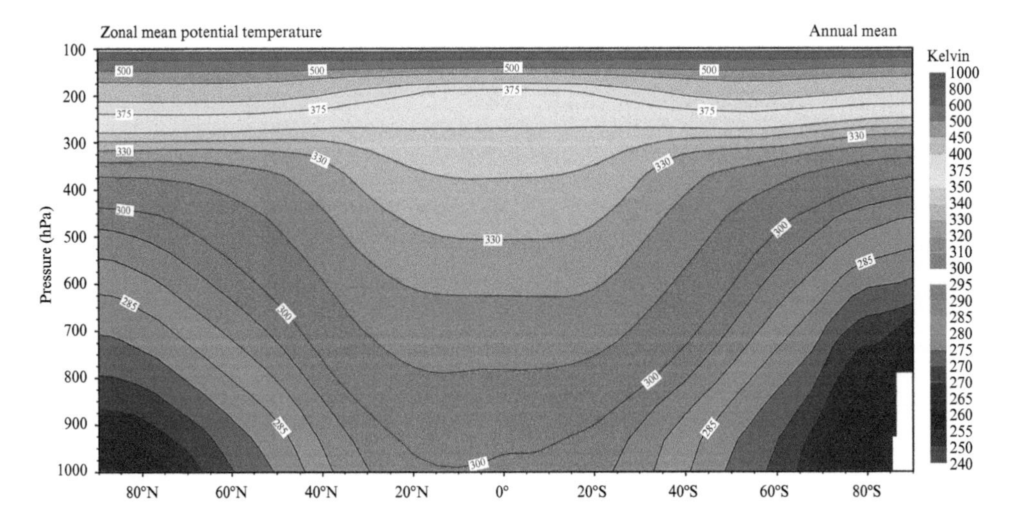

Fig. 4.2 Distribution of annual mean zonal mean potential temperature in the troposphere. This and similar figures are reproduced from the *ERA-40 Atlas*, European Centre for Medium-Range Weather Forecasts (http://www.ecmwf.int/s/ERA-40Atlas/docs/).

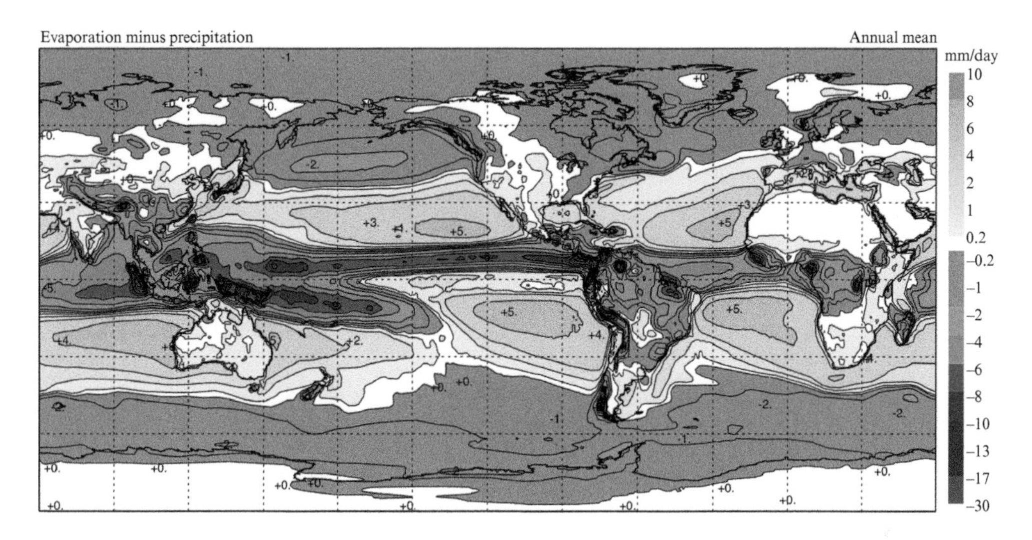

Fig. 4.3 Annual mean evaporation minus precipitation (E-P). From *ERA-40 Atlas*.

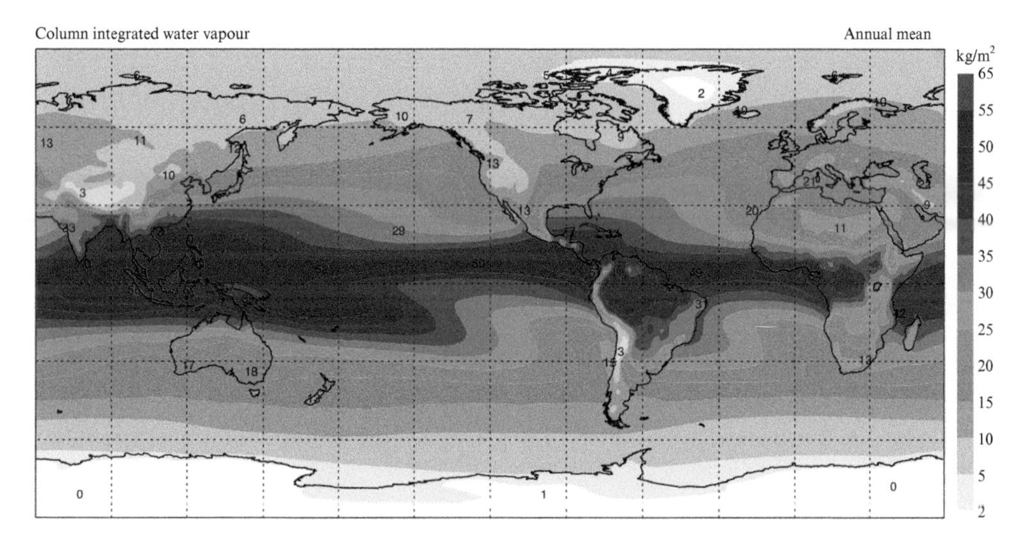

Fig. 4.4 Annual mean column integrated water vapor in the atmosphere. From *ERA-40 Atlas*.

4.2.2 Winds

We start by looking at the zonal mean zonal wind in the troposphere (Figure 4.5). The wind structure in the atmosphere has westerly zonal jets in the subtropics at about 30° latitude, with the jet speed maximizing near the tropopause. The weakening of the westerlies above the maxima reflects the very cold tropical tropopause. We also see that in the Southern Hemisphere, there appears to be a secondary jet at about 55°S.

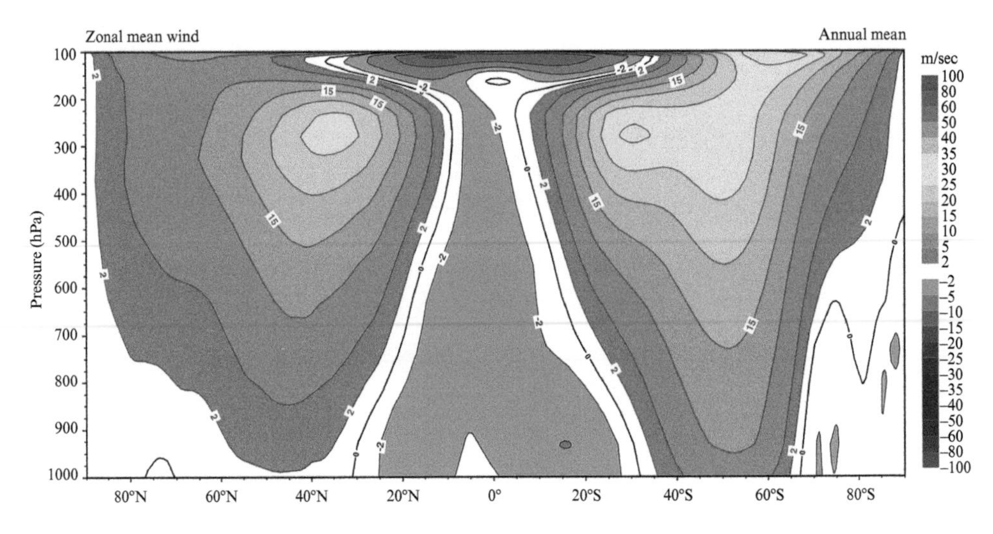

Fig. 4.5 Annual mean zonal mean zonal wind in the troposphere. From *ERA-40 Atlas*.

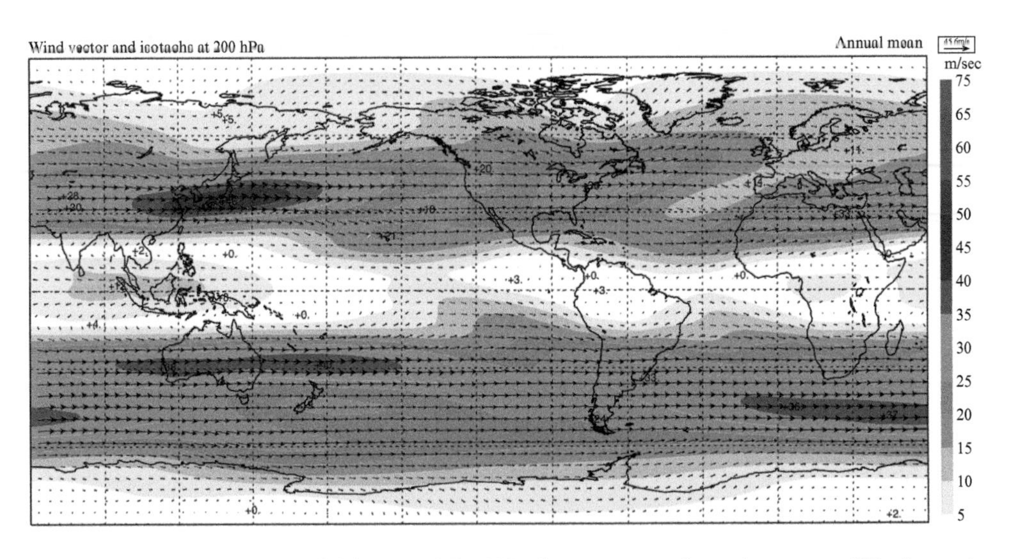

Fig. 4.6 Annual mean wind field at 200 hPa. Wind vectors are shown in arrows. Wind speeds are shown in colored contours (isotachs: contours of constant wind speed). From *ERA-40 Atlas*.

To first order, the existence of the subtropical jets can be explained by the conservation of angular momentum

$$M = a\cos(\phi)(\Omega a\cos(\phi) + u).$$

If we assume $u = 0$ at the equator, then conservation of angular momentum as air moves away from the equator requires that u at latitude ϕ is

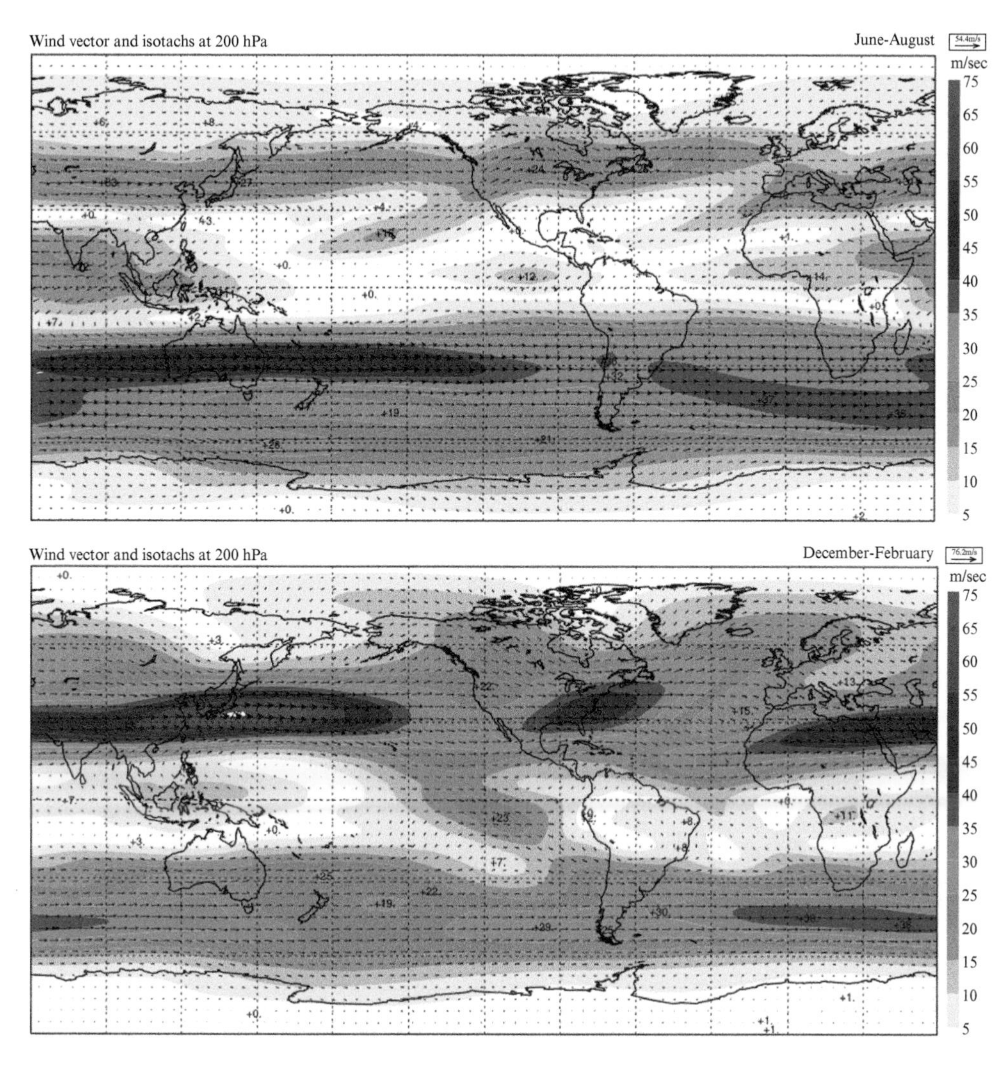

Fig. 4.7 Same as Figure 4.6, but averaged over June-July-August (JJA, top) and December-January-February (DJF, bottom). From *ERA-40 Atlas.*

$$u(\phi) = \frac{\Omega a \sin^2(\phi)}{\cos(\phi)}.$$

This profile is singular at the poles. The Hadley circulation is limited in extent by the equator-to-pole temperature difference, which limits the magnitude of u (Held and Hou, 1980). This requirement sets the meridional extent of an angular momentum conserving flow under Earth-like conditions to around 30°N/S, which is close to what is observed.

The observed winds on earth have a non-trivial zonal asymmetry, most prominently in the Northern Hemisphere (NH) (Figure 4.6). As well as longitudinal variations in amplitude, the NH jet over east Asia and the west Pacific exhibits only a weak poleward tilt, whereas the NH jet over eastern North America and the Atlantic exhibits a prominent poleward tilt. The latter is understood to be mainly due to the effect of the Rockies as well as the tilted coastline of eastern North America. We can see that the apparent "double jet" in the Southern Hemisphere (SH) zonal mean actually consists of distinct structures at different longitudes.

The midlatitude jets are strongest in winter, and are located mainly in the subtropics in both hemispheres (Figure 4.7). The summer jet is located at higher latitudes and is much weaker. The seasonality of the jets is explained to a large extent by the seasonality of the Hadley circulation. The seasonal Hadley circulation has its rising branch located in the summer hemisphere and a strong descending branch in the winter hemisphere (Figure 4.8), which drives the strong winter jets. In contrast

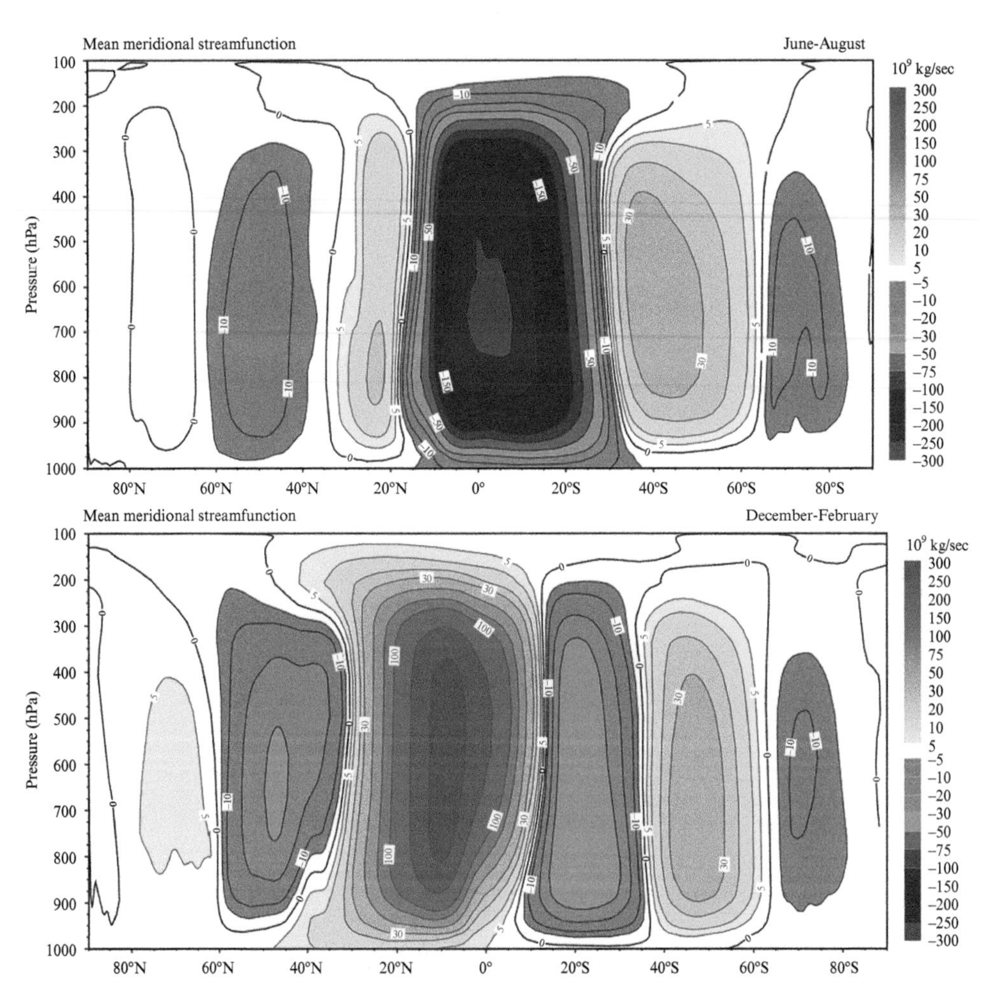

Fig. 4.8 Mean meridional streamfunction for JJA (top) and DJF (bottom). The solstitial Hadley circulation is dominated by a cross-equatorial cell with upper tropospheric flow towards the winter hemisphere. From *ERA-40 Atlas*.

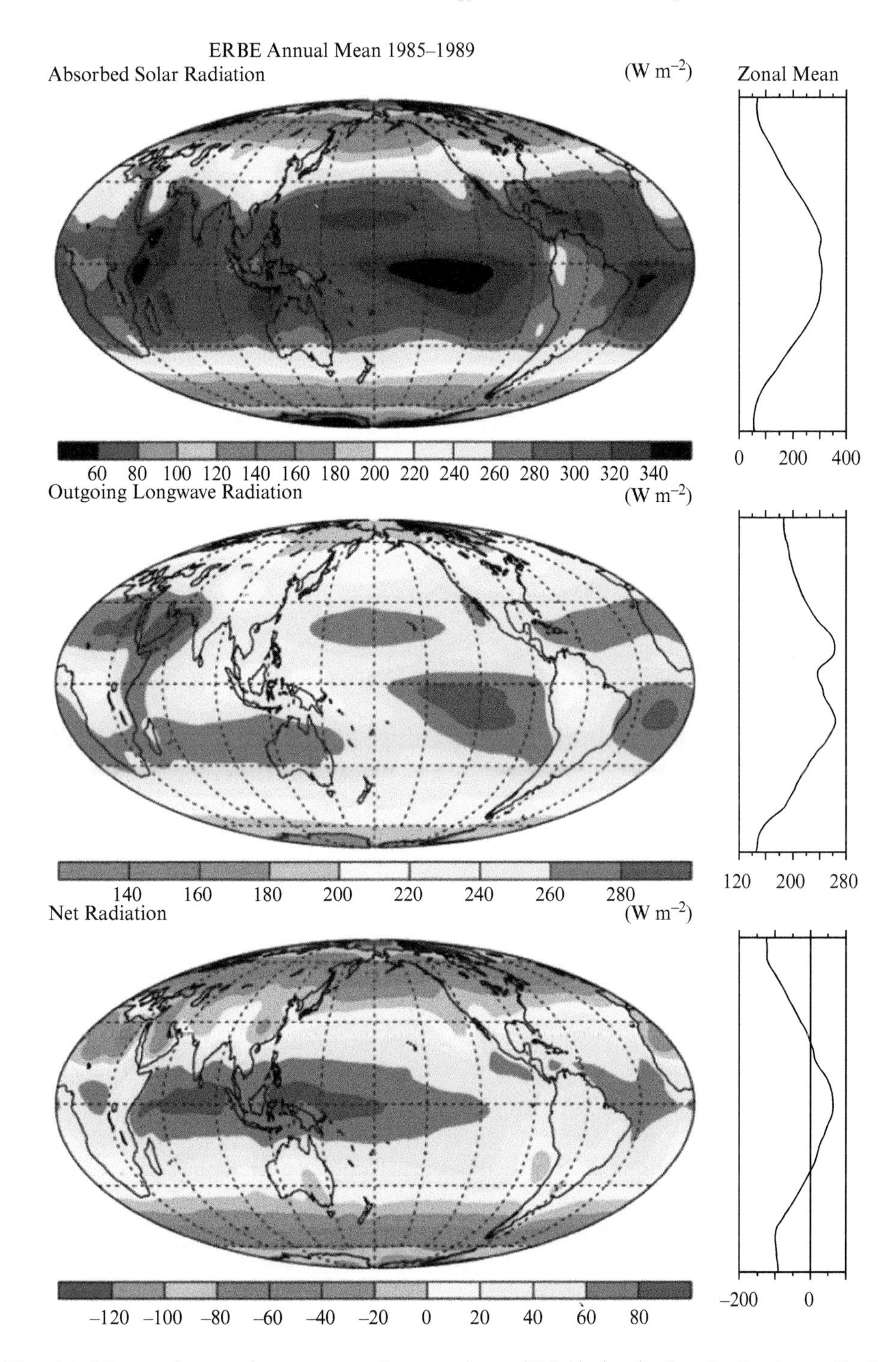

Fig. 4.9 Observed annual mean top-of-atmosphere (TOA) (top) absorbed solar radiation, (middle) outgoing longwave radiation, and (bottom) net radiation. Panels on the right show the zonal mean radiation. Figure from Trenberth and Stepaniak (2003). ® American Meteorological Society. Used with permission

to the zonal mean picture, the Hadley cell is localized near areas of strong convection and uplift, such as the seasonal monsoons in both hemispheres, which can account for some of the longitudinally localized features in Figure 4.7.

The jets exist at finer time scales and are not just an artifact of averaging. The jets experience variability at daily time scales, and meander meridionally as well as changing in strength.

4.2.3 Heat transport

The Earth receives a net input of energy in the tropics and loses energy to space at higher latitudes (Figure 4.9). This implies a poleward transport of energy by the climate system. Since the Earth is heated where it is warm and cooled where it is cold, the pole-equator temperature contrast is maintained, and it behaves like a heat engine which can perform work given two reservoirs at different temperatures. This work drives the atmospheric circulation and turbulence.

The ocean transports substantial heat at low latitudes, but the majority of the heat transport from the tropics to the poles is performed by the atmosphere (Figure 4.10). Interestingly, the net energy transport in both hemispheres looks identical (within observational uncertainties), even though the hemispheres are quite different in terms of amount of land, jet structures, etc.

The poleward transport by the atmosphere is primarily in the form of eddy heat transport (or macroturbulence) (Figure 4.11). The eddies are generated by baroclinic instability in regions slightly poleward of the subtropical jets called "storm tracks" (Figure 4.12). The locations of the maxima in jet speeds are co-located with the maxima in baroclinic storms, which is not surprising since baroclinic instability is

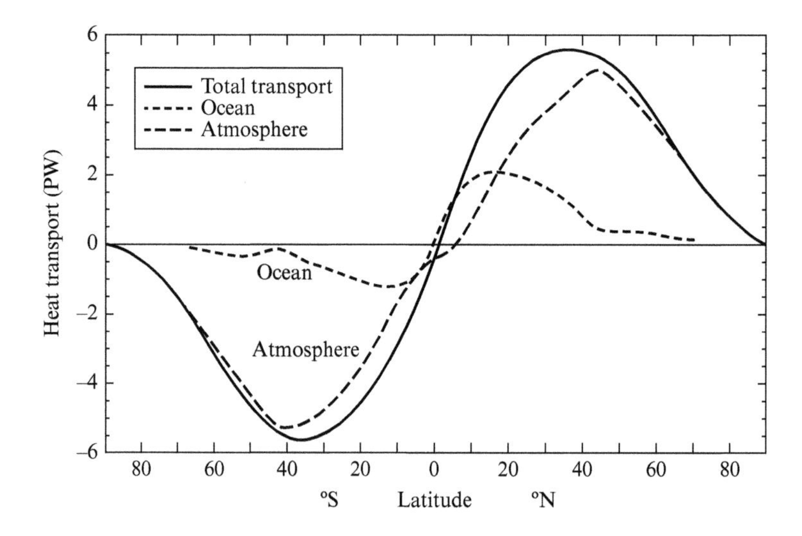

Fig. 4.10 Northward heat transport as a function of latitude, partitioned between the ocean and the atmosphere. Figure from Trenberth and Stepaniak (2004)

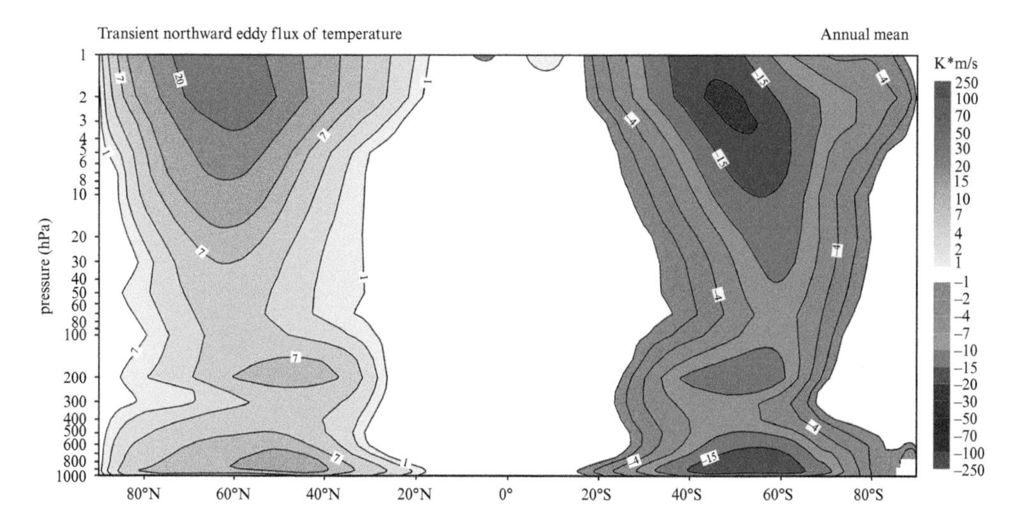

Fig. 4.11 Northward transient eddy flux of temperature as a function of latitude and height. From *ERA-40 Atlas*.

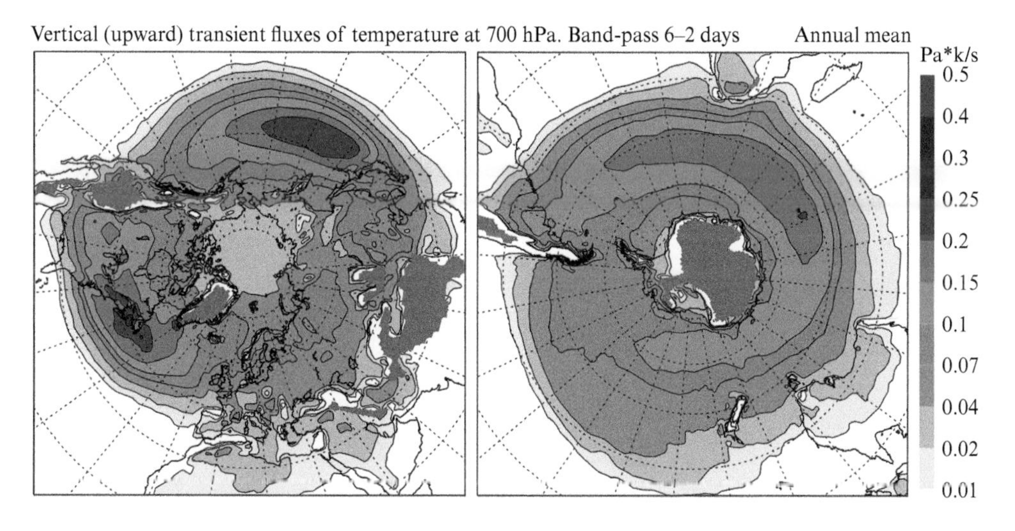

Fig. 4.12 Annual mean upward (vertical) transient fluxes of temperature at 700 hPa. From *ERA-40 Atlas*.

shaped by the vertical shear of the wind (i.e., by the horizontal temperature gradient). A notable exception is the subtropical jet over Australia, which is primarily driven by the strong heating of the Asian monsoon.

The storm tracks have maxima in eddy kinetic energy over the oceans in both hemispheres, and in the Atlantic there is a distinct poleward tilt downstream of the jet maximum (Figure 4.13). The storm tracks have a seasonality as well (Figures 4.14, 4.15), with more storms in the winter. The SH storm track variability is smaller from

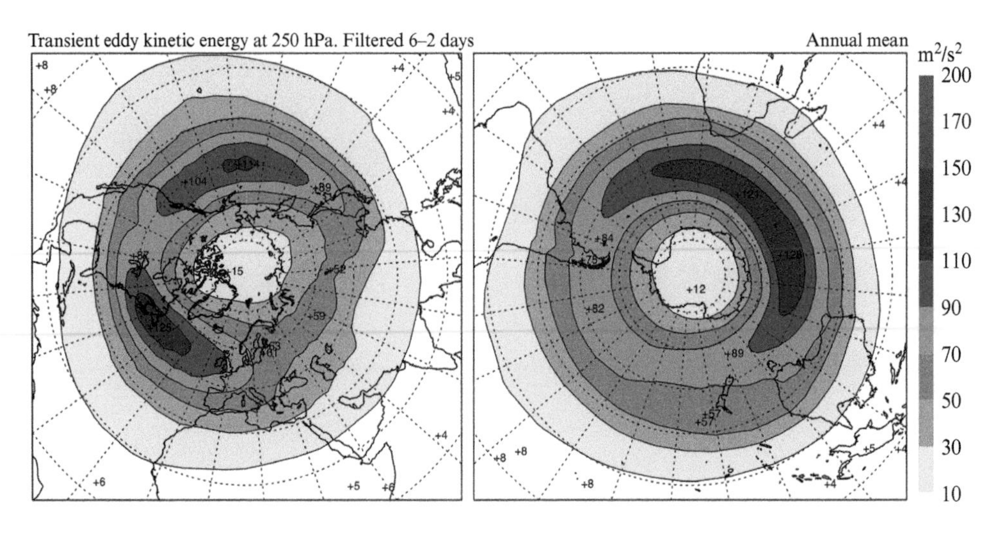

Fig. 4.13 Annual mean transient eddy kinetic energy at 250 hPa. From *ERA-40 Atlas.*

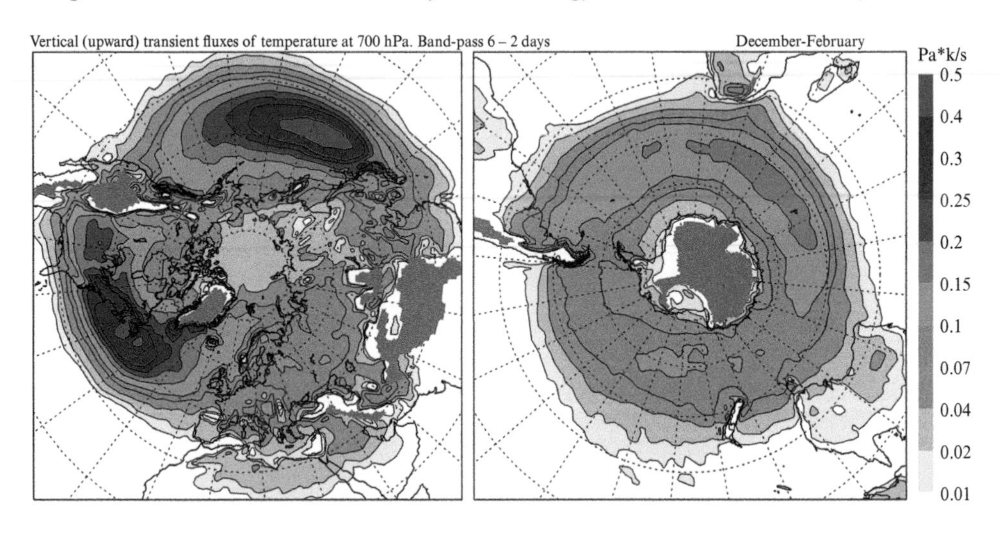

Fig. 4.14 As in Figure 4.12 but for DJF. From *ERA-40 Atlas.*

season to season since Antarctica does not cool or warm much seasonally, and therefore provides a more stable meridional temperature gradient.

In the NH, the meridional heat fluxes vary strongly in the longitudinal direction, and are co-located with the strongest meridional gradients in surface temperature. Although strong meridional temperature gradients would be expected to generate baroclinic instability, we would also expect the eddy heat flux to weaken the meridional gradient. Thus, the observations suggest that the meridional temperature gradient has a rapid diabatic restoration that prevents eddies from erasing the gradient, presumably from the warm western oceanic boundary currents.

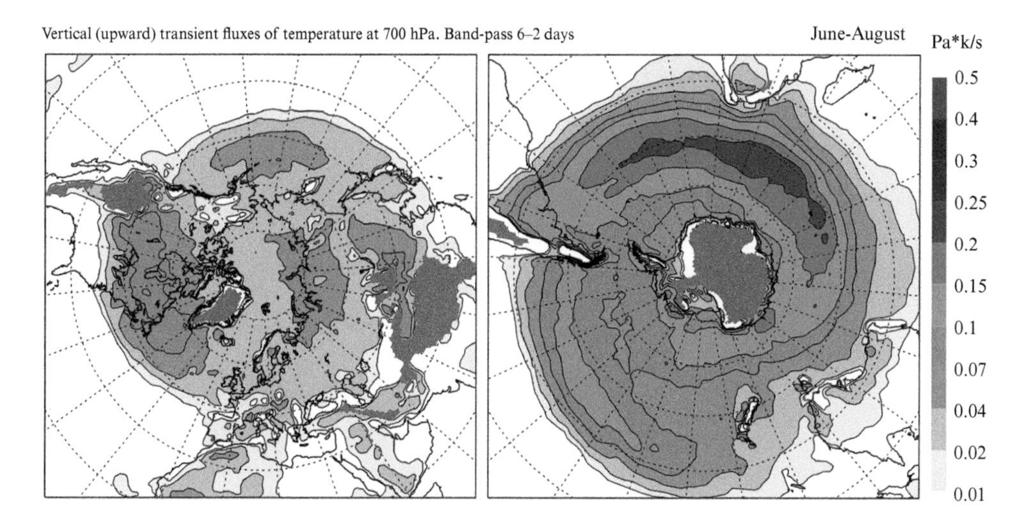

Fig. 4.15 As in Figure 4.12 but for JJA. From *ERA-40 Atlas*.

4.2.4 Momentum transport

The eddies in the mid-latitudes which transport heat poleward also transport zonal momentum, which acts to maintain the westerly winds. There is a net convergence of momentum into the jet core and divergence from the jet flanks. In addition, there is net angular momentum (with reference to the Earth's axis of rotation) convergence into mid-latitudes and angular momentum divergence in the tropics.

The zonally averaged angular momentum budget is given by (overbar is zonally averaged):

$$\frac{\partial}{\partial t}\overline{\int_o^{p_s} a\cos\phi u\frac{dp}{g}} - fa\cos\phi\overline{\int_o^{p_s} v\frac{dp}{g}} =$$
$$-\frac{1}{a\cos\phi}\frac{\partial}{\partial\phi}\left(\cos\phi\overline{\int_o^{p_s} acos\phi uv\frac{dp}{g}}\right) - \overline{p_s\frac{\partial h}{\partial\lambda}} - a\cos\phi\overline{\tau_s^{PBL}}.$$

The right-hand side (RHS) consists of torques applied to the system, while the left-hand side (LHS) represents the response to those torques. The second term on the LHS is proportional to the meridional mass transport, which can be interpreted as a tendency of the planetary angular momentum (the distribution of mass relative to the pole), while the first term on the LHS is the tendency of the relative angular momentum. The first term on the RHS is the angular momentum flux convergence in the free atmosphere, which is mainly associated with eddies and mainly comes from the upper troposphere. The second term on the RHS represents the mountain torque, while the last term represents the frictional surface stress from the planetary boundary layer (PBL).

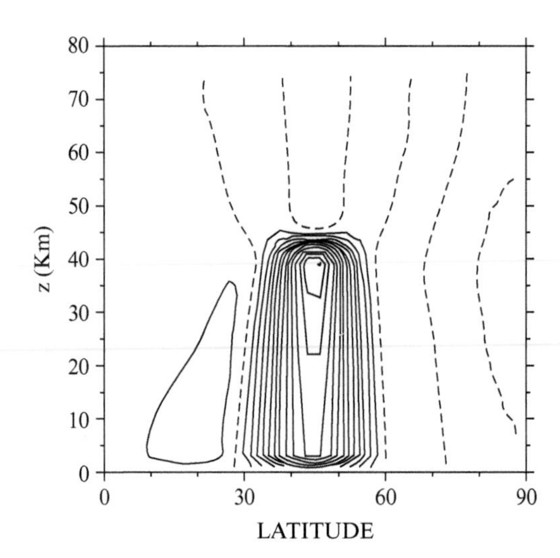

Fig. 4.16 Mean meridional circulation (stream function) response to an imposed torque in the free atmosphere, with a relaxational surface drag and Newtonian cooling. Figure from Haynes *et al.* (1991). ®American Meteorological Society. Used with permission.

In steady state, the momentum flux convergence is balanced by the other terms on the RHS:

$$-\frac{1}{acos\phi}\frac{\partial}{\partial\phi}\left(cos\phi\overline{\int_o^{p_s} acos\phi uv\frac{dp}{g}}\right) = p_s\overline{\frac{\partial h}{\partial\lambda}} + acos\phi\overline{\tau_s^{PBL}}.$$

It is generally assumed that the surface terms act as a drag on the flow, although this is not necessarily the case with the mountain torque. To the extent this is true, and that the surface drag responds passively to the momentum flux convergence, this leads to the picture of surface drag providing the drag required to balance the angular momentum fluxes (Figure 4.16).

Thus, the angular momentum convergence into the midlatitudes is balanced by surface drag acting on the midlatitude westerlies, while the angular momentum divergence out of the tropics implies an eastward drag (to supply angular momentum to the atmosphere) and thus, surface easterly winds. Indeed, the surface winds are observed to be easterly in the tropics (the "trade winds"), and westerly in midlatitudes (Figure 4.17).

These surface winds play an important role in the ocean circulation, and thereby in heat transport. For example, the exchange of heat between the atmosphere and oceans happens mainly over western boundary currents (where the ocean provides heat to the atmosphere) and over equatorial "cold tongue" regions (where the atmosphere provides heat to the ocean). Both oceanic features are wind-driven.

The momentum fluxes also play an important role in the Hadley circulation. Although the angular momentum is homogenized within the deep tropics, the Hadley circulation is seen to cross angular momentum contours in the subtropics (Figure 4.18).

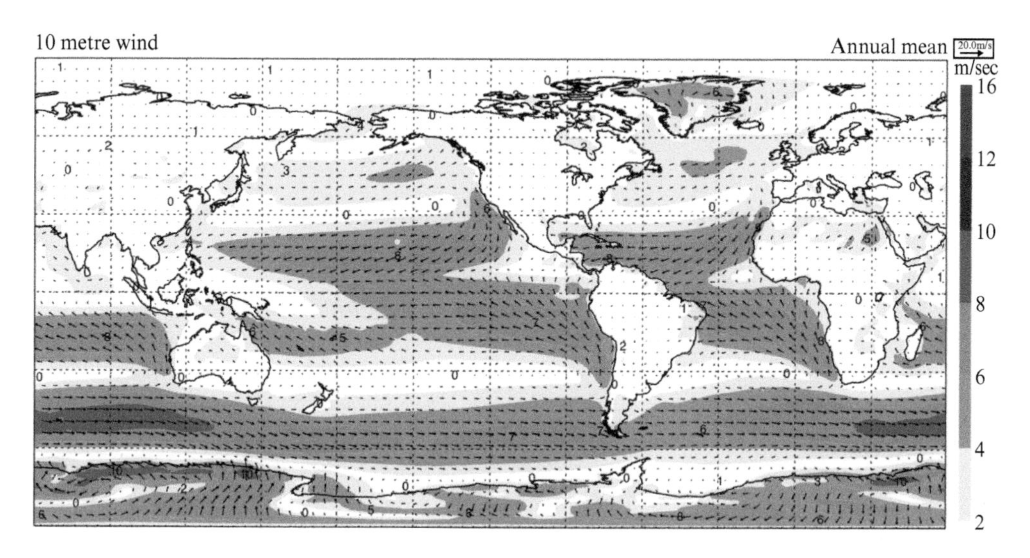

Fig. 4.17 Annual mean surface winds. From *ERA-40 Atlas*.

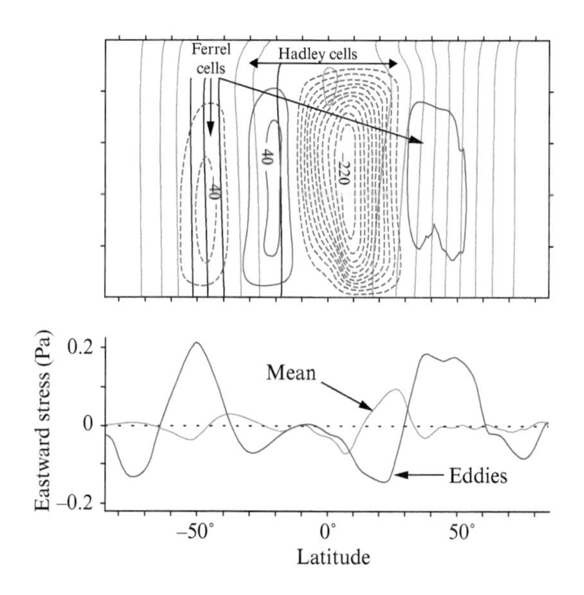

Fig. 4.18 Observations show (top panel) that the Hadley cell (red) crosses angular momentum contours (blue). Hence, the Hadley cell terminus is determined by angular momentum flux convergence (bottom panel). Figure from Schneider (2006).

This can only happen in the presence of torques. Thus, the Hadley cell terminus is determined by the eddies (and not just thermal driving), as the latitude where the angular momentum flux convergence changes sign. The Hadley cell terminus in turn affects subtropical descent zones and the hydrological cycle.

4.3 Balanced and unbalanced dynamics

4.3.1 Why balanced dynamics?

If one examines the observed surface pressure during the passage of a front, which generally occurs over a timescale of less than a day, the high temporal resolution timeseries is seen to be very smooth, despite including the sharp transition associated with the front (Figure 4.19). This may seem surprising, since the atmosphere is capable of supporting much higher frequency oscillations, notably inertia-gravity waves. This suggests that the atmosphere somehow remains close to a "slow manifold" where the inertia-gravity waves are weak, and motivates the study of so-called balanced, or slow, dynamics. This has been a central theme in large-scale dynamical meteorology.

In a system capable of supporting both fast and slow modes, an arbitrary initial condition will project onto both. Although the fast modes will eventually radiate away—the so-called geostrophic adjustment problem—any error in the observed initial conditions for weather prediction will have a spuriously large projection onto the inertia-gravity waves, and generate unphysical oscillations in the forecast. This problem was initially remedied using balanced models to produce the forecasts, and later by initializing the data so that it projects mainly onto the balanced dynamics (Temperton and Williamson, 1981). The effect of different levels of initialization in controlling the gravity-wave oscillations is shown in Figure 4.20. Hence, the requirement to develop balanced systems was a practical requirement in numerical weather prediction, as well as in the theoretical development of dynamical meteorology.

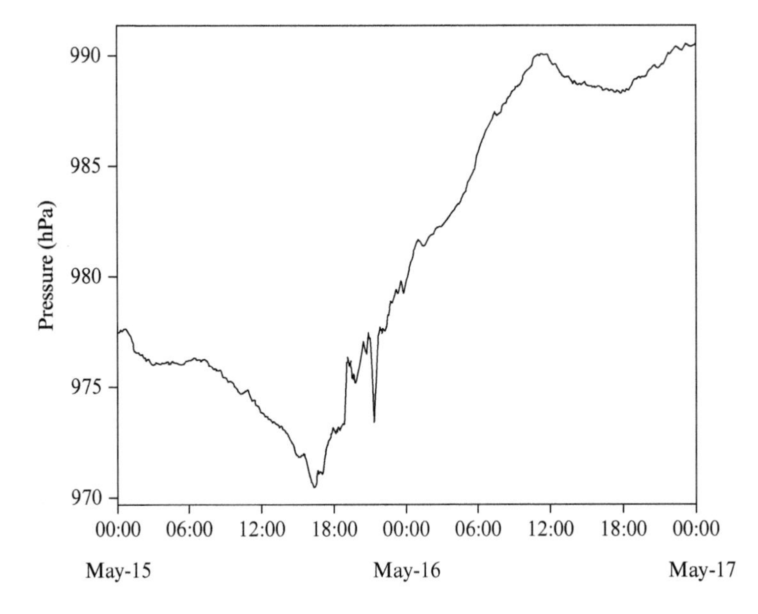

Fig. 4.19 Surface pressure during passage of a cold front and associated squall line at a weather station in Oklahoma. Data from NOAA.

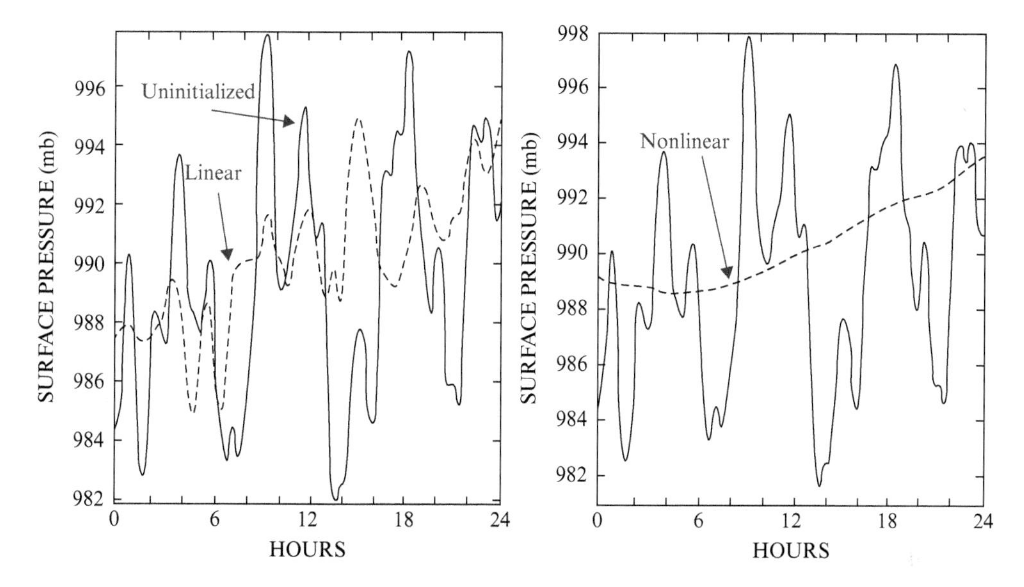

Fig. 4.20 Twenty-four-hour forecast of surface pressure at a particular location in a simplified model, with the initial condition uninitialized and initialized under linear or nonlinear balance conditions. Figure from Temperton and Williamson (1981) and Williamson and Temperton (1981). Ⓡ American Meteorological Society. Used with permission.

4.3.2 Shallow water equations on the f-plane

The canonical model for balanced and unbalanced dynamics is the shallow water equations (SWE) on the f-plane. The system is analogous to the horizontal component of the hydrostatic primitive equations in isentropic coordinates, so is a useful model for understanding stratified flows as well. The equations are:

$$\partial_t u + (u \cdot \nabla) u + f\hat{z} \times u = -g\nabla h \tag{4.1}$$

$$\partial_t h + \nabla \cdot (hu) = 0. \tag{4.2}$$

Linearizing about a state of rest with $h = H =$ constant and substituting the ansatz $\exp i(kx + ly - \omega t)$ for all variables results in the following solutions for the frequency,

$$\omega = 0, \ \pm\sqrt{f^2 + gH\kappa^2} \tag{4.3}$$

where $\kappa^2 = k^2 + l^2$. $\omega = 0$ is a zero-frequency mode representing the slow dynamics, whereas $\omega^2 = f^2 + gH\kappa^2$ represent the inertia-gravity (IG) waves. When $\kappa^2 \ll f^2/gH$ rotation dominates, and when $\kappa^2 \gg f^2/gH$ gravity dominates. Since $|\omega_{IG}| > f$, there is a low frequency cutoff for the IG waves. (This is in contrast to sound waves, which do not have a low frequency cutoff (Saujani and Shepherd, 2002).) Thus there is a clear distinction between fast and slow dynamics in the linear system.

We can introduce non-linearity heuristically by adding a Doppler shift $U\kappa$ to the frequency, where U is a characteristic velocity. Then the ratio of the frequencies is given by

$$\frac{\omega_0}{\omega_{IG}} \approx \frac{U\kappa}{U\kappa + \sqrt{f^2 + gH\kappa^2}}. \tag{4.4}$$

This ratio is much less than unity provided

$$\epsilon \equiv \frac{U\kappa}{\sqrt{f^2 + gH\kappa^2}} \ll 1. \tag{4.5}$$

Under these conditions there continues to be a separation of timescales in the non-linear dynamics, with fast and slow dynamics. The non-dimensional numbers that are important are the Rossby number $Ro = U/fL = U\kappa/f$ and the Froude number $Fr = U/\sqrt{gH}$. Note that the latter can be generalized to vertically stratified flow, with the surface gravity wave phase speed $\sqrt{gH}$ replaced by the phase speed of internal gravity waves.

It is easy to show that

$$\epsilon = \frac{Ro \cdot Fr}{\sqrt{Ro^2 + Fr^2}}, \tag{4.6}$$

which implies that $\epsilon \ll 1$ if either $Ro \ll 1$ or $Fr \ll 1$, even if the other quantity diverges (Saujani and Shepherd, 2006). The ratio Fr/Ro determines whether rotation or gravity (stratification) dominates, since $Fr/Ro = f/\kappa\sqrt{gH} = L/L_R$, where $L_R = \sqrt{gH}/f$ is the Rossby deformation radius. In classical QG scaling, $Ro \sim Fr$, so rotation and gravity effects are comparable.

We now non-dimensionalize the shallow water equations using the characteristic velocity U and length scale L_R. The slow time scale (advective) is L_R/U, and height is written as $h = H(1 + Ro \cdot \eta)$. This leads to

$$\frac{U^2}{L_R}\partial_t u + \frac{U^2}{L_R}(u \cdot \nabla)u + (fU)\hat{z} \times u = -\frac{gH.Ro}{L_R}\nabla\eta \tag{4.7}$$

$$\frac{H.Ro.U}{L_R}\partial_t \eta + \frac{H.U}{L_R}\nabla \cdot u + \frac{H.Ro.U}{L_R}\nabla \cdot (\eta u) = 0, \tag{4.8}$$

and thus to the non-dimensionalized equations

$$\frac{\partial u}{\partial t} + u \cdot \nabla u + \frac{1}{Ro}(\hat{z} \times u + \nabla\eta) = 0 \tag{4.9}$$

$$\frac{\partial \eta}{\partial t} + \nabla \cdot (\eta u) + \frac{1}{Ro}\nabla \cdot u = 0. \tag{4.10}$$

Thus, if $Ro \ll 1$, then to obtain dynamics on the slow timescale we require

1. $\hat{z} \times u = -\nabla\eta \Rightarrow u = -\frac{\partial \eta}{\partial y}, v = \frac{\partial \eta}{\partial x} \rightarrow$ geostrophic balance,
2. $\nabla \cdot u = 0 \rightarrow$ non-divergence.

These constraints can be equivalently expressed as $\psi = \eta$ and $\chi = 0$ where ψ and χ are the stream function and velocity potential, viz. $u = \hat{z} \times \nabla\psi + \nabla\chi$. This shows that there are only two independent constraints. Eliminating the $1/Ro$ terms between the non-dimensionalized equations leads to

$$(\frac{\partial}{\partial t} + u \cdot \nabla)(\frac{\partial v}{\partial x} - \frac{\partial u}{\partial y} - \eta) = 0, \tag{4.11}$$

which is the QG potential vorticity equation. Since all fields can be expressed in terms of ψ, it is a closed first-order-in-time evolution equation. However we need an extra equation on lateral boundaries, which comes from the conservation of circulation over the domain (or Kelvin's theorem). The geostrophic relation $\hat{z} \times u = -\nabla\eta$ is referred to as a balance relation, while the QGPV evolution equation is referred to as balanced dynamics.

The existence of a single slow non-linear equation is no accident, since it emerged from the slow (zero-frequency) linear mode. The QG dynamics is a reduction from the three shallow-water equations to one equation, by eliminating the inertia-gravity waves. The same procedure can be performed in either the primitive hydrostatic or in the Boussinesq equations by eliminating internal gravity waves. In the same way, either of those two systems can be obtained from the fully compressible equations by eliminating sound waves, which are fast compared to internal gravity waves.

4.3.3 What is a balanced model?

It is useful to provide a more general representation of the derivation that was just performed. A balanced model is a reduced set of evolution equations that filters out fast oscillations and describes the slow-time evolution of a system. It involves two components:

1. A balance relation, which filters out the fast oscillations and thereby reduces the dimensionality of the system;
2. Balanced, reduced, or slow dynamics describing the slow-time evolution.

Following Warn *et al.* (1995), consider a system of PDEs which has a combination of fast (f) and slow (s) modes, represented by

$$\frac{\partial f}{\partial t} + \frac{\Gamma f}{\epsilon} = F(s,f,\epsilon), \quad \frac{\partial s}{\partial t} = S(s,f,\epsilon), \tag{4.12}$$

with $\epsilon \ll 1$ representing the ratio between fast and slow timescales. Here Γ is an invertible operator whose spectrum gives the fast frequencies; on the fast time scale $\tau = t/\epsilon$,

$$\frac{\partial f}{\partial \tau} + \Gamma f = \epsilon F, \quad \frac{\partial s}{\partial \tau} = \epsilon S, \tag{4.13}$$

which reduces to the linear system when $\epsilon = 0$. However we are here interested in the slow non-linear dynamics. To this end, we perform an asymptotic expansion on f but not on s, which amounts to a slaving ansatz: $f = f^{(0)} + \epsilon f^{(1)} + \epsilon^2 f^{(2)} + \ldots$

- At $\mathcal{O}(1)$, we have $f^{(0)} = 0$ and $\frac{\partial s}{\partial t} = S(s,0,0)$
- At $\mathcal{O}(\epsilon)$, we have $f^{(1)} = \Gamma^{-1}F(s,0,0)$ and $\frac{\partial s}{\partial t} = S(s,f,\epsilon)|_{\mathcal{O}(\epsilon)}$

ad infinitum. The asymptotic nature of this series is demonstrated for a low-order ODE system by Bokhove and Shepherd (1996).

In GFD, a slow equation is always provided by the potential vorticity (PV) (Hoskins *et al.*, 1985), which necessarily evolves on the advective timescale.

4.3.4 Higher-order balance in the shallow-water equations

To see how this works in the case of the SWE, assuming small Ro, we first note that the PV is given by

$$Q = \frac{f+\hat{z}\cdot\nabla\times u}{h} \to \frac{f(1+Ro\,\hat{z}\cdot\nabla\times u)}{H(1+Ro\,\eta)} = \frac{f}{H}[1+Ro(\frac{\partial v}{\partial x}-\frac{\partial u}{\partial y}-\eta)+...]. \quad (4.14)$$

From this and the previous linear analysis, we infer:

- A suitable slow variable is $q=\frac{\nabla^2\psi-\eta}{1+\epsilon\eta}$ where $Q=\frac{f}{H}(1+\epsilon q)$.
- The fast variables are $D=\nabla\cdot u=\nabla^2\chi$ and $\Omega=\nabla^2(\psi-\eta)$, the latter being the geostrophic imbalance.

The evolution equations can then be written as (Warn *et al.*, 1995)

$$\frac{\partial q}{\partial t} = -J(\psi,q)-\nabla\chi\cdot\nabla q \quad (4.15)$$

$$\frac{\partial D}{\partial t}-\frac{\Omega}{\epsilon} = -J(\chi,\nabla^2\psi)-\frac{1}{2}\nabla^2|\nabla\chi|^2+\nabla^2 J(\chi,\psi)+2J\left(\frac{\partial\psi}{\partial x},\frac{\partial\psi}{\partial y}\right) \quad (4.16)$$

$$\frac{\partial\Omega}{\partial t}-(\nabla^2-1)\frac{D}{\epsilon} = -J(\psi,\nabla^2\psi)-\nabla\cdot(\nabla^2\psi\nabla\chi)+\nabla^2\{J(\psi,\eta)+\nabla\cdot(\eta\nabla\chi)\}. \quad (4.17)$$

This is in the slow-fast form given earlier, with

$$\Gamma=\begin{pmatrix} 0 & -1 \\ -(\nabla^2-1) & 0 \end{pmatrix},\ f=\begin{pmatrix} D \\ \Omega \end{pmatrix}.$$

Expanding all variables except q in a power series in the Rossby number ϵ:

- At $\mathcal{O}(1)$, $\Omega^{(0)}=0$ and $\chi^{(0)}=0$ and $\nabla^2\psi^{(0)}-\psi^{(0)}=q$. This provides the leading-order slaving relations for the velocity and height in terms of q, as found earlier.
- At $\mathcal{O}(\epsilon)$, we have

$$\Omega^{(1)}=-2J(\frac{\partial\psi^{(0)}}{\partial x},\frac{\partial\psi^{(0)}}{\partial y}),\ (\nabla^2-1)\nabla^2\chi^{(1)}=J(\psi^{(0)},\nabla^2\psi^{(0)}) \quad (4.18)$$

$$\text{and}\ \ \nabla^2\psi^{(1)}-\eta^{(1)}=\eta^{(0)}q. \quad (4.19)$$

In both cases the dynamics is given by PV advection

$$\frac{\partial q}{\partial t}+v\cdot\nabla q=0, \quad (4.20)$$

but the $\mathcal{O}(1)$ system (linear balance) has $v = v^{(0)}$ whilst the $\mathcal{O}(\epsilon)$ system (nonlinear balance) has $v = v^{(0)} + \epsilon v^{(1)}$. The velocity fields are determined given q, so these all represent closed systems, which are inherently slow since the timescale of evolution is advective. Note that there is nothing special about PV. Any variable that projects onto the slow modes at leading order can, in principle, be used as a slaving variable, for example, height (Warn *et al.*, 1995).

4.4 Balanced and unbalanced turbulence

4.4.1 Two-dimensional turbulence

The barotropic vorticity equation is

$$\frac{\partial}{\partial t}\nabla^2\psi + J(\psi, \nabla^2\psi) = 0, \tag{4.21}$$

where $\nabla^2\psi = \hat{z}\cdot\nabla\times u$ is the vorticity and J is the Jacobian operator. The system has two inviscid integral invariants, the kinetic energy and the enstrophy:

$$E = \int\int \frac{1}{2}|\nabla\psi|^2 dxdy,\ Z = \int\int \frac{1}{2}(\nabla^2\psi)^2 dxdy. \tag{4.22}$$

Their wavenumber spectra are related by $Z(k) = k^2 E(k)$, where now k is the total (scalar) wavenumber. Enstrophy conservation prohibits a direct (downscale) cascade of energy since k^2 would thereby increase. This leads to the peculiar properties of 2D turbulence, including an upscale energy cascade which is manifested in the spontaneous emergence of coherent vortices (Bartello and Warn, 1996).

The tendency towards an upscale cascade is evident from the following thought-experiment. If we start from an energy spectrum localized around wavenumber k_0, then turbulence can be expected to cause the spectrum to spread:

$$\frac{d}{dt}\int (k-k_0)^2 E(k)dk = \frac{d}{dt}\int [k^2E(k) - 2kk_0E(k) + k_0^2E(k)]dk > 0. \tag{4.23}$$

But since the first and third of the terms on the RHS are invariant, this leads to

$$\frac{d}{dt}\int kE(k)dk < 0, \tag{4.24}$$

implying an upscale (inverse) energy cascade. The situation is depicted in Figure 4.21. In a similar way, it can be shown that enstrophy tends to cascade downscale.

The classical picture of 2D turbulence was introduced by Kraichnan (1967), with a spectrally localized forcing which injects both energy and enstrophy, the energy cascading upscale and the enstrophy cascading downscale (Figure 4.22). The power laws follow from scaling symmetry (dimensional analysis). The paradigm has been

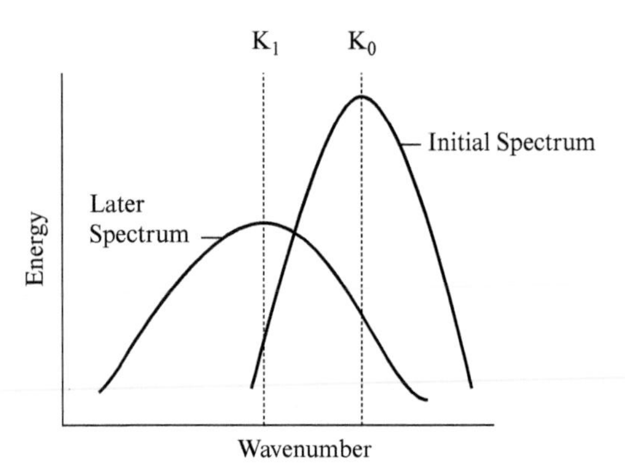

Fig. 4.21 Schematic of spreading of the kinetic energy spectrum in 2D turbulence. Figure from Vallis (2006). Used with permission

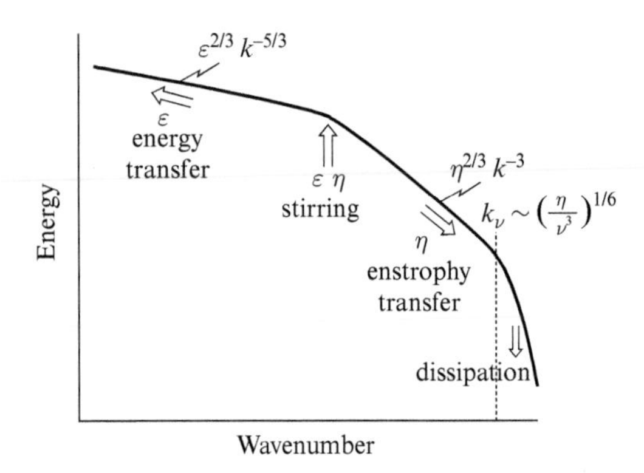

Fig. 4.22 Schematic of inertial ranges in 2D turbulence. Figure from Vallis (2006). Used with permission

argued to be relevant to the atmosphere by Charney (1971), with the forcing provided by baroclinic instability.

4.4.2 Large-scale turbulence in the atmosphere

Global analysis of kinetic energy spectra in the atmosphere revealed that the transient spectra scaled approximately as n^{-3} for wavenumbers (total spherical harmonic index, the analogue of k in planar geometry) larger than $n = 8$ (Boer and Shepherd, 1983). This corresponds to the power law expected in the enstrophy-cascading inertial range (Figure 4.22). The corresponding spectral fluxes confirmed an upscale flux of energy and a downscale flux of enstrophy (Figure 4.23), also consistent with the expectations of 2D turbulence. However, it should be noted that the spectral fluxes are not well resolved by such low-resolution data, since many of the relevant wavenumber triads are unresolved. In particular, the enstrophy flux necessarily goes to zero at the largest wavenumber, whereas physically one expects the enstrophy flux to continue downscale.

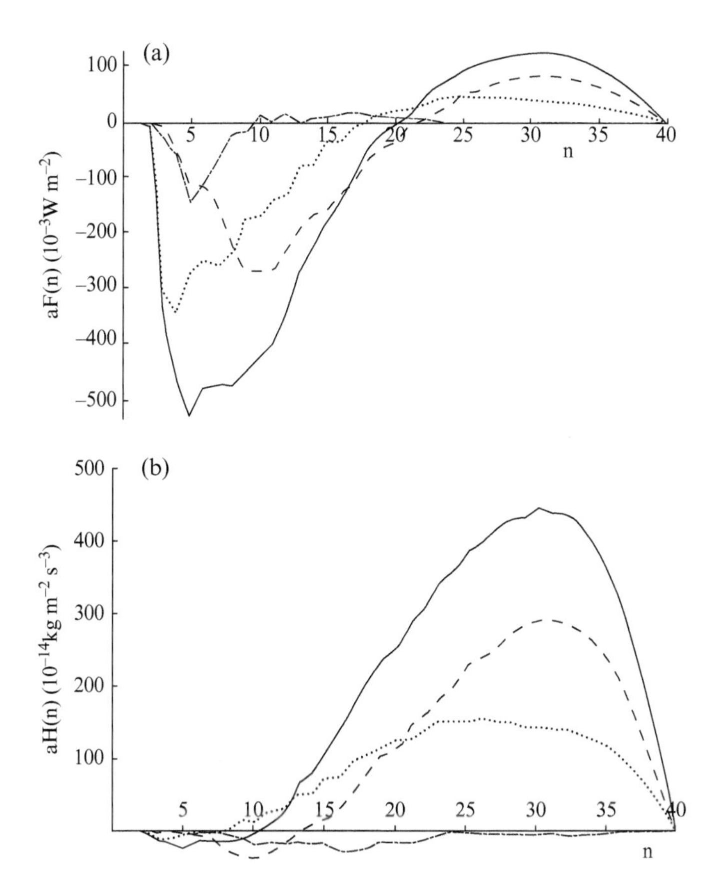

Fig. 4.23 Observed spectral fluxes of kinetic energy (top) and enstrophy (bottom) in the atmosphere, for a data set truncated at spherical harmonic index $n = 40$. Total is solid, transient is dashed, stationary is dash-dotted, and the mixed stationary-transient component is dotted. Figure from Shepherd (1987*b*). ® American Meteorological Society. Used with permission

Another point is that the spectral fluxes can be decomposed into stationary (all three parts of the triad are stationary), transient (all three parts of the triad are transient), and a mixed stationary-transient component (two parts are transient and one is stationary—if only one part is transient, the average is zero by definition). The mixed component is seen to be a very significant part of both the energy and enstrophy fluxes (Figure 4.23). This suggests that mean flows (neglected in the classical 2D turbulence paradigm) play a non-trivial role in large-scale atmospheric turbulence.

The mean flow in the atmosphere is predominantly zonal, and is of larger scale than the transient eddies. This implies that triad interactions between transient eddies and a zonal mean flow are special in two ways. First, they couple eddies with the same zonal wavenumber. Second, the scale separation implies the transient enstrophy is approximately conserved. If the enstrophy transfer is towards higher meridional wavenumbers then the associated energy transfer is to the zonal mean flow from the eddies, whilst if the enstrophy transfer is towards lower meridional wavenumbers then the energy transfer is from the zonal mean flow. It turns out that synoptic-scale eddies lose energy to the mean flow, and planetary-scale eddies gain energy from the mean flow (Shepherd, 1987*b*). We return to this point in the final section of these notes.

As noted previously, the computed nonlinear interactions miss an unresolved component. Leith (1971) used a statistical turbulence model to infer that the interactions with unresolved scales could be represented as an effective diffusion with a negative spectral range, giving zero energy loss. Applying this parameterization to the observed data gave an estimated total energy flux that was purely upscale, and an enstrophy flux that was roughly constant and non-zero at the largest wavenumber, consistent with the expectations of 2D turbulence (Boer and Shepherd, 1983). This suggests that the positive energy flux at high wavenumbers seen in Figure 4.23 is an artefact of the finite resolution, and that in reality, the unresolved scales are providing energy to the resolved scales.

Koshyk and Boer (1995) used a higher-resolution atmospheric analysis (T60 spectral truncation) to compute the effect of nonlinear interactions unresolved at T32 on the scales with $n < 32$, and found that it was consistent with the parameterization of Leith (1971), including the prediction that unresolved scales are a source of energy for the resolved scales. This helped establish the concept of "energy backscatter."

More recently, the spectral fluxes of energy and enstrophy have been revisited with a very much higher resolution atmospheric analysis (T799) (Burgess *et al.*, 2013). At this resolution, the resolved energy cascade is purely upscale, with an inferred baroclinic excitation range between $n = 10 - 30$, whilst the enstrophy cascade has a distinct plateau (Figure 4.24). Interactions with the zonal mean flow remain an impor-

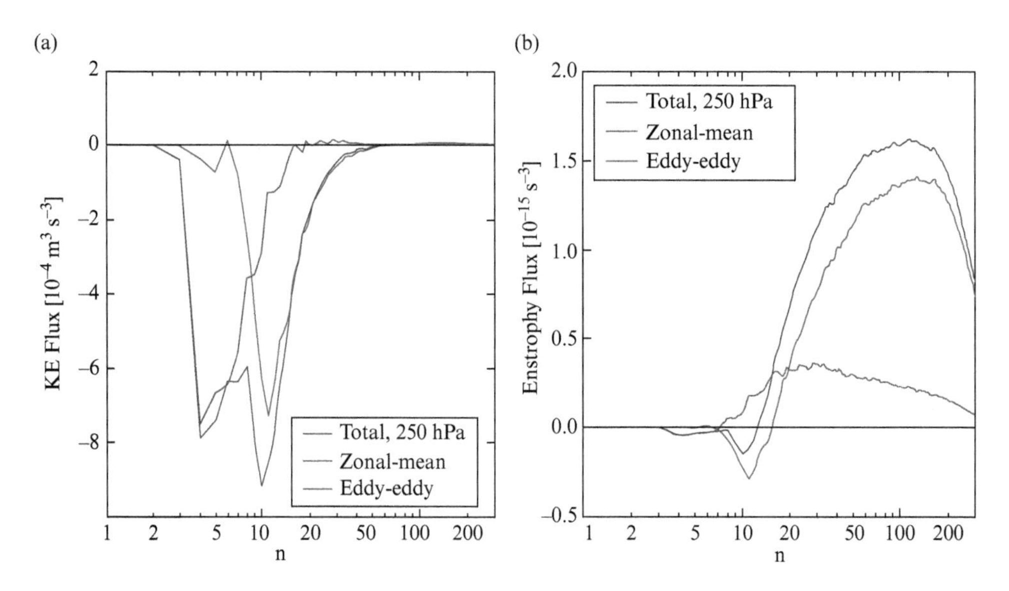

Fig. 4.24 Spectral fluxes of kinetic energy (left) and of enstrophy (right) in the upper troposphere for a modern atmospheric analysis. Figure from Burgess *et al.* (2013). Ⓡ American Meteorological Society. Used with permission.

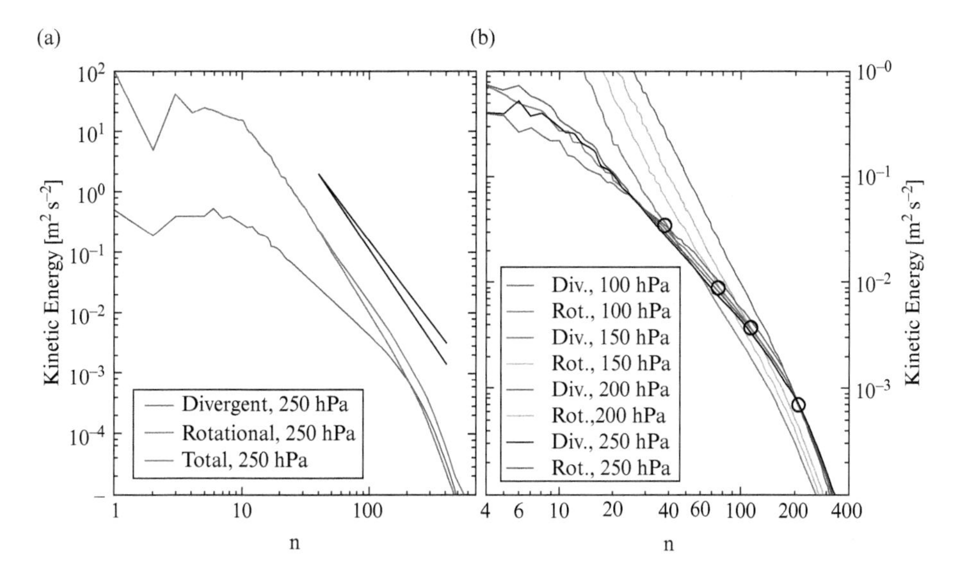

Fig. 4.25 Rotational and divergent components of atmospheric kinetic energy spectra at various altitudes. In the right-hand panel, the scales where the rotational and divergent spectra cross are indicated with circles, which move to smaller wavenumber (i.e., larger scale) with decreasing pressure (i.e., higher altitude). Figure from Burgess *et al.* (2013). ® American Meteorological Society. Used with permission.

tant contributor to the upscale energy cascade; moreover the pure eddy contribution is very limited in spectral range. Thus, the upscale flux cannot really be characterized as a "cascade," as in the classical picture. However, the downscale enstrophy cascade is now dominated by the pure eddy interactions (Figure 4.24). The high resolution analysis also gives a clean n^{-3} spectrum in the enstrophy inertial range (Figure 4.25).

Direct observations of winds in the upper troposphere from commercial aircraft (Nastrom and Gage, 1985) revealed a $k^{-5/3}$ energy spectrum at wavelengths smaller than about 500 km (Figure 4.26), or n larger than about 100. The origin of this Gage-Nastrom spectrum has been a source of controversy. Lilly (1983) argued for an inverse cascade of balanced (quasi-2D) energy from the mesoscales. However, the evidence seems to be consolidating in favor of a downscale cascade of energy due to unbalanced flow, which is not inhibited by the potential enstrophy constraint (Lindborg, 2006; Waite and Bartello, 2006). An unbalanced spectrum can be generated by a variety of mechanisms, and one can expect upward radiation of internal gravity waves from any such spectrum. There could be many waves to get a $k^{-5/3}$ spectrum theoretically—all one needs is the appropriate scaling symmetry.

The Gage-Nastrom spectrum has been reproduced in atmospheric models. In atmospheric analyses, Burgess *et al.* (2013) show that the divergent flow has a comparatively shallow spectrum whilst the rotational spectrum is much steeper (Figure 4.25). Balanced flow has divergent energy that is much weaker than rotational energy (see previous section), whereas the two components are of comparable magnitude for unbalanced flow. This suggests co-existing balanced and unbalanced

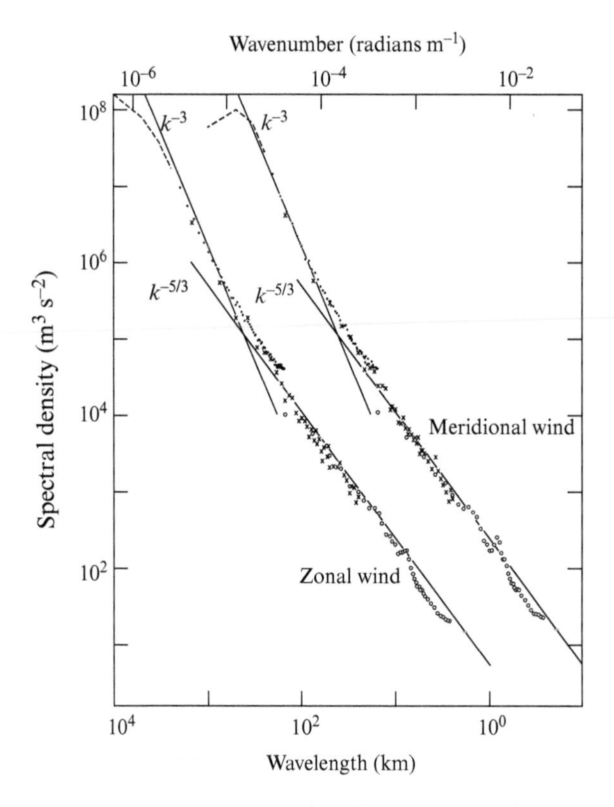

Fig. 4.26 Upper tropospheric spectra from aircraft data. Figure from Nastrom and Gage (1985). ®American Meteorological Society. Used with permission. Vallis, G. K., (2017). *Atmospheric and Oceanic Fluid Dynamics: Fundamentals and Large-scale Circulation*, 2nd edn. Cambridge University Press, p. 946.)

spectra, with the former dominating at large scales and the latter dominating at small scales. The balanced part of the flow decays preferentially with altitude due to Charney–Drazin filtering and Rossby-wave breaking in the stratosphere, meaning that the unbalanced spectrum emerges at smaller wavenumbers (or larger scales) with increasing altitude (Figure 4.25). Even low resolution atmospheric models exhibit an unbalanced spectrum at sufficiently high altitudes (Shepherd *et al.*, 2000).

4.4.3 Predictability

The spectrum of atmospheric turbulence has implications for atmospheric predictability. The classic paradigm is to assume we initially have some error in the small scales, which works its way to the larger scales (Lorenz, 1969). The question is, how long does this take? A heuristic argument can be provided as follows, assuming an inverse cascade of error with the scale doubling in each step (Vallis, 1985). The time taken for the error to propagate from an initial small scale $L(1/2)^N$ to large scale L is then the sum of N steps,

$$\Sigma_{n=1}^{N} \tau_{L(1/2)^n}, \tag{4.25}$$

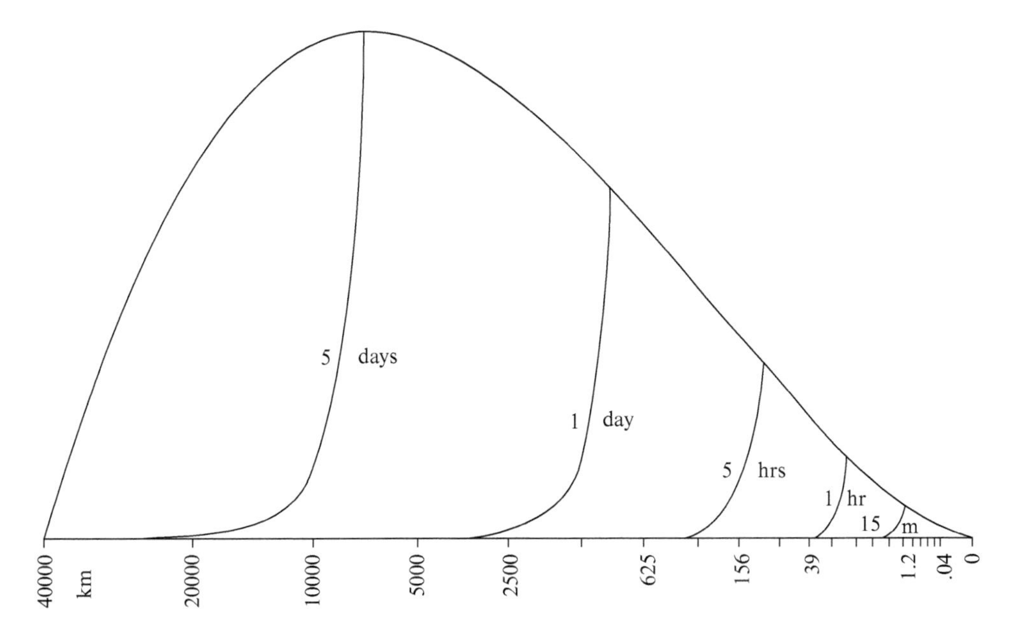

Fig. 4.27 The upscale cascade of error for a $k^{-5/3}$ energy spectrum. Figure from Lorenz (1969).

where τ_L is the error-doubling timescale at scale L. Dimensional analysis suggests that τ_L scales as $(k^3E(k))^{-1/2}$, where $k = 1/L$. If $E(k) \sim k^{-3}$, then τ_L is a constant which basically says that the time taken for errors to contaminate the large scales is unbounded as the initial error is confined to increasingly smaller scales (i.e., as $N \to \infty$). This means there is no inherent limit to predictability.

On the other hand, the Gage–Nastrom spectrum $E(k) \sim k^{-5/3}$ implies that τ_L decreases with decreasing L, and the previous sum converges even in the limit $N \to \infty$. For example, an error-doubling timescale of a day at a scale of 1000 km decreases to an hour at a scale of 10 km (Figure 4.27). This implies finite predictability—a multi-scale "butterfly effect"—and limits the gain in predictability that can be obtained as we increase the resolution of our models and observing systems. Lorenz (1969) obtained an upper limit of about two weeks.

Operational weather prediction systems are still far below that upper limit. However Bauer *et al.* (2015) show that the forecast skill has been increasing since 1980 by about one day of lead time every decade, and that the historical difference in skill between the Northern and Southern Hemispheres has been closed in this century.

4.5 Pseudomomentum and wave, mean-flow interaction

4.5.1 Non-canonical Hamiltonian dynamics

The classical formulation of Hamiltonian dynamics concerns the time evolution of generalized coordinates q_i and generalized momenta p_i, where $i = 1 \ldots N$, which is described by Hamilton's equations

$$dq_i/dt = \partial H/\partial p_i$$
$$dp_i/dt = -\partial H/\partial q_i,$$

where H is the Hamiltonian function. In the special case of a Newtonian potential system

$$H = |p|^2/2m + U(q),$$

from which Hamilton's equations yield Newton's second law. For an autonomous system $\partial_t H = 0$, in which case Hamilton's equations ensure conservation of the Hamiltonian itself (identified with energy):

$$\frac{dH}{dt} = \frac{\partial H}{\partial q_i}\frac{dq_i}{dt} + \frac{\partial H}{\partial p_i}\frac{dp_i}{dt} = 0.$$

(Here and in the following, repeated indices are summed.)

More generally, a Hamiltonian system is one representable in the so-called "symplectic formulation"

$$\frac{du_i}{dt} = J_{ij}\frac{\partial H}{\partial u_j},$$

where J is a matrix with certain mathematical properties. Hamilton's equations are a special case of this formulation, called *canonical*. One of the key properties of J is skew-symmetry, which ensures energy conservation:

$$\frac{dH}{dt} = \frac{\partial H}{\partial u_i}J_{ij}\frac{\partial H}{\partial u_j} = 0.$$

The canonical J is invertible, but in general J may be non-invertible (then called *non-canonical*), in which case $J\partial C/\partial u_j = 0$ has a non-trivial solution C. Such C are called Casimirs. Casimirs are invariants since

$$\frac{dC}{dt} = \frac{\partial C}{\partial u_i}\frac{du_i}{dt} = \frac{\partial C}{\partial u_i}J_{ij}\frac{\partial H}{\partial u_j} = -\frac{\partial H}{\partial u_i}J_{ij}\frac{\partial C}{\partial u_j} = 0.$$

The best-known example of a non-canonical Hamiltonian system is Euler's equations for a rigid body, which comprise three evolution equations for the three components of angular momentum about the principal axis of rotation. (The fact that the number of evolution equations is odd immediately implies that the representation is non-canonical.) The total angular momentum $C = m_1^2 + m_2^2 + m_3^2$ is a Casimir invariant.

In Hamilton's equations, cyclic coordinates are generalized coordinates that do not explicitly appear in the Hamiltonian, i.e., $\partial H/\partial q_i = 0$ for some i, meaning that there is a translational symmetry in that coordinate. Conservation of the corresponding generalized momentum follows immediately from Hamilton's equations: $dp_i/dt = 0$ for the same i. For example, translational symmetry implies conservation of linear momentum.

More generally, Noether's theorem links symmetries and conservation laws. Given a function $F(u)$, we can define

$$\delta_F u_i = \epsilon J_{ij}\frac{\partial F}{\partial u_j},$$

where $\epsilon \ll 1$, which is called an infinitesimal generator. Then the infinitesimal variation of H induced by the function F is

$$\delta_F H = \frac{\partial H}{\partial u_i}\delta_F u_i = \epsilon\frac{\partial H}{\partial u_i}J_{ij}\frac{\partial F}{\partial u_j}.$$

But the time evolution of F can be written

$$\frac{dF}{dt} = \frac{\partial F}{\partial u_i}\frac{du_i}{dt} = \frac{\partial F}{\partial u_i}J_{ij}\frac{\partial H}{\partial u_i} = -\frac{\partial H}{\partial u_i}J_{ij}\frac{\partial F}{\partial u_j}.$$

It follows that

$$\frac{dF}{dt} = 0 \iff \delta_F H = 0.$$

Thus, conservation laws are associated with symmetries of the Hamiltonian. Casimir invariants are associated with invisible symmetries since $\delta_C u = 0$. Consider, for example, the rigid body. In canonical coordinates, the rotational symmetry is explicit and leads to angular momentum conservation through Noether's theorem. But in Euler's equations, angles have been eliminated and the rotational symmetry is now invisible; thus angular momentum (which is still conserved) enters instead as a Casimir.

4.5.2 Barotropic dynamics as a Hamiltonian system

It turns out that barotropic dynamics

$$\partial_t \omega = -J(\psi, \omega)$$

is a Hamiltonian system, albeit an infinite-dimensional one. The state variable (analogous to u_i in the finite-dimensional case) is the vorticity field $\omega(x,y)$, and the Hamiltonian is the kinetic energy,

$$H = \int\int \frac{1}{2}|\nabla\psi|^2 dxdy.$$

Taking a variation of the Hamiltonian yields

$$\delta H = \int\int \nabla\psi\cdot\delta\nabla\psi\, dxdy = \int\int\{\nabla\cdot(\psi\delta\nabla\psi) - \psi\delta\omega\}dxdy.$$

The first term in the last expression is zero since we integrate over the domain, and therefore the functional derivative of H is

$$\frac{\delta H}{\delta \omega} = -\psi.$$

The functional derivative is the infinite-dimensional analogue of the partial derivative, and is what we need to generalize Hamiltonian dynamics to PDEs. Note that the functional derivative can reflect non-local properties, e.g., in this case $\psi(x, y)$ is not a local function of $\omega(x, y)$ but depends on the vorticity field over the entire domain.

Barotropic dynamics can be written in symplectic form as

$$\partial_t \omega = J \frac{\delta H}{\delta \omega}$$

where $J = -\partial(\omega, \cdot)$. It can be shown that this J satisfies all the relevant properties required for the system to be Hamiltonian (McIntyre and Shepherd, 1987).

The Casimir invariants are the solutions of $J\delta C/\delta \omega = 0$, which implies

$$\frac{\delta C}{\delta \omega} = f(\omega) \text{ and hence } C = \int\int g(\omega)\, dx dy,$$

for some functions f and g, where f is the derivative of g. The fact that these quantities are conserved in time can be seen from the Lagrangian conservation of vorticity, which implies that any function of vorticity is conserved. Thus there are an infinite number of Casimir invariants.

This system is symmetric in x, so we can seek conservation laws by Noether's theorem. Translating x to the right is equivalent to translating ω to the left, which can be represented by the infinitesimal variation

$$\delta \omega = \omega(x - \epsilon) - \omega(x) = -\epsilon \partial_x \omega.$$

Let M be the conserved quantity corresponding to such a variation. Noether's theorem then implies

$$-\epsilon \partial_x \omega = \delta_M \omega = \epsilon J \frac{\delta M}{\delta \omega} = -\epsilon \partial(\omega, \frac{\delta M}{\delta \omega}),$$

which modulo Casimirs has the solution

$$\frac{\delta M}{\delta \omega} = y \implies M = \int\int y\omega\, dx dy.$$

This quantity M, which is guaranteed to be conserved, is known as Kelvin's impulse. Apart from boundary terms (which are separately conserved by Kelvin's circulation theorem), it is equivalent to the zonal momentum

$$M = \int\int u\, dx dy.$$

4.5.3 Pseudomomentum

The Hamiltonian structure of barotropic dynamics (and of geophysical fluid dynamics in general, Shepherd (1990)) is especially useful in the construction of disturbance invariants. It is well known that in the presence of inhomogeneous background states, the momentum and energy of waves are non-trivial to understand. This has historically led to a great deal of confusion. Hamiltonian structure explains why this is the case, and also provides a remedy.

If $u = U$ is a steady solution of a Hamiltonian system, it follows that

$$\partial_t U = J \frac{\delta H}{\delta u}\bigg|_{u=U} = 0. \tag{4.26}$$

If the system is canonical, then J is invertible, which means that $\delta H/\delta u$ vanishes at $u = U$ and H is locally quadratic in disturbance amplitude, i.e., there is a quadratic invariant. This is the textbook situation in classical mechanics. In a non-canonical system, however, J is not invertible, which means that $\delta H/\delta u$ does not necessarily vanish at $u = U$ and H is generally linear in disturbance amplitude. This means that the disturbance energy does not have a definite sign, and one therefore cannot establish stability, define normal modes, etc.

However, there is a remedy which leads to the concept of pseudoenergy (McIntyre and Shepherd, 1987). The analogous quantity for momentum conservation is the pseudomomentum. For a basic state $u = U$ that is invariant in x, then by Noether's theorem,

$$J \frac{\delta M}{\delta u}\bigg|_{u=U} = -\partial_x U = 0. \tag{4.27}$$

As was the case with H, the non-invertibility of J means that M is linear in disturbance amplitude. However, the gradient $\delta M/\delta u$ is tangent to the kernel (null space) of J, which implies that $\delta(M + C)|_{u=U} = 0$ for some Casimir C. Thus we can define a new quantity,

$$A = (M + C)[u] - (M + C)[U], \tag{4.28}$$

which is both conserved and locally quadratic in disturbance amplitude. Voila!

We now see how this unfolds in the case of the barotropic β-plane, which supports Rossby waves. All the previous derivations apply with $q = \omega + \beta y$ in place of ω, hence we can write

$$\frac{\delta M}{\delta q} = y, \frac{\delta C}{\delta q} = g'(q), \tag{4.29}$$

where, at this point, g is undetermined. Now consider a disturbance to an x-invariant basic state $q_0(y)$. We determine g by enforcing $\delta(M + C) = 0$ at $q = q_0$, which implies

$$g'(q_0) = -y. \tag{4.30}$$

The right-hand side of this equation can be interpreted as a function of q, allowing the implicit definition of the function $Y(q)$ via the relation $Y(q_0(y)) = y$. This then defines the function g, whence the pseudomomentum can be written

$$A = \iint [yq - yq_0 + g(q) - g(q_0)]dxdy = \iint \left\{ -\int_0^{q-q_0} [Y(q_0 + q') - Y(q_0)]dq' \right\} dxdy.$$

Note that A is negative definite for $\partial_y q_0 > 0$, which is the usual situation in the presence of β.

If q_0 is the zonal mean, and we take the small-amplitude approximation, then the zonal mean of A is $-\overline{q'^2}/2\overline{q}_y$. Exactly the same expression can be derived for stratified QG flow, with q now the QG PV, where it turns out to be the negative of the Eliassen–Palm (E–P) wave activity. Thus, the conservation of the E–P wave activity in the interaction between waves and mean flows reflects the underlying fact that the E-P wave activity is just the (negative of the) pseudomomentum.

The negative sign of A corresponds to the negative intrinsic phase speed of Rossby waves, which have the dispersion relation

$$\omega = Uk - \frac{\beta k}{k^2 + l^2}. \tag{4.31}$$

Rossby waves account for the stationary and low-frequency wave features of the atmosphere and ocean, and are not usually associated with large-scale turbulence. However, even though synoptic-scale eddies are clearly not linear waves, the properties of their macroturbulence are constrained by the positive definiteness of the E–P wave activity, which applies at finite amplitude but is ultimately traceable to the dynamics of Rossby waves. In this way, (finite amplitude) Rossby waves can still be regarded as the building blocks of large-scale atmospheric turbulence.

4.5.4 Relationship between pseudomomentum and momentum

It is instructive to directly show how pseudomomentum is related to momentum. Because $\overline{v} = 0$, where the overbar denotes the zonal mean, the zonally averaged (unforced, inviscid) zonal momentum equation for the barotropic β-plane simplifies to

$$\frac{\partial \overline{u}}{\partial t} = -\overline{\frac{\partial u^2}{\partial x}} - \overline{\frac{\partial uv}{\partial y}} + f\overline{v} - \frac{\partial \overline{p}}{\partial x} = -\frac{\partial \overline{u'v'}}{\partial y}, \tag{4.32}$$

where the prime denotes the deviation from the zonal mean. So the momentum interpretation is that the zonal mean flow is driven by eddy momentum flux convergence. While this sounds physically compelling, it is not very useful because it is not clear how to determine the eddy momentum flux convergence. Indeed, the upgradient character of the observed atmospheric eddy momentum flux was for a long time a source of confusion and puzzlement. But there is an alternative and more informative way of looking at this equation. We first rewrite the equation as

$$\frac{\partial \overline{u}}{\partial t} = \overline{-v'\left(\frac{\partial u'}{\partial y} - \frac{\partial v'}{\partial x}\right) + \frac{1}{2}\frac{\partial}{\partial x}[u'^2 - v'^2]} = \overline{v'q'}. \tag{4.33}$$

This shows that eddy momentum flux convergence is equivalent to the eddy flux of PV. Now, q' is governed by the linearized PV equation,

$$\frac{\partial q'}{\partial t} + \overline{u}\frac{\partial \overline{q'}}{\partial x} + v'\frac{\partial \overline{q}}{\partial y} = 0, \tag{4.34}$$

hence (provided $\overline{q}_y \neq 0$) we can write

$$v' = -\frac{1}{\overline{q}_y}\left(\frac{\partial q'}{\partial t} + \overline{u}\frac{\partial q'}{\partial x}\right) \tag{4.35}$$

and thus,

$$\overline{v'q'} = -\frac{\partial}{\partial t}\left(\frac{1}{2}\frac{\overline{q'^2}}{\overline{q}_y}\right) = \frac{\partial A}{\partial t}. \tag{4.36}$$

It follows that

$$\frac{\partial \overline{u}}{\partial t} = \frac{\partial A}{\partial t}.$$

This important relation (known as the Taylor identity) shows that for barotropic flows, zonal mean flow changes are related to changes in eddy pseudomomentum.

4.5.5 Wave, mean-flow interaction in the atmosphere

We now see how these ideas apply to the baroclinic atmosphere. In stratified QG dynamics, combining the zonal momentum and temperature tendency equations constrained by thermal wind balance, one obtains a similar equation for the zonal mean acceleration,

$$\mathcal{L}\left(\frac{\partial \overline{u}}{\partial t}\right) = \frac{\partial^2}{\partial y^2}(\overline{q'v'}), \tag{4.37}$$

where

$$\mathcal{L} = \frac{\partial^2}{\partial y^2} + \frac{1}{\rho_o}\frac{\partial}{\partial z}\frac{\rho_o}{S}\frac{\partial}{\partial z}$$

and S is a stratification parameter and ρ_0 is density. So it's essentially the same physics as in the barotropic case, but now the zonal-wind response to mixing of potential vorticity is spatially non-local (the Eliassen balanced response). This follows from the non-local nature of PV inversion (Hoskins *et al.*, 1985).

In order to apply these ideas to the maintenance of the atmospheric circulation, we need to allow for source/sink processes on the waves, e.g., radiative damping or the dissipation of waves following wave breaking. Denoting such processes by D, the pseudomomentum conservation law takes the local form

$$\frac{\partial A}{\partial t} + \nabla\cdot F = D, \quad \nabla\cdot F = -\overline{v'q'}, \tag{4.38}$$

where F is the negative of the Eliassen–Palm flux, and represents propagation of pseudomomentum. Thus,

$$\mathcal{L}\left(\frac{\partial \overline{u}}{\partial t}\right) = \frac{\partial^2}{\partial y^2}(\overline{v'q'}) = -\frac{\partial^2}{\partial y^2}(\nabla \cdot F) = \frac{\partial^2}{\partial y^2}\left(\frac{\partial A}{\partial t} - D\right). \tag{4.39}$$

Since the operator $\mathcal{L}$ is elliptic, this shows that mean flow changes require either wave transience or non-conservative effects; this is known as the non-acceleration theorem.

In the extratropical atmosphere we can assume $\overline{q}_y > 0$ since $\overline{q}_y$ is dominated by β. Hence, $A < 0$, as noted earlier. Therefore, Rossby waves carry negative pseudomomentum, and where they dissipate, there must be a convergence of this negative pseudomomentum, and a negative torque exerted on the mean flow. If one assumes that waves dissipate through wave breaking, and that wave breaking will mix PV downgradient, then the deceleration can also be inferred on that basis. By the same token, a positive torque must be exerted where the waves are generated. This phenomenon is very generic, and is seen in laboratory rotating-tank experiments (Whitehead, 1975).

In the atmosphere, synoptic-scale Rossby waves are generated by baroclinic instability, hence, within a jet region. In idealized baroclinic lifecycles, the waves are seen to grow baroclinically within the jet region, and then propagate upwards and outwards (mostly equatorward) where they decay barotropically in the subtropical upper troposphere (Simmons and Hoskins, 1978). The same behavior is seen in atmospheric observations (Edmon *et al.*, 1980). Thus, baroclinic lifecycles seem to capture the essence of what is going on in the real atmosphere.

The non-localness of the mean-flow response to the eddy forcing is reflected in the fact that the response is deep, and the mean-flow acceleration in the core of the jet, even in the upper troposphere, is due to $\nabla \cdot F$ near the lower surface, where the wave activity is generated (Haynes and Shepherd, 1989). This is the essential mechanism behind the eddy-driven midlatitude jets in the atmosphere.

The observations (Edmon *et al.*, 1980) actually show two regions of E–P flux convergence, the main one in the subtropical upper troposphere and a secondary one in the midlatitude middle troposphere. Thorncroft *et al.* (1993) showed that modest changes to the barotropic component of the zonal mean flow in the baroclinic lifecycles could change the location of the breaking region from the former region to the latter region. The implication is that the atmosphere can exhibit both kinds of lifecycle, with wave breaking occurring sometimes on the equatorward and sometimes on the poleward flank of the jet.

Wave breaking is facilitated by the presence of critical layers, where the wave phase speed equals the background flow speed. Randel and Held (1991) computed a phase speed spectrum for the atmospheric E–P fluxes, and showed that both regions of E–P flux convergence followed the zonal winds in a way that would be expected from critical-layer control, with subtropical critical layers in the upper troposphere and midlatitude critical layers in the middle troposphere (Figure 4.28). Hence, the jet both shapes, and is shaped by, the eddies. Michael McIntyre has called this interaction the "wave-turbulence jigsaw puzzle."

The theory of baroclinic lifecycles and wave, mean-flow interaction thus explains the nature of the observed eddy momentum fluxes in the atmosphere (see lower panel of Figure 4.18), and in particular how the eddies act to strengthen the zonal mean flow.

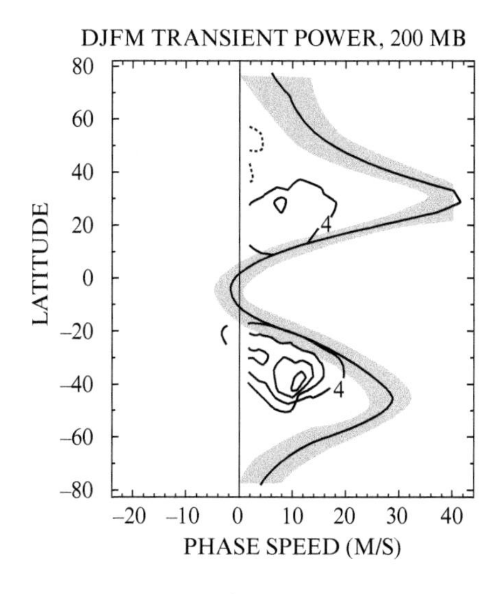

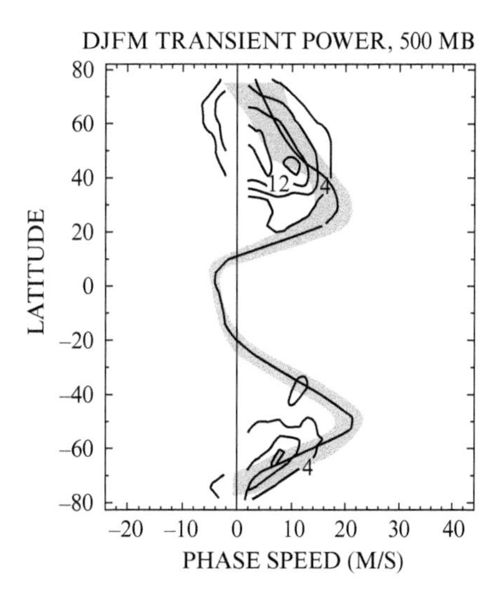

Fig. 4.28 Observed E-P flux convergence as a function of zonal phase speed (contours) and zonal mean flow (thick line), plotted for boreal winter (DJFM) in the upper troposphere at 200 hPa (left panel) and in the middle troposphere at 500 hPa (right panel). Figure from Randel and Held (1991). ® American Meteorological Society. Used with permission.

4.6 2D turbulence and zonal jets

4.6.1 Relation to the upscale energy cascade

As discussed earlier and shown in Figure 4.24, atmospheric observations show an upscale transfer of kinetic energy in the upper troposphere, but the transfer into the largest scales mainly occurs through eddy-mean flow, not eddy-eddy interactions (Shepherd, 1987*b*). Moreover, even the turbulent cascade associated with the eddy-eddy (transient) interactions is very limited in terms of spectral range.

Schneider and Walker (2006) argue that this limited transient upscale energy cascade is no accident. They argue that the atmosphere adjusts towards a state of weak nonlinearity, where the energy-containing scale of the eddies is similar to the scale of the linearly most unstable baroclinic waves. This precludes an extensive upscale energy cascade. A more extensive cascade is found in the ocean (Schlösser and Eden, 2007).

But then the question becomes, why is the mixed (eddy-mean) component of the atmospheric energy flux upscale, i.e., from the eddies into the mean flow? We cannot just appeal to the textbook arguments for an upscale energy cascade mentioned in Section 4.4.1, because they tend to focus on spectrally local interactions and the interactions here are spectrally non-local. In any case, those textbook arguments actually have many loopholes (Holloway, 2010).

In general, for a random collection of disturbances in the presence of a large-scale flow, the shearing of the disturbance vorticity by the large-scale flow means that some disturbances will extract energy from the large-scale flow, in a phenomenon known as the "Orr effect" (first stage of Figure 4.29) and thereby leading to a downscale energy flux (from the mean flow to the eddies), while others will give energy up

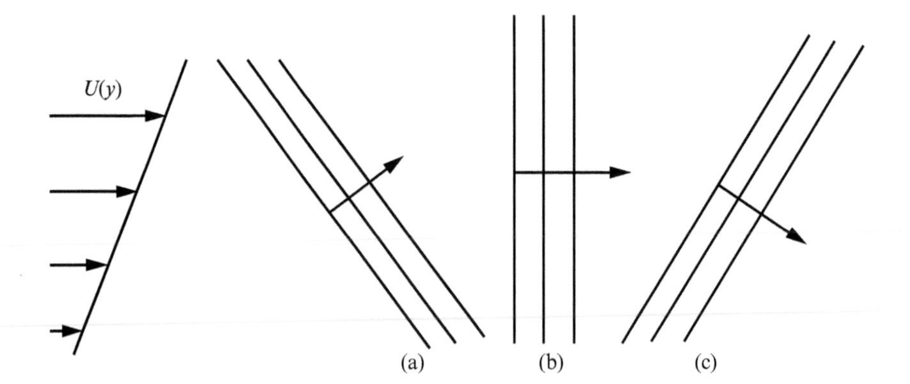

Fig. 4.29 The Orr effect demonstrated for linear Couette flow. The zonal wavenumber is fixed while the meridional wavenumber is continuously varying, and the disturbance initially leans into the shear. As the disturbance is sheared by the mean flow, the disturbance energy grows during (a), peaks at (b), and decays in (c). Figure from Shepherd (1987*a*).

to the large-scale flow, in a process of barotropic decay and leading to an upscale energy flux.

For any single plane wave, the "Orr effect" is transient and all disturbances must eventually decay, as in Figure 4.29, in which case the energy transfer is necessarily from the eddies to the mean flow. Indeed, in a quasilinear 2D simulation with a sinusoidal jet, initially random eddies decay rapidly and develop an anisotropic spectrum, as expected from the Orr effect (Shepherd, 1987*a*). However in the nonlinear version of the same simulation, the eddies do not decay at large scale, as the spectrum is isotropized by the phase scrambling associated with nonlinear interactions. Wave-wave interactions thus render the upscale cascade irreversible, reducing the transfer of energy into the mean flow.

A similar effect is seen in a realistic simulation of the atmosphere using an idealized GCM (O'Gorman and Schneider, 2007). An n^{-3} eddy kinetic energy spectrum is still present (though less cleanly) when wave-wave interactions are suppressed, but the wave-wave interactions indirectly affect the wave-mean flow interaction. In particular, the jets become too strong if the wave-wave interactions are suppressed. However, this result may depend on the parameter regime (Ait-Chaalal *et al.*, 2016).

4.6.2 Complexities of Earth's atmosphere

In the real atmosphere, the transient planetary-scale eddies extract energy from the zonal mean flow, whilst the synoptic-scale eddies give energy up to the zonal mean flow (Shepherd, 1987*b*). The reason the net energy transfer in the atmosphere is upscale is simply because the synoptic-scale eddy contribution is larger. But if the jets are not eddy-driven (e.g., driven instead by radiative forcing), then there is no reason that the eddies would have to maintain them. Thus in general, we cannot expect eddies to always act to strengthen a jet. In barotropic simulations with an imposed jet and random forcing, the sign of the eddy-jet energy exchange depends on the parameter regime (Shepherd, 1987*a*).

In the atmosphere, the stratospheric polar vortex is driven radiatively and weakened by eddy forcing. This is because the jet is dynamically stable, and the eddies are generated elsewhere, in the troposphere. Thus the stratospheric polar vortex is the opposite of an eddy-driven jet. And as already noted, the origin of the subtropical jets lies in the Hadley circulation, with the eddies acting to damp the winds in this region.

Even in the case of an eddy-driven jet, the question arises of what sets the latitude of the jet. It is not enough to attribute this to the eddy forcing, since the eddy forcing depends on the jet itself through the baroclinicity that drives the eddies. The question is an important one, because climate models tend to locate the tropospheric eddy-driven jet too far equatorward, in both hemispheres (Gerber *et al.*, 2010), for reasons that are not understood. The biases are similar when observed SSTs are imposed, implying that atmospheric processes are the issue.

One influence on the mid-latitude jet is the tropical circulation itself. Observations show a zonally symmetric midlatitude tropospheric response to ENSO, with the mid-latitude jet shifting equatorward during El Niño. This is attributed to a meridional shift in the eddy momentum flux convergence, induced by a shift in the critical layers arising from the subtropical zonal wind changes (Lu *et al.*, 2008).

Another influence on the mid-latitude jet is the planetary boundary layer (PBL). It turns out that the PBL does not just respond passively to the eddy momentum flux convergence in the free atmosphere, as assumed in the usual picture. Chen *et al.* (2007) found that the jet in an idealized atmospheric model moved poleward as the surface drag weakened. The mechanism was again explainable in terms of critical-layer control, this time through a change in the phase speed of the waves.

To further complicate matters, Polichtchouk and Shepherd (2016) repeated this experiment with a full-physics PBL, through a change in roughness length. The mid-latitude jets again moved poleward as the surface roughness decreased, but the driving mechanism turned out to originate in the tropics, and to involve changes in air-sea moisture fluxes. The coupling to the mid-latitude jet then followed much as in Lu *et al.* (2008).

On top of this, especially in the NH, there are significant zonal asymmetries, as noted earlier. The longitudinally varying jet does provide waveguides and preferred pathways for Rossby-wave propagation. However since the jet is not zonally symmetric, one cannot use psuedomomentum to describe the wave propagation. For stationary waves one can use the psuedoenergy, but cannot relate it back to the zonal flow. As a result, there is no closed theory for wave, mean-flow interaction in this situation, as there is for zonal mean flows.

The mid-latitude jets can be expected to change location and strength with climate change. This is a very active area of research, which is posing very challenging questions for atmospheric dynamicists. The interaction between jets and eddies (storm tracks) lies at the heart of these questions.

References

Ait-Chaalal, Farid, Schneider, Tapio, Meyer, Bettina, and Marston, J. B. (2016). Cumulant expansions for atmospheric flows. *New Journal of Physics*, **18**(2), 025019.

Bartello, Peter and Warn, Tom (1996). Self-similarity of decaying two-dimensional turbulence. *Journal of Fluid Mechanics*, **326**, 357–72.

Bauer, Peter, Thorpe, Alan, and Brunet, Gilbert (2015). The quiet revolution of numerical weather prediction. *Nature*, **525**(7567), 47–55.

Boer, George J. and Shepherd, Theodore G. (1983). Large-scale two-dimensional turbulence in the atmosphere. *Journal of the Atmospheric Sciences*, **40**(1): 164–84.

Bokhove, Onno, and Shepherd, Theodore G. (1996). On Hamiltonian balanced dynamics and the slowest invariant manifold. *Journal of the Atmospheric Sciences*, **53**: 276–97.

Burgess, B. Helen, Erler, Andre R., and Shepherd, Theodore G. (2013). The troposphere-to-stratosphere transition in kinetic energy spectra and nonlinear spectral fluxes as seen in ECMWF analyses. *Journal of the Atmospheric Sciences*, **70**(2), 669–87.

Charney, Jule G. (1971). Geostrophic turbulence. *Journal of the Atmospheric Sciences*, **28**(6), 1087–95.

Chen, Gang, Held, Isaac M., and Robinson, Walter M. (2007). Sensitivity of the latitude of the surface westerlies to surface friction. *Journal of the Atmospheric Sciences*, **64**, 2899–915.

Edmon, Jr., Harry J., Hoskins, Brian J., and McIntyre, Michael E. (1980). Eliassen-Palm cross sections for the troposphere. *Journal of the Atmospheric Sciences*, **37**(12), 2600–16.

Gerber *et al.*, Edwin P. (2010). Stratosphere-troposphere coupling and annular mode variability in chemistry-climate models. *Journal of Geophysical Research*, **115**, D00M06.

Haynes, Peter H., Marks, Crispin J., McIntyre, Michael E., Shepherd, Theodore G., and Shine, Keith P. (1991). On the "downward control" of extratropical diabatic circulations by eddy-induced mean zonal forces. *Journal of the Atmospheric Sciences*, **48**(4), 651–78.

Haynes, Peter H. and Shepherd, Theodore G. (1989). The importance of surface pressure changes in the response of the atmosphere to zonally-symmetric thermal and mechanical forcing. *Quarterly Journal of the Royal Meteorological Society*, **115**(490), 1181–208.

Held, Isaac M. and Hou, Arthur Y. (1980). Nonlinear axially symmetric circulations in a nearly inviscid atmosphere. *Journal of the Atmospheric Sciences*, **37**(3), 515–33.

Holloway, Greg (2010). Eddy stress and shear in 2D flow. *Journal of Turbulence*, **11**, doi:10.1080/14685248.2010.481673.

Hoskins, B. J., McIntyre, M. E., and Robertson, A. W. (1985). On the use and significance of isentropic potential vorticity maps. *Quarterly Journal of the Royal Meteorological Society*, **111**, 877–946.

Koshyk, John N., and Boer, George J. (1995). Parameterization of dynamical subgrid-scale processes in a spectral GCM. *Journal of the Atmospheric Sciences*, **52**(7), 965–76.

Kraichnan, Robert H. (1967). Inertial ranges in two-dimensional turbulence. *Physics of Fluids*, **10**(7), 1417–23.

Leith, Cecil E. (1971). Atmospheric predictability and two-dimensional turbulence. *Journal of the Atmospheric Sciences*, **28**(2), 145–61.

Lilly, Douglas K. (1983). Stratified turbulence and the mesoscale variability of the atmosphere. *Journal of the Atmospheric Sciences*, **40**(3), 749–61.

Lindborg, Erik (2006). The energy cascade in a strongly stratified fluid. *Journal of Fluid Mechanics*, **550**, 207–42.

Lorenz, Edward N. (1969). The predictability of a flow which possesses many scales of motion. *Tellus*, **21**(3), 289–307.

Lu, Jian, Chen, Gang, and Frierson, Dargan M. W. (2008). Response of the zonal mean atmospheric circulation to El Niño versus global warming. *Journal of Climate*, **21**, 5835–51.

McIntyre, Michael E., and Shepherd, Theodore G. (1987). An exact local conservation theorem for finite-amplitude disturbances to nonparallel shear flows, with remarks on Hamiltonian structure and on Arnold's stability theorems. *Journal of Fluid Mechanics*, **181**, 527–65.

Nastrom, Greg D., and Gage, Kenneth S. (1985). A climatology of atmospheric wavenumber spectra of wind and temperature observed by commercial aircraft. *Journal of the Atmospheric Sciences*, **42**(9), 950–60.

O'Gorman, Paul A., and Schneider, Tapio (2007). Recovery of atmospheric flow statistics in a general circulation model without nonlinear eddy-eddy interactions. *Geophysical Research Letters*, **34**(22), n/a–n/a. L22801.

Polichtchouk, Inna, and Shepherd, Theodore G. (2016). Zonal-mean circulation response to reduced air-sea momentum roughness. *Quarterly Journal of the Royal Meteorological Society*, **142**, 2611–22.

Randel, William J. and Held, Isaac M. (1991). Phase speed spectra of transient eddy fluxes and critical layer absorption. *Journal of the Atmospheric Sciences*, **48**(5), 688–97.

Saujani, Simal, and Shepherd, Theodore G. (2002) Comments on "Balance and the Slow Quasimanifold: Some Explicit Results". *Journal of the Atmospheric Sciences*, **59**(19), 2874–7.

Saujani, Simal, and Shepherd, Theodore G. (2006). A unified theory of balance in the extratropics. *Journal of Fluid Mechanics*, **569**, 447–64.

Schlösser, F. and Eden, C. (2007). Diagnosing the energy cascade in a model of the North Atlantic. *Geophysical Research Letters*, **34**, L02604.

Schneider, Tapio (2006). The general circulation of the atmosphere. *Annual Review of Earth and Planetary Sciences*, **34**(1), 655–88.

Schneider, Tapio and Walker, Christopher C. (2006). Self-organization of atmospheric macroturbulence into critical states of weak nonlinear eddy–eddy interactions. *Journal of the Atmospheric Sciences*, **63**(6), 1569–86.

Shepherd, Theodore G. (1987*a*). Rossby waves and two-dimensional turbulence in a large-scale zonal jet. *Journal of Fluid Mechanics*, **183**(1), 467–509.

Shepherd, Theodore G. (1987*b*). A spectral view of nonlinear fluxes and stationary-transient interaction in the atmosphere. *Journal of the Atmospheric Sciences*, **44**(8), 1166–79.

Shepherd, Theodore G. (1990). Symmetries, conservation laws, and Hamiltonian structure in geophysical fluid dynamics. *Advances in Geophysics*, **32**, 287–38.

Shepherd, Theodore G., Koshyk, John N., and Ngan, Keith (2000). On the nature of large-scale mixing in the stratosphere and mesosphere. *Journal of Geophysical Research Atmospheres*, **105**(D10), 12433–46.

Simmons, Adrian J. and Hoskins, Brian J. (1978). The life cycles of some nonlinear baroclinic waves. *Journal of the Atmospheric Sciences*, **35**(3), 414–32.

Temperton, Clive and Williamson, David L. (1981). Normal mode initialization for a multilevel grid-point model. Part i: Linear aspects. *Monthly Weather Review*, **109**(4), 729–43.

Thorncroft, Christopher D., Hoskins, Brian J., and McIntyre, Michael E. (1993). Two paradigms of baroclinic-wave life-cycle behaviour. *Quarterly Journal of the Royal Meteorological Society*, **119**(509), 17–55.

Trenberth, Kevin E. and Stepaniak, David P. (2003). Seamless poleward atmospheric energy transports and implications for the Hadley circulation. *Journal of Climate*, **16**(22), 3706–22.

Trenberth, Kevin E. and Stepaniak, David P. (2004). The flow of energy through the earth's climate system. *Quarterly Journal of the Royal Meteorological Society*, **130**(603), 2677–701.

Vallis, Geoffrey K. (1985). Remarks on the predictability properties of two- and three-dimensional flow. *Quarterly Journal of the Royal Meteorological Society*, **111**(470), 1039–47.

Vallis, Geoffrey K. (2006). *Atmospheric and Oceanic Fluid Dynamics*. Cambridge University Press, Cambridge, UK.

Waite, Michael L., and Bartello, Peter (2006). Stratified turbulence generated by internal gravity waves. *Journal of Fluid Mechanics*, **546**, 313–39.

Warn, T., Bokhove, O., Shepherd, T. G., and Vallis, G. K. (1995). Rossby number expansions, slaving principles, and balance dynamics. *Quarterly Journal of the Royal Meteorological Society*, **121**, 723–39.

Whitehead, Jr., John A. (1975). Mean flow generated by circulation on a β-plane: An analogy with the moving flame experiment. *Tellus*, **27**(4), 358–64.

Williamson, David L. and Temperton, Clive (1981). Normal mode initialization for a multilevel grid-point model. Nonlinear aspects. *Monthly Weather Review*, **109**(4), 744–57.

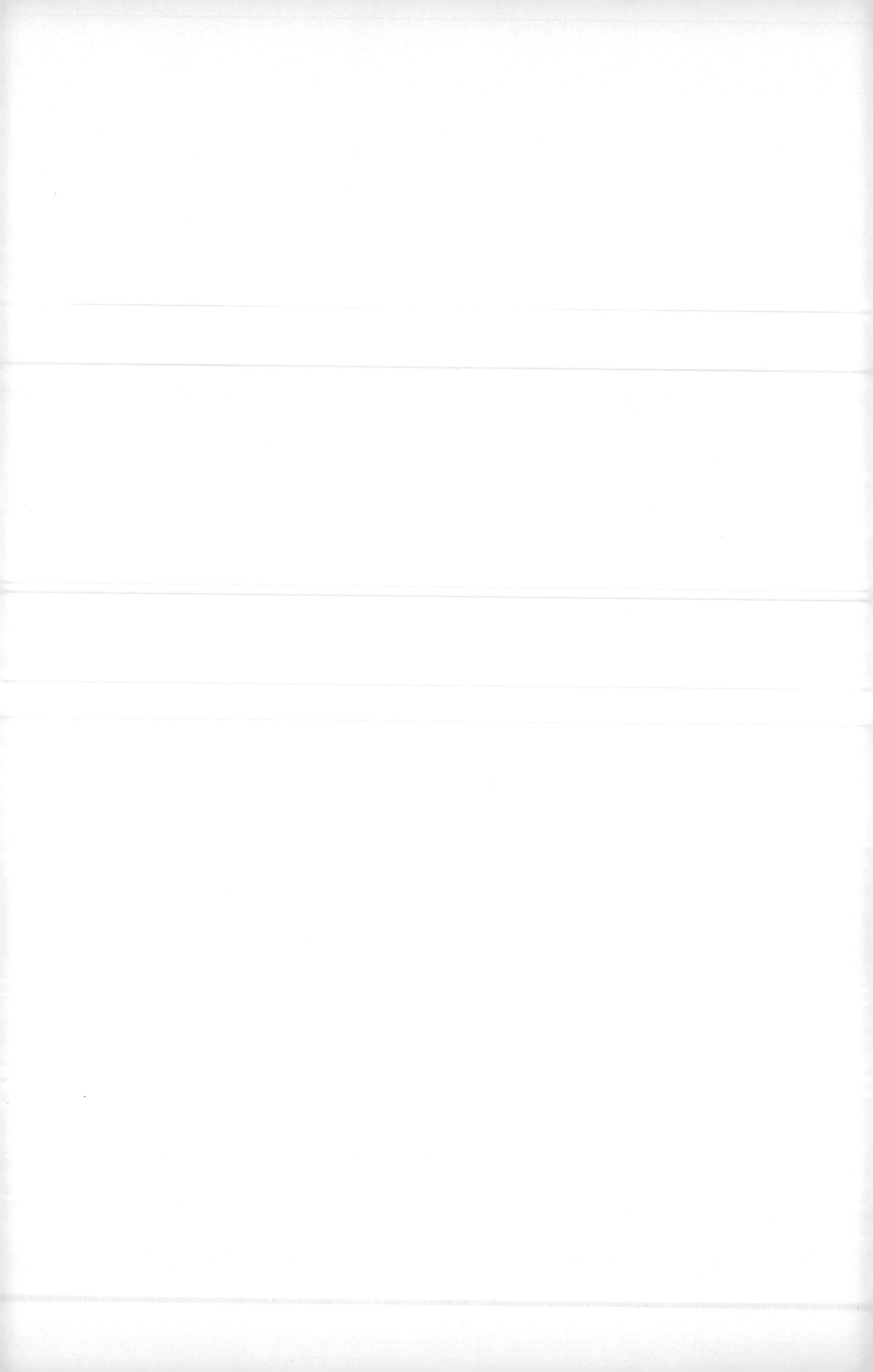

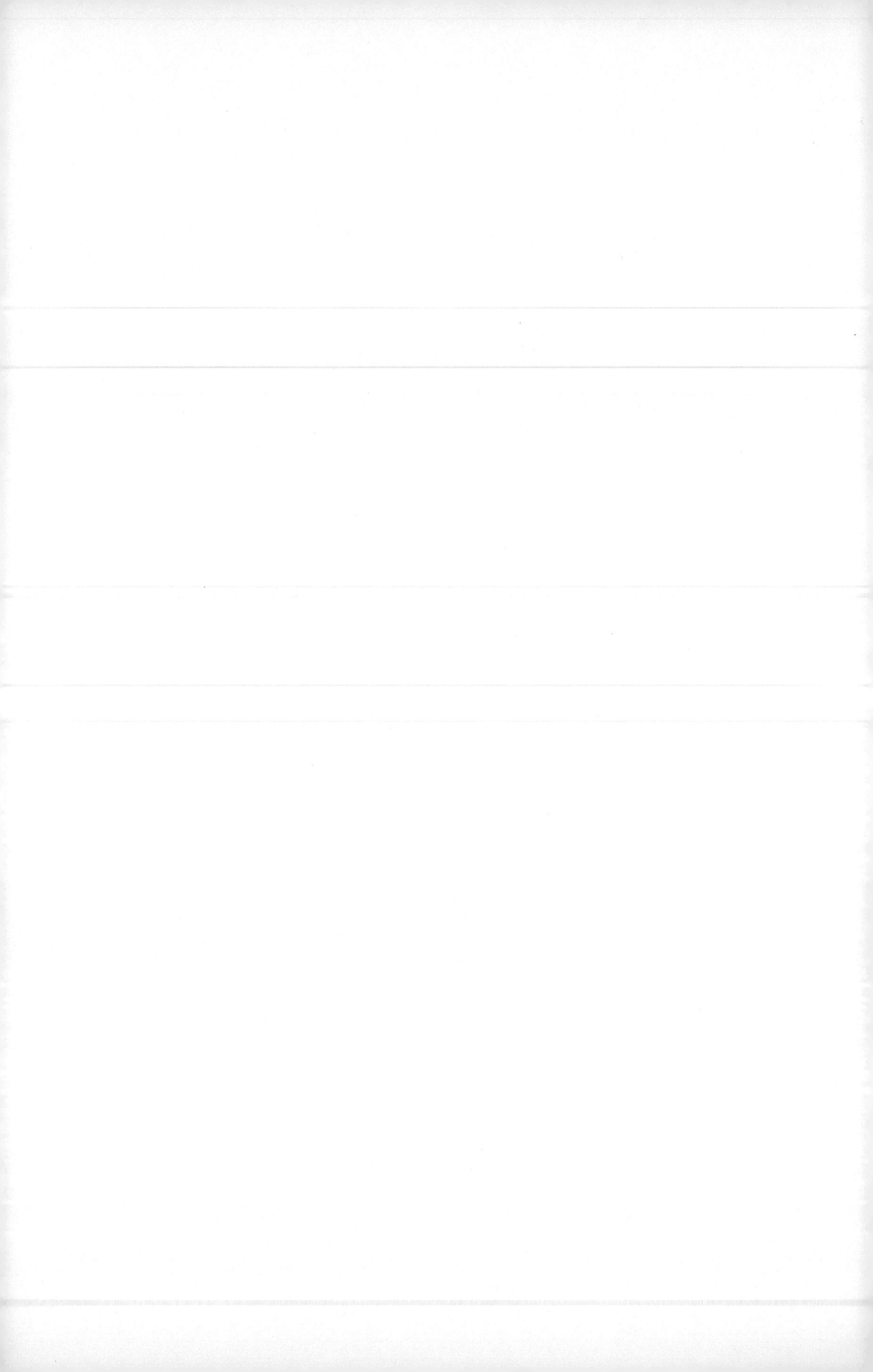

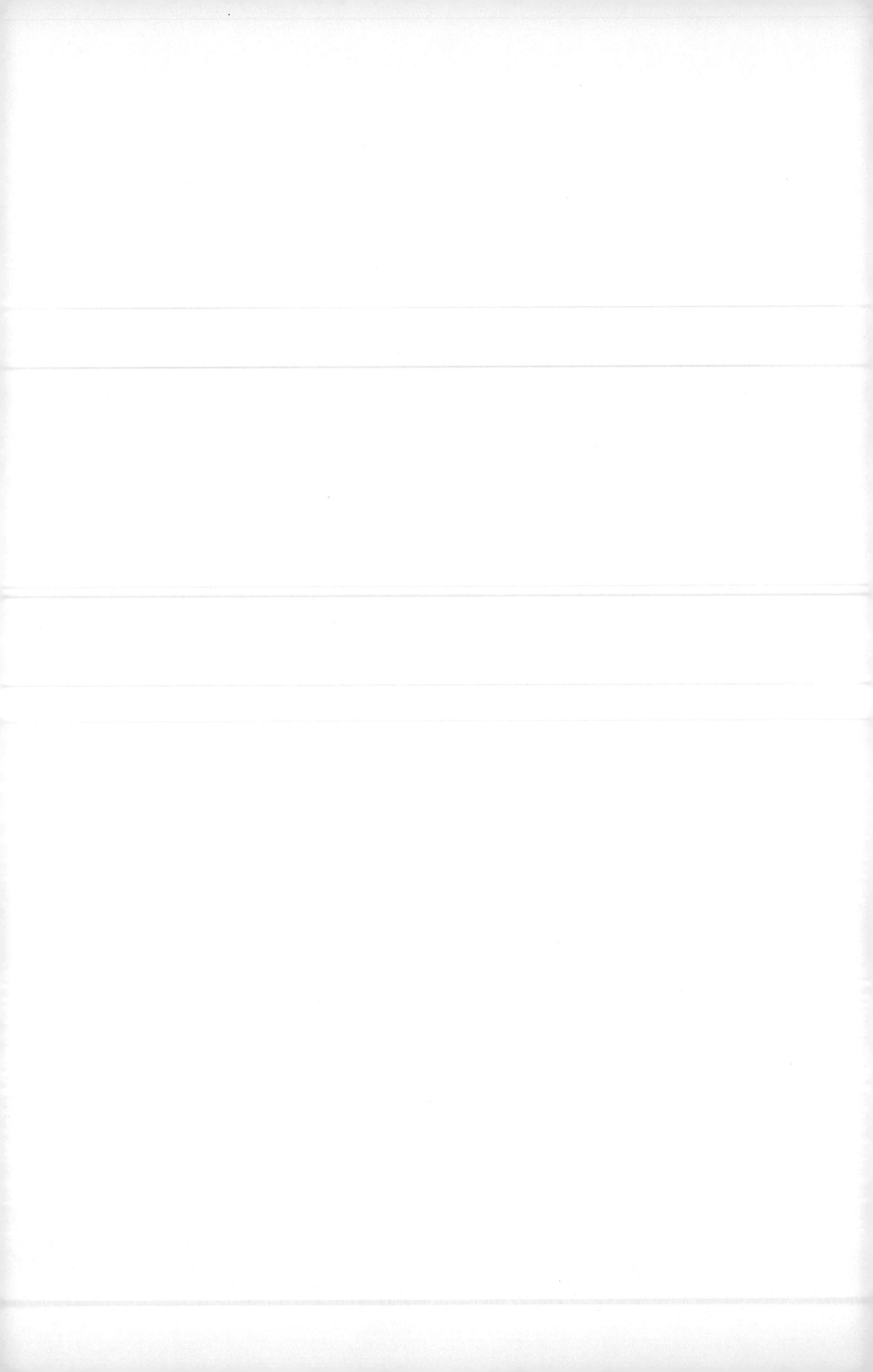